# SEND THE ALABAMIANS

# SEND THE ALABAMIANS

## World War I Fighters in the Rainbow Division

NIMROD T. FRAZER

Introduction by
EDWIN C. BRIDGES

THE UNIVERSITY OF ALABAMA PRESS
Tuscaloosa

Typeface: Perpetua and Corbel

Cover photograph: The Rainbow Division Memorial stands at Croix Rouge Farm near Château-
Thierry (France) on the site where the 167th Alabama Infantry Regiment distinguished itself
on July 26, 1918; courtesy of Ludwig E. Stoeckl, honored member of the RDVF.
Cover design: Todd Lape / Lape Designs

∞

The paper on which this book is printed meets the minimum requirements of American
National Standard for Information Sciences—Permanence of Paper for Printed Library
Materials, ANSI Z39.48-1984.

Library of Congress Cataloging-in-Publication Data

Frazer, Nimrod T. Send the Alabamians : World War I fighters in the Rainbow Division /
Nimrod T. Frazer ; introduction by Edwin C. Bridges.
pages cm
Includes bibliographical references and index.
ISBN 978-0-8173-1838-3 (trade cloth : alk. paper) — ISBN 978-0-8173-8769-3 (e-book)
1. United States. Army. Infantry Regiment, 167th. 2. World War, 1914–1918—Regimental
histories—United States. 3. World War, 1914–1918—Campaigns—France. 4. United States.
Army. Infantry Division, 42nd. 5. Alabama—History, Military—20th century. I. Title.
D570.33167th .F37 2014
940.4′1273—dc23
2013040330

In time of war, send me all the Alabamians you can get . . .
Brigadier General Edward H. Plummer, Commander of Nogales district

# Contents

Photographs follow page 161

# Maps

*Battle maps based on H. J. Reilly's* Americans All *and on maps from the National Archives.*

# Preface

William Johnson Frazer, my father, a native of Greenville, Alabama, served as an enlisted man in the 167th Infantry and its predecessor, the 4th Alabama Infantry, from 1916 to 1919. I knew about Will's service before I could read. I carried his Purple Heart medal to my first grade class and considered his wartime helmet and kit my playthings. At an early age I knew about the regiment's advanced training on the Mexican border and its campaigning in Europe during World War I. I knew how Will—as I referred to him when I outgrew childhood—fought with that regiment in the Rainbow Division in France at Baccarat, in Champagne, and at Aisne-Marne in the battle of Croix Rouge Farm. Hospitalized in Paris for wounds he incurred at Croix Rouge, Will missed the fighting on the Ourcq River but returned to the regiment in time for its battles at Saint-Mihiel and the Côte de Châtillon. He also served in the Army of Occupation in Germany.

Although my parents separated when I was seven, Will and I continued to share a common interest in the 167th Infantry. It remained our strong bond, representing my father's greatest life achievement and an inspiration for my own life. Will taught me an appreciation for military service, and some of my earliest memories are of thumbing through his copy of Captain William H. Amerine's *Alabama's Own in France*.[1] Although considered the official regimental history, Amerine's text is as fragmented as Will's stories. Some scholarly articles consider the 167th, but the complete story of the regiment's moves and battles in 1918 remains untold.

As I grew older and read more, this started to bother me. Were omissions of the role of the Alabamians just a coincidence, or did they arise from more insidious causes? I considered a number of possible causes: prejudice against those mostly southern boys, some of whom may have been racist and wild; bias against uneducated people with a different manner of speaking; an attempt to cover up the number of killed and wounded due to mistakes and failure of officers and military higher-ups.

I remained convinced that the 167th deserved more recognition than it received. One of the first American units committed to combat in France, the regiment served in a number of operations between February 1918 and war's end. It moved constantly, as evidenced by the seventy-seven command posts on its station list. It served in both American and French corps and armies. In the July 26, 1918, battle at Croix Rouge Farm—the 167th's bloodiest battle and one of the hardest American battles in World War I—the Alabamians secured a victory that caused the Germans to retreat twelve miles and set into motion a series of crucial Allied successes.[2] In that two-battalion bayonet assault, which included hand-to-hand fighting, the 167th captured, without artillery support, a fortified farmhouse and the huge area surrounding it. Croix Rouge was just one of the 167th's many successes. The V Corps commander later observed that without the Alabamians' efforts at Côte de Châtillon, the advance by the American army would have been impossible.[3]

The 167th represented a wide range of Alabamians, and it accrued most of the state's World War I deaths. Amerine lists 592 of the regiment's officers and men as dead or missing, 17 percent of the regiment's original 3,677 individuals.[4] Of the 95,000 Alabamians who served in the war, 814, or approximately 1 percent, were killed or died from wounds.[5] The 167th accounted for 73 percent of the Alabamians who gave their lives.

The 167th Infantry was deployed for a tour of duty in World War II and another during the Korean War. Elements of the regiment exist today in the Alabama National Guard, and some of its officers and men have served in Iraq and Afghanistan. Most recently, the 167th Infantry Battalion, consisting of over five hundred men, was deployed to Afghanistan in 2012. Although the 167th continues to perform valuable service, for now the significance of its 1918 tour remains unparalleled.

The 167th's association with the flamboyant Douglas MacArthur from the time it joined the Rainbow Division in the summer of 1917 until the war's end makes its scarcity in the war record even more puzzling. As a major in the War Department, MacArthur helped organize the Rainbow Division, and the 167th's Colonel William P. Screws served directly under him until the end of the war. As division chief of staff, MacArthur occupied the traditional army role of "bad cop" to the division commander's "good cop" and interacted with Screws and other regimental commanders in that capacity. After promotion to brigadier general,

MacArthur commanded the 84th Brigade, of which the 167th was always an organic part. In a 1950 letter to Screws, MacArthur wrote, "During this campaign [Korean War] and the last war I have missed you and your grand Alabama Regiment. I have seen some great units in that time but never one which surpassed that which you so brilliantly commanded in France."[6] MacArthur lavished such praise only in private correspondence, however, and ultimately Alabama proved more loyal to MacArthur than MacArthur was to Alabama. Many felt the general favored the 168th (Iowa) Infantry, whose predecessor, the 1st Iowa Volunteers, had served under MacArthur's father in the Philippines.[7] Whatever the reason, the 167th rarely received such public affirmation from MacArthur.

One of the regiment's most significant battles, at Croix Rouge Farm, was similarly slighted. The fighting along the Ourcq River, where three other Rainbow regiments—the 165th (New York), 166th (Ohio), and 168th (Iowa)—joined the 167th, remains more dominantly etched in American memory and literature. Of nine reference books describing the fighting along the Ourcq, only four include the Battle of Croix Rouge Farm. General orders issued by Major General Charles T. Menoher on August 13, 1918, summarizing the deeds of the 42nd Division, do not mention that costly victory.[8] Although some official accounts, composed later, do mention Croix Rouge, far more omit it.[9] The Summary of History of the 42nd Division begins the story of the Aisne-Marne fighting on July 27, 1918, the day after the 167th pushed the Germans back from Croix Rouge Farm.[10] The victory at Croix Rouge Farm opened the path to the Ourcq River.

While some Rainbow Division regiments had celebrities or politicians as promoters and endorsers, the Alabama regiment had almost none. Contemporary accounts, particularly newspaper articles, repeatedly failed to mention the Alabama regiment in 1918, and no evidence suggests that any newspaper reporter from Alabama visited the 167th during the entire time it served overseas. Alabama senator John Bankhead and his son, congressman Will Bankhead, supported President Woodrow Wilson's efforts to keep the United States out of the war—a factor that likely prevented either of them from visiting the regiment or speaking of its achievements to the press or on the legislative floor. Although it lacked influential boosters, the 167th earned acclaim through its actions. It finally garnered mention on the floor of the US House of Representatives on February 12, 1919, when Iowa congressman Horace M. Towner remarked, "Its name is on every tongue."[11]

In composing a complete account of the regiment's 1918 tour, I often consulted John H. Taber's *The Story of the 168th Infantry*.[12] Although poorly organized, Taber's two-volume history stems from his experience as a lieutenant of the 168th (Iowa), the 167th's sister regiment in the 84th Brigade. I checked his text against *Americans All: Official History of the Rainbow Division* by Brigadier General Henry J. Reilly, ORC.[13] Although work on the official division history was discussed at every national Rainbow Division convention since 1920, Reilly, who served with the division during the war, published his text in 1936.[14] Working years after the events described, Reilly collaborated with a committee and used multiple sources. Reilly's text also proves convoluted at times, but invaluable details are buried within it.

Unlike those authors, Captain William H. Amerine, who served in Signals and Supply, had not served in the Rainbow or the 167th in combat. He had no training as regimental historian and did not ask for the job. It was thrust on him at the suggestion of the highly regarded battalion commander Major Dallas B. Smith and at the command in Germany of Colonel William P. Screws on March 29, 1919.[15] Amerine wrote most of *Alabama's Own in France* while in the Army of Occupation in Germany. He had access to everyone in the regiment, but the few months between his writing and the book's publication in the United States offered little time for further research. Amerine himself believed corrections were in order.[16]

All of the participants in the 167th Infantry of 1916–19 and its battles are now dead, so my firsthand accounts are limited to the stories Will told me as well as my knowing his best friend and fellow soldier Chester Scott. My primary source materials consist of diaries, letters, and general orders. For general knowledge of the war I have found Martin Gilbert's *The First World War* to be the authoritative text. In addition to extensive reading, I have conducted substantial research in archival material in France and the United States. I have visited each of the regiment's battlefields in France, the site of its advanced infantry training in Nogales, Arizona, and Malabang in the Philippines, where Screws served as a combat soldier and an administrator.

In retracing the 167th's steps, I have been reminded that most of its men enlisted as ordinary men with simple ways. Their military service enabled them to participate in a complex, life-wrenching event, an adventure larger than they were. It also forged their identity. They left home as small-town southerners, but they returned as Americans.

# Acknowledgments

During my research, I was fortunate to benefit from the help and insights of Doran L. Cart and Jonathon Casey (National World War I Museum, Kansas City, Missouri), Norwood Kerr and the late Rickie Louise Brunner (ADAH, Montgomery, Alabama), Dwayne Cox and John Varner (Special Collections and Archives, Auburn University), Patrick Osborn (NARA, College Park, Maryland), Jodie Wilson (Crawfordsville District Public Library, Indiana), Colonel Gregory C. Camp (The Infantry Foundation, Fort Benning, Georgia), James W. Zobel (MAMA, Norfolk, Virginia), and Axel C. F. Holm (Pimeria Alta Historical Society, Nogales, Arizona).

Dalton Kenneth Barr Jr. reviewed my research in local newspapers and the war records of the 167th in the Alabama Archives. Ms. Aude Rœilly, conservateur du patrimoine, directeur des Archives départementales de l'Aisne, provided the beginning of research in French archives. I thank them both for their help.

I want to thank Ruth Truss (University of Montevallo, Alabama) for sharing a copy of her pioneering dissertation on the Alabama National Guard from 1900 to 1920.

Thanks to W. Craig Remington, Cartographic Library director in the Department of Geography at the University of Alabama, and to his graduate assistant Laura Wesley. They drew the detailed maps that accompany the various chapters of this book, and I am very indebted to both of them. I would also like to thank USAF General Lance Smith, who, when commander of the LeMay Center at Maxwell Air Force Base, kindly provided me with copies of the period battle maps pertaining to the Rainbow Division.

Thanks to the generosity of Josephine Lahey Screws McGowin, Elizabeth Jordan Simmons, Borden Burr II, and Wade Watts Kuisel, we were able to read all or parts of their respective grandfathers' diaries, scrapbooks, or personal correspondence.

To the late Margaret Thorington Kohn McCall I am indebted for the 1923 photograph of General Henri Joseph Gouraud with Montgomery ladies at the Montgomery Country Club.

The American Battle Monuments Commission—from its former executive director, Brigadier General William J. Leszczynsky Jr., to its then director of public affairs and now chief of staff, Mike Conley, to the then American cemeteries superintendents: Jeffrey Aarnio, at Oise-Aisne American Cemetery; Phil Rivers, at Meuse-Argonne American Cemetery; and Bobby Bell, at Saint-Mihiel American Cemetery—all provided me with kind assistance, information, and welcome. Jeffrey Aarnio welcomed me several times on the site of the battle of the Croix Rouge Farm, and I am exceedingly grateful to him for his time and commitment.

At the Côte de Châtillon, I had the good fortune to visit the site twice with the welcoming owner of the land, Jean-Pierre Brouillon, who showed me the Musarde Farm, the Tuilerie Farm, the German bunkers, and the remains of the small gauge railroad the Germans used. During my visit to the training grounds and battlefields of Lorraine, I benefited greatly from the recommendations of Jacques Bourquin, who introduced me to collector Lionel Humbert and scholar Eric Mansuy.

I am very grateful to John W. Cork (Los Angeles) and to the late Yetta Samford (Opelika) for their encouragements, as well as to Bob Martin (*Montgomery Independent*) for his guidance regarding publication of the book. In this regard, but also concerning the style and the scope of this book, as well as the importance of detailed maps, the advice of my friend Dr. Edwin C. Bridges (ADAH, Montgomery, Alabama), was absolutely invaluable, and I will always remain in his debt.

Dan Waterman and Donna Cox Baker of the University of Alabama Press made possible the assignment of Dr. Elizabeth Wade as consulting editor of this book. Her assistance has been invaluable. Once my manuscript was completed, Dawn Hall, copyeditor, added her light and masterful touch before Jon Berry, project editor at the Press, prepared it for publication with an admirable professionalism.

My longtime assistant, Mary Romano Rembert, helped me keep files and the various iterations of this text organized while Katie Chase did the original copyediting. My colleague Paula Mims, who served as treasurer of the Croix Rouge Farm Memorial Foundation, delivered the utmost assistance.

Finally, the contribution of Dr. Monique Brouillet Seefried to this work, from its inception to the final product, can never be properly acknowledged. Without her passion for the subject, her historical background, her research skills, her ability to locate and translate for me French and German sources, and her repeated proofreading of my work, *Send the Alabamians* would never have been written. To her, as well as to all of those named above, my most sincere thanks for having helped me bring alive those whose names and sacrifice should never be forgotten.

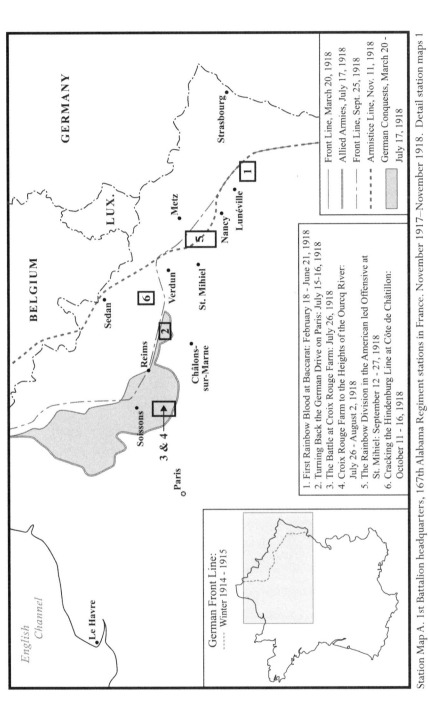

English Channel

Le Havre

GERMANY

BELGIUM

LUX.

Strasbourg

Metz

Nancy

Lunéville

1

5

Verdun

St. Mihiel

Sedan

6

2

Reims

Châlons-
sur-Marne

Soissons

3 & 4

Paris

Front Line, March 20, 1918
Allied Armies, July 17, 1918
Front Line, Sept. 25, 1918
Armistice Line, Nov. 11, 1918
German Conquests, March 20 -
July 17, 1918

1. First Rainbow Blood at Baccarat: February 18 - June 21, 1918
2. Turning Back the German Drive on Paris: July 15-16, 1918
3. The Battle at Croix Rouge Farm: July 26, 1918
4. Croix Rouge Farm to the Heights of the Ourcq River:
   July 26 - August 2, 1918
5. The Rainbow Division in the American led Offensive at
   St. Mihiel: September 12 - 27, 1918
6. Cracking the Hindenburg Line at Côte de Châtillon:
   October 11 - 16, 1918

German Front Line:
----- Winter 1914 - 1915

Station Map A. 1st Battalion headquarters, 167th Alabama Regiment stations in France. November 1917–November 1918. Detail station maps 1 to 4 appear in the text. All maps were produced by the Cartographic Lab of the Department of Geography, University of Alabama.

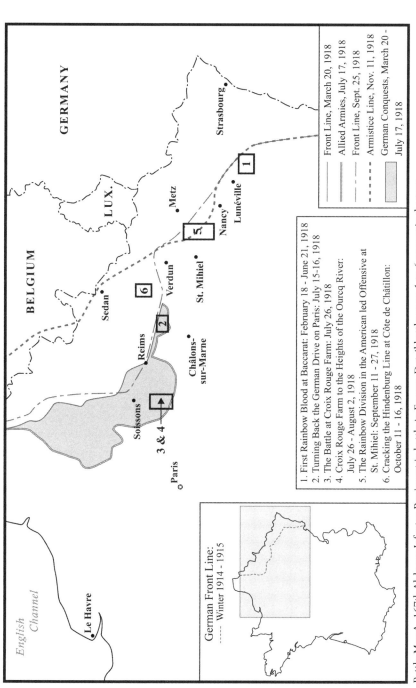

GERMANY

BELGIUM

LUX.

Strasbourg

Metz

Nancy

Lunéville

Sedan

Verdun

St. Mihiel

Reims

Châlons-sur-Marne

Soissons

3 & 4

Paris

Le Havre

English Channel

**German Front Line:**
----- Winter 1914 - 1915

Front Line, March 20, 1918
Allied Armies, July 17, 1918
Front Line, Sept. 25, 1918
Armistice Line, Nov. 11, 1918
German Conquests, March 20 - July 17, 1918

1. First Rainbow Blood at Baccarat: February 18 - June 21, 1918
2. Turning Back the German Drive on Paris: July 15-16, 1918
3. The Battle at Croix Rouge Farm: July 26, 1918
4. Croix Rouge Farm to the Heights of the Ourcq River: July 26 - August 2, 1918
5. The Rainbow Division in the American led Offensive at St. Mihiel: September 11 - 27, 1918
6. Cracking the Hindenburg Line at Côte de Châtillon: October 11 - 16, 1918

Battle Map A. 167th Alabama Infantry Regiment in battle in France. Detail battle maps 1 to 6 appear in the text.

# SEND THE ALABAMIANS

# Introduction

*Edwin C. Bridges*

As time passes, memories fade. World-shattering catastrophes of one generation thin out into old stories for the children of the next generation. For later generations, they are merely the stuff of history. Thus nearly a century after their heroic service in World War I, the men of Alabama's 167th Infantry Regiment—called "The Immortals" in their time—have been largely forgotten. In *Send the Alabamians*, Rod Frazer helps bring their story back to life. And it is a story that for many reasons deserves to be kept alive.

World War I may have been the shaping event of the twentieth century. It led to the breakup of European dominance in the world and ushered in a new era of horrific, mechanized total warfare. It gave birth to communism and fascism and new vitality to militant nationalism. In many ways, much of the rest of the twentieth century can be seen as the playing out of forces World War I either unleashed or accelerated.

In the spring of 1918, after almost four years of carnage, France and England were in desperate straits. The Russian communist government had signed a treaty of peace with the Germans in early March. The Germans were moving hundreds of thousands of soldiers westward for a great final push against the French and English, whose armies were depleted and worn. The Germans held numerical superiority. Without help, the French and English lines would probably have broken.

By May, however, as the Germans were intensifying their attacks, more than a million American soldiers had arrived in France. These fresh troops made the difference in the outcome of the war. One of the most effective units in the US forces was the famous "Rainbow Division," and one of its strongest regiments was Alabama's 167th Infantry. *Send the Alabamians* is an account of this remarkable regiment.

In addition to serving as a regimental history, *Send the Alabamians* also helps us see how World War I engaged and affected the people of Alabama. When we think about the war now, almost a century later, we visualize photos of trench lines and the pulverized terrain of "no man's land" in between. We think about the war's massive destruction and its disastrous aftermath. We do not think much about how important World War I was for people in Alabama or the role Alabamians played in its outcome. But it was a life-changing experience for many Alabamians as well as for people in Europe, and it was a major chapter in the state's history.

The 167th Infantry Regiment of the US Army grew out of a 1916 mobilization to protect American interests along the Mexican border. That June, President Woodrow Wilson ordered National Guard units totaling more than 150,000 men from across the United States into active service. They were to protect the American border against raids by Pancho Villa and spillover damage from internal turmoil inside Mexico. One of the Alabama units Wilson mobilized was the 4th Alabama Infantry Regiment.

The 4th Alabama was led by William Preston Screws, a native Alabamian who had been the training officer for the state's National Guard. He was then Captain Screws in the Regular Army, but he was also the lieutenant colonel of the 4th Alabama militia, when officers were still elected by their men. The 4th Alabama trained at Vandiver Park in Montgomery and added new men to bring it up to strength before shipping out in October.

By the time the 4th Alabama arrived in Arizona, much of the hard fighting had already taken place. The role of the new National Guard units was nominally to police the border, but American leaders had been watching the war in Europe for two years. They knew the United States was unprepared for serious, large-scale warfare. So the Mexican Expedition also became a training program. Through the winter of 1916/17, under the command of General John J. Pershing, the Guard units carried out extensive exercises in trench warfare.

In early 1917, as this training progressed, the Germans began an expanded offensive against the English and French, including unrestricted submarine warfare against American supply ships. In response, President Wilson broke off relations with Germany in February, and Congress officially declared war with Germany in April. When the 4th Alabama returned home from Arizona that March, its men were immediately dispatched to guard strategic positions across the state—railroads, bridges, and industrial sites—against possible sabotage by German agents or sympathizers (for instance, from the German immigrant community in Baldwin County).

That June the 4th Alabama reassembled in Montgomery at Vandiver Park. New men were added, and the regiment began another round of intensive training. In this reorganization and enlargement, the 4th Alabama National Guard Regiment was renamed the 167th United States Infantry of the US Army. At the same time, Vandiver Park experienced its own transformation. It was expanded to accommodate at least thirty thousand men and renamed Camp Sheridan.

When the new 167th shipped out from Montgomery in August 1917, it numbered 3,677 men. At Camp Mills in New York, the 167th joined National Guard regiments from other states. "The Alabam" became part of the southern spectrum in a newly formed division dubbed the *Rainbow*, because it was comprised of units from all across the United States.

The new Rainbow Division, numbered the 42nd, embarked for France in October of 1917 and there received more training through most of the winter. It became one of the first American divisions committed to full combat, and it continued to be engaged, often intensively, for the duration of the war and into the occupation of Germany.

Starting in February 1918, the Rainbow Division, including its 167th Infantry Regiment, served in three successive defensive areas alongside the French. Each deployment brought greater independence and harder fighting. At Souain in July, the unit's third deployment, the 167th helped bear the brunt of the last desperate German offensive of the war. In a fierce and bloody stand, they held their positions and repulsed the attacking Germans.

By the end of that month and without any letup, the Rainbow Division moved to the offensive. In two successive assaults at the Croix Rouge Farm and then at the Ourcq River, the 167th attacked entrenched German positions. They charged through established defenses in the face of murderous machine gun fire, artillery shelling, and poisonous gas. They drove the Germans back, but at a very heavy price in killed and wounded. The 167th entered the fight with just over 3,500 men. In these two attacks alone—and in less than ten days—it lost 1,785 killed or wounded, a casualty rate above 50 percent.

After a brief period of recovery and the incorporation of replacement troops, the 167th led another assault in September at the new American sector of Saint-Mihiel, pressing relentlessly against flagging German defenses. In early October they hit one of the key German posts of the Hindenburg Line at the Côte de Châtillon. Another bloody victory there against a seemingly impregnable German position helped break the back of effective German resistance. The regiment's success at Châtillon also cemented its reputation as a truly distinguished fighting unit.

After another brief time of rest, the 167th joined French and other American forces in the final push toward Sedan. The 167th was the first unit of the Rainbow Division to reach the Meuse River as the war ended. After the armistice on November 11, it moved on into Germany and became part of the Army of Occupation.

At the conclusion of *Send the Alabamians*, Rod Frazer is able to reassert convincingly the claim of the Rainbow Division in 1919 that "it had spent more days in the trenches in the face of the enemy, gained more ground against the enemy, and marched further in its operations than any other division in the American Expeditionary Forces." And the 167th Infantry Regiment, "the Alabam," was at the front in every one of the division's major engagements.

When the 167th returned to Alabama in May 1919, its surviving officers and men were honored in a series of huge, emotional homecoming ceremonies. A total of 616 men had been killed, with many others wounded. But the pride of Alabama in its sons made the survivors' return a landmark moment in the state's history. Alabama gloried in the courage and skill of her fighting men. The honors won by the 167th in France marked Alabama soldiers as among the best of a victorious nation. Their service also marked a major step in the reintegration of Alabama back into the life of the nation following the great divisions of the Civil War.

Alabama newspapers of the time hailed these men as "The Immortals," but as we read their story today, we are all too conscious that "The Immortals" have largely been forgotten. Rod Frazer's excellent research and forceful writing, however, will help a new generation understand and appreciate their story. With each new reader, their memories will live again, and the honors claimed for them by the orators and writers of 1919 will not be entirely mocked by the passage of time.

*Send the Alabamians* is a unique book in several respects. Frazer is not a professional historian. He has undertaken this work out of his own long interest in the 167th, inspired by his personal experience of the way the war shaped his father's life. This book represents the collected conversations, reading, research, and reflections of a lifetime. As he has pursued this interest, Frazer has repeatedly walked the original battlegrounds with local guides and followed the movements of the 167th using copies of battle maps, after-action reports, and later memoirs. His careful descriptions of the battles make this book the new basic resource on the military actions of the 167th. He has even purchased one of the battle sites, the Croix Rouge Farm, and built a memorial there to honor the memory of those who served.

But Frazer is also a gifted storyteller. He has a great eye for details of the ordinary soldier's life that makes his narrative lively and interesting at a personal level. His pacing is as steady and driving as a fit unit on the march. He was a soldier himself, serving with distinction in the Korean War. This story is greatly enriched by his soldier's appreciation for the many "little" things that fill in the huge gaps between the adrenalin surges of combat—from food service and latrine practices to leave days and rivalries with other units. We learn about ordinary soldiers struggling with cooties and the officers' struggles to prove themselves to Regular Army superiors.

The narrative also covers higher-level military planning and strategy considerations that governed the deployments of the 167th. The role of Douglas MacArthur, the man who helped give the Rainbow Division its name and who ended as its commanding general, is particularly fascinating. His leadership of the division showed in full flower the combination of drive, ability, ambition, and calculation that marked his entire career. He was clearly an important part of the division's success, but his leadership also left a cloud of uncertainty about his manipulation of subordinates and self-promotion that still lingers unresolved.

Another important individual story is that of the unit's only commanding officer, Colonel William P. Screws. He was a Regular Army officer, but not a product of West Point. Before the war, he had been assigned to training National Guard units. Screws was from Alabama, and he was pleased to return home from Missouri in 1913 to the Alabama National Guard. He knew and trained the officers and men of the old 4th Alabama Infantry Regiment before it was nationalized for federal service in 1916.

Screws continued training the expanded regiment after nationalization and led it to the Mexican border. He brought it back to Alabama for still more training and led it to France. He commanded the 167th in every action in France and Germany except for a few days when he was hospitalized with the flu. He was hard working, conscientious, demanding, wise, energetic, and able. Screws was concerned for his men, but when the time came to fight, he expected every man to do his duty, and he pushed them hard. His aggressive but intelligent and straightforward leadership compares favorably to that of his occasional leader, MacArthur.

*Send the Alabamians* is greatly enriched by Frazer's generous use of quotations— taken from letters soldiers sent back to their families, their writings after the war, and after-action reports, as well as from descriptions by observers who were occasionally associated with the regiment. He has gotten to know many of the soldiers as well as someone living many years after their deaths can. Because of his detailed knowledge and the many direct quotations, readers are able to get a sense of who these men were beyond the level most military histories are able to convey.

One frequently quoted source, for example, is Mortimer Jordan, a physician from Birmingham who was also an officer in the 167th. His letters to his wife are lively and filled with rich details about the unit's daily experiences. They also reveal Jordan's own intelligent, insightful character. His death was just one of many losses for the unit, but it still comes as a blow even for the reader today. In fact, the losses of officers and men in every engagement are stunning. We hear a man's voice in one letter and then learn of his death in another. One wonders today how the survivors were able to keep going as they watched one colleague after another fall.

A unique feature of this regimental history is that it is also a personal story. Will Frazer, a sergeant from Greenville, Alabama, returned home after the war, wounded in body and also in soul. His service as a member of the 167th was the great, shaping event of his life, but he never readjusted fully to civilian life or found a place for himself where he could be happy and productive. Will's two sons grew up in the shadow of his war experiences, and for the younger, this book has been a journey back through his father's life. Details about Will and his circle of friends add another personal dimension and help the reader see through accounts of unit movements and action reports into the lives of real people and their families.

Three other features contribute substantially to this book's interest and usefulness. One is the author's success in placing the story of the 167th Infantry Regiment in the larger context of the war. While general information about World War I is fairly limited, the reader can easily understand and follow the big picture of what was going on and how the 167th fit into that picture.

A second strength is the truly wonderful set of photographs Frazer has been able to uncover and incorporate into the book. Many of these are pictures that few living Alabamians have ever seen. They provide a great visual reinforcement to the story narrative.

A third feature is the substantial appendix section, which includes a complete roster of all Alabamian soldiers and officers at Camp Mills, a list of stations, and an overall war chronology. These appendixes make *Send the Alabamians* a valuable new reference resource for Alabama history.

I would like to close this introduction with a personal note. Rod Frazer has been a friend for many years, and his support of the Alabama Department of Archives and History goes back to the time of Milo Howard, who preceded me as director. I heard Rod present a paper on the 167th to a literary group in the early 1990s, and he gave a talk at the archives on the subject as well. I have watched as his knowledge of and passion for this story have increased over the years— talking with him frequently about sources he found after one of his research visits or listening after he returned from walking over a battle site.

After Rod's semiretirement from a distinguished business career, he pursued this work with even more vigor, which, as all his friends know, is considerable. In conversations, he has said repeatedly that he wants to pull together the incredible number of different pieces that are part of the scattered documentation of the 167th and to present the whole story in a way that keeps it alive. Thanks to his work, Alabamians today and in years to come can easily learn about this important and now generally unappreciated chapter in our history. With the publication of *Send the Alabamians*, Rod has achieved his goal, and I am very happy to have this opportunity to thank and commend him for this fine work.

# 1
# Mobilization of the
# Alabama National Guard, 1916

On June 19, 1916, the *Montgomery Advertiser* reported the mobilization and federalization of the Alabama National Guard by the Militia Division of the War Department.[1] The "call up" was a nationwide order for possible duty on the Mexican border. The Alabama regiments, having previously served at the state level, were to enter federal service.[2] They were ordered to Montgomery's Vandiver Park.[3]

The National Defense Act, passed on June 3, 1916, was considered "Milestone Legislation" and stated that when in federal service, the Guard was an integral part of the Army of the United States.[4] When mobilized on June 16, it was unprepared for the possibility of war and had to adjust rapidly to its new, higher status.[5] According to Henry Reilly, these units faced two primary adjustments: "The first was the dismissal from the ranks of the officers and enlisted men unwilling to enter Federal service or physically unfit for such service. The second was the raising to war strength of those units by a large number of green recruits who were recruited for war service."[6]

Alabama units, the 1st, 2nd, and 4th Alabama Infantry and the 1st Alabama Cavalry were provided with uniforms, weapons, equipment, and some training by the army, but the Guard was a second-class service. Most officers in the Regular Army were West Pointers serving full time. Officers of the militia were part-timers and usually had no more than a high school education. Enlisted men usually needed the part-time work of soldiering.

The Guard, despite having "been ill trained and poorly equipped in the past," suddenly offered young men an opportunity to walk away from the simple lives that many had never been able to escape.[7] Now they might travel to unknown places, eat healthy food, wear good clothes, and earn income for doing work that upright citizens respected and valued. Many young men without money, education, or training relished this new kind of work. It promised a better way to make a living than jobs that usually required long hours, often combined with sweaty, dirty, sometimes dangerous labor for little pay. Few Alabama men could rise above that kind of work, but some were intelligent enough and adventurous enough to take advantage of an opportunity to do so.

Not many in those days traveled outside of the South, or even across the state. Most were skeptical about the unknown, but some possessed enough imagination to think that enlisting in the National Guard could mean opportunity. Especially those with no family farm to inherit or business to enter saw the Guard as a possible chance for promotion and adventure. Raised on the stories of Confederate veterans, most boys in 1916 knew tales of heroes finding glory in faraway places. Almost every town or courthouse square in Alabama boasted a Confederate memorial, such as a rifleman facing north. Under their shadows many Alabamians coveted their own chance at glory.

## Trouble in Mexico

Their new opportunity to fight would come from the south, after trouble arose in Mexico. Civil war was raging and the US Army was going there out of fear that it might spill over into the United States. Revolution was respected as an internal matter, but Mexico and the United States shared a two-thousand-mile border that had been troubled since 1910.[8] In January 1916 the Mexican irregular leader "Pancho" Villa launched the first of two significant attacks on Americans.[9] The first, a train attack in Mexico, led to the deaths of nearly all the American workers present.[10] Later "a band of nearly 500 Villistas" entered American territory to invade Columbus, New Mexico, where they again killed American citizens.[11] Many US citizens, "especially those living in fear near Mexico, demanded retribution."[12] President Wilson authorized sending 15,000 Regular Army troops and 156,000 National Guardsmen to the border.[13] At the same time Wilson was conducting peacekeeping efforts with Germany and seeking reelection on the campaign slogan "He kept us out of the war" raging in Europe since 1914.[14] His response to the Mexican conflict surprised some and angered those who considered it a "politically ill considered foray."[15]

The army mission was announced in a State Department message on March 14, 1916. They would "enter Mexico with sole object of pursuing and capturing Villa and his band."[16]

Two cavalry brigades and one infantry brigade led by Brigadier General John J. Pershing immediately penetrated four hundred miles into the interior.[17] On

March 16 the US Congress passed a resolution authorizing "the use of the armed forces of the United States."[18] Thereafter the expedition was referred to as the "Punitive Expedition."

## The Alabama National Guard

Captain William Preston Screws (see fig. 1), having served as training supervisor of the Alabama National Guard since it was established in 1912, was mustering officer of its four militia regiments.[19] Few companies had the authorized strength of three officers and sixty-five men.[20] The *Montgomery Advertiser* described Screws as lieutenant-colonel-elect of the 4th Alabama, his having been put in charge in February by a vote of the soldiers.[21] The new commander replaced Colonel E. H. Graves.[22] Mortimer Jordan, a medical doctor and K Company commander from Birmingham, expressed his satisfaction with the choice: "This is the best thing that could happen for all of us. We are now assured that we will have the best regiment in the Alabama service."[23]

Most in the Guard were proud to be involved and derived prestige from being members. John H. Gardiner, a cavalry man who joined the military because he "wanted to see some action," remembered: "In 1917 joining the service was 'the thing to do.'"[24] It set people apart in a world where there was little distinction. Without education to fall back on, some turned to the military. It also held allure for some with education. Jordan, who balanced his medical practice with his dedication to serve, wrote his wife, "I can't tell you how fine I feel. This is certainly the life. Money could not buy the benefit I am deriving. Then, of course, the military training is of great value," adding in the next letter, "This fascination of soldiering, especially with a company to command is irresistible."[25]

Local units were anxious to be called up for service on the Mexican border. Screws told the *Montgomery Advertiser* that those nearest full strength would be summoned first. This brought on a flurry of activity as units worked to sign up new men.[26] K Company, Birmingham, was typical. With about ninety-five men, it reached Vandiver Park on June 26, 1916.[27] Its captain, Mortimer Jordan, said, "We are still up in the air. We are working early and late on our paper work. In order to get mustered in we must do a month's book keeping in two days. Have been at it since we got here."[28] Officials took in many new recruits without proper physical examinations or full equipment. President Wilson activated the entire National Guard—123,605 enlisted men and 8,589 officers—on June 16.[29] The Alabama men passing physical examinations were sworn in at Vandiver Park on June 28, 1916.

## Muster at Vandiver Park

At the time of mobilization, Montgomery had a population of about forty thousand.[30] Vandiver Park was about four miles north of town. It had an active racetrack that had long been used for militia training and was a good place to camp, shoot on rifle ranges, drill, and from which the men could go on road marches.

During the mobilization process an army doctor visited every company in its hometown armory. All personnel were examined, and anyone medically unfit for military service was supposed to be discharged.[31] There was lobbying for exceptions, as "Most men were willing and even eager to go overseas."[32] Disease among the units was rampant, and the rejection rate was generally 25–30 percent.[33] About 60 percent of men in the state later examined for selective service had hookworm.[34] However, most dismissed by the Guard were put out for "being underweight or having venereal diseases (gonorrhea and syphilis), 'bad teeth,' tuberculosis, or heart disease."[35] With such high rejection rates, "Civilian recruits became a necessity."[36] Beginning on June 18, 1916, National Guard recruiters covered the state, posting notices in public places.[37]

Governor Charles Henderson decreed that Alabama join fifteen states in celebrating the Fourth of July holiday of 1916 as "Preparedness Day." It commemorated the call-up of the Guard, called attention to the recruiting drive, and announced the beginning of training at Vandiver Park. It was a national event. Civilians visited the camp on Sunday of the holiday weekend and bands played in downtown Montgomery until the parade of new troops began at three that afternoon.

Some 2,600 soldiers marched before 30,000 civilians—quite a turnout for units that had never been on extended active duty and included some marchers with less than two weeks of military training.[38] Only the original Guard members knew the arcane way to stay in step as they headed up Commerce Street on the traditional parade route. This show of strength was an opportunity to build confidence and perform military exercises as a unit.[39] Recruiters brought in scores of new men, and individual volunteers showed up at the camp gates every day. Some eager recruits paid their own fare to get there quickly and enlist.[40]

## Basic Infantry Training in Montgomery

The 4th Alabama included three rifle battalions of three companies and a support battalion. Every company commander bore responsibility for training his men, for turning civilians into infantrymen. Like the men they supervised, most of the regiment's officers had been recruited as local youth and worked up through the ranks in the National Guard. Doing a good job of soldiering bestowed hometown status. Although most officers held jobs in small businesses or management of larger companies, people knew them more for their leadership in the local units than for their civilian careers. They were believed to be good men making themselves fit for war, and parents entrusted their sons to them.

Like those sons, every officer in the 4th Alabama was a volunteer. Many Alabama youth had not worked outside their own family. Few had experience with a chain of command, had received orders backed by the force of law, or had been yelled at by strangers. Some people struggled with these realities.

A lot of confidence came from their commander William P. Screws. At age forty-one, he knew the men, having professionally evaluated every officer in the unit and written efficiency reports on them. Screws had made many visits to each of the hometown units, had looked into the eyes of every member of the regiment during inspections in ranks, and knew which promotions had taken place during his tenure. It was said that "he knew his bunch as their own fathers never knew them."[41] The men trusted him and understood his authority, surreptitiously granting him the nickname "Boom-Boom" to refer to his loud and direct manner of presenting commands.[42] There was never doubt as to who was in charge, and the men responded well to Screws's leadership. Captain Jordan said, "He really commands all the time."[43]

Born in Montgomery, Alabama, on January 1, 1875, and raised there, Screws spent a year as a cadet at Marion Military Institute in Marion, Alabama, making the honor roll one time. He was commissioned second lieutenant in the 3rd Alabama Volunteers in 1898 at age twenty-three, just in time for the Spanish-American War. Promoted to first lieutenant of volunteers in 1899, he went to the Philippines. In 1901 he returned to the United States, where he was appointed second lieutenant in the Regular Army in 1902.[44] On subsequent tours in the Philippines, Screws took part in combat operations during the Moro uprising and served as president of Malabang, governing its civil affairs in a force like an Army of Occupation. On returning to the United States he supervised National Guard units in Wisconsin, Illinois, Kansas, and Missouri before returning to Alabama for similar duty.

Screws carried himself well and was carefully turned out, whether in uniform or civilian clothes. He displayed command presence and set a good example in personal appearance.[45] A lifelong Presbyterian, he was not given to flamboyance or gossip, but he did swear freely, which likely helped make him appear more approachable to his men. Profanity and gambling were common-place in his regiment.

Walter E. Bare joined Screws as executive officer and second in command. Employed by the Southern Bell Telephone Company, he organized Company F in Gadsden and was called to active duty with the regiment in 1916.[46]

Chapel services, with voluntary attendance, at Vandiver Park were conducted by First Lieutenant Emmett P. Smith.

Most officers needed the extra income. Even Jordan, more sophisticated and better educated than most, acknowledged the value of his National Guard income in a letter to his wife: "Am glad the cheques came so nicely. We will be paid again in a week or so, and then I will send you a better cheque."[47] Even while preparing for deployment to the Mexican border, Jordan and others remained acutely aware of the demands from home.

## Daily Life at Vandiver Park

Everyone knew they faced a bigger undertaking than ever, and some aspects of the transition were nearly overwhelming. However, they were not rookies. They wore the same uniforms as Regular Army soldiers, with whom they had trained previously at Camp Chickamauga near Chattanooga.[48] They knew elements of soldiering and camp life, and they understood how things were done in a proper army. They were not equal to the regulars in training and experience, but order started to emerge from the confusion of mobilization, and they built leadership skills on the job.

Recruits learned the routine of camp life and were assigned to tents, squads, and platoons. Formations were held in the dirt company street in the early morning, at the end of the day, and as needed in between. Men gathered there for roll call, training, work details, and mail. Every recruit learned his blood type and unique serial number. Later he received a metal identity tag to wear.

The camp experienced a shortage of clothing and blankets. Even cots were scarce. The parsimonious US Army quartermaster tried to give full support to the new regiment, but it, too, was short due to the nationwide troop buildup.[49] Despite the scarcity of some items, the first trip to the supply room felt like Christmas for most recruits, who had rarely owned such amounts of good quality clothing and equipment.

Everyone received inoculations against typhoid and smallpox. Some laughed when officers scheduled sex hygiene classes, but the lessons proved important.

For small-town men unaccustomed to urban standards and economic freedom, the proliferation of brothels—and the cash to spend at them—posed a temptation and a threat. With the assistance of bellmen, prostitutes discretely conducted their trade in practically all downtown hotels. Regulations forbade consorting with prostitutes, but many soldiers flaunted the rules and discussed their disobedience openly. Medics cautioned men about syphilis, gonorrhea (commonly called the clap), and vermin called crabs. Men learned to inspect their bodies for bugs and infection, and they were urged to turn themselves in to a medical facility called a "prophylactic station" for treatment after exposure to prostitutes.

Screws carefully followed VD infection rates of his men. If unusually large numbers visited the Sanitary Department with infections, he required medics to conduct mass "short arm" inspections.[50] In these inspections, units of soldiers formed a line before a doctor. In turn, each lowered his pants and underwear, stripping down his penis with his hands for the doctor to see if anything came out. Symptoms of infection included swelling, inflammation, or fluid coming out of the penis. It took about a week from the time of exposure for the infection to develop and for the head of the penis to swell and turn blue. Once a soldier had been diagnosed with VD, he would be administered a painful treatment, consisting of an injection of a solution of protargol into the penis.[51] VD caused a lot of suffering, but more importantly, it disabled men and interrupted their training. Despite these problems—and the officers' attempts to prevent them—many men continued visiting local prostitutes.[52]

The guardsmen still accomplished a great deal, and in September Screws led the 4th Alabama out of Vandiver Park for its second parade to the capitol.[53] Large crowds turned out for it—a milestone for the unit—and cheered the 4th Alabama, whose soldiers paraded better than in July. Eager to go to New Mexico or Arizona to fight, the troops complained when they heard of matters there calming down.[54] Captain Jordan wrote, "I am crazy to go—for the sake of the experience and the soldiering."[55] In an article titled "Uncle Sam's Soldiers," the Greenville newspaper outlined the advantages of deployment: "A soldier is given the opportunity to travel without expense to himself . . . the Alabama troops will unquestionably be sent to the border for training of about two months and will be equal in its benefits to a year in school or college."[56] This experience was important to men with little education—and to their families.

Alabama newspapers treated the mobilization and training on the Mexican border positively. Military matters assumed a heightened relevance, and papers such as the *Montgomery Advertiser* reported news about the war in Europe. Stories datelined London or Paris extolled the achievements of the British and French armies. War was in the air, and the Alabamians longed for their own wartime experience.[57]

They had only a short wait. Great excitement met the *Montgomery Advertiser*'s October 13 announcement that the regiment would move to the Mexican border, to depart Montgomery by train.[58] The destination was Camp Little in Nogales, Arizona. Officers and men hastened to settle any outstanding arrangements. In one of his last letters to his wife from Montgomery, Jordan wrote, "The bugles blew 'pay day' today so I am sending you $150 in money orders. . . . The other $50 will pay up whatever little expenses I have and get me safely to Nogales."[59] With that, the units were on their way. The Alabama National Guard was headed to war.

# 2
# Pershing's Force on the Mexican Border

Fall brought crisp, clear, and invigorating weather to Montgomery, where a chill marked the air.[1] Vandiver Park opened to civilian visitors on October 22, 1916, and spectators flocked from around the state to see the troops off to the Mexican border.[2]

Two days earlier the regimental commander, regimental surgeon, and a railroad official inspected the trains for damage, cleanliness, working toilets, and adequate potable water. Upon inspection, Colonel Graves and Lieutenant Colonel Screws—who had pointed the troops to this trip as a reward for twelve weeks of hard training—found the cars dirty. Refusing to allow their soldiers to be treated poorly or taken for granted, Graves and Screws demanded that the railroad clean the cars to the highest possible level. The extra cleaning delayed the troops' departure by a day, but men took pride in their accommodations, and Jordan boasted to his wife, "The other regiments left in dirty old cars but we go in style."[3] In looking out for the welfare of his people, Screws had passed an important test of his leadership skills.

Sleeping and eating meals aboard the train while crossing the country was exciting to everyone. The trains stopped approximately every hundred miles to take on water and sometimes coal for the steam engines. Troop trains were often put on sidetracks so that civilian passenger trains could pass, always bringing on lots of waving and cheering. Many locals along the way learned train schedules and stood alongside the tracks when the troops came through. Bystanders talked to the soldiers during stops and shouted encouragement at moving trains. After the cotton fields of Alabama and Mississippi, the soldiers saw the sugarcane plantations and lily-pad-covered bayous in Louisiana.[4] Chatting with Cajun locals they heard French patois spoken for the first time. Derricks and oil tanks in East Texas offered light shows—flares of burning natural gas spouting from wells. After that, scenery mostly consisted of flat plains, mesquite trees, cattle, and cowboys.

A few issues dampened spirits or caused dissention. There was water for shaving and sponge bathing, but the toilets were hard to keep clean. Flush arrangements were primitive. Other disgruntlement arose from passengers themselves. The wives of Captains Lacey Edmundson, Bessemer, and Gardner Greene, Pell City, traveled to Arizona on the troop train, causing some officers to complain. Jordan called the decision, "about the commonest thing I ever heard of."[5] The grumbling came to nothing, however, because Screws had approved their travel with the troops.[6]

The regiment traveled six days and nights with excitement and anticipation building. According to Jordan, "The trip here was delightful."[7]

## John J. Pershing

Like all of the National Guard, the 4th Alabama was placed under the command of Brigadier General John J. Pershing when it reached the Mexican border. Despite being first captain and president of his class at West Point, Pershing had only an average academic record, coming in thirtieth out of seventy-seven in his class.[8] He entered West Point at age twenty-two—later than most cadets—after an unusual path. A formal, tough Missouri farm boy with an influential and ambitious father of limited means, Pershing taught in a school for blacks as a teenager. Income from it allowed Pershing to enter Kirksville Normal School, which helped qualify him for appointment to the United States Military Academy.[9] There he became "the model American soldier: no-nonsense, obedient, quietly forceful and a little dull."[10] Regarded by some as an unexceptional officer, Pershing was not a polished speaker. However, he gained distinction as a reliable troop leader in Cuba and a careful tactician in combat and good negotiator with insurgents during service in the Philippines. When General Joe Wheeler—a West Point graduate, a Confederate general from Alabama, and a US Army general during the Spanish-American War—recommended him for promotion, he spoke of Pershing's "untiring energy, faithfulness and gallantry."[11]

Along the way, Pershing made influential friends. He and Theodore Roosevelt met in 1897, when Roosevelt served as police commissioner of New York City.[12] Service in the Spanish-American War strengthened their bond and mutual respect. At age forty-five Pershing married Frankie—the attractive and vivacious daughter of Francis E. Warren, the powerful Wyoming senator and chairman of the Senate Military Affairs Committee. Roosevelt attended the ceremony at the National Cathedral in Washington.[13] Such connections caused suspicion that Pershing received unfair advantages. These suspicions escalated when President Roosevelt arranged for Pershing's promotion from captain to brigadier general, skipping more than eight hundred officers on the traditional list and causing quite a stir.[14]

Although some doubted his abilities, Pershing demonstrated leadership skills. His best quality was to critically judge the officers of the primitive, poorly trained US Army. He allowed for no excuse, working in a dispassionate and firm way, putting in fourteen-hour days, seven days a week. His demeanor was harsh but effective, and the men working under Pershing "thought he was strict, but fair. Nor did they doubt his competence as commander. One veteran who called him an 'S.O.B.' and said he 'hated his guts,' added: 'But as a soldier, the ones then and the ones now couldn't polish his boots.'"[15] Others reported on his softer side: "His fierce mien, said one, which tended to freeze up everyone, considerably softened when he opened his mouth and began to speak. And he could tolerate human foibles. When he encountered a group of soldiers squatting behind an overturned wagon which served both as a windbreaker and concealment, he said not a word about their playing craps, which was against regulations, but told them to move away from the trail 'or some lieutenant might see you.'"[16]

Pershing's service on the Mexican border rewarded his ability to deal with people of opposing views and offered both a training ground and a showcase.[17] It also helped him cope with grief over the death of his wife and three small daughters, who died on August 27, 1915. The tragedy took place in a house fire at the Presidio, an army post in San Francisco, while the general was on the Mexican border.[18] A six-year-old son, Warren, survived.

Among those offering condolences was Francisco "Pancho" Villa—the man Pershing would soon try to capture. Villa, who was twenty-five when he learned to sign his own name, was an influential guerilla leader.[19] The two men first met in 1914 when Pershing was stationed at Fort Bliss and Villa was fighting a new Mexican president, General Victoriano Huerta. They took to each other: "Villa thought that the American general was *muy simpatico*, while Pershing found Villa a genial, rough-and-ready sort, not unlike some of the guerilla chieftains he had fought against in the Philippines."[20] This experience gave Pershing a firsthand knowledge of the complexities of the Mexican situation.

The Mexican Revolution started in 1910. A year later, President Porfirio Díaz, whom President Taft had met in 1909 on the border, was overthrown by the leader of the constitutionalist party, Francisco Madero.[21] Taft stationed five thousand troops along the Rio Grande to protect American interests. After two years in power, President Madero was deposed and assassinated by General Huerta, the army officer he had called upon to suppress the numerous army rebellions that plagued his regime.[22] President Wilson refused to recognize Huerta because he had seized power by killing Madero.[23] Under Huerta's rule, an incident with the US Navy at Veracruz caused the death of seventeen American marines and led to an American occupation of the city.[24] Meanwhile, Pancho Villa, the popular bandit leader, a Mexican Robin Hood who took the side of the poor against the wealthy landowners, joined the fight against Huerta. He and another revolutionary leader, Álvaro Obregón who commanded a guerilla army made of thousands of fearless Yaqui Indians, allied themselves with the Constitutionalists, favored by the Americans.[25] Huerta was eventually forced out by the constitutionalists, Venustiano Carranza became head of the government, and the Americans withdrew from Mexico. Emiliano Zapata, another revolutionary leader whose guerilla bands roamed the country north of Mexico City and who had also been allied previously with Carranza and the constitutionalists, resumed revolutionary activities while Villa started targeting American interests on the border. This was observed with great interest by German officials eager to see the United States engulfed in the Mexican imbroglio and therefore less apt to become involved in the European conflict.[26]

## Advanced Infantry Training in Arizona

Many National Guard troops had been in Bisbee, Yuma, Tucson, Nogales, and other towns and villages since 1914, and a large force still trained and maneuvered all over the countryside when the Alabamians arrived "bag and baggage" in Nogales (see fig. 2) on October 28, 1916.[27] Soldier Dan Vann described it for people back home: "This is not a big town, [sic] there are about fifteen hundred people here beside soldiers. There are about fourteen thousand soldiers."[28]

The men, stiff from the journey, welcomed the three-mile march to Camp Little, named for Private Stephen Little, killed in the crossfire of a skirmish between Mexican revolutionaries on November 26, 1915.[29]

The actual skirmish involved only Mexican troops, but "the eleven-strand wire fence separating Nogales, Arizona, from Nogales, Sonora, gave little protection against flying bullets."[30] A stray bullet killed Little, who was serving guard duty nearby.[31]

Upon arrival Jordan wrote his wife, "There are so many wonderful things to see, we hardly know where to turn."[32] The air was clear, clean, and dry. All 4,955 men in the Alabama National Guard would train together there.[33] The regiments' camp, a discrete place within Camp Little, was strung out along a line of steep hills on the eastern end of the main camp.[34] Recently vacated by the 5th Infantry of the California National Guard, it was a ready-made site, complete with screened-in tent kitchens, dining rooms, and terraces for the pyramid squad tents (see fig. 3).[35] Company streets were parallel and stacked one above the other like a flight of steps. It lacked the wooden cottages with modern facilities boasted by the main camp. Still, the location, described as "high enough to get a good view but not too high to climb," was desirable.[36] There was a 360-degree view of mountains, some with streaks of snow on top. The most prominent were Mount Hopkins and Mount Wrightson, named for early mining engineers. The Mexican border was a mile and a half south of the camp, though men knew not to cross it for fear of "a fine of 6 months and $30.00."[37]

Danger lurked nearby, but things were stable. The few married officers and their wives lived in what was known as the Squaw Camp.[38] Captain Edmundson, whose wife's presence angered men on the train, had borrowed a tent from the quartermaster, boarded the sides, added a floor and several pieces of furniture purchased cheaply, and moved in.[39] Compared to soldiers, the Edmundsons lived in luxury.

The Alabama regiments were fully equipped and physically fit when they reached Nogales. The men could generally hit a target with a rifle, pistol, and machine gun; they could march long distances; and they assembled and disassembled camp quickly. Four months of advanced infantry training in Arizona were started with confidence and high morale. The band put on concerts. The colorful places and people excited everybody.

The troops, for the first time in their lives, were in the midst of mountains, extinct volcanoes, canyons, and plains. They marched near cottonwood trees, tall oaks, and flowing willows, some of which arched over the road. Cacti of all sizes, some huge, dotted the surrounding desert, and tall cattails sprung from the riverbed. Colors were varied and breathtaking, including sand-colored adobe houses, as the men marched through plains, hills, mountains, and canyons. Streams were nonexistent or very shallow, and the riverbed offered good campsites in dry weather, though flash floods posed a danger. Occasional grasslands nourished grazing cattle. Mesquite was everywhere, and flat, barren deserts contrasted with massive thunderstorms, dust storms, and fluctuating temperatures.

The climate was desertlike. Jordan described it as "dry and bracing, the days . . . pleasantly warm, almost hot, and the nights unpleasantly cold. It began to cool off at sunset and by nine o'clock we are ready for overcoats. By three A.M. it is almost freezing."[40] The 4th Alabama received extra clothing when they arrived in Arizona.[41] On some nights the temperatures plummeted to fifteen degrees, as desert sand would not hold the heat from the day. Men used small, wood-fired Sibley stoves for warmth.[42] As many as wanted could be drawn at no cost. Jordan wrote, "It seems that the quartermaster department here has everything we are apt to need and does not hesitate to turn it loose!"[43]

The Mexican border was a busy place. Such a large deployment of American infantry had not occurred since the Civil War. Beyond providing advanced infantry training for the 4th Alabama and others, the overall Mexican border operation was the first large-scale testing ground for the modern American army. Pershing, denied full use of railroads by the generally uncooperative Mexican government, rebuilt trails and successfully delivered over ten thousand tons of supplies by wagons, army trucks, and trucks purchased from civilian dealers in Texas. He learned that the army needed better rolling stock and that underpowered airplanes were of little use even for scouting or communications.[44] Men used telephones and tested technology such as wireless communication. The Signal Corps implemented photography, including aerial photography.[45]

Special equipment was everywhere. The camp had mechanics, repair shops, and dumps for gasoline, oil, and spare tires. Armored cars were tried out, and there was talk of introducing tanks and phasing out cavalry. However, mules, wagon trains, and horse-drawn artillery continued to be the mainstay of US Army transportation. Two-mule and four-mule army wagons, driven by soldiers called mule skinners, triumphed when trucks reached rivers without bridges or hopelessly sank into mud holes. The cavalry practiced old-fashioned mounted charges. Most camps had picket lines of horses and mules, whose daily care required substantial manpower. Trainloads of alfalfa hay, corn, and oats arrived constantly.[46]

New weaponry accompanied the new technologies. Although there was very little artillery on the border, and the Alabama regiments did not train with it, observation balloons were used for adjusting its fire. Small trench mortars were introduced as infantry weapons.

Pershing's soldiers spread from Texas to New Mexico to Arizona. The logistics of moving troops, food, and supplies in the field are always complicated, but the relatively recent (1912) statehood of Arizona and New Mexico added improved roads. These maneuvers also tested the army's ability at large-scale field sanitation.

A reliable water supply required constant attention by the Sanitary Department. The camp had showers, but streams and rainwater were sometimes used for bathing. Potable water for cooking and filling canteens came from regulated water points. The supply for Nogales was controlled by a heavily guarded pumping station on the Santa Cruz River, about nine miles east of Camp Little. A robust river flowed underground, but the riverbed above ground was dry.[47] Elements of the 4th Alabama frequently pulled guard there, as did the 1st Alabama, 2nd Idaho, a battalion of California engineers, and a California mounted engineer unit.[48]

Each unit was responsible for its own water supply while in the field. Soldiers kept canteens filled to the top, not waiting until they were empty before refilling. Chlorination helped make water safe. An American firm, Wallace & Tiernan, was incorporated in 1913 for the manufacture of the world's first chlorination machines.[49] They were a big improvement over earlier processes, and the American and British armies purchased three hundred units in 1916. Army kitchens used chlorinated water to wash aluminum mess kits when boiled water was unavailable. Still, illness and injury occurred. Camp Little had a permanent wooden hospital, and circus-sized tents housed hospitals elsewhere along the border.[50]

Beyond Nogales were the "Old West" villages of Lochiel and Arivaca. Three or four shabby wooden structures on dusty streets, they offered glimpses of frontier life. Many Alabama men liked soldiering and adventuring. There was always a chance of combat. It was remote, but their training never let them forget why they were there.

## Daily Life on the Border

Bayonet training had been introduced in Montgomery, but in Arizona it was practiced seriously. The armies in Europe used bayonets and the men from Alabama believed their time would come if the United States entered this conflict. A rifle with a bayonet on the end of it was heavy and awkward to handle, and the notion of killing a man face to face was not easy to get used to. The US Army tried to overcome that with an extraordinary amount of practice. Regularly on the training schedule, bayonet work required as much as four hours work at a time, making soldiers physically stronger and more confident. Thrust techniques were taught for offense, and parry exercises were conducted in defense. The men learned to use the rifle as a club.[51] On the bayonet course men ran from station to station at assault speed and thrust the bayonet into straw men. The Manual of the Bayonet became second nature. For combat purposes it was the most important part of the Manual of Arms and trained men for close combat.

Poor weather never delayed training, and pneumonia developed. Amerine records: "Deaths occurred daily and at times as many as four bodies were escorted to the railroad station in a single procession, all to be shipped back to Alabama."[52]

Major Dallas Smith's 3rd Battalion undertook a big desert project—the construction of a full-sized trench line with dugouts, shooting steps, and lookout points.[53] Army manuals included plans for these structures, which were the same size and type as those the French used in combat—just one indication of the influence of the war in Europe.[54]

All three battalions practiced patrolling techniques and defensive combat training from Smith's newly constructed trenches.[55] Rifle companies became expert in using lightly armed reconnaissance patrols to gather information. More complicated, heavily armed combat patrols of platoon size and larger were organized.[56] These were usually used to set up ambushes for the capture of prisoners or to raid, surprise, and kill groups of the enemy. Techniques to get relief parties out to and back from listening posts and outposts in no-man's-land were part of advanced infantry training. Various methods of rotating platoons and companies were practiced. Procedures were rudimentary, but executing the smallest detail perfectly could aid in a unit's success.

Jordan wrote his wife, "Our crowd continues to thrive. We are being put through by the regular officers and although we are not as good as we might be, we believe there have been worse troops than ours."[57] The men continued drills and practice, gaining confidence with each exercise.

## Road March

Fourteen hundred men in the 4th Alabama left Nogales for Tucson on November 21, 1916, their longest road march ever.[58] Everyone walked except for those on kitchen and supply wagons, machine gun carts, and ambulances. A medic accompanied each company, a doctor was assigned to each battalion, and a dentist and a veterinarian served the regimental surgeon, a major. The regiment's ambulances followed the column, and medics with a pack mule trailed each battalion. Mule-drawn machine gun carts hauled weapons and ammunition.

The column followed the riverbed up the San Rafael Valley. Hills, mesas, and mountains flanked the road about two miles to the east and to the west. The tops of some hills were dusted with snow. Carrying full field packs with weapons and wearing sweaters, overcoats, and gloves, the regiment hiked 18.5 miles on the first day.[59]

Reaching Tucson late on November 24, 1916, after a four-day march, they made camp and rested before being reviewed by the regimental and brigade commanders.[60] A maneuver was practiced with the 2nd Alabama Infantry and the regiment participated in a war exercise on the last leg of the four-day return march. The round trip totaled 140 miles, with twenty-one miles marched on the last day.[61]

Despite the rigor, Jordan observed "everybody in fine shape and high spirits."[62] A few weeks later, the 2nd Alabama Infantry Regiment took twelve days to make the same march that the 4th Alabama had completed in nine. Screws and his leaders were proud of their men. Everyone knew that the standard for Roman legionnaires was twenty-four miles a day. The US Army standard was fifteen miles a day, which is what they did on that 140-mile march. With large groups the regulation rate was eleven miles a day.[63]

In late November Jordan learned that civilians at home were attempting to have Birmingham's artillery battery returned home by Christmas. This caused disgust among the K Company riflemen, but Jordan wrote his wife, "Of course, we would all be glad to go but we infantry boys intend to stick it out and do our work as long as Uncle Sam needs us."[64] He continued to growl in a letter the following week, "We have all been amused at the efforts of some of our 'prominent citizens' to get the batteries home by Christmas. . . . Why is it Birmingham people always try to do the wrong thing at the wrong time? They haven't a chance of getting their boys home, for the g'vt is going to send those who have been on the border longest home first, and the Alabamians are the newcomers. . . . The boys in my company declare they will stay here 'til they rot' before they will go begging anybody to send them home."[65]

## Dividing Lines

A racial incident occurred when soldiers of the 4th Alabama and two troops of the 10th US Cavalry of black Buffalo Soldiers met in Nogales.[66] Pershing had served with the 10th Cavalry in Cuba, where he earned the nickname "Black Jack Pershing."[67] On the border Pershing had requested the 10th to accompany his force for its first penetration deep into Mexico.

Later, when the 10th came to Nogales, some Alabama soldiers spoke of the black cavalrymen as wanting to "clean out" the 4th. The men of the 10th were the only armed, uniformed black men the soldiers from Alabama had ever seen. Tensions erupted, and "in several street fights groups of black men, when they attacked the Alabamians, were severely beaten by the 'tenderfeet' of the Guard."[68]

General Plummer, the district commander in Arizona, solved the problem by dividing the 10th Cavalry and sending half of it to Lochiel and half to Arivaca.

## Social Life and Recreational Activities

This episode added to the reputation for fierceness the Alabama men earned on the border. General Plummer reportedly exclaimed, "In time of war, send me all the Alabamians you can get, but in time of peace, for Lord's sake, send them to somebody else."[69] Plummer recognized an Alabama trademark: the energy and enthusiasm that could lead men into distraction and trouble when they grew bored were the same qualities that allowed them to thrive in the chaos of war.

There is little evidence of much contact between American enlisted men and Mexican civilians, although occasional references to interactions appear in letters. For example, Dan Vann reported that he could understand enough to converse with some of the area's natives.[70]

Some ventured into the section of downtown Nogales that was known for brothels. In a feeble show of curtailing soldiers' behavior, "Commanders made contraction of venereal disease punishable by court-martial based on the idea that the prophylactic treatment could prevent infection. But they failed to attack the problem at the source, making little effort to prevent the men from visiting houses of prostitution."[71]

Other distractions existed. Vann, for example, bemoaned the high inflation of luxury items in a letter home: "Yes there is whiskey out here but it cost [sic] 3 or 4 dollars a pint."[72] Many men were court-martialed for "use of alcohol and drunken behavior."[73]

Privates earned $15 a month, less 40 cents for the soldier's home, a net of about $307 a month in 2009 dollars. Captains earned $200 a month in 1917 dollars, the equivalent of about $4,320 in 2009 currency.[74] (See fig. 4.)

The men took full advantage of every opportunity for small pleasures. Vann reported playing in daily football games.[75] K Company bought a phonograph with $50 from the Company Fund, and nightly concerts took place in the mess hall or in First Sergeant J. P. Davis's tent. Some even kept the machine going while off duty during the day. The company cooks were in the habit of starting the music when they reported to prepare breakfast at 4:30 A.M.[76]

As 1916 waned, members of the regimental and battalion staffs planned for a big Christmas tree as an opportunity for officers to entertain selected local civilians. A sudden death changed those plans. Lieutenant Hughes, a popular, hard-working, and big-hearted fellow from Supply Company keeled over from an aneurysm. After a memorial service an honor guard and the band escorted his body to the railroad station where it began the journey back to his family.[77]

K Company still held a celebration but omitted the civilian guests. It worked out well. Jordan reported home about the hard wind and "once a year snow" that covered everything, then added, "We had our Christmas dinner on Christmas Eve . . . and it was a dandy. We had a regular spread, turkey and all the usual fixings. Cost about $50.00 of the Company Fund in addition to the regular issue. The boys had a fit over it."[78]

An inspector general reviewed Camp Little on January 12, 1917.[79] It was serious business for the camp's ten thousand men. The regiment paraded for the brigade commander, a regular army colonel named Jenkins. Jordan relayed the day's success in a letter, "Colonel Screws announced to the whole regiment, 'The Brigade Commander wishes to especially compliment Captain Jordan's company. The marching of this company is as good as that of any troops he has ever seen.'" Jordan acknowledged his pleasure to his wife, admitting, "Poor as I am, I would not have taken anything for it."[80]

The men continued to develop through training exercises, but illness always threatened. Papers at home reported flu on the border, and two Butler County soldiers—Will Frazer and nineteen-year-old Cleveland Campbell of D Company—were listed in their hometown paper as ill. It was later learned that Frazer had been confused with a Birmingham man, also named Will Frazer, who died on the border.[81]

The Greenville paper published a letter from Captain Ashworth of Ambulance Company to G. W. Campbell, father of the deceased. Ashworth reported that young Campbell had died of pneumonia, received a funeral service attended by his company with tent mates as pallbearers, and was accompanied by the regimental band to the railroad station. In that same issue of the paper, Greenville's Sergeant Earl Godwin of D Company reported that there were only eight deaths from flu in the entire regiment.[82] Jordan wrote his wife: "A good many of the boys had grippe, some with pneumonia. A mild type of measles developed a short while ago. . . . As is always the case in armies, any contagious disease spreads rapidly . . . a wise order from headquarters forbids any soldier from going to a picture show or any crowded place."[83]

Soldiers' complaints about the flu reached Alabama's governor Charles Henderson, who responded by visiting Nogales. Along with Screws, he inspected the unit's camp and hospital on January 15, 1917. Henderson spoke with about two hundred men and found everything in order.[84] Announcements of departures of US troops would come soon enough, but high-level international politics would trigger them, not the flu.

## Breaking Camp

In early February, shortly after the War Department had published an order calling for withdrawal, the Alabama National Guard troops were sent on border patrol. On February 7, 1917, the 2nd Battalion, 4th Infantry went to Lochiel, about fifteen miles due east of Nogales. The 1st Battalion, 2nd Infantry moved to Arivaca, about thirty-five miles northwest of Nogales and twelve miles from the border. Almost eight months after mobilization Alabama National Guard troops finally were guarding the border.[85]

Mexico's president Venustiano Carranza had promised cooperation with US forces, but little materialized. Public opinion there opposed having Americans within Mexico's borders. Although Pershing remained unable to engage Villa's forces in decisive battle, he penetrated into the country during his eleven months there.[86] He demonstrated that the United States would not be controlled by those operating beyond properly constituted authorities. Upon his departure, he received a new appointment to command the Southern Department of the Army from San Antonio.[87] This appointment was facilitated by the death of Pershing's former rival, Major General Frederick Funston, whose position he assumed.[88]

Internal disturbances in Mexico continued after Pershing's departure. Emiliano Zapata attempted to overthrow Carranza but was assassinated, then Carranza was assassinated.[89] Turmoil prevailed, but for the Americans, the most important outcome of the Mexican Punitive Expedition was intensive training for a large number of American soldiers.[90] They had ostensibly gone there to patrol the border and prevent raids, but they had emerged better prepared for future conflicts—and at least a few of them believed those conflicts awaited them in Europe.

## Homeward Bound to Crisis

Following the withdrawal order of January 28, 1917, the Alabamians left the area. Twenty-six cars carrying troops from the 1st and 2nd Alabama left on March 15.[91] The 4th Alabama departed on March 16, 1917.[92]

Rumor was that some National Guard units had been immediately discharged upon returning home, and most Alabama soldiers thought that would happen to them. A few, including Jordan, believed that they would eventually serve in France, but President Wilson continued his posture of international neutrality.

The return train trip to Montgomery was much like the one out to Arizona, though the troops—more confident and suddenly released from discipline and routine—were more boisterous. Some of the Alabama regiments returned to Montgomery through Oklahoma, Memphis, and Birmingham, while others followed a southern route.[93] Three trains coming from San Antonio stopped in Greenville, Alabama. Sidetracked, they were met by a large crowd in a gala event lasting almost two hours.[94] The welcoming group included Butler County native Robert E. Steiner, a National Guard brigadier general.[95]

The regiments pulled into Montgomery that same afternoon, March 22. In a ceremony at Vandiver Park, each returnee received a service medal paid for by civilian subscription.[96] About four hundred young lady sponsors participated in those festivities, and the newspaper estimated the total civilian crowd to be fifteen thousand.[97] Governor Henderson attended, and Secretary of War Newton D. Baker sent a telegram of congratulations. Jordan wrote his wife, "Our badges were pinned on yesterday amid great enthusiasm. The sight of so many pretty girls made me think all the more of you."[98]

The big question was whether troops would be mustered out or sent immediately to Europe. Some felt they would be dismissed, while others argued that "despite many weaknesses shown during their service on the border there was overwhelming evidence that the National Guard of this period was a very different force from the Militia which on numerous occasions in the past combat history of the country had proven itself unreliable in battle."[99]

The answer came in the form of a warning order instructing all Alabama regiments to guard railroads, bridges, and industrial sites in Alabama and Tennessee. Neither state harbored any known German saboteurs, but previous acts of sabotage—the most famous being the July 1916 destruction of the munitions terminal at New York's Black Tom Pier—were attributed to the Germans, and this left the country with a lingering sense of insecurity.[100] The threat provided a reason to keep the regiments intact while the United States remained outside of the war.

## The United States Enters the War

A lot had changed during the five months on the Mexican border, but even more significant developments in Europe took place after the regiment returned from

Nogales. President Wilson's January 27 inaugural address called for "Peace without Victory"—a clear overture to the Germans, who totally ignored it.

After the sinking of the *Lusitania* and with the Arabic pledge in 1915, and the Sussex pledge in 1916, Germany had tried to keep the United States unprovoked and out of the war by drastically restricting its use of submarine warfare, although it never stopped it fully.[101]

By 1917, they had calculated that if they acted quickly on restoring full submarine warfare, they could force the British to ask for peace before the United States could join the Allies. They believed that "Britain would sue for peace, so long as unrestricted warfare began not later than February 1, 1917."[102]

Germany warned that after that date German U-boats would target all ships, regardless of their flag. Germany hoped to stop the Americans from sending unlimited supplies to the exhausted Allies, but Germans no longer feared the possibility of the United Sates entering the war—in fact, they knew their actions would provoke it.[103] Rather, they now reasoned that German submarines could stall American shipping effectiveness by stopping most supplies from reaching England and France. They believed their submarines would delay the American war effort enough to stop it from tipping the balance of power to the Allies. This rationale allowed a narrow and uncertain strategic window for German success.

However, Germany's change in policy helped push Wilson from his position of neutrality. American public opinion was also shifting and becoming more anti-German. This was not only due to the new German policy of unrestricted warfare but also to the acknowledgment at the end of March by German Foreign Minister Zimmerman that he had sent a telegram in January to Mexican President Carranza specifically asking Mexico to join Germany in a war against the United States, with Japan as an ally. As a consequence, Mexico would be able to recover Texas, New Mexico, and Arizona.[104]

Wilson had labored to keep the United States outside the war, "but when the time for action arrived he threw his whole weight behind both the war and the peace efforts."[105] He broke off diplomatic relations with Germany on February 13, immediately after the Germans returned to the policy of unrestricted submarine warfare. Then, on February 26, in an effort to protect American commerce, the president asked Congress to adopt a policy of armed neutrality.[106] American merchant vessels began carrying deck guns, an aggressive step toward the "preparedness movement" that former president Theodore Roosevelt and business interest groups began advocating in August 1914.

There had been considerable support for the preparedness movement throughout the country in 1916. The banner was taken up by Chambers of Commerce throughout the United States where organizations "in twenty-six states unanimously approved compulsory military training along with a majority of chambers in sixteen states. . . . Only one, Alabama, took an anti-preparedness stand."[107]

One product of this preparedness movement were the Businessmen's Military Training Camps originally operated by the army on an unofficial basis in Plattsburgh, New York. In April 1916 Secretary Baker expressed his admiration of the summer encampments for students at Plattsburgh and elsewhere. This time, the preparedness movement was embraced by some in Alabama as the president of the University of Alabama joined a large group of other university officials in endorsing these military training camps.[108] These camps allowed eager volunteers to receive advance training and preparedness, and some forty thousand men had been put through a month-long basic training course by the summer of 1916, long before the May 1917 enactment of the Selective Service Act.[109] Unlike the typical National Guard population, the Plattsburgh camp model generally attracted men from an upper echelon of society.[110]

Although the Plattsburgh men proved eager to enter the European conflict, not all Americans agreed. The hit song "I Didn't Raise My Boy to Be a Soldier," by lyricist Alfred Bryan and composer Al Piantadosi, represented the sentiments of many Americans.[111] German and Irish interest groups and immigrants "attempted to pressure the government to keep Americans out of the conflict and actively promoted a course of strict neutrality."[112] However, Germany's change in submarine warfare policy pushed the nation toward war. Whether or not Americans wanted it, their nation was headed for it.

Wilson issued a special call to Congress for April 2, two weeks sooner than originally scheduled. In the speech he said, "Right is more precious than peace."[113] He felt that the thinking and feeling of the people had reached such an inflection point that he could support war on Germany "and bring the American people with him in such a momentous decision."[114] German U-boats sank a number of American merchant ships on the day of Wilson's speech, adding further fuel to the fires of international conflict.

On April 6, 1917, the United States declared war on Germany. The country was emerging from two decades of divisive political struggles and social change, and it had struggled for three years to remain neutral. The United States entered the war at a low point for the Allied Army, which had seen every major offensive fail and was making no gains. Wilson asked Congress to commit the United States to a distant war that had already "butchered men by the millions."[115] Only time would reveal whether this was a reckless choice or a bold decision.

Ten days later, the French Army launched an ill-fated offensive on the western front. Called the Second Battle of the Aisne, it took place on the Chemin des Dames, causing an Allied defeat rather than the expected success. Preceded by a six-day barrage of French artillery, the attack across a ten-mile front was met by strongly dug in German troops. The French suffered forty thousand dead.[116] French commander General Robert Nivelle, after predicting a great triumph, was forced to resign, and the battle was a disaster in the eyes of the French people. As a result of the doomed offensive, poor food, and lack of leave, French troops staged a series of mutinies. Eventually, officials found 23,385 soldiers guilty of mutiny. Many were reduced in rank and more than four hundred were sentenced to death, but only fifty were executed.[117]

On April 22, 1917, a British delegation arrived in Washington and appealed for help. A few days later, French delegates—including Marshal Joseph Joffre, "The Hero of the Marne"—arrived. Joffre was especially well received in New York and Washington.[118] He asked Wilson for at least one division, but his request was denied, as there was not a single formed and equipped combat division in the United States.[119]

In an emergency move, General Philippe Pétain, a hero from the defense of Verdun, received command of the French Army on May 15. The mutinies continued until he successfully reorganized the army. Pétain worked hard to build back shattered morale. He won the confidence of the country, and of the poilus, the ordinary soldiers who did the fighting.[120]

A letter from Secretary of War Baker on May 27, 1917, organized the US Army and Marines committed to the fight in France into the American Expeditionary Forces (AEF). Funston would have been the obvious choice to command it, but he was dead. Pershing, who had recently replaced him as commander of the Southern Department, became the favorite candidate to head the force, originally a single division, and Baker's letter put him in charge of the AEF.

Pershing arrived in Liverpool, England, on June 8, 1917. Baker placed great confidence in him, saying, "I will give you only two orders, one to go and the other to come home."[121] Pershing later described the state of affairs when he reached France:

In the five months ending June 30, 1917, German submarines had accomplished the destruction of three and a quarter million tons of Allied shipping. During three years Germany had seen practically all of her offensives except Verdun crowned with success. Her battle lines were on foreign soil and she had withstood every Allied attack since the Marne. The German general staff could now foresee the complete elimination of Russia, the possibility of defeating Italy before the end of the year and, finally, the campaign of 1918 against the French and British on the western front which might terminate the war. . . . It cannot be said that German hopes of final victory were extravagant . . . conditions made it apparent that Americans must make a supreme material effort as soon as possible. I cabled Washington on July 6, 1917 that plans should contemplate sending over at least a million men by next May.[122]

Pershing and the 1st Division crossed the English Channel to France where huge crowds and elaborate ceremonies welcomed them. An old veteran in charge of Napoleon's personal effects held out the emperor's sword for Pershing to touch in Paris at Les Invalides.[123] Thought stiff and cold by many, the general created a high sense of drama by kissing the relic. Brigadier General James G. Harbord, Pershing's chief of staff said, "The story was told in every bivouac and barracks in France and ran through the drawing-rooms of the capital like a bulletin from the Grande Armée."[124]

## Developments in Alabama

On April 7, the day after the war was declared, the 4th Alabama broke camp in Montgomery to assume its new duty as sentries. Captain Edmundson, D Company, established guard posts throughout Baldwin County along the L&N railroad tracks and at all railroad bridges and viaducts. Bay Minette, the county seat, stood about 150 miles south of Montgomery. Its population included many German immigrant growers and shippers of cabbage and other vegetables, but they exhibited no hostility and behaved as loyal Americans. D Company pitched pyramid squad tents on the courthouse grounds in the town square. The men performing guard duty lived in two-man pup tents and rotated assignments with soldiers from the base camp on the courthouse grounds.[125]

The other Alabamian guardsmen conducted the same type of activities throughout Alabama and parts of Tennessee. Many disliked the work of civilian watchmen and considered it beneath their skills as trained infantrymen.[126]

When soldiers from the 4th Alabama returned to Vandiver Park from sentry duties in April, it was the only place in the state where civilians could join the National Guard. Volunteers arrived every day. President Wilson signed into law the Selective Service Act on May 19, 1917, but the draft did not start until July 20, 1917.[127] Due to the time it took to execute the law, the draft was not yet in place, and it remained controversial: "House Majority Leader Claude Kitchin, who had voted against the war resolution, was even more vehemently opposed to a draft. The chairman of the Military Affairs Committee, Alabamian S. Hubert Dent, Jr., had made his opinion clear by refusing to bring the bill to the floor, handing the task to the ranking Republican on the committee. Dent insisted the government should try to raise an army of volunteers before resorting to the draft."[128]

Many believed it unpatriotic and unmanly to be drafted, and they preferred going into the National Guard as volunteers. The final legislation of the Selective Service Act "allowed for volunteering only in the Regular Army, the Navy and the National Guard, but not in the new 'National Army.'"[129]

Only about 13 percent of Alabamians who registered for the draft in 1917 and 1918 were inducted.[130] This low acceptance rate stemmed from poor health and illiteracy. Draftees had to demonstrate basic literacy skills, though many servicemen possessed only rudimentary reading abilities. According to intelligence testers, 21.5% of all white troops were illiterate. World War I men as a group averaged a sixth-grade education.[131] Other than doctors, dentists, and veterinarians, few officers in the Alabama regiments boasted a college education. Captain Herman W. Thompson of H Company attended Marion Military Institute and had a distinctive academic record at Howard College; Captain Mortimer Jordan, though a rifle company commander, held a medical degree; and Captain Gardner Greene graduated from George Washington University Law School.

Many other good men were recognized on the basis of their leadership rather than their educational background. The 4th Alabama promoted Ozark's Captain John W. Carroll to major in May 1917. He got the job through the popular vote of troops, apparently the last of the regiment's officers to be promoted through that process.[132] Jordan described him as "the best fellow in the world, very unassuming and modest, a good officer and fine fellow . . . has been homesick for his old Company G ever since his election."[133]

Authorized strength for rifle companies in the 4th Alabama increased from sixty-five men to 150.[134] The unit established another basic training schedule for newly recruited men. Screws ordered a big parade in Montgomery for July 29, 1917. It had been ten months since the last parade.[135] Old hands as well as new recruits needed the precision drill. Time spent on sentry duty in poor conditions dulled the edge and professionalism gained on the Mexican border. The July parade coincided with the beginning of the draft and was regarded as motivation for people to register for the draft. Screws led the regiment's best "spit and polish" show thus far; all wore felt campaign hats, and the mounted regimental staff preceded the twenty-two-member band. It was the 4th Alabama's last parade under its Civil War name.

Everything seemed to be coming together for the unit, but that stability was threatened. On August 2, 1917, while preparing for the possibility of fighting forces abroad, the 4th Alabama faced difficult politics. In a letter to Senator John Bankhead, the adjutant general of the United States announced that Regular Army officers would no longer be permitted to hold commissions in National Guard organizations below the grade of general officers. The shocking news, which appeared on the front page of the *Montgomery Advertiser*, meant that Lieutenant Colonel Screws might be forced to leave the regiment.[136] Lieutenant Colonel Bare was mentioned in print as a possible successor. Civilian and political leaders in Alabama raised a flurry of support for Screws. Among those writing to Washington on his behalf was Marie Bankhead Owen, daughter of Senator John Bankhead and sister of Congressman William Bankhead.[137]

An army-wide competition for commands was taking place, and Screws was far down on the promotion list. Many envied him and wanted his plum job. The War Department decision meant that Screws would lose his command of the 4th Alabama and be sent to a Regular Army unit, most likely in a lower position than regimental command.

However, the *Montgomery Journal* forecast Screws's retention despite official word that Regular Army members would be retained by their old commands in the regular service.[138] He was far better equipped to lead an infantry unit in combat than most National Guard officers, and—luckily for his men—he ultimately kept the command because he had done a good job in Alabama. He was respected by politicians in the state and had served as a Regular Army officer supervising National Guard and militia in various parts of the country without interruption since his combat and administrative experience in the Philippines. The unit had faced yet another challenge, but it had survived intact. Now the men awaited the larger challenges to come.

# 3
# Making an Infantry Division

Given the War Department's recent concern with the relationship between Regular Army officers and National Guard units, Lieutenant Colonel Screws seemed unlikely to receive a promotion. However, on August 14, 1917, not two weeks after Screws was threatened with the loss of his command, the War Department ordered the name of the 4th Alabama changed to the 167th United States Infantry.[1] In the process, it elevated Screws to full colonel, thus validating his leadership.[2] He now held a coveted army officer job—and the promise of leading into combat the infantry regiment he had trained.

The change from the 4th Alabama to the 167th carried more than a new name. Orders authorized the regiment to grow from approximately 1,400 to 3,720 officers and men. As part of the transition, rifle company strength increased from 150 to 250, and even the band expanded from twenty-two men to forty-nine.[3] The 1st Alabama Infantry, 2nd Alabama Infantry, 1st Alabama Cavalry, and 4th Alabama Infantry had a total of 5,025 men.[4] Screws knew all the units, which helped him select men among them for the new regiment.

The troops learned of the changes while on a road march near Ware's Ferry, north of Montgomery, but not all was in flux. The field grade officers and company commanders from the 4th Alabama continued to hold their ranks and positions in the new 167th US Infantry Regiment. Everybody seemed to benefit from the regiment's new name and new future. While acknowledging that the transitions would take some effort, Captain Mortimer Jordan shared with his wife the enthusiasm of most that surrounded the changes: "The new men seem to be highly pleased with the transfer and have already begun to accuse their former comrades of being 'tin soldiers' while they belong to the 167th US Infantry. Some of our new men from the 1st Infantry had several fights on that account the day they transferred. They were 'rearing' to go with us."[5] For most of the men chosen, the prospect of travel across the ocean for wartime action far outweighed the irritation of changing companies or platoons or of taking a stranger into their squad. Overall, the men met the changes with excitement and energy.

## Origins of the Rainbow Division

On the day after the name-changing order, the *Montgomery Advertiser* announced that the 167th United States Infantry Regiment would become part of a new full-strength US Army division, the 42nd, to be called the Rainbow Division.[6] Secretary of War Newton D. Baker asked Major General William A. Mann, chief of the Militia Bureau, to form a new division that would "cover the United States."[7] Earlier, the War Department had successfully created the 1st Division by selecting and synthesizing into it superior elements of the Regular Army. Major Douglas MacArthur, who worked as the War Department's press censor, suggested a similar approach in amalgamating elements of the National Guard. Baker asked for the most highly trained people possible, so Mann created the 42nd from elements of National Guard units drawn from twenty-five states and the District of Columbia, each filled with men having Mexican border experience.[8] Many states had lobbied Washington to be first to send troops overseas, and news of the new division offered some of them immediate satisfaction.

MacArthur described the unnumbered division as stretching like a rainbow across the United States. Building on this comment, a reporter called it the Rainbow Division, and the name stuck.[9] Deciding on the division's official numerical designation proved somewhat more complicated. The War Department reserved numbers 1 through 25 for Regular Army divisions and 26 through 41 for National Guard divisions. Therefore, the number 26 marked the New England Division (known most commonly as the "Yankee Division" or YD), and the system continued until the last regional division, that of the Pacific Northwest, received number 41. However, as a composite of units from across the nation, the Rainbow Division differed from these geographically defined divisions, and "throughout all the organization of the national guard divisions it stuck out in everyone's mind in the War Department as a special division. Finally, it was decided to give it the number forty-two."[10] In time, the division's numerical designation proved somewhat inconsequential, as "its nickname became more universally recognized than its number."[11]

Of even greater significance was the division's actual existence. As Reilly observes, "The decision that the National Guard could be trusted to fight in France, and in fact was a distinct military asset, prepared the way for the conception and birth of the Rainbow Division."[12] The Rainbow was the first National Guard unit specifically organized for service in France.[13] The second National Guard unit organized for such service, the 26th Division, drew members from New England only and not from the nation as a whole.[14] Thus from its very conception, the Rainbow was unique.

The War Department immediately changed the numbers of the National Guard units joining the 42nd Division. In addition to renaming the 4th Alabama, it changed the 69th New York to the 165th United States Infantry, the 4th Ohio to the 166th, and the 3rd Iowa to the 168th. This meant that numbers used by Civil War–era militia units no longer appeared on the army rolls, and eventually an excellent esprit de corps developed among the new units.[15]

However, not every aspect of the transition ran smoothly. Practical problems arose from bringing together units with various levels of training and dedication. Initially, everybody in the Rainbow Division was a volunteer. Eventually, replacements arrived, either draftees–Regular Army men or men from other Guard units, along with officers straight from training camps. Such diverse backgrounds offered potential conflicts, as the core troops believed themselves tougher, better trained, more experienced, and more filled with the spirit of the volunteer than people who waited to enlist or be drafted. The Alabama soldiers openly spoke of draftees as "slackers."[16] One of the 167th's rifle company commanders used the word in a letter home.[17] By April 1918 all references to National Guard and Regular Army backgrounds were eliminated, but the 42nd Division always unofficially maintained its volunteer distinction. Members of the division never abandoned their pride in this lineage, and replacements longed to join the division and share in its growing reputation.[18]

Mann received promotion to major general, a title that elevated him from a desk job to wartime command of the new division.[19] He appointed MacArthur to be chief of staff and promoted him to colonel.[20] MacArthur, whose father Major General Arthur MacArthur had received a Medal of Honor for his Civil War service, was an army aristocrat. He gained further distinction by earning West Point's all-time best academic record and becoming first captain of the Cadet Corps. Screws, whose National Guard rank was colonel, was listed on the Regular Army promotion list as a captain. Although ten years younger than Screws, MacArthur far outranked him. MacArthur almost certainly would have replaced Screws with another had he failed to motivate and discipline the Alabama regiment properly throughout the war. Luckily for all involved, Screws kept his job and excelled at leading his men and cultivating their strongest qualities.

North toward War

Less than two weeks after joining the Rainbow, the 167th received orders to proceed to Camp Mills, New York, for further training and preparation to deploy
overseas.[21] The final days in Montgomery were a flurry of paperwork, logistics,
and fresh inoculations. Soldiers could purchase reasonably priced war insurance
of up to ten thousand dollars, with claims proceeds to be paid to beneficiaries
over twenty years.[22]

The regiment's move to the Mexican border ten months earlier had involved
about 1,400 men.[23] The troop movement to New York involved 3,677 officers and
men.[24] On August 27, 1917, soldiers at Camp Sheridan, formerly Vandiver Park,
loaded packs and equipment on eight trains and received assignments on wooden
tourist sleepers.[25] The next morning they boarded the trains under the cavernous
L&N shed facing the Alabama River. The *Montgomery Advertiser* was barred from
printing anything about the departure of the troops, so crowds were scarce. Although the men felt hurt that so few people came to see them off, the clanging
drive wheels, bells, whistles, and cheering from the few onlookers brought excitement among the soldiers to a fever pitch.[26] Steam and smoke filled the tall
shed as the trains pulled out.[27]

The journey to Garden City, New York, took nearly three days—a crowded
and sometimes excruciating journey. A member of the Machine Gun Company
bemoaned, "Some had to sleep two to the bunk and believe me this was some
crowded."[28] Guards manned each door, preventing troops from exiting during
stops.[29] As they progressed up the Eastern Seaboard, the soldiers used windows
to chat with civilians—especially females—whenever the engines sidetracked for
water and coal. And the train's kitchens (located in the old baggage cars, which
had been converted for military use) served hot meals en route. One soldier recognized that the journey was relatively comfortable, writing, "The trip up here
was worth a great deal to me but I expect it preceeds [*sic*] the hardest work any
of us ever saw in the army."[30] Upon disembarking, the men hiked from the station
to the five-hundred-acre sea of canvas squad tents set up to house thirty thousand
men.[31] They had arrived at Camp Mills—and moved one step closer to the war.

Quarantine

However, the 167th would not enter training initially, as it arrived with seven
cases of measles and was quarantined by both the Regimental Sanitary Depart-

ment and the Division Surgeon. Jordan wrote his wife: "The measles situation is excellent but we are under quarantine again. We're out for two days, then back again. Naturally, the men are fretting over it and getting very restless. It looks to me as though some medical officers higher up have been afraid to take the responsibility of turning us loose."[32] Despite the men's restlessness, the quarantine worked, and only two isolated cases appeared in camp.[33]

Other illnesses occurred, too. Major James W. Frew, "while screening new soldiers, wrote of the Alabamians of the 167th Infantry, 'From a medical standpoint the Alabama regiment caused us a great deal of worry and trouble. They were nearly all boys from the mountains and rural districts and as soon as they hit camp they began to have their baby diseases. Measles, diphtheria, and scarlet fever were soon raging and the whole regiment was put under strict quarantine.'"[34] The September 18, 1917, *Montgomery Advertiser* reported that Wilber Riley of Ozark's G Company died from pneumonia, the regiment's fourth death in camp.[35] The Alabamians had not yet entered the war, but they had already experienced casualties.

## Settling In to Camp Mills

Once out of quarantine, the regiment went to work, spending daylight hours in hands-on training and evenings receiving instruction.[36] Rain or shine, physical training, classes, and drills proceeded, and all worked hard. Companies conducted daily bayonet practice. The physical work exposed troops to the feeling of violent and close combat. The Rainbow Division had about two months at Camp Mills in which to bring together 27,000 soldiers uneven in training. Melding them into a fighting unit was a challenge.

This was complicated even more by the numbers of junior officers added to the unit at Camp Mills.[37] Most were northern officers with a few years of college, which was more than most of their better-trained counterparts from Alabama. All had volunteered for officer training. Their inexperience caused even more work to prepare the regiment, but they were welcome additions to the chronically shorthanded regiment. One new officer, Second Lieutenant John Donaldson, recalled being greeted warmly: "A mighty fine bunch of fellows that treated us like Princes. . . . The officers [*sic*] mess is a dandy and if today's food is any criterion, Glory, Glory!"[38] Still, the men worked hard, and Screws continued to demand discipline and rigor, even adding additional schooling sessions for the new officers.[39]

As preparation for imminent departure, the division was reequipped with

machine guns, wool uniforms, short trench coats, blankets, gas masks, trench
knives, rolling kitchens, food, medical supplies, and munitions. Individuals who
could afford it, usually officers, purchased personal items in New York stores.[40]
In addition, some hired Long Island seamstresses to adorn their uniforms with
Rainbow Division patches: strips of felt on squares of brown wool uniform cloth.
Although individual seamstresses offered their own variations on the rainbow
theme, the patch symbolized the division's unity and the men's loyalty to it. Men
wore the patch with pride.[41]

## Tensions and Loyalties within the Rainbow

The Rainbow Division became more cohesive and unified, but the transition took
time. In the early days at Camp Mills, fights often erupted between Alabamians
and the mostly Irish soldiers of the New York 165th—the first two units to arrive at the camp. The Alabama soldiers had earned a rowdy reputation on the
Mexican border. Others sometimes viewed them as undisciplined troublemak-
ers. From the Mexican border Jordan had written, "We had to be especially vigi-
lant as the entire Alabama brigade had been 'thrown off' guard by Gen. Plummer a week or more ago because of the disgraceful conduct of some of the men
on guard."[42] Although Jordan did not specify the nature of the "disgraceful conduct," he had indicated that the issue was rampant rather than isolated. The result had been a form of mass punishment, and General Plummer had disgraced
the Alabama soldiers by declaring them unfit to pull guard duty, a serious matter.

Indeed, the rambunctious ways of the Alabamians continued in New York and
included gambling fights. The 167th's reputation as a bunch of rough necks blossomed when I Company's cook, Bud Fletcher, died from injuries received in a
brawl following a crap game. The company held a military funeral for him.[43]

But the tensions arose from more than just the Alabamians' rowdiness. Men
of the Rainbow represented most of the nation's ethnic and immigrant groups.
Their ideals, religions, and backgrounds were often different. Private Thomas
S. Neibaur, a Mormon replacement brought to the Rainbow from Idaho, was
placed in the 167th's M Company in February 1918. In a letter home he wrote,
"The boys I am with now are from the south. Of course they are good fellows
and all that but still they have different ways that seem a bit funny to me."[44] In a
postwar interview, he would give a vivid description of the Alabamians: "They
were a bit rough and a bit rowdy. But, there were no boys who'd stand by closer.
I'll tell you how it was. They were so full of life and pep they had to be doing

something all the time. If there was nothing doing, then they's [sic] have to do *something*. They's [sic] raise hell."[45]

Many Alabamians had been raised to despise all Yankees—their term for anyone from the North. Likewise, the New Yorkers and Ohioans often looked down on the southerners, considering them to be ignorant country bumpkins. The tension between the New York and Alabama soldiers reached back to the Civil War, when their predecessor regiments fought each other at Manassas, Fredericksburg, and other blood-soaked sites. The New York colors carried names of all the principal battles of the Army of the Potomac from Bull Run to Appomattox.[46] That history was well known to both of the modern regiments, and some resentments lingered.

The drama continued when African American soldiers of the 15th New York National Guard arriving at Camp Mills were told by a soldier from another New York unit, "The Alabamas are coming over and clean you out."[47] Despite such comments—or perhaps in response to them—officers of the 167th played down, even to the point of outright denial, such incidents. And in at least some cases, more objective sources concurred. Responding to news that a racial melee had erupted at the camp, a *New York Times* article stated, "Sensational reports of fights between a battalion of the 15th New York Negroes and the 167th (Alabama) Infantry soldiers proved to be based only on reports of one or two fist fights."[48] At the time, Jordan, trying to defend his men, called the accusations "absolutely erroneous." Father Francis Duffy, chaplain of the New York regiment, agreed, describing one such happening as "a small family row at Camp Mills."[49] Tensions did exist, and some violence occurred.[50] But it was never as sensational as some sources claimed, and over time, some even began to suspect people sympathetic to "German interests" to be at work.[51]

Conflicts among the ethnic and geographical groups were also being addressed at the highest national level. President Wilson created the Commission on Training Camp Activities (CTCA) immediately after the nation entered the war. It was charged with "protecting the newly mobilized American soldiers from the ravages of venereal disease" but was also concerned with the cultural influence of others viewed as "marginal Americans."[52] The reformers' goal was to reshape the country's culture and society in the image of their white, urban middle-class background, to make all soldiers fit their vision of a new American man.[53]

This progressive effort had not yet reached its full extent when the men of the 42nd arrived at Camp Mills. The Rainbow soldiers would eventually learn the value of fellow countrymen, regardless of their race or state of origin, and the tensions—both founded and exaggerated—would fade, subordinated to the pressures of war. Later, once the division entered France, Reilly observes, "every sectional, racial, religious and vocational prejudice sank far into the background before the deep bond of comradeship which being a member of the Rainbow Division came to mean and which nothing could disrupt."[54]

## Diversions and Distractions

Although the men trained hard at Camp Mills, some events disrupted the routine. Officers—and a few lucky privates—received passes to travel into New York City, a place few of the Alabama men had seen. Many members of the 167th found themselves unable to escape quarantine, but Private Gary A. Roberts of B Company wrote his grandmother about being "in the great city having a most enjoyable time."[55] The city may have intimidated some of the more rural men, but reports remained positive and filled with tales of patriotism. One soldier recounted, "I don't know how many men came up and wanted to shake hands and wish me well. It is hard to say but these people are more patriotic than ours and show it more."[56]

Those who could not leave Camp Mills sought diversion there. The Aviation School at nearby Mineola Field fascinated many. The wonder proved short-lived, however, as Private Franklin Ashton Clark noted: "there are several machines in the air all the time but they have gotten old now."[57] Many distractions arose from the YMCA, the official partner of the CTCA.[58] Manned by civilians, the YMCA organized most recreational activities, from religious services to boxing and staged shows featuring "flat foot dancers, humorists, cornet [sic] quartets, contortionists, cards and other tricks, piano solos and several quartetts [sic] and solos," all drawn from the soldiers.[59]

Visiting civilians provided respite. People took great interest in the men, and many visitors without a personal connection to the soldiers just wanted to encourage them. Jordan described one such set of visitors to his wife: "A crowd of ladies from Port Washington have adopted our regiment and are loading us down with gifts. They came to K Company yesterday with an auto load of eats and smokes."[60] Of course, some visitors did have connections to the 167th. Alabamians visiting Camp Mills included Helen Keller, the deaf, blind, and mute native of Tuscumbia. An inspiration to the world, she was the state's most famous citizen. Despite being opposed to the war, she was one of the most important visitors to the regiment at Camp Mills. Others were Dan Pratt, a prominent Birmingham industrialist, and Oscar W. Underwood, a US senator from Alabama who was twice nominated Democratic candidate for vice president.[61] Leo Strassburger of Montgomery, a member of the Alabama governor's honorary staff, also visited with a message from the governor.[62] Few Alabama families could afford to travel north for a last farewell, but the sister and widowed mother of Worth Lewis from Greenville, who had taken up residence in New York, visited him and D Company.

The Rainbow Division also received official visits from military dignitaries, and these provided a different sort of break from routine. While visiting family members and local ladies bringing snacks and hand-knitted sweaters generally offered a pleasant distraction, the visit of "higher-ups" caused a flurry of work and preparation. Every man had to be on his best appearance, and the units had to function seamlessly. No visit evoked more anxiety than that of Secretary of War Baker, who reviewed the division in a spectacular ninety-minute parade on September 23, 1917.[63] Not all of the men had rifles, but all marched in felt campaign hats in columns of platoons, four abreast on a company front stretching from curb to curb.[64] Baker created excitement, because the men knew he had participated in organizing and naming the 42nd the "Rainbow Division" and had addressed the Alabama Bar Association following the regiment's mobilization the previous summer. Baker's visit aroused excitement outside the camp as well as within it, and one newspaper estimated the civilian crowd for this Camp Mills event as fifty thousand.[65]

The 167th Alabama occupied that parade's post of honor, marching at the head of the two-and-a-half-mile-long column.[66] Jordan's letters indicate his pride in the regiment's performance: "Today we passed in review before Secretary Newton D. Baker. It was the most wonderful and impressive sight I ever saw and everything moved like clockwork. Am sending a newspaper account from the *Telegraph*. It made one grave error—the 165th is NOT the best of the infantry regiments. The 167th is."[67] The men were as inspired as the officers, as evidenced by a letter Private Clark wrote: "As we marched about three miles back to camp between double ranks of soldiers at attention on each side of the road we came to the conclusion that Germany will be quickly beaten when we get there."[68]

On September 26, three days after the division review for Baker, the 84th Brigade, consisting of the 167th and 168th (Iowa) Infantry Regiments and the 151st (Georgia) Machine Gun Battalion, paraded 8,324 men for Iowa's US senators and governor. Those units were to fight side by side in every action of the Rainbow and were always friendly and mutually respectful.[69] This might have been because the Iowa and Alabama soldiers were the country boys, looked down on and treated as inferiors by the Ohioans and New Yorkers in the Rainbow. As Private Robert D. Pickel of D Company said in a postwar survey, "people from the rest of the country in the services did not like Alabama or Iowa boys."[70] It was the Iowans who first called the 167th "The Alabam," a practice picked up with affection by the other regiments and eventually used throughout the division.

The Rainbow's final parade at Camp Mills took place on Hempstead Plains on October 7, 1917. A news story datelined October 8 reported sixty or seventy thousand in attendance.[71] News of the happenings at Camp Mills reached Alabama, and around this time the *Montgomery Advertiser* reported that motion pictures of the 167th filmed on Long Island had been shown at Montgomery's Grand Theatre, located near the capitol on Dexter Avenue. The silent film included shots of regimental officers and men. The audience applauded vigorously, as many of them knew the regiment was en route to Europe and that it was led by Bill Screws, a man many knew or knew about.[72]

## Battalions Massed

With each day, the distance separating the Rainbow Division from the war grew smaller. However, on October 12 some men learned that they would not be going to war with the 42nd. The division surgeon announced that 325 men were being discharged as physically or mentally unfit.[73] For most of the men, though, war was imminent.

Two National Guard divisions—the 42nd (Rainbow) and the 26th (New England)—were to join the Regular Army 1st Division in France, along with the Regular Army 2nd Division, which was being assembled there from independent units already sent over.[74] These four divisions, about equal in training, would be the only American combat units in France through the winter of 1917/18, and they were essential to the war effort.[75]

The 167th had a good opinion of itself, as evidenced by a letter Jordan sent his brother, the last before sailing. He wrote, "Our division is in the peak of condition and the morale is very high. Our regiment is the most feared and respected here. The 165th have long ago learned that there is one regiment that they had better not fool with. It is a solemn fact that the Alabamians have got the goat of everything here. A New York officer told me that our boys are the only ones his crowd ever saw that were not afraid of them."[76] The regiments' respective opinion of themselves is best captured by these words written ten years later, "As to which the best regiment of the four, do not ask the division staff who thought that all belonged to the best division. But a member of the Ohio regiment would give you an answer gladly without waiting a second for consideration; and so would a member of the Iowa, the New York or the Alabama regiments."[77]

## Shipping Out of New York

The first of the US convoys to France departed in June 1917. Few embarked in July and August.[78] Nearly 80 percent of the AEF left from New York harbor, while most of the others departed from Newport News, Virginia.[79] The men of the Rainbow reached France on a number of different transports, as every available American and confiscated German passenger vessel, large and small, was being converted to carry troops.[80]

The Alabamians left Camp Mills in early November. 1st Battalion, Machine Gun Company, and the 117th Signal Battalion boarded the *Lapland* on November 3. Companies G and H of 2nd Battalion and its Headquarters Company left by train for Canada on November 5 to board a converted small German ship while the rest of the battalion left from New York Harbor.

The 3rd Battalion of the 167th, under Major Dallas B. Smith of Opelika, was the last of the regiment to go to the docks from Camp Mills. The troops awoke at 2:00 A.M. on November 6, received sandwiches, and marched to the station. The train chugged through fields white with frost and amid cheering civilians at Long Island City.[81] They went by ferries down the East River and under the Brooklyn Bridge, giving those denied passes to visit the city a long-awaited glimpse of New York City and the harbor.

Off-loaded at a Cunard Line dock in Hoboken, New Jersey, the men were checked, given bunk and lifeboat assignments, and issued meal times. They boarded the crowded Canadian ship *Andania*, with weapons, duffle bags, and full field packs with helmets, blankets, and bayonets strapped on them. The ship headed to sea about noon, though with scant fanfare as no bands, noise, or passengers were allowed on deck.[82] Soldiers kept watch for submarines. Trips to the galley for meals of Australian rabbit were an ordeal. Seasickness was widespread. Several hundred men had mumps on the voyage. Joseph J. Patton, from Battles Wharf, Alabama, died from pneumonia on November 16. A medical officer embalmed the body, which was taken to England for burial.[83]

The regiment had its first test of wartime discipline. Crowded into narrow and closely stacked multitiered bunks, the men lacked even the solace of an evening cigarette. Boat drills required them to rush to assigned lifeboats to practice abandoning ship. Ships were in total darkness at night. Decks emptied at sundown, portholes closed, and the only illumination was from a few small globes of blue glass. Sailors were not allowed to wear white caps in evening hours.[84]

The voyage took two weeks and the 167th, other than the companies of the 2nd Battalion leaving from Canada, traveled from Hoboken to Liverpool. Their journey to the war was underway.

## Change of Command

Unknown to Rainbow men, they were the subject of serious discussion while at sea. On November 10, 1917, Colonel Fox Conner, a right-hand man of Pershing, issued a memo recommending the 42nd Division be broken up. According to policy, every fourth division arriving in France was to be used for replacements.[85] The division was to be disbanded with everyone going as individuals, called "casuals," as fillers to other units. Then, on December 15, 1917, Mann was replaced as commanding general of the Rainbow.[86] As the United States entered the war, Pershing replaced older officers in poor physical shape with younger ones better suited to fulfill his "drive 'for results.'"[87] Major General Charles Menoher, a schoolmate of Pershing's from West Point, replaced Mann. His chief of staff, Colonel Douglas MacArthur, appealed to Pershing's chief of staff, James Harbord, with a request that the Rainbow Division remain intact, and the next division arriving, also a National Guard division, was broken up instead.[88] The Rainbow had been threatened, but it survived.

## England

The 167th started its short, cold, and miserable stay in England on November 19, 1917. After a train ride from Liverpool the regiment spent five days in a squalid replacement depot at Winchester. The band played a downtown concert for locals, and a picture of it appeared on the front page of the *Montgomery Advertiser*.[89] The unit also earned coverage from the Winchester newspaper, which lionized Colonel Screws. He found local English ladies entertaining and welcoming, but for the men, conditions—marked by a scarcity of food—were terrible.[90] They amused themselves, despite the scarcity—some frequenting "seedy bars" while others chose museums and other cultural offerings.[91]

The Rainbow never served alongside or worked with the British, though many soldiers in the AEF did. Alabamians were not unmindful of the vast British involvement in the war, their great losses, and their heroic sacrifices. Alabama newspapers regularly printed articles with London datelines showing the results of British fighting. Most Alabamians were of British descent and were naturally sympathetic. There was the advantage of a common language in creating a warm relationship between the soldiers of the two armies that facilitated joint training.

However, some disagreements existed. The British had always wanted US soldiers to fight under their leadership, as replacements for the huge numbers of British soldiers killed, wounded, and taken prisoner. The British high command maintained a negative opinion of American officers throughout the war and never considered placing its divisions under American command.[92]

Although British military leadership remained resistant to US leadership, the British people and soldiers reached out to the Americans, whose arrival was to make a huge difference in their morale. The British government lent all the transports it could, and its people expressed heartfelt welcomes.[93] In a December 10, 1917, speech at the Corn Exchange in Bedford, England, Winston Churchill said:

> If Russia has, for the time being, fallen out of our ranks, the United States of America have entered them. The great Republic of the West, more than a hundred millions, of the most educated and scientific democracy in the world, are coming to our aid, marching along all the roads of America, steering across the ocean, organizing their industries for war, spending their wealth like water, developing slowly but irresistibly and unceasingly the most gigantic, elemental forces ever yet owned and applied to the triumph of a righteous cause. The appearance of this mighty champion at the other end of the world has restored to us the fortunes of war, and has repaired and more than repaired all that we have suffered in the loss of Russia.
>
> The intervention of America means the uniting of practically the whole world, and the whole of its resources against the German Power. It cannot fail in the end to be decisive. It will secure us victory.[94]

Such faith in the Americans proved common—and while it inspired confidence in the troops, it also underscored their great responsibility. Their stay in England was brief, but their significance potent.

## France

The weather was terrible when the 167th crossed the English Channel to France on November 25. One of the three boats carrying the regiment across the channel had to turn back, causing further delay. Men from the first two boats were put up for a night at Le Havre in a squalid and overcrowded replacement depot before the incomplete regiment crowded into two French trains on the night of November 26, 1917. Each passenger car held straight wooden benches and an overhead rack for storage. Despite the discomfort of being crowded, the cars were warmer than boxcars. During the thirty-hour trip to Vaucouleurs, about 150 miles east of Paris, the men ate only hardtack. They sat bolt upright and caught what sleep they could in that position, eagerly awaiting the welcome stops at French canteens, where French Red Cross ladies served coffee with rum.[95]

Screws and his men reached their first destination in Lorraine on November 28, 1917, at the beginning of one of the worst winters in many years. The railroad station at Vaucouleurs was fifty-one miles from Chaumont, which had been AEF headquarters since July. It was far away from the temptations of Paris and what one officer called *la guerre de luxe*, or the war of luxury.[96] Located on a plateau, the town dominated the woods and fields for miles around and brought a rare bit of drama to the ordinary landscape of eastern France. The French offered Pershing a large compound of brick barracks and buildings there, to which he moved his headquarters in early September.[97] The French company of Wagons-Lits (sleeping cars) put a special train at his disposal, just as it had done for the French chiefs.[98]

The French did not hesitate to commingle their army with Pershing's. Like the British, they preferred total command, even down to battalion level, but they were willing to integrate American help where they could get it. Gratitude and admiration existed between the French and the Americans, but it did not come easily. French liaison officers criticized their own soldiers for failing to salute American officers and observe proper military decorum as a good example for the newly arrived Americans.[99] The French resented the slow pace at which Americans entered the actual fighting and Pershing's insistence on an All-American army. Despite these differences, which were largely confined to the higher-level officers, the soldiers of both countries cooperated well.

In that cooperative spirit, France provided the Americans with two large maneuver areas and twenty-one smaller training areas with rifle, machine gun, and grenade ranges. Each stood near a village with billets or barracks. All were functional and had been used by the French forces. Since the 1st and 26th Divisions were training in other parts of France, the Rainbow was the first American unit to receive training in the Chaumont region, and they were the first Americans that many local people had ever seen.

Vaucouleurs and Uruffe

The regiment's trains arriving at Vaucouleurs disgorged equipment on the mile-long stone quay, the unloading platform, near the railroad station. The cold at Vaucouleurs was penetrating. The men had been on irregular rations with virtually no exercise for a long time. They were in bad shape but happy to have finally reached a place that made sense, one step closer to their reason for being in France. Men poured out into platoon, company, and battalion formations, facing west to the fortress town built on the hillside. The Meuse River flowed behind a large open field to the east. A prosperous looking town, Vaucouleurs boasted mostly paved streets and upscale old homes. The railway station faced an ancient church dedicated to Joan of Arc, the young woman known as the savior of France and sometimes referred to as the Virgin Warrior. The town had been an early source of support for the fifteenth-century martyr, regarded as an electrifying leader who rose to save France from England.

It was an auspicious site for the soldiers to disembark. With packs and rifles, steel helmets, and web ammunition belts, they wasted no time lingering in the bitter cold. Crossing a canal, the men struck out toward a bridge spanning the Meuse, which ran north–south through a valley flanked by wooded ridge lines. They crossed the river and swung south, marching in route step past ancient winding stone walls unlike any the men from Alabama had ever seen. En route to Uruffe, the six-mile stretch of road ran past an ancient cemetery and a small country chapel. It seemed idyllic, save for the red flashes and echoing dull thuds of enemy cannon fire. Rather than fearing the signs of action—which seemed like watching and hearing a distant storm—"Alabamians were again thrilled at the thought of fighting."[100] The newcomers felt excited, braced, and encouraged by being there.

Upon reaching Uruffe, Colonel Screws established headquarters in the *mairie*, or town hall. Although not war damaged, the village was old and gloomy. Stone buildings lined its few muddy streets. Supply Company and 1st and 2nd Battalions were billeted in wooden barracks on the outskirts of town, while 3rd Battalion and Machine Gun Company marched on to Gibeaumeix, a mile north.

Once in the village, officers were assigned spaces in family-occupied homes.[101] Captains Ravee Norris and Mortimer Jordan shared a billet in the house of a kind and accommodating Frenchwoman, who offered cozy feather beds built into wall alcoves.[102] A group of 3rd Battalion officers organized a unit mess in the home of a local dignitary, whose wife cooked their rations into tasty meals

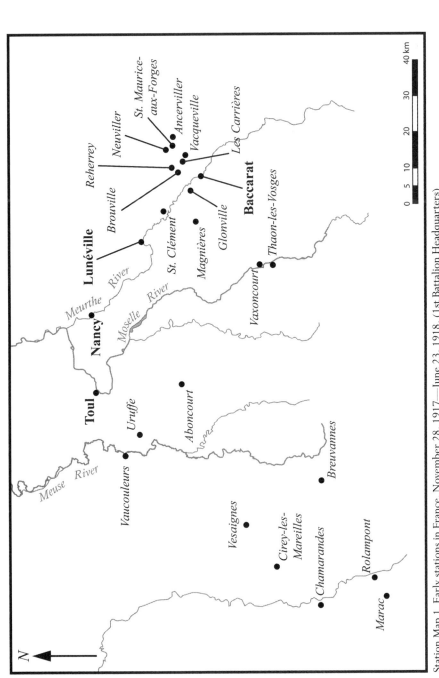

Station Map 1. Early stations in France. November 28, 1917—June 23, 1918. (1st Battalion Headquarters)

warmed in a large open fireplace and even served goose as a belated Thanksgiving dinner.

Life for the men lacked such luxuries. Barracks housed some, while others occupied billets in dirt-floored barns and vacant houses. According to the regimental surgeon, "The billets, mostly barns and cattle sheds, were cold and miserable and unsanitary, with no provision for heat. There were no bunks, the men sleeping on louse-infested straw piled upon the floor or ground."[103] Officers maintained a festive and gentlemanly spirit, reminding troops that "he who quits smiling is lost," but the days were short and gloomy.[104]

In the villages, Alabamians had their first look at French civilians. All showed the hardships of war, but despite poverty and shabby clothing, they were friendly. All young, healthy Frenchmen had been conscripted into military service, leaving only the elderly or disabled behind. Many women wore widow's black, something the Americans kept noticing. Almost none of the villagers spoke any words of English, but the children were bright and filled with admiration for the newly arrived soldiers.

French villages proved fairly standard. All soldiers of the Rainbow were learning about the French. An officer of the 166th wrote: "The towns occupied by the regiment were typical French country villages. A winding street, lined with stone and plaster houses, each one like its neighbor, and all like those in every town of the district—red-tiled roofs and cobble-stone streets—no gutters, and before every house the inevitable pile of manure—such is the prevailing pattern on which the French villages are cut."[105] Dwellings stood side by side like row houses. Most had cellars for storing vegetables with wooden foldout doors opening from the ground on the street side. They also contained sections for livestock. Manure piles littered the front yard. To the French people a big heap of manure indicated a family prosperous enough to own livestock, but the American soldiers never grew accustomed to the sight—or the smell.[106] Most families also stacked split firewood in front of their houses for heating and cooking. Uruffe had a communal *lavoir*, a wash house consisting of a stone shed built on a running stream, and despite the cold, soldiers immediately started using it alongside the local civilians.

The YMCA set up a recreation center in a barn, providing free writing materials and selling tobacco and candy. American soldiers roamed everywhere, and hospitable civilians repeatedly told the Alabamians in the best English they could muster that America, France's savior, would win the war. Villagers always spoke of the "American" or "United States" language rather than "English."[107] Some officers studied French systematically, pairing with upscale civilians and trying to teach them English. That brought them closer to the misery, suffering, and signs of sacrifice the locals had endured for three and a half years in the war's back yard.[108] Soldiers acquired a smattering of French through contact with civilians, which included everything from encounters at the wash house to playful snowball fights with the village children.

Official training started when thirty new American officers and two French instructors joined the regiment on December 3, 1917. All of the American newcomers had some college education or were experienced "mustangs," former enlisted men picked for officer training. They had been trained in the United States before attending a French school for company grade officers at La Valbonne. The two French officers were experienced and charming veterans.[109] Most soldiers in the 167th understood themselves to be untested, so they welcomed both the French and American instructors. Tensions arose as all Americans and French adapted to each other. With their plentiful cash and wasteful habits, the American soldiers puzzled the war-weary people of the French countryside. Rowdy drunken behavior upset people accustomed to controlling their drinking habits. But the healthy and cheerful American soldiers also delighted people whose villages had been without men or optimism for nearly four years. They played with the children, helped in village life where they could, and—despite their occasional boisterousness—left a lasting good impression on the villagers.

## Saint-Blin

The regiment left Uruffe on December 12 for a twenty-two-mile, two-day road march to Saint-Blin.[110] En route, the 167th passed through Domrémy, the tiny birthplace of Joan of Arc, where the 3rd Battalion stayed overnight.[111] Men told each other how she had started her quest to save France from the English in that tiny village, and later they saw numerous signs reading *Jeanne d'Arc, P.P.N.* An abbreviation for *Priez Pour Nous*, the pleas asked the saint to pray for them.[112]

In many ways, Saint-Blin resembled the other villages, though its row houses boasted flat-tiled roofs and better construction than those in Uruffe, and many had decorated stone arches over entrance doors. Most backyards had fruit trees and pens for rabbits—a valuable source of meat. The primary distinction arose from the natural surroundings: the area possessed few hills, and the increasingly cold wind swept through the open village.

Army life went on. Outgoing mail was censored, and all mail—incoming and outgoing—spent three to six weeks in transit. Soldiers were prohibited from describing or naming their location or activities. Incoming mail arrived in bunches and out of sequence. Regulations forbade American soldiers from acting as correspondents for newspapers, though many letters home found their way into local papers.

A mail delivery reached the regiment several days before Christmas, and heavy snow fell on Christmas Day. Some soldiers shared sugar, sweets, and tobacco sent from home with locals. Some men received fruit cakes soaked in whiskey. Company cooks had hoarded for a bountiful holiday meal. Town criers invited all children from surrounding villages to be guests of the Americans, who offered the youngsters turkey, cranberries, figs, English walnuts, and dates.[113] Good feelings abounded between the locals and the men of the 167th, who did their best to ease the villagers' suffering.

The stay at Saint-Blin included several morale-boosting events. The arrival of G and H Companies and 2nd Battalion headquarters people serving under Major Hartley A. Moon (the men who had been delayed leaving Camp Mills) completed the regiment, bringing it to the full complement of 3,770 men. Because accommodations were limited, the battalions ranged across several villages on the road to the headquarters town of Chaumont: 1st Battalion billeted at Vesaignes, 2nd Battalion and Regimental Headquarters in Saint-Blin, and 3rd Battalion at Humberville.[114] In exciting news, the men learned that the long-anticipated 10 percent pay increase for overseas service had taken effect, along with longevity pay of up to 20 percent. Since many men had served for a decade prior to the National Guard's federalization, this was especially welcome news.[115]

Still, some unpleasant aspects did exist. Cooties (the soldiers' slang for lice) were first reported in I Company at Humberville, but they spread quickly, and soon everyone had them. Living in dirty surroundings without washing caused the soldiers to suffer from these rapidly multiplying vermin. No matter how carefully the men searched their bodies, how often they visited the rare delousing stations, or how vigorously they boiled clothes to get rid of the cooties, the critters returned. Amos D. Brenneman, a C Company soldier wrote home, "these darn lise [sic] first keep us wored [sic] to death all the time."[116] The bugs annoyed the men, but they appear not to have affected their health. Brenneman marveled that the men were so healthy, and Jordan boasted that he had "not had one day's sickness since the war started."[117]

The weather was extremely cold, but the AEF men marched well and appreciated hot meals of canned corn beef and hardtack. Food was scarce and appetites ravenous. Guards protected kitchens and food supplies against those men hoping to sneak an extra ration. Living in cold barns and cattle sheds strewn with manure was rough, but the unit's Sibley stoves helped.[118] Snow covered everything, and men struggled to keep their shoes dry. This seemed difficult enough, but even more strenuous times awaited them.

## The "Valley Forge" March

Around Christmas, orders from Colonel MacArthur informed the division that it would move immediately following the holiday.[119] Reilly notes that the heavy snowfall and subfreezing temperatures, combined with the scarcity of vehicles available to help with the movement and the difficulty of providing meals for men in transit, encouraged officers to expedite the march as much as possible.[120] On December 26 the 42nd Division started the three-day march from Saint-Blin to Rolampont. Although the troops needed to be closer to Chaumont in order to train with and assist the French, the march also constituted part of Pershing's attempts to toughen up his soldiers. This march was the 167th's most challenging trip yet—a test of endurance and tenacity. The unit carried everything it owned, and each man was heavily loaded with packs and weapons. At night they stopped in unheated billets, barracks, and barns that offered little protection from the cold. The regimental surgeon recorded temperatures as low as minus seven degrees Celsius. Some men lacked overcoats and gloves. All wore the same blouse and pants they wore when Secretary Baker reviewed troops on a balmy afternoon back at Camp Mills. Although made of wool, these did not provide sufficient warmth for the frigid conditions.

The conditions tormented everyone, but the Alabamians in particular had never experienced anything like the French cold, wind, and snow. They suffered more from weather and lack of rest than from fear of being killed in unknown battles. What might happen to them in a future battle was vague, something they had not experienced and that was not then hurting them. Cold was different. It was present and hurt desperately. The mufflers, sweaters, and helmets knitted for the soldiers by the ladies at home and on Long Island were valuable, but even they left some skin exposed, allowing the wind to hit like needles. Toes and fingers ached. Some shoes were badly worn, as the constant drying of wet leather caused them to crack and tear.[121] Several men's feet had deteriorated so drastically that their snowy path bore trails of blood.[122] A New York soldier remembers: "There were so many complaints about the quality of the footwear that reports were required. One officer wrote a memorandum calculated to require the supplier of these boots to wear them in hell."[123]

As if the shoes were not bad enough, heavy packs, rifles, and ammunition threw bodies off balance as men struggled to overcome snowdrifts and slipped on ice. Everybody yearned for the end of the day, for any kind of barn or house to offer some protection, however meager, from the penetrating wind and cold. They thought about, spoke of, and longed for hot coffee or food and a trusty portable stove.

Despite these hardships, the men marched (see fig. 5). Routes varied slightly, and not all men marched the same average of forty-six miles.[124] One participant, Lieutenant Isaac G. Walker of Company A, 151st Machine Gun Battalion, reported a much greater distance of "a hundred and eighteen miles through snow, ankle to knee deep in drifts to the Rolampont area."[125] Columns headed southwest during a snowstorm, toward the Meuse River. On the second afternoon they turned south at the base of the cliff of Chaumont alongside the Upper Marne River. AEF headquarters staff in Chaumont watched from far above as the men passed in the freezing wind on the snow-covered roads, agreeing that "it was a great march."[126]

Villagers were eager to help when they could. Cheseldine notes: "The French people, knowing that the division was on the march, gathered in groups and broke trails through the worst drifts near their villages. It was a mark of devotion that did not go unnoticed."[127]

Units maintained integrity on the road, marching in route step but with battalions, companies, platoons, and squads keeping together. Regular breaks spanned ten minutes of each hour. Soldiers propped against a tree or tried to catch a few winks of sleep in a snow-filled roadside ditch. They soon learned, however, that stops in the whipping wind became almost unbearably painful when blood stopped circulating and the body stopped producing heat. Stragglers were not treated kindly, and men cursed each other to keep the columns moving. The division's march order stated that only those physically unable to walk were allowed to drop out and be picked up by wagons and the few ambulances following the columns.[128]

Despite all the challenges it held, the men completed the march, allowing the entire combat-loaded division—a force now including over 3,700 men of the 167th—to shift its base thirty-six miles in three days.[129] Only enemy opposition could have made the operation more daunting. Father Duffy was writing about the division, not just the 165th when he identified the march as "everybody's hike and everybody's purgatory," noting both the difficult and unifying nature of the task: "in the morning their shoes were frozen stiff and they had to burn paper and straw in them before they could get them on. . . . Soldiers fell in the snow and arose and staggered on and dropped again. The strong helped the weak by encouragement, by strong biting words when sympathy would only increase weakness and by the practical help of sharing their burdens. . . . It was a terrible experience. . . . We have not the slightest doubt that men who have shown the endurance that these men have shown will give a good account of themselves in any kind of battle they are put into."[130]

This was not just a successful winter troop movement or simply a huge forced march. And it became more than a commander's challenge to the Rainbow Division and the Alabama regiment in France. Later, men identified it as the beginning of the division's reputation for reliability and toughness. The 42nd Division had not yet seen combat, and this experience brought the men and units closer together than anything they had previously endured. It instilled commanders and planners with confidence that the unit would not quit and could perform under difficult conditions.[131] It made the officers and men, who emerged with increased confidence and strength, more trusting of one another. And it also brought recognition to the unit. Throughout the AEF, regard for the Rainbow blossomed. In stressing the importance of this event, the *Official History* of the Rainbow Division notes: "It was a great march . . . full of courage and determination . . . from which the spirit of the Division was made."[132] Jordan summarized it succinctly in a letter to his wife: "That march will be talked of for a long time, and all over the country. It has been called the best ever."[133]

## Faverolles and Additional Training

The "Alabam" column reached its destination, a cluster of villages in the training area of Faverolles. Machine Gun Company, Supply, and 1st Battalion were billeted at Marac, 3.7 miles from the 2nd Battalion at Leffonds, which was 1.2 miles from the 3rd Battalion at Villiers-sur-Suize.[134] Soldiers moved into family homes and enjoyed their relative luxury after the roadside barns occupied on the march from Saint-Blin. Marac's town square and watering trough for horses distinguished it somewhat from the other villages, but for the most part, life in the communities proved typical. Soldiers noticed simple crosses and crosses with more elaborate models of Jesus on roads throughout the area, and Lieutenant

Langworth of the 168th admiringly credited the country's "real religion" with its wartime successes.[135]

There were tensions, but the acknowledgment of linguistic and cultural differences helped bridge misunderstandings. The Americans had heard rumors of French civilians calling Americans "Sammies," a nickname the men found initially objectionable. To them, it suggested the folk character Little Black Sambo from Helen Bannerman's 1899 children's story. Despite the talk, the Alabamians were not labeled with the epithet. One officer wrote home, "no one has called us 'Sammy' yet. I have been waiting and longing for someone to so address me, but so far in vain. Evidently the simple villagers whom I have met never heard the word. . . . I think this foolishness started when the first American troops landed in France. The delighted populace embraced the soldiers with cries of 'amis' (friends). . . . The French call us 'Américains,' and the British call us—mark the word—'Yankees.' Think of it! Southern troops being called 'Yankees'! Am not minding it in the least, either. Surely times do change."[136]

Conventional wisdom held that American help would be decisive in the spring of 1919, but the French needed immediate reinforcements. Scheduled to enter the line in forty-five days, the Rainbow Division received preference in the matter of supplies, including scarce motor vehicles. The French pushed the AEF, and in turn, the AEF pushed the Rainbow to finish preparation for combat. Some French people doubted the Americans' ability to engage and stand up to the Germans. While the French had their own demands, the Americans identified some weaknesses as well. Some US officers expressed doubts about the National Guard leaders.[137] Pershing attempted to balance these demands with his troops' welfare, and he worked to ensure adequate training for his men.[138] On January 15, 1918, he ordered the establishment of the 1st US Army, moving forward in the plan to create an American sector on the Lorraine front—and moving the troops, logistically if not yet physically, one step closer to combat.[139]

## Specialty Schools

Another step in the plan called for additional training of as many US personnel as possible. Training was done in the early months with the French, although the British conducted some specialty training.[140] The National Guard made every effort to more closely resemble the Regular Army, and training fostered this. To facilitate it, Pershing created an AEF school system and selected the trusted Major

General Robert Lee Bullard, a native of Lee County, Alabama, to head it. Meanwhile, Colonel James A. McAndrew established a Staff College at Langres. Overwhelmed by French management methods, Bullard asked the YMCA—which he "thought more efficient than the army"—to organize his program.[141] French capabilities provided for four additional schools to train infantry officers as platoon commanders and weapons specialists. They furnished the 167th with additional technical skills and flourishes.

The 42nd Division entered a flurry of training activity. Colonel Screws attended staff school in nearby Langres from January 20 to 30. There, British and French instructors taught upper-level courses. Attendance was required for all regimental and brigade commanders, colonels, and brigadier generals.

Three-fourths of the original officers of the 167th and many noncommissioned officers attended the US First Corps School at Gondrecourt.[142] Most trainees hated it.[143] They understood that many of them had been judged inadequate, and they complained that the school was boring and repetitive. Some resented being put back, while others found the close-order drills required of officers demeaning.

Captain Mortimer Jordan's opinion differed. He called Gondrecourt a "wonderful old town," romantic and interesting, unlike other villages he had seen. He enjoyed being back in school with captains and field grade officers, some of whom had been his classmates at a war college in Washington the previous summer. The school drew a hand-picked, upscale lot consisting of West Pointers and well-educated former civilians. Jordan joked with his wife about this "bomb proof" duty preparing him to become the regimental S-3, operations officer, a new post and the third most important position in the regiment, behind the executive officer.[144] In that capacity he would control training and coordinate combat operations. Pershing created a similar job for each command, including the divisions and his own command at Chaumont.

At the school Jordan's workload shifted from the physical demands of commanding a rifle company to the mental demands of staff work. Exercise came from gentlemanly afternoon horseback rides. However, studies of maps, planning orders, and classes consumed all free time from morning until midnight.[145]

The US First Corps School at Gondrecourt also offered lectures and demonstrations in tactics, grenades, map reading, and gas defense. Every officer performed bayonet drills despite snow and mud.[146] They received some instruction in trench warfare, but more training focused on the open order formations being devised by the AEF to employ in subsequent campaigns.

The school was demanding, and even majors were required to carry rifles, wear web equipment, and keep leather polished. Leaders of doubtful ability were being weeded out.[147] Despite their disgruntlement, the work was valuable. None of the men were tested veterans. Soon they would enter the war against a tough professional German army, and they desperately needed any additional edge possible.

## Further Training

While Screws and other officers attended specialty schools, the core of the regiment, the doughboys, underwent training closer to the villages to practice maneuvers and spend more time on the rifle and machine gun ranges. They were to serve as riflemen and to provide men for patrols, assault troops, and shock troops. Their morale was boosted when they received copies of the January 5, 1918, issue of the *London Globe* with a headline heralding their presence: "A Famous American Regiment Reaches Europe. The Gallant Alabamas Land at a French Port." Always the faithful correspondent, Jordan mentioned the article to his wife, telling her the paper "has made us very stuck up and tickled us mightily. . . . Evidently, over here, we are thought pretty well of."[148]

The thirty new American officers and two experienced French officers, with the regiment since early December, conducted classes in platoon, company, and battalion attack; operated machine gun and rifle ranges; and held daily bayonet training (see fig. 6). Training proceeded for seven to eight hours a day, regardless of weather.[149] The circumstances often proved challenging, as Private Ben Allender described: "Jan 31st 1918 Worked all day on trench detail. For dinner we had two pieces of dry bread and one piece of bacon. We stood muster of pay tonight in the dark after supper."[150]

Each soldier trained on French- and British-model gas masks, and some even took both models with them in the early combat situations until they decided which they preferred. The initial experience of putting on a gas mask was claustrophobic and asphyxiating, terrifying but necessary. They mastered putting them on in six seconds and conquered the panic of breathing through a rubber mouthpiece.

The regiment's three rifle ranges, one for each battalion, were in constant use. Longer machine gun ranges had also been constructed for the French automatic rifles, the crew-served 30 calibers, and the US Browning automatic rifle. An officer and six men of the 167th received instructor training at two French machine gun schools.[151] All of the 167th soldiers—not just those designated automatic riflemen—were introduced to the French automatic rifle, or Chauchats. Designed for walking fire, the lightweight weapons held a half-moon clip under the barrel and had a bad reputation for jamming. British Hotchkiss machine guns, more reliable and holding more rounds than the Chauchat, quickly gained popularity. Many soldiers in the 167th trained with it and the English 1914 Lewis automatic rifle, which had a large pan magazine holding forty-seven cartridges on top of the barrel. The regiment used all three automatic rifles, even after the US Browning automatic rifle, a fine weapon that could be fired in single shots or short bursts, entered regular service. Training helped men master the variety of weapons and anticipate a number of possible combat situations, from walking fire to firing from a prone position. Other training covered intelligence capabilities, cartography, and composing after-action reports.[152]

Before going to staff school, Jordan assisted in training troops prior to their departure for the trenches. His letters to his wife describe it as a busy time: "No idle time anywhere. Have hardly any time, even, to think about you and none to get homesick."[153] Just as on the Mexican border, men built practice trenches with dugouts, observation posts, rifle steps, and fighting positions. They were laid out for practice rotations of front, support, and reserve units. Men practiced responding to alerts and alarms, learned defense tactics, and practiced getting small units into and out of trenches, including the rotation of two platoons at a time. Defensive training, the tactic of holding long fronts with weak forces, stressed economizing troops on a front, with reserves held elsewhere. It also involved training in making a counterattack from fixed positions.[154] Every American learned that the Germans always counterattacked after being attacked. The men practiced offensive raids and assaults into trench positions. They launched simulated recon patrols from the trenches. Everybody drilled in throwing dummy grenades from pits, though no live grenades had yet been issued to the 167th because of a recent accident in which a member of the 168th was killed by a dropped bag of grenades.[155]

Some members of the regiment received specialized weaponry training, and others received signal training to educate them on both old-fashioned and updated technology. Along with training fifteen thousand pigeons for use in France, the Signal Corps also trained its engineers for a joint telephone-telegraph job.[156] Although useful and efficient, the phones required near-constant maintenance, as wire strung on top of the ground had to be spliced every time artillery fire hit it. Lineman supporting infantry units had one of the most dangerous and least glamorous jobs around.[157] Operating alone, usually at night, they were almost always in the open and frequently exposed to fire while splicing wire. Few soldiers wanted the danger and loneliness that came with being a telephone man supporting a front line unit.

The 167th received a warning order in early February. Two battalions of the 32nd French Infantry joined the regiment to serve as school troops and assist in getting the 167th ready during the last weeks before it entered the war.[158] Training gave the regiment a harder edge. Each man received new clothes and equipment: two pairs of hobnail boots, two uniforms, and plenty of socks. They wore steel helmets and web equipment at all times. They packed the distinctive felt campaign hats in duffle bags stored with division trains, not realizing they would never see them again.

After daily training, men received much-appreciated free time to explore local cafés and wine shops. Some lucky officers found a last opportunity to enjoy visiting larger cities. Colonel George E. Leach, commander of the Rainbow's 151st Field Artillery Battalion, recorded in his diary on February 17, 1918, "Arrived in Paris at five A.M., went to the Hotel Meurice. Spent the day seeing the sights of the city and one of my life's ambitions realized—I saw the tomb of Napoleon. Went to church at Notre Dame. Dinner at seven at Maximes [sic] and to the Casino in the evening. While I am writing this, the German planes are bombarding the city. It is a wonderful moonlight [sic] night."[159]

Even the men consigned to the countryside enjoyed diversions. Like every American in France, the men had money in their pockets and did their best to spend it. Although beneficial to the food and beverage business, this created inflation that hurt the poor civilians. The problem nagged at the French government, which complained to the Americans. No real changes occurred, however, and the men, unaware of the difficulty it posed to the civilians, enjoyed their leisure.

Despite such hardships, the locals knew what awaited the 167th, and they treated the men kindly. A bar owner in Marac had seen many French regiments pass through the village while training in the area, with the men becoming his customers and friends. As they proceeded to war, he followed their involvement, posting lists of dead and wounded on the café walls. He asked his new American customers to send him their casualty lists as well—a sobering reminder that village life was an interlude, and not the endpoint of the men's journey. The war waged on, and they were about to enter it.

# 4
# The Rainbow in the Trenches

### The 167th Reaches the Baccarat Sector

On February 16, 1918, the regiment marched from Faverolles to the Rolampont railhead, where it boarded trains of "40 and 8" boxcars heading for Baccarat.[1] These standard wooden boxcars for French troop trains took their names from their design, which accommodated forty men or eight horses. The cold, open cars had no toilets, and "As these troop trains sped through the French towns and countryside the undraped posterior of soldiers usually shone protruding from open doors with shirttails flapping in the breeze."[2]

Baccarat was approximately nine miles from the 1871 French-German border. Like all towns and villages near the front, it was all too familiar with the cost of war.[3] Having a population of about seven thousand, the prewar city was a thriving center for the manufacture of crystal. But the town suffered extensive damage in the opening days of battle. In August 1914 the German Army overran a French garrison there of three thousand, torching 120 houses in the process.[4] When the French retook Baccarat from the Germans on September 12, 1914, they caused further damage.[5] They also established an Allied trench line about five miles east of the city. The Germans conducted aerial reconnaissance when French units relieved one another in the trenches, but other than a few dropped bombs, the sector remained relatively quiet.[6] From then on by unspoken accord, the Germans and French demonstrated restraint in this area, firing weapons only infrequently.[7] Thus, in 1918, the Americans arrived at a relatively calm place and saw war damage for the first time.

André Thirion, a member of the French surrealist movement, remembered witnessing the Americans' arrival as a child: "Some towering Model T's brought soldiers dressed in khaki. . . . They installed themselves at all crossroads with orderlies on motorcycles and arranged a new invasion. New, handsomely equipped soldiers arrived from everywhere—at the small depot, in trucks and even on foot. Beneath our windows . . . huge caterpillar tractors dragged heavy cannon behind them. It was the 42nd US, the 'Rainbow' Division."[8] The American soldiers—aggressive, physically strong—soon gave hope and new life to the town and countryside. One soldier recalled the exuberant welcome the men received on their arrival in Baccarat, writing, "At the word 'American!' the cry 'Vive l'Amerique' leaped from mouth to mouth and the villagers swarmed about, anxious to get close-up views of the men from over the seas."[9] Such greetings were common, and they bolstered the Americans' enthusiasm.

On February 18, in the middle of the exceptionally cold winter, the 167th marched from Baccarat to Glonville. Ben Allender of the 168th described the area in a letter dated February 26: "The more we see of the town, the worse it looks, for nearly all of it has been destroyed. . . . There are also many graves of French soldiers scattered all over the town and country, wherever they fell."[10] The Meurthe River was so solidly frozen that horse-drawn artillery passed directly over it.[11] Four days later the 167th marched to Brouville, several miles nearer the front, and heard artillery rumble and saw German and Allied airplanes skirmish. Roads and friendly artillery were elaborately camouflaged, and everywhere they looked, they saw "a skeleton of a village shot to a crumbling ruin."[12]

## Entering the Trenches

By February 1918 the AEF decided that the Rainbow's "fighting spirit, which was already very high . . . should be sharpened to a fine point."[13] For its first official action, the Rainbow entered trenches in the Lorraine northeast of Baccarat, where it faced the 96th German Infantry Division and the 6th German Cavalry Division.[14] This quiet sector southeast of Nancy bordered Germany to the east and continued to Switzerland farther south.[15] The AEF planned to battle-train the 42nd Division by having it face the enemy while under the supervision of the VII (French) Corps, "who were temporarily holding the extreme right of the line in Lorraine on a front which extended from Dombasle to Baccarat."[16] Three French divisions—the FR 128th, 14th, and 164th—helped with this work.[17] Each of the four Rainbow regiments relieved a French unit or units. The 167th (Alabama) and 168th (Iowa) US Infantry Regiments were assigned to the 128th (French) Division, a division of Alpine chasseurs nicknamed the "Wolves."[18] The French provided on-the-job instructions until March 21, when the Rainbow assumed sole responsibility for the Baccarat sector. Under this "twinning" arrangement a US company, battalion, and regiment replaced French counterparts, but

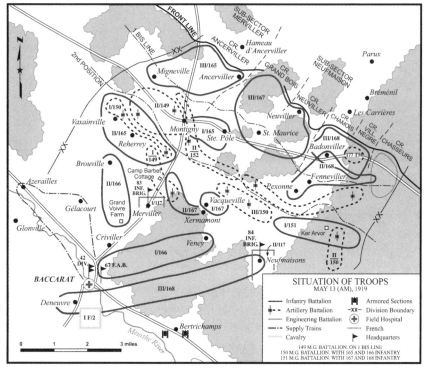

Battle Map 1. First "Rainbow" blood at Baccarat, February 18–June 21, 1918.

French officers retained initial command of the operation. Once the US troops grew accustomed to the responsibilities, the command passed to the Americans, and the French assumed positions in reserve. Eventually, the French pulled out completely.

A battalion shifted assignments every eight days, moving from the front line to the support position of that line and then to the reserve position, just as fully engaged units did.

The sector was mostly rolling farmland with mixed forests and crops. Farther back, villages were intact and provided billets—places for the American soldiers in reserve to stay, often either a space in a barn or, for the luckier ones, in a civilian home. Abandoned houses were also used for sheltering troops not being used on the front line or in immediate support. The Vosges Mountains were in the distant east. The black mud left both physical and emotional marks on the soldiers, as Louis Collins, a Rainbow artilleryman, who later became lieutenant governor of Minnesota, explains: "Never will the men of the 42nd Division forget the mud of Lorraine. Comrades may be forgotten, details of fighting go glimmering, marches and campaigns become hazy, but that awful February–March battle with the mud of Lorraine will stand out in their memories until final taps are sounded over the last surviving member of the division. For ten days the men of the 151st ate in mud, worked in mud, slept in mud, and dreamed of mud—when the mud would let them sleep. The picket lines in the echelons were in the mud; the men had to wallow through mud to get to the horses; and the horses had to wallow through mud to get to water. Every day it rained or snowed and the already villainous character of the mud became ever more villainous. . . . There is no mud like that of Lorraine."[19]

Other aspects of the trenches proved equally bleak. The sky was almost always overcast. Aircraft either operated below ceilings or during occasional breaks in the cloud cover. On the ground some German fighting bunkers, made of white concrete, loomed even in darkness. An eerie area called "no-man's-land," spotted with holes and debris from previous conflicts—stood between the German and Allied trenches, which were from three hundred to three thousand yards apart.

The trenches offered little respite. Communications trenches connected all positions except for Observation Posts (OPs) well in front of the trenches. They had duckboard floors—if they had floors at all—and walls made of saplings laced together. Some were in good condition since there had been little fighting in this sector for some time, but many were in bad shape.[20] Sandbags reinforced some trench walls and each trench had multiple shooting steps, lookout points, and firing positions. Narrow passageways made it difficult for men to pass through, particularly while carrying stretchers of wounded.[21] As R. M. Cheseldine observes, "Life in those days was anything but pleasant."[22]

The dugouts were reinforced to prevent caving in and had bunks, but were shallow, damp, and smelly. Charles MacArthur recalled, "[They] looked like four frail piano boxes on end, roofed with tin to make them bomb-proof. Every time we fired a gun fifty-seven rafters caved in. Each dugout was equipped with running water. Sometimes it ran down the walls—more often through the door. The place was full of rats addicted to creeping across faces or chewing up shoes."[23] Bunks consisted of boards.[24] Men were required to wash their feet and change socks daily to avoid foot rot, the condition brought on by constantly wet feet and socks. It causes skin to waste away and soft decay sets in.[25] Cooties flourished in such filthy conditions, aided by the soldiers' louse-infested straw bedding and their inability to bathe.[26]

Mobile kitchens served the trenches. Troops received two hot meals a day, delivered in insulated metal containers carried by two men or, more frequently, by a mule- or soldier-drawn machine gun cart. Men often used Sibley stoves to heat coffee or food in the trenches, but those without such luxuries improvised by punching holes in a tin can, adding wood and candle shavings sprinkled with gun oil, and lighting the mix with a match. The standard menu for hot meals was "slum," a mixture of meat and canned vegetables served with boiled rice. Despite its unappetizing name, one appreciative soldier described it as an appetizing and nourishing stew. Soldiers also received bread, butter, coffee, and condensed milk. For sweets, they had molasses or jam and an occasional bread pudding. They learned to keep canteens and extra water cans filled with chlorinated water.

Feeding the Alabama regiment was the responsibility of Captain J. Miles Smith of Montgomery. His Supply Company drew cases of rations at Baccarat and hauled them to Glonville by trucks and mule-drawn wagons for distribution, a complicated process. To reach Companies A, B, and D the rations were transferred at Montigny to a flat car pulled by a mule over the narrow railway running behind the trench lines. The jitney railroad crossed a creek at a small railway station. Mule-drawn wagons took rations directly to C Company's kitchen behind GC (Groupe de Combat) Number Ten, or strong point number 10.[27]

Men were uneasy on first reaching the trenches, but eventually settled in to a sort of equilibrium. Cheseldine recounts, "In the inky blackness wire posts looked like Germans and many an unoffending stick of wood was made the target of a shower of rifle bullets and hand grenades. Many flares were sent up, another habit of the beginner. As the nervousness wore off, however, these symptoms disappeared and things settled down to the tedium of trench warfare which, as our English Allies so aptly said, is 'damned dull, damned damp and damned dangerous.'"[28] For many men, the trenches mixed apparently opposing forces—terror and boredom.

## French-American Relationships

While the men of the 167th got their introduction to trench warfare, the question of who was actually commanding them became the subject of debate in the rear. On the ground, the troops enjoyed camaraderie, but higher headquarters expressed substantial differences on how the Americans should be involved in the war effort—and what shape that effort should take.

The foundations of Franco-American cooperation were formed through the

Joffre-Baker Agreement in May 1917 in which the United States rejected the commingling of its troops with those of France. The French referred to American collaboration, not help.[29] General Pershing and his staff always resisted French tutelage over training Americans. The first US divisions arriving in France received training from French units, but that system was soon replaced by US training schools with some French help. Pershing agreed to use French instructors and school troops but insisted on maintaining control over the process. The influence of the French trainers slowly waned.[30]

A primary source of disagreement was the perceived value of trench versus open warfare. The division commander, Major General Charles Menoher, and his chief of staff, Colonel MacArthur, worked closely with the French and accepted the challenge of the trenches, but they did not forget that Pershing, their commander, wanted training for open warfare to prepare his army for a drive to Germany. The French were committed to trench warfare, which required less training. They wanted the US Army to go into their trenches under their officers. The British advocated a similar plan, but the Americans refused them both. The French and the British, whose offensive approach led to hundreds of thousands of casualties in 1914, favored defensive warfare from then on—a tactic the Americans resisted.

The British and French also expected American involvement to end the war, and they pressured Pershing to expedite this process. For months Georges Clemenceau, the prime minister of France, had spoken of adding newcomers "into the fighting as soon as possible," and British Commanding General Haig also wondered how to expedite the preparation and deployment of American forces.[31] Pershing knew that fighting from trenches could be done with less well-trained troops and fewer of them, but he did not believe it was a way to achieve decisive results. Rather, he looked for plans beyond sticking his men in a trench. Pershing knew that he must find a way to run the Germans out of France, and to do that, he believed he would need offensive, rather than defensive, warfare.

Therefore, while the Rainbow spent time in the trenches, its trench warfare training was subordinated to training for more aggressive warfare in the open. Patrolling from trenches into no-man's-land—the disputed territory between the opposing trenches—eventually became the principal part of the Rainbow mission. It practiced raids or minor attacks on German trenches, and it dealt with German retaliations—large raids backed up by heavy concentrations of artillery.[32] MacArthur participated in one aspect of this firsthand on February 20, 1918, when he accompanied a French raid toward German trenches, advancing eleven hundred meters through German artillery fire and taking several prisoners.[33]

Such real-life training situations offered significant tests for members of the regiment, who were well trained but had not previously been under much fire. They wanted to perform well and prove themselves before their fellow soldiers and the French. Several aspects of their prior experiences helped prepare them. Most of the men in the 167th had been together for a long time, and they had been tested—and unified—by the epic march a month after their arrival in France. A bond of mutual confidence and understanding existed between officers and the men and from the men to each other. The friendships between some of the Alabama men further substantiated such confidence. The 167th also exhibited a substantial amount of satisfaction in its identity as a volunteer unit belonging to the first National Guard division to see combat in the war.

All this combined to instill a great deal of pride in the 167th. Although tensions existed among high-level officers responsible for planning the strategic aspects of the war, the twinned American and French troops coexisted amicably. One illustration of such mutual respect arose in a February 22, 1918, meeting between the officers of the 167th (Alabama) and the 167th (French). The official diary of the French noted that date as George Washington's birthday, showing French respect for American history.[34] The French appreciation for Washington proved more than an idle gesture, and his birthday was celebrated in a dinner held by the staff of the 166th and their trainers, the French 60th.[35] Another demonstration of this respect existed in a survey of letters from French military personnel. As Robert E. Bruce notes, "As early as January and February 1918, when Americans soldiers were still rarely seen at the front line, French military censors noted that approximately 20 percent of the letters they had surveyed not only mentioned Americans but gave glowing appraisals of their military capabilities, even though hardly any had been in action yet."[36]

Even Germans recognized the affection shared between French and American troops. General Erich Ludendorff, the chief of the German Army, later observed, "Inasmuch as the French greeted the sons of the new world with enthusiasm, as their saviour in time of need, friendly relations were quickly established. Frequently the memory of General Lafayette was invoked."[37]

## Amalgamation in the Trenches

On the night of February 24 the 1st Battalion of the 167th assembled in Brouville to head into the trenches for the first time.[38] Two lieutenants from every company, each with thirty men, formed units of half-platoon size in the main street of Brouville and marched from the village to their posts in the trenches facing the enemy.[39] Although individual Alabamians may have already entered the war, the 1st Battalion of the 167th was the first element of the Alabama regiment to engage the Germans in combat. On its first night an enemy airplane came over and dropped a bomb. Another bombing occurred in the morning.[40]

The initial group of D Company men had French soldiers with them until February 26. Each American had a poilu as an instructor. The French offered practical briefings on the details of trench life, day and night. They also advised on how best to defend each position and where to look for trouble. The second two platoon groups, with the remainder of the men in D Company, then relieved the last of the French still in the trenches, who took their weapons with them upon completion of the relief. The 167th Machine Gun section attached to D Company fired test rounds. Rainbow artillery relieved the French artillery and established its own fire direction centers, maps, concentrations, and limits before the French Army was completely relieved in the sector. The final turnover took place on February 28, 1918.[41] Nearby village streets were filled with French and American soldiers coming and going to billets in reserve areas as they awaited duty at the front.

Although the American men got along with their French counterparts, the twinning of units caused some anxiety. One captain recalled the stressful experience: "Will you ever forget that first time you fell in with the 'picked men' and your skin felt like a picked chicken, to [sic] out in no man's land to see what was to be seen? How you repeated to yourself over and over and over again that fool French pass word, and wondered how in the name of common sense a perfectly good American was going to remember in time of need all that frog lingo."[42] Now that the Americans were proving their competence, they gained familiarity, but they also gained responsibility, and that brought its own stressors.

As part of its twinning at Baccarat, the 167th Sanitary Detachment, the medical detachment, took over responsibilities from its French counterpart in the aid stations. French medics explained procedures, including the evacuation of wounded, and left some equipment with the Americans.[43] The 167th assumed the French unit's six Groupes de Combat (GC), or strong points, assigning two to each rifle company. Captain Edmundson's D Company (Bessemer) held numbers five and six. Two men at a time manned each fighting position, which were connected by communications trenches.[44] Throughout the night, men stood two-hour watches spelled by four-hour breaks in the underground log dugouts.

The most dangerous assignments were Observation Posts (OPs) in no-man's-land, in front of the trench lines. They were exposed to raids, and the two men on each OP served twelve-hour shifts, all night or all day, with relief at dawn and dusk. They stood in the open and under constant surveillance, so daylight shift changes were too dangerous.

Soon the men learned some characteristics of incoming rounds. They usually heard a "swish" or "flutter" when one passed overhead. If a round came in close, depending on the angle of fire, there might be a quick "whistle" or "scream" followed by the explosion. Although one rarely heard a small mortar hitting nearby— hence the saying that you never heard the one that would kill you—everyone instinctively listened for incoming fire.

The Alabamians were in range of enemy artillery, and tension built. Green American flares frequently signaled gas attacks, but they were mostly false alarms.[45] Both sides spasmodically exchanged fire with rifles, machine guns, and artillery. The realities of war set in.

While the men got along, the groups possessed different energies and characteristics. This sector had remained fairly quiet since the French reclaimed it in 1914. At that time Germans typically fired a quota of shells at the front lines, communications trenches, and artillery emplacements, and each day usually held some brief machine gun fire whether or not targets appeared. But neither German nor French gunners liked shooting unless there were real targets. That simply meant more work cleaning weapons. Raids were expected, but the periods in between were more like an armed truce. Both German and French divisions had arrived after their heavy fighting on more active fronts, and neither sought trouble in the Baccarat sector. The relative stability offered both sides a respite from the conflict.[46]

Things heated up when the Rainbow entered the picture and the Americans started shooting. The French appreciated the newcomers, but some of their behavior concerned experienced veterans. French officials noted that Americans frequently relied on telephones to exchange "important tactical information" and that they chattered on the phones all night, opening themselves to infiltration by wiretaps.[47] Additionally, they would often "show themselves carelessly in the trenches, providing German observers with opportunities to record the routine of the troops, and, worse, to ascertain American schedules such as time and method of feeding and the relief of outposts and guards."[48]

Raymond S. Tompkins, war correspondent of the *Baltimore Sun*, describes one incident involving the Alabamians of the 167th, noting their disruptive behavior but calling them the story's "heroes." He recounts:

The Germans had washed clothes in that shellhole before and nothing had happened. . . . On their side the French had peacefully smoked their pipes in the cool of the evening on the very top of the trenches. It was simply one of the workings out of the tacit agreement.

But a little outpost of Alabamians got one glimpse of this group of Boche in undershirts arrogantly dipping dirty clothes in the water of No-Man's-Land, and they opened fire. The Germans scattered like rabbits, some of them hugging wounds.

A French officer came rushing to the outpost in a fury of excitement. What did the Americans mean? They had done a terrible thing! Now the Germans would be angry and everybody was in for a period of shelling and gas and raids! He rebuked the hot-headed Yanks sternly.

"What the hell?" said one of the men later. "I came out here to kill these Boche, not to sit here and watch 'em wash clothes."[49]

Alabamians were among the most boisterous of the Rainbow Division, lending the 167th the description "the most aggressive."[50] In a letter to his wife, "Wild" Bill Donovan of the 165th Infantry noted that the men of 167th "wander all over the landscape shooting at everything."[51] Even the Germans quickly understood the character of their opponents, who boldly "crossed No Man's Land one night and put signs in the German wire facing their trenches which read, 'Germans, give your soul to God because your ass belongs to Alabam.'"[52] The Alabama men remained undaunted in the face of danger, united by faith in their cause, each other, and their own abilities. Officials concurred, noting the unit's abilities and positive demeanor. In late February, Colonel Galbrunner, commander of the 167th FR Division, reported his delight with the "outgoingness, good behavior, discipline, and spirit of the American soldiers."[53] Both the French and the Americans appeared pleased with the arrangement.

## The 167th's First Patrol

Although the 167th had been engaged on the Baccarat front since February 24, its first patrol was on the night of March 4, 1918. After substantial planning, D Company was chosen for the job. After dark, Sergeant Varner Hall led a hand-picked group of five volunteer noncommissioned officers into no-man's-land, where they located a German trench and followed it until encountering nine Germans.[54] Hall challenged, and the leading German soldier lunged at Hall, who shot the German in the stomach. The remaining Germans evacuated the trench and surrounded the Alabamians. A brawl followed, and another German was wounded. One attacked Hall. Corporal Homer Whited of Bessemer jumped into the hand-to-hand fight. Another Alabamian, Corporal E. H. Freeman of Montevallo, shot the German Whited held. The other Germans fled.

Hall's patrol emerged with a prisoner, one enemy killed, and two enemy wounded. Five Germans got away, though later that night, D Company's Lieutenant Shelby V. Gamble, of Lamar, Colorado, led a larger patrol that returned with one of the wounded.[55] The Hall patrol's prisoner was the war's first for the Rainbow Division and possibly the entire AEF. Corporal Whited was cited for his hand-to-hand fighting.

But the celebrations soon ended. The escaped Germans reported the patrol, and the 77th Bavarians raided the neighboring 168th the next night.[56] The stakes spiraled up. First one side struck, then the other, with increasingly stronger blows.

German artillery became more active and used 88 mm flat trajectory guns for the first time against the 167th. In the March 5 attack, the Germans also fired a professionally executed walking box of indirectly fired artillery shells around their own infantry, protecting it from counterattack. The two Iowa platoons, badly mauled but not overrun, sustained losses of twenty-two killed, including the company commander, and twenty-two wounded. Despite the casualties, this National Guard unit successfully withstood attack by professional German soldiers. Officials noted the accomplishment. It was the first significant test of the staying power of the National Guard troops and was regarded as a major milestone by the troops and commanders.[57]

## General Pershing Visits the 167th

Despite American successes, the situation was tense. During the twenty-four-hour period beginning at noon on March 6, Germans fired 1,571 rounds into the Baccarat subsector, 1,237 into the Saint-Clément subsector, and 309 into the Lunéville subsector.[58] Pershing visited the regiment, arriving at 84th Brigade Headquarters on March 6 with two Rolls Royce automobiles. Escorted on foot by Lieutenant Colonel Walter E. Bare, executive officer of the 167th and the 84th Brigade's acting adjutant, Pershing lunched on canned corned beef, hardtack, and Roquefort cheese and drove to a position about three hundred yards from the German line in the Alabama sector. He spoke with several officers and men and inspected a section of trench. Bare then accompanied the general by car on a route parallel to the front lines and connecting Pexonne, Badonviller, Ogeviller, and Lunéville.[59]

Pershing's visit was part of a broader interest in the area's troops. The high command of the AEF watched every detail of the Rainbow Division's maiden performance. Some doubted that National Guard divisions could demonstrate reasonable value.[60] The French and the British, who were eager to see how their allies performed, also watched the division's development, as did the Germans, who hoped to assess their new foe. To the delight of the French and the dismay of German intelligence service, the AEF declared the Rainbow to be a first-class combat division.[61]

The Germans continued to retaliate, launching a March 7 attack into a battalion-sized sector of the Rainbow's 165th (New York) Infantry. The Alabama D Company was nearby when two officers and about fifty men of the 165th received fire and held a strong point called Rouge Bouquet. More than thirty New Yorkers were killed, mostly in a bunker cave-in.[62] Sergeant Joyce Kilmer of the 165th, already famous for his poem "Trees," memorialized the event in a poem titled "Rouge Bouquet."[63]

D Company's Corporal Gentry Herman of Huntsville was killed on March 8. According to the June 9 edition of the *Birmingham Age Herald* Herman was the first member of the 167th to be killed in action. Herman was awarded the Distinguished Service Cross (DSC) by the US Army.[64]

By successfully launching small patrols the Americans proved they were ready for greater challenges. On March 9, the 128th French Division planned and led two company-sized patrols jointly with the Americans in the vicinity of Badonviller. These were carefully rehearsed, with each patrol using a French company of Alpine chasseurs to guide the newcomers.[65] The Rainbow's 168th Regiment provided both American companies, and Colonel MacArthur accompanied them as an observer. Advancing in two columns after heavy artillery preparation, the US forces remained in the center with the French units on the flanks. They found no opposition on reaching the first trench line, largely destroyed by artillery. The patrol turned back at the second line after encountering gas and receiving artillery and machine gun fire. American losses for the patrol were nine killed and thirty-three wounded.[66]

Although American casualties at Baccarat were relatively light, they did occur. Casualties shocked the units, and "the whole outfit bristled" at the losses.[67] French villagers also mourned the deaths. Thirion remembers, "We treated their first casualties with great love. They were brought to Baccarat and buried in a new cemetery. . . . The procession was led by a slow moving infantry band playing Chopin's Funeral March, the first time I ever heard it."[68] The Americans quickly realized that even in a "quiet" sector, casualties were inevitable. The American units were not emerging unscathed, but they were gaining valuable combat techniques.

## The Rainbow Receives Recognition

As it proved its merits, the Rainbow garnered official recognition in the form of visits and decorations. The senior American member of the Allied War Council, General Tasker M. Bliss, as well as practically all of the AEF section chiefs from Chaumont, visited for a close look at the Rainbow soldiers. No visitor proved more important than Secretary of War Newton D. Baker. Although Baker hailed from Ohio and wanted to visit the Rainbow's 166th Infantry Regiment from his home state, his visit proved significant to men from other areas.[69] He was escorted by Colonel James G. Harbord, chief of staff of the AEF, who had accompanied Pershing to France and continued to serve him. Harbord, who served at headquarters but visited the front line, described the scene: "Very sturdy and soldierly they looked, with the unmistakable air of men who have had their experience in the trenches. Not clean or spick and span, not much like militia such as they were a few month ago, but real field soldiers swinging by at a good steady step, their clothes showing signs of wear; and over it all the stars shining down, the Germans guns booming in the hills. The officers were called to the roadside and the Secretary made them the first of several very clever little speeches I was to hear that day. . . . He told of his interest in this particular battalion, of the interest of the whole country in the Rainbow Division."[70]

Baker also urged the men to ask for needed assistance, declaring himself their ally in all matters, from the organizational to the culinary.[71]

While in the field, Baker witnessed carrier pigeon demonstrations, seeing an important mechanism for communication between troops. (See fig. 7.) The French VII Army Corps instructed the 42nd Division in Glonville and Baccarat to issue four pigeons per post, recording the time of departure and arrival of pigeons in each flight with a message while making an effort to keep two in reserve.[72] Captain Jordan had earlier written home to explain the pigeon training to his son, who expressed concern for them. Jordan responded, "Tell Mort to cheer up about the pigeons. . . . They have men to look after them and have fine houses for them, and whenever the army needs any message sent, they send a basket of pigeons to the front and the pigeons then bring the messages back. They say that they will fly through a barrage and above the gas to get home."[73] Later in the day Baker insisted on visiting a listening post after trudging through trenches for half an hour. A German shell exploded about fifty yards from his car, underscoring the area's danger.[74]

Members of the Rainbow also received official decorations for their accomplishments. The French IV Corps awarded each member of Sergeant Hall's March 4 patrol a Croix de Guerre, and the AEF followed with a DSC. The US Congress passed a law legalizing American soldiers' acceptance of French medals. Around this time Pershing recommended the creation of a combat medal that would be less conspicuous than the US Medal of Honor or the DSC. To be named the Citation Star, it would recognize soldiers cited for honors by their regimental, brigade, or division commanders.[75] Pershing, along with many others, felt that awards were too freely distributed, and the creation of an award for smaller honors would help maintain the distinction of decorations such as the Medal of Honor and the Distinguished Service Cross.

In early 1918 the only other existing American awards were marksmanship medals and campaign ribbons. All members of the 167th who had gone to the Mexican border were eligible for the Mexican Border Campaign Ribbon, and members of the regiment who served on active duty in France would become eligible for the AEF Victory Medal, with a clasp naming every battle its wearer participated in. The men in the 167th were already eligible for the ribbon with a clasp for Lorraine. Those wounded in battle after April 5, 1917, the last day before the United States entered into war with Germany, were authorized to wear a wound stripe. The men of the Rainbow Division were already receiving recognition for their efforts.[76]

## Coming of Age in the Trenches

The three battalions of the regiment had all served reserve, support, and front line duty in four-day rotations, half the duration of standard rotations. Thus each stint of service on the front line was followed by time in the rear. When Colonel Screws's unit rotated out on March 13, it had been in the trenches, faced the Germans alone, seen some members lose their lives, and taken German lives. They were veterans—something that could be said of very few Americans in France at the time. On returning to Glonville each platoon was met by the regiment's band, which followed the standard practice of escorting every unit rotating from the front lines, a ceremony the women and children in nearby villages enjoyed.[77]

As some troops rotated out, others went back in, and despite the routine, action picked up as the Americans settled in. German observation balloons always hovered aloft. During a twenty-four-hour period spanning March 18–19, twenty-two German planes appeared over Baccarat, four over Saint-Clément, and eight over Lunéville. For the same period Germans fired 5,503 rounds of artillery into the sector.[78] In a March 18, 1918, letter to his mother, Lieutenant Duncan Campbell described the sound of a German rifle, "The only way to tell it is by the words Tack Oh, or Tacko."[79]

The stress caused disruptions in other ways. First Lieutenant Hugh Thompson, Company L of the neighboring 168th Infantry, reported patrols of the 167th coming through their lines from no-man's-land: "The Southerners couldn't be bothered with rifles; a grenade in the hand and another in the otherwise empty canteen cover was worth 'beaucoo' [sic] small artillery. The boys from Alabama did not think much of our passwords and countersigns which came from French sources. Their own signals, sent us each day were more original 'Big Boy,' 'Come seben—come eleben' from their stock of slang."[80]

Regular reporting of frontline activities appeared in some US newspapers beginning in March, and complete casualty lists were published in the Minneapolis, Minnesota, papers.[81] The March 16, 1918, *Montgomery Advertiser* included an article about the 167th's contact with the enemy. The front page named the Alabamians decorated for bravery by the French.[82] Subsequent stories appeared in the *Montgomery Advertiser* on March 18 and 20. The latter named Alma W. Martin of Castleberry as a regiment member killed in action. The first report at home of the combat death of an Alabama soldier was partially in error: Martin, of I Company (Opelika), actually hailed from Girard, Alabama.

## The Spring Offensive

On the day Baker visited the Rainbow trenches (see fig. 8), the division was ordered to return to the Rolampont area. Everyone thought, incorrectly, it would be for another round of training for open warfare.[83] While the Rainbow emerged from the trenches and headed to the rear, the Germans launched a peace offensive against exhausted French and British troops in the north. This followed the March 15, 1918, abdication of the Russian czar and subsequent declaration of Russia as a republic. That event ended Germany's war with Russia and freed troops on the eastern front to participate in the war against the Allies on the western front. In November 1917 the Germans had used 144 divisions against 108 French and 52 British. After the treaty of Brest Litovsk—the peace treaties Russia signed with Germany, Austria-Hungary, Turkey, and Bulgaria in March 1918—Germany could bring sixty divisions—600,000 men—from Russia, and an additional 450,000 recruits entered the German army with the class of 1919.[84] The Germans were becoming very good with the war of movement, and they suddenly had more troops for it.[85] With the additional forces, they set their sights on Paris.

On March 21, 1918, the opening day of the German offensive, the British line in the Somme gave way.[86] The German efforts were impressive, as they retook ground "the British had struggled six months to capture in the Somme," along with thousands of British prisoners.[87] The French immediately rushed every available unit to the north to stop the German advance and close the widening gap between the Allies there. The British Army was running out of men. It was in such despair that despite the opposition of Irish nationalists to the war, it extended conscription to Ireland for the first time, gaining fifty thousand Irish soldiers.[88]

It was a replay to veteran German soldiers. The first day, when the offensive started after long preparations and the arrival of the troops from the eastern front, reminded soldiers of the beginning of the war in 1914. One soldier's letter notes: "The Spring has started today and not only this, since 4 o'clock the cannons are thundering without interruption . . . it is again war and I think we are finished with rest. . . . Everywhere people are working feverishly and the sight of the roads is so busy, like in the first months of the war."[89]

On the evening of March 21, the 167th (France) replaced the 167th's 3rd Battalion in the Center of Resistance (CR), Ancerviller. When leaving, Colonel Screws asked Colonel Galbrunner to thank the French 167th—which he called by its nickname, "the Wolves"—for its fraternal reception and helpful instruction. Screws added that he was happy to have had his regiment's first feat of arms with his French sister regiment. The colonels decided to celebrate the anniversary of the units' first encounter, February 22, with an annual exchange of letters to maintain their brotherly bond.[90] The Rainbow was part of the VII FR Army until March 23, 1918—not quite as long as planned initially.[91] The training period was ended by the German offensive, which required that French troops be reassigned to other areas, leaving Americans with responsibility of the sector.

The French and British situations grew dire. On the offensive's first day, March

21, 1918, 300,000 American soldiers were in France. Of these, the 1st, 2nd, and 42nd Divisions were in the trenches, and the 26th was ready for service. In their new offensive to take Paris the Germans launched by far the most formidable force the world had ever seen: forty mobile divisions with full attack battalions of 850 men each, along with thirty attack divisions and a rumored "1,569,000 rifles to the Allies' 1,245,000."[92] Within eight days the Germans practically destroyed the 5th (British) Army and penetrated to a depth of almost forty miles—an extreme distance, as previous advances averaged between one and five miles.[93]

The British and French "were just a step away from panic" when facing the German offensive, "which smashed into the junction of Allied armies between Cambrai and St. Quentin and seemed unstoppable."[94] British commander Douglas Haig said, "With our backs to the wall and believing in the justice of our cause, each of us must fight to the end. . . . Every position must be held to the last man. There must be no retirement."[95] Many French divisions rushed to aid the British. In that time of crisis, on March 26, 1918, the British and French in a meeting at Doullens saw the need for unified command and named General Ferdinand Foch supreme Allied commander.[96]

The Americans remained concerned, as this meant that Pershing would not exercise any tactical control over the AEF.[97] Baker allowed Pershing free rein to act. On March 27, 1918, Pershing visited Foch in his headquarters in the field and announced a relaxing of the American position as to the use of its troops. Using halting French, he said, "the American people would consider it a great honor for our troops to be engaged in the present battle. I ask you for this in their name and my own. At this moment there are no other questions but of fighting. Infantry, artillery, aviation, all that we have is yours; use them as you wish. . . . They are yours to dispose of as you will. . . . More will come, in numbers equal to the requirements."[98] Because of the critical nature of this time, the Americans agreed to increased French leadership, but they made sure that they could withdraw if action was against their national interest. On the same day, Straub, a sergeant in the 150th Field Artillery wrote: "last night they had received over wireless a message saying the Germans had started their great offensive extending from Luneville to the North Sea."[99]

At a meeting at Beauvais on April 3, Foch requested authority to coordinate commands and to initiate action as commander in chief over armies led by Pétain, Haig, and Pershing. All who attended—including Clemenceau and David Lloyd George, prime minister of Great Britain—agreed. When Lloyd George asked for Pershing's opinion, the American general acknowledged that the only way to assure cooperation was to have a single leader.[100] Foch became strategic commander of all operations on the western front, but each commander had the right to appeal to his government if safety of his forces was compromised by an order given by Foch.

A month later in Abbeville, the Supreme War Council added the Italian front to Foch's command. The British and French asked once more that American battalions be merged into Allied armies. Pershing pounded on the table to make his point.[101] Despite his having offered in March to furnish troops to fight alongside the Allies, he would not settle for less than an American army under an American flag and American command. Pershing's original concession to Foch was only temporary, and he continued advocating for increased American responsibility.

## Responsibility for the Baccarat Sector

Although the Rainbow planned to continue training with the French for several months, the German offensive expedited matters, and the Rainbow became "the first American Division to be entrusted with the command of a Divisional sector."[102] On March 28, 1918, the 42nd Division, barely out of the trenches, received orders to return to the defensive positions in the Baccarat sector.[103] D Company marched to its new billets near Vaxainville, a village run down by war but that still boasted some older houses with arches over the doorways and remnants of backyard gardens.[104] In going back to the trenches, the Rainbow replaced the 128th French Division, this time as a full-blown replacement, not as troops twinning with it for training. The division went back in with brigades abreast, but at slightly different places than its former position. Now it was on the right flank of the VIII (French) Army, which remained in overall command of the Lorraine front. The 167th's order to move, published at Screws's PC (Post of Command) at the village of Hablainville on April 6, 1918, described placement of guides and units, routes of march, and march discipline to include orders to move platoons at intervals under combat rules.[105] Otherwise, life in Hablainville was more or less normal for the Americans and the villagers, who continued operating the local school and town hall.

The entire division sector—a specific portion of the front that was to be defended and from which combat and reconnaissance patrols were launched—was entrusted to the Americans. The additional training schedule planned for the Rainbow was shortened, because the division was now believed to be capable of trench fighting.[106] All of its infantry and artillery were engaged. Despite the

Rainbow's proving itself, French leaders were cautious about allowing it sole responsibility for the sector. The Germans had enjoyed a string of recent successes and held superiority in numbers along the entire western front. The French worried that the Germans might catch the relatively green Rainbow by surprise and defeat it in the Baccarat sector. It was unnaturally quiet there as German activity diminished in the first half of April. Expecting a trap, alarmed French commanders asked the Rainbow to step up patrols, both day and night, and to make raids to test the combat intelligence gathered from reconnaissance patrols.[107]

MacArthur asked for more aggressive operations. On April 13, after the 167th took over the Neuviller and Grand Bois Centers of Resistance controlling the area east of Ancerviller and Neuviller, he instructed brigade commanders to conduct nightly patrols "to capture prisoners."[108] The 167th responded promptly, sending D Company on a record-setting, long-range patrol that evening.[109] It entered the Salient du Feys to a crossroads well within German lines, was discovered but escaped without loss. D Company's already successful patrol leader, First Lieutenant Shelby V. Gamble, led it. Other officers were Second Lieutenants George Berriman and Dick Breeding.[110] As they made the deepest penetration of any of the patrols up to that time, they killed seven Germans and shot up more.

Not all patrols enjoyed such success, and on April 18, Major General Menoher reinforced MacArthur's order, offering something that might be construed as a motivational speech: "prisoners must be obtained . . . our patrols are timid . . . the 42nd Division has so far been able to establish a most enviable reputation in everything it has undertaken except in the matter of patrolling. Is it going to fail to establish a reputation for fighting spirit? If it fails in this point, it fails in everything."[111] From then on lieutenants Gamble, Breeding, and Berriman led patrols into no-man's-land practically every night that the 167th remained in the sector.

Two of the other officers leading these patrols were first lieutenants. All others were second lieutenants; eight were recent arrivals from officer training. They obtained prisoners and gathered useful information, but, most importantly, they learned to patrol and be better infantrymen. This was the most dangerous work of the regiment, and leaders carefully documented each operation with a strip map and written report.[112] Every officer other than commanding officers and staff was required to patrol, as were all riflemen, mortar men, and machine gunners. These patrols used substantial manpower and drained the men emotionally and physically. Every person going out into no-man's-land was in danger of being killed, captured, or wounded. Duty rosters were posted a day in advance, causing nerve-wracking waits, briefings, and rehearsals. There was waiting time, allowing one to take counsel of his fears. The patrols were pressured to secure prisoners—to capture or kill a tough and experienced enemy by going out after dark and returning before dawn, staying out even if no contact was made. Germans responded to those pressures with a fourteen-man ambush of a 167th OP relief. It netted them two captured Alabamians.[113] The Rainbow was getting its first look at the *Sturmgruppen* (deep penetration groups) tactics. These German infiltration methods started in 1917 to replace the casualty-heavy "over the top" attacks of 1914–15. The Germans now planned to look for Allied weaknesses, infiltrate men into the area, then swarm and run over the weaker positions. The classic infantry assaults would be preceded by specialized light infantry shock troops going into target areas and building up local superiority at various places along the front. By 1918 raids were conducted by large groups, and neither side put out raiding parties simply for demonstrations or shows of strength. Some raids served strictly for reconnaissance or ambushes. Members of those operations would move by stealth and maintain fire discipline—a policy of firing only when absolutely necessary so as not to disclose position—while lightly armed with a rifle, pistol, and a few hand grenades. They carried no machine guns or mortars. In contrast, combat patrols were deadly serious, purposeful affairs that involved as many as fifty men attacking strong points or capturing sections of trenches and holding them for a time.[114] Within the division, the 167th distinguished itself, gaining a "reputation as indomitable fighters [that] continued to grow."[115] (See fig. 9.)

On May 2 a French artillery unit took up a position in the Alabama area and fired twenty thousand rounds in preparation for two companies from the 166th to pass through the lines of the 167th and go "over the top"—the soldiers' term for initiating contact or beginning a mission—at dawn on May 3. The next night, one of the most promising patrol leaders in the regiment, F Company's Second Lieutenant Alton P. Woods of Boston, Massachusetts, was wounded on an ambush patrol. He died in the Evacuation Hospital at Baccarat.[116] His assistant patrol leader, Private First Class John B. F. Walters, of Gadsden was missing in action.[117] Prisoners offered great value in terms of information about the enemy, and the raids to secure them refined the infantryman's confidence and skills. However, Woods's death and Walters's being missing served as a reminder that these expeditions were costly.

After another raid on May 12, one of the Alabamians failed to return, and two second lieutenants, including Dick Breeding, volunteered to lead a patrol to search for him. Breeding approached enemy lines, killing a combatant in the process, and brought the body into American lines.[118] Breeding received a DSC.[119]

The regiment rotated all three of its infantry battalions to the trenches and was doing its most dangerous work ever, but Screws still insisted on maintaining standards and discipline. On May 4 he issued a written order requiring units to keep harnesses oiled and animals groomed. Those with animals were to submit written reports on their condition to his headquarters by Sunday morning of each week.

Men never enjoyed the trenches, but morale went up briefly when pear trees bloomed and trees started to bud. Ben Allender from Ottumwa, Iowa, wrote on Sunday, May 12, "Mother's Day. This day is sure a great day to us over here. The little French children have been at the 'Y' all day with baskets of flowers, pinning them on every American soldier they see. We have a swell program at the 'Y' tonight and our Chaplain is going to give us a talk on 'Mother and the Bible' and I know it will sure be good for us. He is a wonderful talker."[120]

After that it rained most days, and skies were overcast—typical weather for early spring in eastern France. Days and nights were wet, dirty, and depressing. The work was hard. Men rotated duty on the dangerous observation posts, firing steps, and machine gun positions, sometimes using carrier pigeons to deliver messages. Rifles, pistols, and machine guns were cleaned after every firing, or every other day if they were not fired. Reserve ammunition was kept clean. Guard duty, lasting two hours on and two hours off, continued during darkness. The dugouts did not have enough bunks, and arguments broke out among the tired and irritable men. Rats abounded, along with bedbugs and lice. It took great effort to properly dispose of human waste, maintain dry socks, or obtain hot food. Even getting a "whore's bath" or "spit bath" with a few quarts of water proved challenging to the point battalions.[121] Reading the Bible or playing cards or checkers offered occasional relief. The initial enthusiasm and excitement from proximity to danger were over and the days dwindled on.

On May 25–26 the Germans made an aggressive gas attack, killing about a hundred men of the flanking 168th (Iowa).[122] Bulky containers of odorless and colorless phosgene gas wobbled through the air. In almost no time fumes drenched the large area, and one whiff killed. Men could not remove their gas masks to speak. That same night, Huntsville's Lieutenant Stephen W. Harris, Company C of the 167th, bumped into a strong enemy patrol while leading twenty men on patrol. No casualties occurred, as both sides disengaged.[123]

On the next day, the Germans launched a major attack on the Chemin des Dames, a sector much farther north. The French suffered reverses there in April 1917, but Foch held such faith in its current strength that he unwisely allocated some of its troops to other positions.[124] This operation, created with care and secrecy by the Germans, was part of the Hindenburg Offensive. Its success damaged French morale and created a temporary panic in Paris, alarming the French high command.[125]

The 168th suffered another brutal gas attack at midnight on May 28th. It was a wet, dismal time—perfect for gas. Thick mists caused gas vapors, heavier than the natural atmosphere, to hold close to the ground in low terrain. Men sought higher ground to avoid it. Gas attacks were especially terrifying and confusing when followed by artillery attacks at night. Gary Roberts described two such attacks in a letter home: "A week ago yesterday the air was full of poison and of course some of the boys 'had a hard day' as we call it. The huns followed in behind the gas but as they reached the barbed wire they came to a dead halt. The boys took their masks off and let them have it so there was a few of the bloody huns that had a bad day too. They tried the gas again on Monday night and followed it up but they found the boys right on the job so the huns were beaten off again and some prisoners taken in return."[126] Men did not have to be told to keep their gas masks with them, as they understood the consequences of being without—and what could be achieved when the men were well prepared.

In the midst of combat, the 167th endured an irritating wave of flu, typically lasting three days and spreading through units. Cooties continued to inflict misery—a misery that would only abate when men could wash regularly.

The Rainbow believed it had reached the point of controlling its no-man's-land. A lot more experienced, it patrolled with confidence, pushing far into enemy lines and crisscrossing the front. It regularly moved into temporarily vacated sections of German trenches and stayed in them for as long as three days, hoping to ambush enemy soldiers returning to the area. This intense pressure caused the Germans to practically desert their front line OP by day and to change strong points most nights. It was a fluid and unpredictable situation.

Edward Wren, a former Auburn football player in B Company of the 167th, wrote his father from a reserve position on May 29: "I had the experience of going out on patrol our last time up to the trenches out in No Mans [sic] Land and that is some excitement and will sure cause a man to use his head when a machine gun is shooting over your head and you don't know how far the bullets are missing you. But it is something about it that you can't help liking and I want to go out every chance I have."[127]

## Away from the Front

In reserve for eight days, K Company settled into a village behind the trenches. Having just returned from staff school, Jordan wrote, "It was a scene with demolished houses and debris everywhere, but with flowers growing from every patch of ground, and swallows nesting in the ruins. We made ourselves comfortable in an ancient garden, with hammocks and easy chairs. In the close up villages there are no civilians left, but farther back, the poor devils go on making the best of life. And it must be a pretty hard life at that. The villages are always full of soldiers, waiting orders to move forward, and the poor people have hardly room for themselves in their own houses. But they are uniformly cheerful and lively, and live in hope of 'after the war.' It is a hard sight to see babies have gas masks."[128]

While in reserve some lucky Rainbow soldiers attended a performance by internationally celebrated singer Elsie Janis, who had been cleared by Pershing to visit the division. She performed about ten miles from the front—not far removed from the danger, but safe enough, by wartime standards. Traveling with her mother, she went wherever she could find a crowd, and sang for large and small audiences, including 1,500 at Gondrecourt; 5,000 at Langres; 2,500 wounded French and American servicemen in a hospital, where her repertoire included songs in both French and English; and later in an all-American Fourth of July show for 7,000.[129]

As another distraction between rotations, some enterprising soldiers in reserve positions visited a bordello until the military police put it off limits. It was in a fine seventeenth-century house standing on a hill near old Roman fortifications and centered between Baccarat and Deneuvre.[130] The French called the brothels "pleasure palaces" and the women inside "butterflies," but the meaning of such sites transcended language barriers. The brothels were generally protected spaces, the province of officers or French soldiers.[131] However, this did not prevent men from congregating nearby, sometimes in the guise of gentlemanly behavior. Leslie Langille, a soldier from the 149th artillery from Illinois, recounts, "the old Southern spirit of chivalry, aided and abetted by a few 'shots,' causes those boys to go out trouble bent, and gives us no end of concern when they meet up with such lines of waiting 'gents,' as it is no easy matter to keep our Alabamans, Georgians, etc., from cleaning up the assembled mob, very often not even overlooking the 'babes' themselves."[132]

Other men improvised more subtle ways to gain entrance. One recalled, "We could visit provided we wore French uniforms. Consequently, impoverished Poilus did a thriving business in the rental of blue helmets and overcoats. Fee, two francs an hour; three francs for two hours; and ten francs for the evening. Our own coats and helmets were kept for security."[133] Along with issues of order—not the least of the officers' worry—came concerns over venereal disease. One approach, suggested by Clemenceau, considered licensing brothels so that the AEF could better regulate the men's visits and practices. However, Pershing resisted this idea, and upon seeing Clemenceau's letter suggesting the plan, Secretary of War Baker exclaimed, "For God's sake . . . don't show this to the President or he'll stop the war."[134] Pershing maintained strict orders concerning the prohibition of brothel visits, as he understood that National Guard units consisted primarily of respectable men who were not to be tainted by disease and immorality.[135] He was also fully aware of the Progressive movement and of the plans of Raymond B. Fosdick, chairman of the CTCA, to keep soldiers morally and physically pure and healthy.[136]

## On the Front Lines

Although the men found some respite when serving in reserve, they never relaxed for long. The time was coming for the first big American offensive operations, which would move battles from trenches and no-man's-land to open fields, employing the fire and maneuver doctrine Pershing advocated for a drive into Germany. Americans were arriving in France in great numbers, and the French and English expected a decisive blow. Pershing believed his 1st US Army could deliver, but it required mobility. In another sector, on May 28, 1918, the US 1st Division, commanded by Major General Robert Lee Bullard, made a carefully rehearsed, though costly, regimental attack at Cantigny. It was the division's first battle and cost 1,607 casualties. The French had taken and lost the village twice, but the Americans held it against German counterattacks, despite some of Pershing's French and British associates doubting the Americans' ability to retain the position. The AEF gained greater confidence in itself and was coming to be more highly regarded by its Allies.[137]

On May 30 troops in the Baccarat area celebrated Memorial Day with a band concert in the rear. A local French dignitary spoke, as did Father Duffy, chaplain of the 165th (New York) Infantry. Duffy spoke of the division's dead, saying, "our first duty was to pay them solemn honors." After French children placed wreaths on the graves, he continued, "and the last resting place of our French companions was not neglected." That afternoon Duffy visited Croixmare, another cemetery, along with Colonel MacArthur and Generals Menoher and Lanihan. He recalled, "We found that the Curé and his parishioners, as also the French soldiers, had kept the graves there in beautiful condition—a tribute to our dead which warms our heart to the people of France."[138]

Despite such warm feelings the men had to keep their attention focused on the war. The 167th continued patrolling, and from June 1 to June 15 the regiment sent out a total of thirty-five patrols of about twenty men each.[139] The 1st Battalion and its D Company got their worst artillery bombardment so far on the night of June 18/19, just as they were being relieved by elements of the 77th (New York) Infantry Division, regarded by some as the best of the new National Army Divisions.[140] It cost a number of killed and wounded. Bringing in this new division continued the ongoing French-American twinning and training process.

Meanwhile, the US 2nd Division, with its brigade of marines, set new standards for "toughness and determination" in two weeks of battle at Belleau Wood.[141]

When Jordan took up his new S3 duties, he wrote home: "The regiment still collects notoriety and local color. It seems that every time anybody hears a good story, he hangs it on the Alabama crowd. We deserve most of it, for we have certainly got a hard bitten, desperate bunch of dare devils. And the funny part of it is, that a great many of them are from other parts of the country and never saw Alabama in their lives."[142] Although the regiment had originally consisted solely of Alabamians, the first available and able men, regardless of their geographic origins, replaced casualties. Thus the regiment's identity shifted over the course of the war.

By the end of June, the 61st French Infantry Division relieved part of the Rainbow, and the 42nd's men were happy to be leaving the trenches. Alabama soldiers had been in Europe for six months and had earned the right to wear a gold chevron on their left sleeve to signify overseas service. Colonel George C. Marshall and his 1st US Army planners at Chaumont regarded them as veterans. During four months of trench warfare, the Rainbow accrued casualties of eighty-one officers and 1,815 men killed or wounded.[143] The 167th had the lowest casualty lists in the division and regarded itself as the toughest of the regiments. The constant patrolling and trench operations helped the Alabamians, along with the entire division, to establish a reputation for fierceness and reliability.

On June 15, 1918, the commanding general of the French VI Corps, General Duport, commended the Rainbow in General Order No. 50. The division had been part of his French corps since March 1. He wrote of the division's fighting qualities, discipline, initiative, and of the affectionate bonds of friendship between the French and Americans. He promised that American dead would be guarded with all sympathy by France and asked that the units, side by side, valiantly contribute to "the triumph of justice and right."[144] Pershing's June 17 diary entry notes the French praise for the 42nd.[145]

Meanwhile, the French suffered further losses in the Chemin des Dames region, and their VI Army was forced back to the Marne. On June 9 the III French Army was pushed back about nine miles.[146] In preparation for this new attempt the Germans assembled near the Marne in June, placing them within "stirring distance" of Paris, just as they had been in the summer of 1914.[147] Faced with the successful German offensive, Foch called on the celebrated Rainbow to help the French save Paris in what would be called phase one of the Second Battle of the Marne. It was a vote of confidence in the 42nd Division.

On June 21, 1918, the Rainbow issued orders at Baccarat for its units to leave the trenches and proceed northwest by rail. It had completed eighty-two continuous days of sole responsibility for an increasingly active sector in the trenches. Coupled with its earlier "twinned" trench service with the French, the 42nd was one of the most experienced AEF divisions, having spent a total of 110 days in the trenches, and, according to general orders of the division dated August 13, 1918, having served continuously in the trenches for a longer period of time than any other American division.[148]

The men of the Rainbow took great satisfaction from learning they were to join the fight to defend Paris. The city had not been threatened with capture, as it was then threatened, since 1914 when the French turned back the Germans in the epic First Battle of the Marne that saved the nation. The Americans felt certain that their battle would be no less epic.

# 5
# Champagne-Marne, July 3–18, 1918

Approximately three miles north of the village of Souain near Châlons-sur-Marne, a stone marker displays the description "Ici fut repoussé l'envahisseur" (Here the invader was pushed back).[1] It stands across the road approximately five hundred yards from the final resting place of General Henri Gouraud, whose body is in a massive ossuary on the old farm of Navarin, where the worst fighting occurred in Germany's July 1918 attempt to take Paris. This stone stands where the 167th Infantry validated its reputation for excellent fighting qualities, where the Rainbow and the Alabama regiment helped the French turn the tide of victory to the Allies in one of the decisive battles of the Great War.

## The Rainbow Division and the 13th French Division

The 167th started its move to the Champagne when its lead elements left the trenches of Baccarat on the night of June 18/19. The 2nd and 3rd Battalions marched through the city that night, and the last of the Alabama regiment to leave, the 1st Battalion, pulled out on the night of June 21.[2] The battalions took different routes on their long march to the railhead at Thaon-les-Vosges. The 1st Battalion walked twenty miles from Vacqueville to Vaxoncourt, where the men spent the night of June 22 in local barns.[3] Despite mud and low-hanging clouds, the countryside was open and picturesque. Located well behind the front lines, the villages bore no signs of war damage. Rabbits and small deer called roebuck abounded. Marchers traversed winding roads that followed the contours of the hills, valleys, and flat land under cultivation. Church steeples were generally visible from one village to the next.[4] A hike of about three miles on the morning of June 23 took the 1st Battalion into the railhead village just north of Epinal. The other two battalions also arrived that day, completing the regiment's second tour of duty on the Lorraine front.[5]

Spirits were high. General headquarters at Chaumont made staff studies to carefully plan the logistics for the rail and road trips for the entire division, and they went smoothly. Historians later praised the order as "a model for such a movement."[6]

The division move was on the way on June 21, and MacArthur was supervising the loading of the first troops when he received the visit of General Pershing and members of his staff. Pershing was known for the habit of showing up without warning and for putting down his field officers to keep them under pressure. The surprised MacArthur, surrounded by his men, had to take the criticism, "This division is a disgrace, the men are poorly disciplined and they are not properly trained. The whole outfit is just about the worst I have ever seen. They're a filthy rabble." MacArthur tried to defend his men by replying that they had just come out of three months in the trenches. This only added to Pershing's irritation: "Young man, I do not like your attitude." He further lashed out, "MacArthur, I'm going to hold you personally responsible for getting discipline and order into this division—or God help the whole pack of you."[7]

Despite all this criticism, the 167th Regiment had grown expert at moving wagons, equipment, kitchens, ammunition, machine gun carts, and livestock by train or foot. On the afternoon of June 23, the 1st Battalion boarded trains and headed northwest on a miserable twenty-four-hour ride to Vitry-la-Ville in the valley of the Marne. The 2nd Battalion boarded about midnight, and the 3rd Battalion left the next morning. After reaching Vitry-la-Ville (see fig. 10) the battalions marched to their assigned bivouacs.[8] Except for daily sessions in gas warfare instruction and intervals of actually wearing a gas mask, the regiment finally rested for four days. There, on June 26, MacArthur learned that, despite Pershing's outburst, he might be promoted to the rank of brigadier general.[9]

After two night road marches of about eighteen miles, the regiment reached Camp de la Noblette, close to Suippes, where the division was attached to the 13th French Division under General de Bouillon.[10]

The 167th's battalions were scattered around Châlons, a longtime training area for the French army. The 1st and 2nd Battalions were at La Noblette and the 3rd at La Cheppe (see fig. 11).[11] Upon arrival at La Noblette, the regiment immediately joined General Bouillon's men for training on open warfare assault problems and rehearsing for an actual attack.[12] That work helped the Ala-

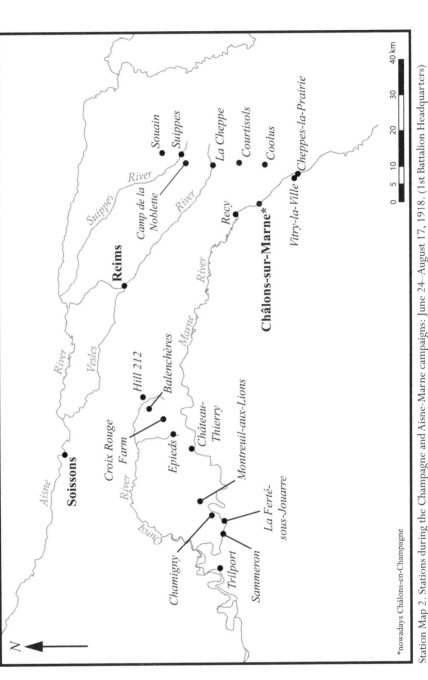

Station Map 2. Stations during the Champagne and Aisne-Marne campaigns: June 24– August 17, 1918. (1st Battalion Headquarters)

*nowadays Châlons-en-Champagne

bama soldiers refresh after their long tours in mud trenches. They also wanted to impress their counterparts in the 13th French Division, who wore the distinctive Fourragère, a braided cord around the left shoulder with the green and red colors of the Croix de Guerre.[13] The decoration was unique to the French. Fourragère could also have the colors of other military medals. They were almost always worn as a collective decoration, given to a unit as a whole, but the Croix de Guerre was also given to individuals, and some Americans received it.

Colonel Screws, in his best Regular Army mode, set out to make a "spit and polish" impression on the regiment's new French comrades. A special order dated June 26 required twenty bugle calls every weekday, with seventeen on Saturday and fifteen on Sunday. Officers were required to attend reveille and retreat and to report daily roll to the battalion adjutant. An officer in each battalion was required to attend "stables" and inspect each animal for grooming.[14]

The *Stars and Stripes*, the iconic army newspaper published in France from February 8, 1918, to June 13, 1919, described the Rainbow as combat effective and said it was a unit "far separated from other American Divisions."[15] The Alabamians embraced the challenge and enjoyed the vision of *la gloire* surrounding the French.[16] They understood that serious combat was imminent and that American forces would fight as equals alongside experienced veterans.

As the regiment's new operations officer, Captain Jordan frequently relayed orders from Screws to the battalion commanders, who, as majors, outranked him. In his new job Jordan maintained responsibility for coordinating all operations with his division and with the French infantry and artillery. That meant feeding troops, supplying them, planning for evacuation of wounded, and dealing with prisoners. Colonel Douglas MacArthur explained that supply, the evacuation of wounded, and all functions of that character were completely under US control. Such coordination served to instill a sense of camaraderie and to counteract German propaganda arguing that "the American reinforcement was a myth or greatly exaggerated."[17]

## Germany's Last Great Offensive

The Germans knew Pershing's forces in Europe were growing fast. They knew France and Britain were weak and could not hold out much longer. General Erich Ludendorff advocated attacking before the United States reached full force, stating, "we should strike at the earliest moment . . . before the Americans can throw strong forces into the scale."[18]

In June the German high command planned two major offenses for July, "one against the French in Champagne and the other against the British in Flanders."[19] They knew they must take Paris before the Americans could send more troops. The Germans believed the imminent battle in Champagne, which the Allied called the Second Battle of the Marne, would win the war for them.[20]

The Germans called the broader series of battles the *Friedensturm*, which translates as the Peace Offensive or the Drive for Peace. The German commander received an order to take Paris with fifteen divisions.[21] They were about seventy-five miles from Paris, and fifty thousand French and American soldiers stood between them and the city. Georg von Hertling, the German chancellor, believed the great German offensive of mid-July would succeed. It would use traditional mass troops as well as *Sturmtruppen*, the highly motivated, majority-volunteer force, and implement new deep penetration tactics.

Ludendorff, Germany's most senior commander, and Crown Prince Wilhelm, the Kaiser's son, did not expect a quick victory but gambled on winning.[22] The Germans believed they held the upper hand and that waiting would waste that advantage by allowing time for more Americans to come into the war.[23]

## The Rainbow Division in the Champagne Region

On June 28 the entire Rainbow Division was placed in reserve at Châlons-sur-Marne and assigned to the French IVth Army under General Gouraud. MacArthur described him, "With one arm gone and half a leg missing, with his red beard glittering in the sunlight, the jaunty rake of his cocked hat and the oratorical brilliance of his resonant voice, his impact was overwhelming. I have known all of the modern French commanders . . . he was the greatest of them all."[24] (See fig. 12.)

The French were complimentary of the 42nd's service at Baccarat. The division's actions earned it widespread recognition, and "Every French corps commander in and near the Champagne knew that near Chalons-sur-Marne there was a fresh American division of more than twice the strength of the average French division, which in five months' trench service had proven itself to the Germans, the French and the American High Command, a first-class combat division."[25]

From that time on, all movement by the Allies in the Champagne was at night for secrecy. The region was arid, chalky, and without much agriculture. One could pick up a lump of earth and use it to write on glass or wood, just as if it were a piece of chalk. The desolate landscape had open trenches of white lines in the chalk, and large craters were gaping from four years of exploding mines. There had been massive struggles over every bit of the land by German and French forces. Barbed wire clung to saplings and vegetation.[26] Father Duffy, who had soldiered on the Mexican border, quoted one of his men as saying this country was "just like Texas."[27] More often, though, both French and American soldiers called it "the lousy Champagne."

A relaxed attitude dominated as the men slept and waited. All expected serious combat. With daylight saving time twilight was at ten in the evening. The men enjoyed plentiful *vin rouge*.[28] They welcomed the opportunity to boil clothes and get rid of lice (see fig. 13).

On July 1, Colonel Screws received a civilian visitor from Alabama at his PC (Post of Command). Borden Burr, a forty-two-year-old YMCA representative, had left his law practice in Birmingham to travel to France on a short contract as an adventure-seeking civilian employee. Burr joined B. C. Dunlop, who "served with the 167th as a YMCA man during the major portion of the time they were in combat, including service as a litter bearer, first aid man, ambulance guide and runner."[29] The 167th had at least one Y representative, a civilian, throughout its French service who would carry a rucksack of tobacco, chocolate, cakes, chewing gum, and writing paper to the troops, cashed checks for officers, wrote letters home for men who could not write, and even offered prayers. Burr, a former football player at the University of Alabama, witnessed some of the regiment's hardest fighting, often came under fire, and commingled with the combat troops every day, visiting each company many times while it was actually engaged with the enemy. He compared the regiment to "a football team on edge."[30]

## Gouraud's Complicated Defense Plan

Now furrowed with trenches and cobwebbed with barbed wire, the French Champagne had been an avenue of conquest since antiquity. Germans tried to capture it early in 1914 and 1915. With mostly straight roads it still resembled the original layout the Romans constructed.[31]

The old battlefield provided Gouraud with a good place for his unusual tactic, called "elastic defense."[32] Although successful in past wars, it was complicated and far removed from conventional French doctrine. It required movement and substantial cooperation between the French and Americans, who shared the old, clearly defined trench lines and fighting positions. The idea was to trick the Germans into believing the Allies wanted to hold the first line when they really planned to use the second line as the main line of defense.

The first was a "sacrificial" line, so called because it would be manned by a limited number of French troops that would set off flares, fire, and fall back as soon as the German forces attacked. The second was about two thousand yards behind it where the main battle was to take place.[33]

Behind the main line of defense stood a third line, sometimes called the last-ditch. If it was penetrated, all American and French troops in the sector would immediately come under the command of the US 42nd Division and take orders from it, not the French.[34] At that point the entire Rainbow would then be thrown in to stop the enemy.

At the beginning of the battle the French would contaminate with yperite (a poisonous gas) all of the dugouts of their sacrificial line other than those actually occupied by the sacrificial troops.[35] French survivors of the first German assault on the sacrificial line would retreat to the second line. As they pulled out, Allied artillery would fire on the sacrificial line "for effect," and the attacking Germans would be required to assault a second trench nearly a mile away, the main line of defense.[36] For the attacking Germans this posed a highly unusual, dangerous, confusing, and exhausting requirement before reaching the scene of the main battle.

The plan called for elements of the 167th to be placed in the main line of defense between two French divisions. First Lieutenant Dan Campbell, a platoon commander of Company F, Gadsden, reported his movement into the main line of defense:

> On July 4th all Battalion and Company commanders went forward to look over the positions that we were to occupy with the French troops then in the lines. . . . The evening of the same day . . . orders were received to move our troops up at once. The 2nd Battalion under temporary command of 1st Lieutenant Greet of Company F went forward to the town of Souain, Company F being temporarily under my command. Company F relieved French units in the entrenched positions about six hundred yards northwest of Souain and extending from the Souain-Somme-Py road west. . . . The positions we occupied had a front of about five hundred yards and about seventy five yards in depth, three combat groups in the front line.[37]

Not a solid trench line but a string of fighting positions organized along centers of resistance that offered troops limited visibility.[38]

On the next day, July 5, 1918, all other forces of the 2nd Battalion, under its new commander, Captain Everette H. Jackson, and with its Machine Gun Company, also moved into the main line of defense. The 2nd Battalion was in the most sensitive part of the line defended by the Alabama regiment, straddling the principal road, the German attack's avenue of approach. Screws placed his untried 2nd Battalion commander with Lieutenant Colonel Randier, an experienced French officer whose 109th French Infantry was a very good regiment of comparable size to the 2nd Battalion.[39] The French outfit had many battle credits, and its men wore the Fourragère displaying their Croix de Guerre honors.[40]

Lieutenant Campbell explained F Company's fighting position, which was typical the Champagne defenses: "Our trenches were old and deep for the most part, with good firing step and good wire. There were a number of communicating trenches running out through our wire to the front. There were many trenches and old dugouts in the open ground in front of us. The French occupied the trenches in front of us until the night of July 14th. Until then our duties were to improve our positions and keep out of sight. Our orders were to man the trenches when the attack started. The men dug into the walls of the trenches for protection from the shelling which was due. We did not use our dugouts because should they cave in under hostile fire our trenches would have been left unmanned."[41]

To the right, on a line with the 167th E and F Companies, stood G and H Companies alongside the celebrated 21st French Infantry. That line was also a series of linked centers of resistance. The Alabama regiment's 2nd Battalion was expected to be hit by the Germans as they attacked down the main road.[42] About two hundred Americans and two French platoons of about fifty men flanked each side of the main road. Also present were "The 167th Machine Gun Co. 3rd platoon on left side of road with Co. F and first platoon on right side with Co. E plus French Co. Co. G and H were in support position with 2nd platoon M. G. Co. 167th."[43]

Screws changed many of his officers as he prepared for battle. Command of his 1st Battalion, formerly under Major John W. Carroll of Ozark, went to Captain Gardner Greene of Pell City, formerly C Company commander. Command of the 3rd Battalion, formerly under Major Dallas B. Smith, Opelika, was given to Captain Joe P. Esslinger, formerly L Company commander (see fig. 14). Both were on the third line, the last ditch, using the excellent old trench lines and fighting positions built in 1914 and 1915. Much of the French and American counterattack would be launched from that position.[44] Screws, anticipating a major artillery duel, set up his headquarters bunker there, dug deep in the chalk down a thirty-foot chicken ladder, in a hot, humid, and rat-infested room. The floor and walls were boarded up to prevent the cave-ins common to the muddy Lorraine.[45]

From the time it assumed position on July 4 and 5, the 167th was ordered to lie in wait in camouflaged holes or bunkers. All Allied soldiers were forbidden to show their heads above the parapet.[46] The men lay under cover for ten days. Again and again, officers explained that the enemy attack would be launched against a position to be evacuated by the French at the last minute, thus creating an empty position, the sacrificial line. When the assaulting German forces reached that sacrificial line, the Allied artillery would fire for effect at them. Then all of the French and American rifle, mortar, and machine gun positions in the main line of defense as well as those in the last ditch position would add to the slaughter of Germans. Rainbow forces there included the 1st and 3rd Battalions of the 167th as well as the 2nd Battalion of the 165th Infantry, the 3rd Battalion of the 166th Infantry, and companies E and F of the 168th Infantry.[47]

Not much happened during the first few days of waiting. One Alabama soldier said, "This place didn't seem like a war. It was almost like a rest camp."[48] The sector remained unusually quiet—according to some, more quiet than it had ever been. German artillery seldom fired during the waiting time.

Americans practiced caution, with all labor and construction done in the evenings. They also received rations at night, except for Machine Gun Company, which was rationed through the French. Those lucky soldiers enjoyed the French meals, which reached them more regularly, tasted better, and included *vin rouge* as part of the normal issue. Other traditions, especially regarding hygiene, proved less popular. In an American headquarters company, a soldier spoke of his nervous colonel's picturesque outbursts about the French: "A peculiar odor hung heavy on the air. We walked about the ditch trying to locate the stench. Not knowing the French technique, he stepped on a bunch of leaves and sank ankle-deep in excrement!"[49]

Most of the 167th preferred to pitch tents (see fig. 15) even after the shooting started. Sometimes incoming artillery forced them to roll up blankets and go to fighting positions or dugouts in the chalk, but the men remained unruffled by such "roll-ups."[50]

Despite their bravado, all understood the significance of events to come. Winfred E. Robb, a chaplain of the 168th (Iowa) described the situation in these dramatic terms: "Our Division had never taken part in a great battle and now we were to be suddenly thrown into a fight on which would hang the whole history of civilization. The Germans had broken the British lines on the left in March and had driven through for thirty-five kilometers. In May, they broke the French line and drove through clear to the Marne River and captured Château-Thierry, forcing the French back forty-seven kilometers. Now, the enemy was to attempt an even greater attack and we were to have part in resisting his assault."[51]

The journal of the 17th French Infantry recorded that its officers dined with American counterparts on July 14. Gouraud dined with the generals and colonels: "The food simple but as always in French messes deliciously cooked and hot, was greatly appreciated by the Americans."[52]

## Attack and Counterattack

Spencer Wells, a battalion adjutant of the 167th, stated, "French moral [*sic*] at that time was so low that many of our soldiers received instructions from their French comrades as to the correct procedure to surrender if the [*sic*] became too hot."[53]

Then on July 7, 1918, Gouraud issued his stirring Gallic Order of the Day: "The bombardment will be terrible—you will bear it without flinching. The assault will be fierce—in clouds of smoke and dust and gas. But your position is formidable. In your chests beat the hearts, brave and strong, of free men. No one will glance back; no one will retreat a single step. Everyone will have but one thought—to kill. To kill many of them, until they have had enough. This is why your General tells you this assault will break up and it will be a glorious day."[54]

Colonel George Leach, commander of the 151st Field Artillery, said, "Our information from General Gouraud was of such a nature that no one expected to survive the attack. His order impressed me more than any other I had ever received."[55]

On July 10 a long-range French patrol brought in a German prisoner who revealed that Germany would attack on July 14 or 15. Gouraud urged his army to get ready.[56]

By the time the German attack began, the Allies knew its key details and had a nearly complete picture from prisoners as to German intentions and capabilities. Thousands of Allied guns stood hub to hub. They opened fire over the entire front on the night of July 14/15. The French high command believed the Germans would open preparatory artillery fire at ten minutes past midnight.[57] Gouraud instructed his "heavier long-range guns, and half the lighter guns, to fire at 11:30 P.M."[58] The other Allied fire commenced at midnight. When the Germans joined in it was the greatest concentration of German and American artillery the war had yet seen. One Alabama soldier said, "It sounded like thunder in a mighty storm."[59] Private Neibaur of M Company said, "for a while bullets were falling so fast and guns shooting so rapidly that if one had attempted to count the large shells that struck close to us, he would have had a big job on his hands. These were our first days of real fighting."[60]

The fire covered an overall front, not just the main point of attack at Souain where the Rainbow was dug in. At 12:10 A.M. on July 15, "came the roar of several large-sized projectiles followed quickly by crashes of their explosion."[61] The Germans then sent a large number of red flares and at the same time opened fire with mortars and artillery of all calibers.[62] This fire fell on the first, or sacrificial, position.[63]

Then Allied artillery fired for effect at Germans crossing the unoccupied position. The French reported hearing shots over the telephone and the fire of their last machine guns in place on the sacrificial line.[64] French and American infantry added to the artillery fire with small arms and mortars fired from the main line of defense and from the third lines, the last ditch.

The attacking Germans had to leave their assault position while under constant fire, cross the sacrificial line, and take the thousand-yard journey to the Allied main line of defense. "When the German troops reached the parapets of the real trenches, they were caught by the uncut wire, and the unimpeded machine-gun fire of the defenders; they were, one American officer in the line remembered, 'exhausted, uncoordinated, and shattered, incapable of going on without being reorganized and reinforced.'"[65]

An Alabamian reported: "we saw the attacking Germans literally covering no-man's-land. This was when the boys stood, for their first time, face to face with an army of great force and with a dogged determination of advancing on the iron wall of American 'doughboys.' But to the sorrow of the onrushing Germans it didn't give in."[66] The 168th Infantry was positioned at the 167th's left flank. The Iowa regiment's official history says, "It was as being in the grasp of a great hurricane that tears and pulls, the trees above them were being twisted and battered. Men were torn and blown to atoms before the eyes of their comrades. White chalk was spouting up in cloudy geysers. . . . There were long anxious hours before the German barrage stopped sweeping over the trenches and ravaged woods."[67]

Elements of the Rainbow had the 43rd (French) on its right and the 132nd (French) on its left in the "real front" line.[68] As the battle raged, "watchers in the trenches suddenly saw the sky behind the German lines opposite light with a tremendous flare, stretching farther to the right and left than any individual could see."[69]

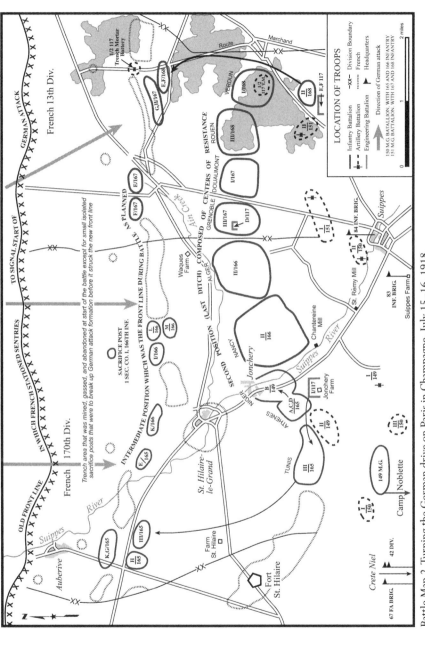

Battle Map 2. Turning the German drive on Paris in Champagne, July 15–16, 1918.

The Rainbow was among those taking the brunt of the assault, but it was girdled by a great semicircle of Allied artillery, firing as fast as possible. Small arms also fired. An observer said, "They worked their machine guns for all they were worth, astonishing both the French and the Germans by the coolness and the directness with which they aimed."[70] The German attack was relentless. Neibaur wrote, "At 6 o'clock the Germans came over in one of their famous mass formations. We didn't think we would be able to stop them . . . the Germans kept coming on, wave after wave, until, I think, about 8 or 9 o'clock in the evening, they kept up a steady fire."[71]

One German column proceeded down the road where Corporal William S. Hughes from Marion, of Machine Gun Company, was waiting. He moved his gun out of the emplacement and put it on the parapet beside the road for "a good field of fire. He let the enemy approach to within 200 yards and opened fire. Many Huns were killed by the first shots and the others fled in panic."[72]

Captain Julian Strassburger served in a volatile position as Machine Gun Company commander supporting Companies E and F. At 8:30 A.M. he composed a faded field message to the battalion commander, Captain Everette Jackson: "Boche dead piled here sky high. *Ils ne passeront pas.*"[73] The French slogan, used widely, translates as "they will not pass." It stemmed from General Pétain's February 25, 1916, speech asking French soldiers to stop the Germans on the right shore of the Meuse River.[74] The slogan was on the wall of the Officers Club in the concrete defenses at Verdun standing watch at the entrance of trench lines.[75]

Lieutenant Colonel Bare climbed a tree and watched two German artillery batteries assume position northeast of Souain. The Germans, not suspecting the Allied soldiers were waiting for them near the main line of defense, were "about a hundred yards in front of Alabama troops. The German artillerymen confidently pulled their guns up to the firing position, sitting on their caissons with arms folded. The French artillery observer gave his guns the coordinates of the German position and the French opened fire, putting those two batteries out of commission."[76]

Germans continued advancing, "reaching the intermediate position only toward 7 A.M."[77] They gained control temporarily, but the Allies succeeded in pushing them "back to the first positions upon which the artillery at once directed a violent fire."[78] Eventually Germans made it into American trenches of the main line of defense in several places but were driven out by counterattacking French infantry and Alabama infantry in small units.[79]

Corporal Major D. Riley, from Ozark, Alabama, "climbed out of his trench to the parapet at the top. Firing from the prone position, he picked off a German machine gunner about two hundred yards away and sought cover. Another German soldier went into the dead man's place and started operating the gun. Riley again jumped to the top, exposing himself to fire as he drew a bead through the haze and killed that man. Five times the gunner was replaced, and each time Corporal Riley exposed himself to shoot the replacement."[80] A sixth German shot Riley in the head, killing him. A French officer witnessed the heroics and returned Riley's body to the trench.[81]

Lieutenant Hackett reported "that E and F Cos., 167 Inf., have taken 25 prisoners and some machine guns. During the attack of the morning 36 German planes flew over the intermediate and second positions firing on men in trenches with machine guns."[82] Among others the planes shot up F Company.[83] Captain F. L. Wyatt, who commanded it, noticed that the planes were "flying low enough to hit."[84] He recruited Private Brock Hill, Gadsden, who had "grown up from childhood with a squirrel rifle under his arm."[85] With only two shots from an automatic rifle, Hill killed a pilot and caused one of the German planes to crash—a deed that would earn him the Croix de Guerre and promotion to sergeant.[86]

At the end of the day Screws knew his men were holding. According to the American Battle Monuments Commission summary, "The Germans attacked again at 6:00 P.M. on both sectors but were repulsed at all points."[87] The artillery continued through the night, and patrols from both sides made continuous contact up and down the line. A Rainbow artilleryman reported, "They say that all along the 88 kilometer front the Germans were repulsed with great losses, the American army is said to have done wonderful work; the Alabama 'dough-boys' having shown up above all the rest."[88]

The next morning brought renewed efforts from the Germans. Father Duffy, who always kept among his men at the risk of his life, reported, "On the morning of July 16, there was another furious assault. A whole German battalion attacked one of the defensive positions."[89] Eventually, the German attack on the ground started to spend itself, faltered, and renewed again before it finally died down and failed.

Both German and American airplanes continued to fly over Souain after the German ground attacks stopped. According to Lieutenant Campbell, "[Allied] planes brought down a number of enemy observation balloons directly in front of us. The enemy planes were numerous and active. On July 16th I counted thirty six red-nose planes in one formation which passed over us firing on the trenches with machine guns."[90] In all, some fifty German planes came over on the morning of July 16, but the battle was essentially over.[91]

The American Battle Monuments Commission chronicled the battle's end: "The German artillery preparations began at midnight July 15/16 and although not as severe as on the previous night, continued on all three lines until 4:20 A.M., when an attack was launched against the Esperance sector. This attack was driven off, and intermittent fighting continued here throughout the morning. . . . The Germans in the afternoon again attacked . . . but their forces were spent, and they were easily driven off. . . . July 17th: The 42nd Division remained in these positions throughout the day without any further attacks."[92]

On the night of July 18/19, the French 109th Regiment, which had sustained heavy losses while serving on the 167th's left side on the line, relieved the Alabama regiment. By the end of day on July 19, the French announced that a successful Allied push in the vicinity of Soissons had taken place and the Germans were retreating on a wide front.[93] Gouraud's unconventional plan was a success.

## Alabama's "American Tigers"

As "the only American division" involved in the battle, the Rainbow gained a great deal of attention for its efforts.[94] Even the Germans recognized the Americans' abilities. Kurt Hesse, a junior officer in the 5th Grenadier Regiment, 36th German Infantry Division, wrote, "The Americans kill everything! That was the cry of horror of July 15th, which long took hold of our men. At home meanwhile they were sarcastic about the imperfect training of this enemy, about the American 'bluff' and the like. The fact that on July 15th more than sixty per cent of our troops led to battle were left dead or wounded upon the battlefield may substantially be charged to his credit."[95]

The Alabamians themselves remained pleased, as evidenced by Jordan's description of events in a letter to his wife: "We have met the Boche and found that we can whip him any day. He is a good mass fighter, but is no match for our men in the hand to hand affair. What pleases me the most is our men have shown the most calm and desperate courage, lying unmoved under continuous shell fire. . . . The French are loud in their praise."[96] Interestingly, in focusing on the accomplishments of his men, Jordan modestly refrained from reporting his own heroics. Other accounts reveal that he left his bunker and rushed to the aid of a private wounded by shell fire. After administering first aid, Jordan carried the private through bombardment for 150 yards to safety. Jordan was decorated with a Distinguished Service Cross for this action.[97]

Many of the 167th's men received recognition for their individual actions. The commanding general of the Rainbow Division cited Lieutenant Hoxie Fairchild, E Company, for his leadership in reclaiming two lost positions. The French commended him as well. According to the French Battle Report, "Fairchild's Support Point LaFayette had to be abandoned at 7:45 A.M. He immediately and spontaneously went into counterattack for which he was later awarded the Legion of Honor by the French government."[98]

The 2nd Battalion's Lieutenant M. L. Marklin retook a third position. As a result, French and American troops captured five heavy machine guns, ten light machine guns, and fifteen prisoners of the 15th and 20th Bavarian Regiments. Thanks to the bravery and initiative of the French and American counterattackers, about sixty German bodies filled the trenches of the reoccupied position.[99]

Company F of Gadsden had distinguished itself throughout the battle and was recognized by the French government by being awarded the Croix de Guerre with one palm.[100] The units receiving the award varied in size from a section (a unit smaller than a squad) to a brigade. The unit receiving such an award was authorized to place on its flag a streamer in the colors of the decoration and to embroider on it the name of the action for which the unit was cited.[101]

French respect for the Americans blossomed after the events in Champagne. A French report stated, "US officers and soldiers in the line had shown extremely good qualities: desire to learn, curiosity, discipline, excellent spirit, silence and order when relieving and in operation, seriousness and exactness in accomplishment of missions. . . . Great courage and ardor in attacks, desire and research of hand to hand fighting. Fundamental qualities are there and will make for an excellent infantry with more experience." It also noted that "the General Headquarters of the 42nd Division had not believed in the Champagne attack. Later on, with the best of grace, they recognized that it had been wrong. The magnificent work of our Intelligence, the skillfulness of the decisions taken by the IVth French Army and our victory made therefore an even bigger impression on the US Headquarters and all American officers."[102]

Individual officers and units lavished unmitigated respect. On July 15 the official diary of a French battalion recorded, "The presence of Allied soldiers creates a strong emulation. The Americans, young in front of fire, want to prove to the old troops that they can hold on as well as the best of experienced troops and they do so."[103]

The 42nd Division was continuing to establish its reputation as splendid fighting men. Gouraud remained pleased with their efforts.[104] Major J. Corbabon, from General de Ragueneau French Military Mission, said, "The conduct of American troops has been perfect and has been greatly admired by French officers and men. Calm and perfect bearing under artillery fire, endurance of fatigue and privations, tenacity in defense, eagerness in counterattack, willingness to engage in a hand-to-hand fighting—such are the qualities reported to me by all the French officers I have seen."[105] Teilhard de Chardin concurred: "I had a close up view of them. Everyone says the same: they're first-rate troops, fighting with an *individual* passion (against the enemy) and a marvelous courage. . . . There's complete comradeship between them and us, born right away, under fire."[106]

Within the division, the 167th earned particular distinction. One French captain reported that an officer from general headquarters had asked if there were any American Tigers in the vicinity. When asked for clarification of who he was describing, the officer answered, "Those Alabamas—the 167th."[107]

Throughout the war, the Alabamians continued to cement their reputation as wild men. Sometimes a bit unrefined—particularly when bored—they always rose to the occasion in battle, proving their tenacity and fierceness. As a Rainbow soldier in another regiment said, "I do not know if they would make good parlor pets or proper chaperons for young ladies at the movies, but they sure are wonderful fighters."[108]

Although the news spread slowly, an article in the important French publication *L'Illustration* on July 17, 1918, praised the French infantry in this great battle and also gave credit to the Americans, stating, "They [The French] had in their midst, in the most perfect fraternity of arms, an American division."[109]

It would prove to have been "one of the greatest battles in history"—and one of the most costly Allied battles yet.[110] The division's casualties, concentrated on July 15, were "256 killed, 71 died of wounds and 1240 wounded or a total of 1567."[111] The loss equaled 152 percent of the division's total losses during the preceding five months in Lorraine.

## The Next Challenge

On July 19 the Rainbow received a warning order. It was to move to a regroupment point in the Châlons area and to expect to participate in exploiting the successful French counterattack begun there on the previous day. The 42nd Division had been placed at the disposal of the commander in chief of the French army.[112]

The 167th started its eleven-mile march to the Coolus railhead at 4:00 A.M. on July 20. A Rainbow soldier said, "When the moon rose that night we pulled out, covered with chalk and glory. The French turned out to cheer and say good-bye."[113] Sergeant Elmer Sherwood wrote in his diary: "The Frenchmen, whose positions were next to ours during the hottest part of the battle, were downcast at our leaving [sic] they are exceptionally generous in their praises saying that the Americans are the best fighters in the world and all that. Well, we did our darn-dest and can only say we have equal admiration for them."[114]

On July 22 the men boarded trains for Château-Thierry. They had made many previous train trips, but this time was special. Charles MacArthur recalled, "Every town through which we passed was hung with American flags. Women and children cheered and threw kisses, and we hit the next line in a swell frame of mind."[115] Men on the five trains carrying the 167th could see the Eiffel Tower. The regiment passed through Paris from July 21 to 23, going into the Gare de l'Est, a civilian railroad station. For four years Paris had not been able to celebrate a victory. Now they had one, and everywhere they lauded the Americans—soldiers who passed by in trains, but who could not join in the city's celebration.

D Company friends from Greenville, Will Frazer, Chester Scott, and Worth Lewis, watched it all as their 40 & 8 railroad car passed through the marshaling yards. The city offered them an unprecedented chance at celebration, but it was not to be.

The 167th detrained with precision at Trilport and La Ferté-sous-Jouarre on July 22 and 23. The regiment was in shape to fight again. Its soldiers, mules, wagons, machine gun carts, and support people moved professionally in the heavy traffic of Allied armies on the move. Replacements came in as soon as the Alabama camps were set up on the Marne. The 167th had a swagger. Its soldiers were experienced veterans led by competent officers. If one asked a soldier what outfit he was in, the answer might now be a confident "Ala-goddam-Bama." The men had what some might consider a lack of refinement, but those who knew of the regiment's battlefield abilities might overlook the rough edges.

At La Ferté there was a semblance of normalcy. Everyone enjoyed a payday. Carter Mastin, Montgomery, wrote home, "It was good to have some Charlies (francs) again. We got two months pay."[116] There was time for haircuts, swims in the river, hot meals, and shopping at the YMCA store.[117]

General Gouraud's July 16 order thanked the Rainbow and the French Fourth Army for the win in Champagne, adding, "It was a hard blow for the enemy. It was a beautiful day for France."[118] The camaraderie between French and Americans transcended boundaries. People from all stations of life united in exuberance and excitement over their common cause. Jordan wrote on July 23, "My present billet is one of the best I have ever drawn. Madame is most solicitous of my comfort, and I am occupying the best room in the house. She cannot do enough for the 'braves Americains.' She is downstairs now, peeling potatoes for dinner, assisted by two of our men, who just wandered in. The three are talking a steady streak, though they cannot understand a word of the other's talk."[119]

Victory in the Champagne had not ended the war, but it stopped the Germans, turning them back for the first time since Russia dropped out of the war. And, for the first time, the supreme commander, Marshal Foch, had the means to order a major counterattack. By the end of July 1918 the AEF in France could count 54,224 officers and 1,114,838 enlisted men—nearly double the number of a month earlier,[120] and they continued to come. The tide of war and the momentum of battle had turned. German Chancellor von Hertling later said, "We expected grave events in Paris for the end of July. That was on the 15th. On the 18th even the most optimistic among us understood that all was lost. The history of the world had played out in three days."[121] Although the Germans had not surrendered, even Crown Prince Wilhelm "no longer entertained any doubt that matters at the front as well as affairs at home were drifting towards the final catastrophe."[122]

The great German offensive, their last real hope for victory, had been stopped. Paris had been saved. At the end of the war Douglas MacArthur pointed out that the Rainbow Division was the only American unit involved in the fighting in Champagne. He wrote, "The Champagne was the high water mark of the War. If it had not been fought, there would have been no counter-blow and the War would have dragged on for an indefinite period. The backbone of the German Army was broken in Champagne and he passed from an offensive status to a defensive one. In many respects it was the most critical battle of the War."[123]

After the Champagne, Foch immediately ordered the Rainbow into the new offensive to begin at Château-Thierry, beginning what became the Second Battle of the Marne.[124] As historian Robert B. Bruce eloquently expressed, "It was in the crucible of the Second Battle of the Marne that the American Expeditionary Forces came of age. A host of high-ranking French officers, including Pétain, Mangin, Gouraud, and Degoutte, were completely convinced by the Americans' performance there that they were ready to assume responsibility for their own sector of the western front."[125]

# 6
# Aisne-Marne, Croix Rouge Farm, July 24–26, 1918

### Move to the Front

Immediately after the Champagne, Foch scheduled the Rainbow Division for more battle, ordering it to join a Franco-American drive to the northeast. The mission was to break up the Château-Thierry salient, where the German battle line projected farthest into the French position.[1] Foch knew the Allies had to capture the Marne Valley to close the road to Paris to the Germans. This called for the kind of open field fighting that Pershing wanted. Foch also understood fully that the Germans had retained strongholds in an area that was well suited for defense and deadly for the attackers.

The Rainbow proceeded to Château-Thierry. They saw "ghastly evidence of the Huns' departure—the ruined homes; the ruthless destruction coupled with the terrible artillery bombardment [had] left the town a scene of desolation."[2] The trip was sobering, "the route was a panorama of panic and sudden death. Pontoons, ripped with shell, stood on the river. A lot of gents had gone to glory there."[3]

Only weeks earlier, the Germans had believed victory at hand. Chancellor von Hertling later admitted, "at the beginning of July 1918, I was convinced, I confess it, that before the first of September our adversaries would send us peace proposals."[4]

The Rainbow was shifted without rest to Château-Thierry. The division was placed in the VI French Army under General Jean Marie Joseph Degoutte, who put I Corps into American control for the first time when command went to General Hunter Liggett. This was an arrangement by which French generals controlled the major operations, but American officers oversaw the details.[5]

"General Jean Degoutte . . . sent word through General Liggett, who passed the order to General Menoher, to attack a German rearguard unit . . . at Croix Rouge Farm . . . To push out the defenders . . . with a bayonet charge. The order . . . went to the 167th Alabama Regiment . . . and the result was a minor chapter in the war's history, but no minor chapter in the history of the 167th."[6] The regiment's fighting skills earned it the point position in the French initiative. The Americans had intense admiration for their French commanders. "All during this time," an American lieutenant observed, "our respect, liking and admiration of the French was unqualified. The good nature of the *poilu* is apparently inexhaustible, and the French officer is nearly always a gentleman . . . which is not so universally true in our army, unfortunately."[7]

The Alabama regiment received its warning order at La Ferté near Château-Thierry at 3:20 P.M. on July 24.[8] The 167th was told to be ready to load on trucks in an hour, but in typical "hurry up and wait" army fashion, departure was rescheduled for 7:45 P.M. The trucks arrived even later, and the troops did not leave Ussy-sur-Marne for the all-night drive until 11:30 P.M.

Moving a combat-loaded infantry battalion required seventy-five solid rubber-tired camions (trucks) with sixteen men crowded onto each one.[9] Traveling over rough roads in thick dust and fumes, they reached Liggett's I Corps in Epieds shortly after dawn on July 25, about the same time as the 168th (Iowa).[10] An overturned German howitzer littered the street. Fires smoldered. German ammunition and equipment was strewn among their dead. There was an active American aid station, and American dead lay in nearby fields. Full of Rainbow soldiers, Epieds was a good target for German artillery, which crashed all around.

Prior to the arrival of the two regiments of the 84th Brigade, I Corps consisted of two divisions: the French 167th and the US 26th, commonly called the Yankee Division or YD. Liggett had nothing but praise for the French, but there were problems. Earlier Liggett had ordered the 26th to take over the sector held by the French, but the task was beyond its capacity. Major General Clarence Edwards, the Yankee Division commander, failed to put the order into effect, and Liggett canceled it, telling Edwards that neither he nor his subordinates obeyed orders. Edwards, a West Pointer with a reputation for being easy on his men, was later deemed not to have pushed aggressively enough in the July fighting.[11] By July 26 the Rainbow took over the entire I Corps front, where the Yankee Division had failed.[12]

Liggett controlled the coming battle from Epieds, using the 39th Division (French), the 167th Division (French), and the just-arrived US 42nd Division.[13] The Rainbow always wanted the infantry regiments and the artillery to go into battle as one unit. French general Degoutte specified in his order that if the Rainbow could not be committed as a unit, it should at least be committed as a brigade.[14]

This time the 42nd was committed piecemeal over several days—"its first and only experience of being thrown into battle pell-mell, by units instead of going in as a whole ready to strike a united blow against the enemy."[15] The Rainbow's men knew they had to follow orders, but they disliked this plan, and the situation caused unease throughout the division. It is officially recorded that "as part of this plan, the divisional artillery of the 42nd Division was to reinforce the 51st F.A. Brigade on the night of July 25/26. The extension of the divisional front of the 42nd Division, however, resulted in diverting the 42nd Divisional Artillery to the support of the 83rd Brigade, leaving the 51st F.A. Brigade in support of the 84th Infantry Brigade alone. The command passed from the 26th division to the 42nd division upon the passage of the first units of the latter through the front of the 26th Division, this actually taking place on the morning of July 26."[16] This documents that the 51st FA Brigade of the 26th Division was assigned to support the 84th Infantry Brigade (the 167th and 168th Infantry Regiments) and was placed at the disposition of the commanding general of the 42nd Division on the morning of July 26. The lack of artillery fire preparation for the ensuing infantry assault that afternoon can only be explained by a breakdown of cooperation between the 84th Brigade and the 51st FA Brigade.

## The 167th Infantry Approaches the Objective

Officers of the newly arrived 167th assembled in Courpoil, approximately a mile and a half northeast of Epieds, around 7:00 A.M. on the rainy morning of July 25. Among the by-now experienced staff was First Lieutenant Maurice W. Howe, a Cornell man with French language skills who established the PC for the 3rd Battalion. After arrival, the wet, chilled troops had a hot meal and tried to rest (see fig. 16). That afternoon, they were alerted to move forward to relieve the Yankee Division. Howe reported that two of them were killed that day by artillery fire—and eleven in all before it was over.[17]

The YD, after advancing ten miles and suffering around four thousand casualties, was at less than half strength when replaced by the Rainbow.[18] Standard procedure called for the New Englanders to furnish guides to the 167th, but there were none. After leaving Courpoil, neither the 167th nor the 168th regiment had guides or knew where the other was. The Alabamians departed Courpoil at

2:30 P.M. on July 25, passing German and American dead on the march through open fields and woods toward the Forêt de Fère.[19] According to John B. Hayes, I Company, "Reconnaissance German planes swooped low over the tree tops every few minutes for a close check of our forces and our movements."[20] They flew low through breaks in the clouds and observed the regiment on the march up while its sister regiment, the 168th, was digging in under the trees behind Bois de Fary.[21] Colonel Screws later said, "the Boche practically saw my troops going forward, as there was no chance to get to the front line without crossing a long open space."[22] Sanitary detachments carried stretchers and boxes of medical supplies. Medics accompanied rifle companies, and men carried hardtack, full canteens, and a basic load of 250 rounds of ammunition in web belts or bandoliers. Machine Gun Companies were at a special disadvantage. They were exhausted from riding in trucks all the night of July 24 and from rolling the heavy guns and ammunition by hand carts through the mud and rain on the five-mile trek from Epieds.[23] Mules would normally have pulled carts, but the animals were marched cross-country for the long journey from La Ferté and did not arrive in time to help with the move to the front.[24] The men, guns, and carts had been hurriedly brought up by camions the night before.[25]

En route to establishing a skirmish line the 167th passed the 111th Regiment of the US 28th Division. Its Lieutenant Allen, who had witnessed the confusion in the area, observed, "the 'Rainbow' did not look nearly as war-worn as the 26th, at least that was our impression."[26]

Yankee exhaustion fails to excuse the absence of guides, however, and as the Rainbow neared enemy lines on July 25, it suffered from a "lack of definite information."[27] When an Illinois officer asked one of the Alabama's officers their destination, the officer told him to ask Screws. Eventually the Illinois officer "easily picked out Colonel Screws because of the large cigar fiercely burning, which he always had in his mouth. He said, 'Hello, Bill. Where are you going?' Screws replied, not even taking the cigar out of his mouth, 'Damn if I know, but I am on my way.'"[28]

## The 167th Establishes a Skirmish Line

These were the worst conditions under which the Alabama regiment had ever entered a fight, and they were further complicated by the fact that this was its most mobile combat operation ever.

At dusk on July 25 the 1st and 3rd Battalions took up lines as skirmishers—

individual scouts on a line rather than part of patrols or assault forces. Each soldier bore responsibility for his immediate front. The Machine Gun Company was attached to 1st Battalion, and Company B of the 151st Georgia Machine Gun Battalion was attached to the 3rd Battalion. All reached their positions by dark.[29] The 1st and 3rd Battalions had been chosen as the operation's assault battalions because they had easier jobs in the previous battle in Champagne. The 2nd Battalion, which received the worst of the German attack in Champagne, was placed in reserve in the rear of the combat for the battle of Croix Rouge Farm.[30]

The battlefield was littered with the debris of the 26th Division and German combat. Hayes recalled, "The sickening smell of rotting flesh and the acrid fumes of high explosive powder combined with the sickly sweetish smell of mustard gas."[31]

Beyond the skirmish line could be seen the German-occupied stone complex— the Croix Rouge Farm (see fig. 17), sometimes called the Red Cross Farm by the Americans. The "farmhouse, a huge walled-in affair of stone and mortar, medieval in style and fortress like effect," offered the Germans excellent cover.[32] Lawrence O. Stewart, a member of the 168th Infantry sanitary corps, later described it: "Imagine a hill crowned by a group of farm buildings, not the more or less perishable edifices common to this country but solid constructions that have withstood the test of time—hundreds of years as reckoned by the French."[33] The house stood "at the apex of a V" of trenches holding machine guns.[34] The arms of the V, with machine gun nests, reached for about two hundred yards to the southwest and northwest toward a line of woods holding the Americans. Other machine gun nests were dug into the north and south along the public road.[35] It was an excellent position to defend—and an extremely challenging one to attack.

The 167th closed into the abandoned skirmish line of the 111th Regiment of the US 28th Division by about 7:00 P.M. on July 25.[36] That night the 42nd Division headquarters reported relative quiet at Croix Rouge Farm after the Alabamians had captured a handful of prisoners and taken only light fire.[37] Things appeared to be going smoothly, but trouble awaited. Artillery support from the US 28th Division did not arrive.

## The 168th Infantry Maneuvers

The 167th reached the front on schedule, but the 168th was late. Seeking shelter from German artillery, the Iowans dug in under the trees of Bois de Fary at noon on July 25. Without guides, they waited. Heavy incoming fire, combined with pitch dark as night came on, hindered movement through the tangled woods. The 168th's 2nd Battalion, commanded by Major Claude M. Stanley, made its first relief of the 102nd Infantry Regiment of the 26th Division at 9:20 P.M.[38] He placed E and F Companies on the battalion's left flank to try to link with the 167th Regiment at the edge of the trees southwest of Croix Rouge Farm. The 168th's 1st Battalion went into position late on the night of July 25 before repositioning later.[39] The 3rd Battalion was in reserve in the rear.

At daybreak on July 26 the 168th's 1st and 2nd Battalions did not know their positions with regard to each other. The 1st Battalion commander, Major Emory C. Worthington, could not be located, and his men did not know their orders.[40] To make matters worse a gap separated the Alabama and Iowa regiments and caused further confusion amid incoming artillery. Both the Alabama and Iowa regiments worked to establish flank contact that morning, but they did not connect until afternoon. By then Worthington's 1st Battalion had moved into the northeast-facing position that it should have occupied all along. Its assault line was in the corner of woods southwest of the fortified farmhouse. The 2nd Battalion vacated its original position for an even more dangerous place in the Forêt de Fère, due south of the fortified Croix Rouge Farm.[41]

Attack orders dictated that the 1st and 2nd Battalions should jump off at 4:50 P.M. on July 26, but the orders did not reach either assault battalion until after the scheduled attack time.[42]

## The German-Occupied Farmhouse

Germans were well set up in defensive positions. They knew what they were doing, having already fought the 26th (New England) Division, the 167th (French) Division, and the 29th (French) Division to a standstill in the vicinity of Croix Rouge Farm. More than a month earlier they constructed a position for four antiaircraft machine guns in a trench in the field east of the fortress.[43] They had transformed the old farm house into a massive machine gun position, capable of all-around fire.[44] Troops from the 23rd German Infantry Division moved into position on July 23. Although weakened by flu, reinforcements from the 10th Landwehr Division replaced a battalion of a Schutzen regiment in the Caesar position on the night of July 25, the night before the battle.[45]

The walled compound of the large farmhouse dominated the open fields around it. The Germans set up interlocking bands of fire over measured distances with big 7.92 mm machine guns. Well-camouflaged and dug in for cover, each was served by a five-man crew. Rifles and automatic weapons there could pump out ten thousand rounds a minute of very accurate fire for distances up to a thousand yards. Riflemen were also in preplanned sniper positions. A German ammo dump located in the Forêt de Fère, about a mile east of the farmhouse clearing, held large quantities of artillery ammunition. Left unused after the failed drive on Paris, it was now available to defend the fortified farmhouse.[46]

A soldier from I Company of the 167th said at the time, "the woods had been carefully cleaned of underbrush to permit an unobstructed view, and the trees were girdled with bands of white paint about waist high from the ground to aid enemy machine gunners . . . in directing their fire. From long experience the Germans had prepared a cunning death trap in which they sat like a great spider, ready to spring on its prey."[47]

The Americans, of course, knew nothing about the German preparation. In fact, the daunting situation differed drastically from what the Alabamians expected. One of their officers recalled setting up positions despite being "in ignorance of where the enemy lay in strength."[48] In his own hand, MacArthur later wrote: "It was presumed that the Germans were pulling back and our orders were to pass. . . . But the high command was just in error. The Germans were not retreating with only a small rear guard left to cover their withdrawal. Instead, strong forces had settled down on rugged slopes and in protecting woods."[49]

Rain continued, and the cold penetrated.[50] German artillery fired preplanned missions throughout the night of July 25/26. L Company's Neil Ford, who had entered the army as an Auburn freshman, was killed by artillery shortly after midnight.[51] The battle had not officially started, but the casualties had begun.

## The 167th Plans to Attack

Screws set up his PC tent that night in a gully alongside a muddy trail approximately half a mile to the rear of his two assault battalions.[52] Early on July 26 efforts were made to locate the enemy's exact positions. Cleared forest was in front of the 1st Battalion to the left of the regiment, leaving little or no protection from fire.[53] On its right, the 3rd Battalion occupied thicker and safer woods—good for cover, but hard to run in. Both battalions were in skirmish lines about a thousand yards east of Croix Rouge Farm but only two or three hundred yards from the nearest German riflemen, in range.

Steak and coffee were brought up at dawn. The two battalions dug in for battle. They were hit throughout the day with intermittent sniper, machine gun, and artillery fire.[54]

Screws worried about where his regiment linked with the weakened French, on the left, where his patrols had been turned back the night before. He sent out a strong patrol under Abbeville's First Lieutenant Robert Espy on the morning of July 26, and it was not turned back.

Both battalions of the Alabamians took casualties all day. Lieutenant Colonel Bare had a close call with a sniper that Espy spotted and killed.[55] An I Company soldier serving as a stretcher bearer, said, "Twigs and leaves cut from trees by the fusillade began falling; whistling machine gun slugs knocked bark from the trees."[56]

Despite having no attack order from the brigade, Screws drew up a plan and reviewed it with his battalion commanders early on July 26, an invaluable precaution. He assigned the executive officer, Bare, and the operations officer, Jordan, to positions behind 1st Battalion on the left, where they were to reorganize casuals—men separated from their units—and disorganized units after the battle started. First Lieutenant John M. Powell, commander of I Company, Opelika, assumed a similar role behind the attacking 3rd Battalion. Both battalion commanders returned to their Posts of Command after the meeting and went over the plan with the company commanders.

The soldiers had slept little in forty-eight hours. Rain fell off and on, but some German planes flew through the overcast skies.[57] There was no observed German artillery fire placed on the Americans in the woods, but the Germans fired preplanned concentrations on them intermittently.[58] At 2:00 P.M. Screws sent a penciled note to Major John W. Watts, the regimental surgeon, giving him a line of departure for the assault on a sketch map and estimating the time of attack to be 4:00 P.M. Screws had previously approved Watts's recommendation for the location of battalion and regimental aid stations.[59]

## The 1st and 3rd Battalion Assaults

The commanders of the Rainbow's 167th and 168th Regiments and the commanding officers of the US 26th Division's 101st and 102nd Field Artillery assembled at about 3:00 P.M. at Brigadier General Robert A. Brown's brigade PC.[60] Brown read out orders to attack that afternoon in broad daylight, jumping off at 4:50 P.M. Screws protested as much as he dared in the face of a direct order and

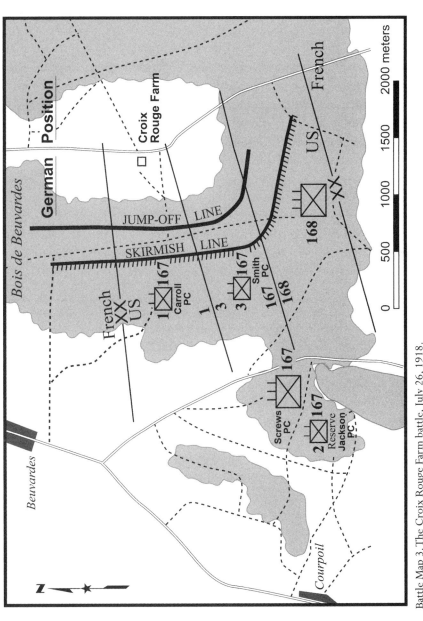

Battle Map 3. The Croix Rouge Farm battle, July 26, 1918.

suggested falling back from the woods and bringing artillery fire on the German position at the Croix Rouge Farm house.[61] Fearing a lack of coordination, Screws asked if the French at his left had received orders and were going to jump off at the same time. The French had no orders and did not attend the meeting. Despite Screws's concerns, "All watches were synchronized, and all regimental commanders left for their respective PC's."[62] Screws's suspicions proved well founded, as the artillery did not fire until that night after the battle was over.

In the Rainbow Division history, Reilly reports that Screws entrusted Bare with delivering the attack order to the 1st and 3rd Battalions. Bare had only fifteen or so minutes to reach the units after receiving the order, but he proceeded immediately, reaching 3rd Battalion's Major Smith before heading to the 1st Battalion. Traveling in the regiment's motorcycle sidecar, Bare reached a felled tree that blocked the road. He ran to Major Carroll, who managed to lead his men into the battle about ten or fifteen minutes later than scheduled.[63]

The 168th and 167th were to attack to the east. The Alabama regiment was ordered to take the farmhouse and go to the woods east of it, while the Iowa regiment's objective was the road.[64] Lieutenant Hackett recalled, "When the order came to 'get up and at em,' there was general rejoicing."[65]

Borden Burr, the civilian YMCA representative, described the first assaults in his diary: "by means of a smuggled Kodak we take some pictures and the films are given to me for development. At five the word comes and we start through very thick woods."[66]

Carroll's battalion, dug in west of the farmhouse, had orders to proceed with the 167th Machine Gun Company, which was to carry its guns with the riflemen as it crossed the open land between the skirmish line and the farmhouse.[67] After reaching the farmhouse the riflemen and machine gunners were to head northeast across the open land beyond the farmhouse until reaching the La Ventellette woods about a mile farther on. None of that worked according to plan.

Smith's 3rd Battalion soldiers were in position west and southwest of the farmhouse. Its orders were to go through the strip of thick forest beyond the skirmish line, then to cross the open land in front of the farmhouse. It was to proceed until it reached the woods about a thousand yards beyond the farmhouse.[68] Again, none of that went according to plan.

Although ordered to attack simultaneously, the two assault battalions advanced from their skirmish lines about fifteen minutes apart. They were in irregular lines, and forward progress was uneven. The 1st Battalion moved ahead much faster than the 3rd. According to Burr, companies and men were mostly unaligned by the time they got to the edge of the woods.[69] The staggered initial advance failed to overrun the enemy. The 1st Battalion attack was kicked off with elements of C and D Companies going through the thin woods on the regiment's left flank. They passed through A and B Companies, which were laying down rifle and machine gun fire.[70] C and D Companies bounded through the field, taking heavy casualties from the beginning. Many were hit by German machine gun fire. German riflemen were also actively shooting into the four attacking platoons. According to the Germans, the attack did not last more than fifteen minutes.[71] Survivors of the failed 1st Battalion assault force were trapped in the open field for more than an hour. American dead and wounded covered the battlefield. The regiment's mortar and machine gun sections proved ineffective. D Company's Sergeant Worth Lewis, Corporal Amos Bush, Private William T. Cheatham of Greenville, and Private Horace Rigsby of Georgiana all died. Private Ben Hope of D Company, wounded in the head, continued to advance against the enemy until he received three additional wounds. He was killed and received a posthumous Distinguished Service Cross.[72] Corporal Usry Burnett of D Company was killed along with many others.[73] Private Carl Lee Canoles was shot through the head and was buried where he fell, alongside ten comrades.[74]

The 167th Machine Gun Company, attacking with the 1st Battalion, was also hard hit. Its commander, Captain Strassburger, was killed in the first hundred yards.[75] Twenty-year-old Private Russell Bowlin of Ashville was killed with him.[76] Private Newell S. Houston of Statesville, Autauga County, also died and was cited by the regimental commander, which entitled Houston to a Silver Star.[77] Corporal William Scott Hughes of Perry County, an outstanding soldier, was killed. France decorated him with a Croix de Guerre with a palm, and he received a citation from the division commander entitling him to a Silver Star.[78]

## Major Dallas B. Smith's 3rd Battalion Attack

L Company's First Lieutenant Howe described the 3rd Battalion's attack as unfolding in degrees when its elements engaged, faltered, and tried again. He described coming to the farmhouse from the south and southwest, progressing at what he called a reasonable battle pace and reaching the fortified house by 7:00 P.M.[79] Major Claude M. Stanley, commander of the 168th (Iowa) Infantry's 2nd Battalion, spoke of "hearing the Rebel Yell as Alabama soldiers held their rifles high and raced across the field."[80]

The shouting raised spirits, but casualties mounted. Burr wrote in his diary, "Wonderful nerve to see them run without protection through machine gun fire. Some are killed and wounded."[81] First Lieutenant Henry L. Griggs, I Company,

Opelika, stated, "this was the hardest fighting my battalion had during the war and was the only hand to hand fighting I saw during the war."[82]

The officer commanding the 3rd Battalion's Mortar Platoon was ordered to fall in with riflemen in M Company, whose first sergeant Norman L. Summers wrote: "Some of our men were blown to pieces. Some had their arms and legs blown into tatters. . . . It began to get dark. Shells were bursting on all sides. . . . Long red flashes came from German machine guns. Heavy undergrowth made progress difficult. As I was advancing a boy at my side was shot down by a German machine gun. . . . I will never forget the look on his face as he went down."[83]

I Company losses in the charge through the woods were about thirty killed and a hundred wounded.[84] Major Smith would later receive a Distinguished Service Cross for his actions, but at that time his mind remained on the cost of the attack.[85] He admitted afterward, "It is difficult for me to comment on the Croix Rouge Farm for the reason that I always felt, and I know our regimental commander felt . . . that it would be a sacrifice of troops to make an attack through those woods without some artillery."[86]

A captured German report written by Battalion Commander Hildebrandt said that the American attack came in very thick lines with one infantry group attacking north of the farm and one south of it, both with several machine guns. Hildebrandt complimented the fire discipline of his men, saying they had stopped and started it several times, which he thought worked. He praised German messengers who brought up ammunition and believed all his men behaved well while receiving fire in a difficult situation—including becoming ill from the German gas and suffering from occasional friendly fire casualties. Hildebrandt wrote that two company leaders had, through binoculars, seen American reinforcements proceeding in columns after the first assault failed. The Germans claimed that fire effectiveness continued to be good, inflicting overall heavy losses on the Americans attacking against his 6th and 7th Companies. The report, making no distinction between the US 1st Battalion attack on the north and the US 3rd Battalion attack on the south, claimed that the attackers were met with machine gun and rifle fire lasting until nine that evening.[87]

## The 1st Battalion's Second Effort

The 1st Battalion's second assault occurred about an hour after the first, around 7:00 P.M. It used men drawn from C and D Company men who had not been in the first effort, along with men from A and B Companies, through which the first assault had been launched.[88] This second attack started when two D Company platoons under Bessemer's First Lieutenant Ernest E. Bell and two B Company platoons under Abbeville's First Lieutenant Robert Espy rushed forward. Their assaults were successful from the beginning. Firing as they went, spread out across the field, the hundred or so Alabamians savagely fought German riflemen and machine gunners in defensive positions. They attacked at a run, killing Germans with the rifle, bayonet, pistol, and rifle butt—essentially anything they could brandish as a weapon. Driving remnants of German units back, they sealed the fate of any Germans on the farmhouse's north and west sides. Those retreating Germans "left their guns, rifles and hundreds of boxes of ammunition and behind them came the 1st Battalion, charging forward."[89]

Although successful, the attackers suffered. Bell received wounds in the assault, and only twenty-three of his initial fifty-eight D Company men were left standing. Espy's group of about fifty from B Company had eighteen survivors.[90] Bare said, "The platoon commanded by Lieut. Robert Espy of Abbeville, Alabama was largely responsible for breaking up all the 27 machine gun nests in the edge of the woods by advancing in double time on the position."[91] As a result, "the dismal state of affairs out front began to clear up."[92] Screws later stated that Espy's efforts saved the regiment.[93] He was awarded the DSC for the action.[94]

Germans counterattacked, but 1st Battalion bayonets met them. Major Carroll, 1st Battalion commander, shouted, "Save your fire men! We'll give 'em hell with the bayonet."[95] Lieutenant Hackett said, "On that instant the fire of our men ceased and with bayonets fixed each man awaited the chance to impale a Boche on his 'toasting fork.'"[96] Again, success proved costly. Sixty-five percent of Carroll's 1st Battalion was killed or wounded that afternoon.[97] D Company, with men primarily from Bessemer, Greenville, and Huntsville, had 80 percent killed or wounded in the two assaults.[98]

## The 3rd Battalion's Final Effort

Smith's 3rd Battalion continued pushing from the south toward the fortified farmhouse. An I Company soldier whose company commander, 1st Lt. John M. Powell, had been killed described it: "Just as it seemed we were surely doomed by the heavy enemy attacks on our left and rear, the issue of the battle then hanging in the balance was suddenly resolved in our favor by unexpected help from two sources. 'Shorty' Wren and his detail came up with their small one-pounder cannon [mortar] to silence machine gun nests in front."[99] Then the tide turned, and "the entire American forces swept forward at bayonet point with great slaughter."[100] These events marked the battle's first effective use of mortars. The 1st Battalion continued to force its attack and the German retreat.[101] Witnesses recalled, "Line after line of grey-green forms began to crumple up and disappear."[102]

Smith's force pushed through where others had been stopped by German fire and where some companies had failed to maintain organization. A mixed group of infantrymen and machine gunners, thrown together by Lieutenants Murphy and Kairn of B Company's 151st Machine Gun Battalion, charged the farmhouse. K Company's Lieutenants Roy Sharp and Alan K. Smith and I Company's Lieutenant Harry Young also led small groups in charges. When Young was seriously wounded, another force from K and I Companies took out German machine gunners east of the farmhouse.[103]

With all the attacking forces under heavy fire, the remnants of an L Company platoon swept forward. Led by First Lieutenant Howe, approximately twenty men reached the house about 7:00 P.M. They were a mixed group of Alabamians and Iowans. The Iowans, members of F Company, 168th Iowa, had fixed their bayonets, started from the angle of the woods in the southwest, and ran through the open land in front of the Fère-en-Tardenois Road, which ran north–south. The 168th's E Company did the same, making it to the safety of the road before being stalled. Seven hundred yards due south of the farmhouse, Iowa's F Company linked up with the 167th's M Company. The combined force, "which bore the brunt of the fighting, advanced on the farm," taking heavy losses in the open.[104] Lieutenant Harold T. Fisher, whose fourth platoon of the attacking 168th F Company had dwindled from thirty-five men to ten, told the leader of the Alabama M Company assault force, "We will join you." When the Alabama officer was wounded, Fisher assumed command.[105] His leadership also proved brief, as he suffered a facial wound after advancing only "twenty-five or thirty yards."[106]

Those who reached the farmhouse included some able men, two machine gun lieutenants, and twenty-five or thirty wounded. About that number died in the final fight. They cleaned out German soldiers dug in along the west side of Fère-en-Tardenois Road and in the large vegetable cellar. After dark, they moved American wounded to the woods.[107] Germans were still active, and the Americans sent a runner asking 3rd Battalion Commander Smith for help in holding the position. He replied that he had no help to offer. The Americans reorganized lines and established contact with Carroll's 1st Battalion on the left and with Worthington's 1st Battalion of the 168th Infantry, which had advanced its troops, on the right.[108]

B Company's Captain Bryan Whitehurst took command of the mixed group, which repelled counterattacks and suffered through German artillery, which "kept up a constant fire all night long."[109] As combat slowed, drizzling rain continued through the early night, and a storm erupted at 10:00 P.M. After midnight the retreating Germans burned stores and exploded ammunition, causing great lights and explosions in the east as they withdrew the last of their forces to their Dora position beyond the Ourcq River.

## After the Battle

It took a huge effort to find wounded and get treatment for them that night. Medics were shorthanded; the 1st Battalion Aid Station had two doctors and a dozen assistants, and five of them were wounded.[110] The regimental band, every member of the sanitary staff, and all available soldiers served as litter bearers. Narrow paths with mud-and-water-filled shell holes made stretcher bearing harder than usual.

Huts at the battalion stations offered little protection from weather, and covered space was limited. The Alabama and Iowa regimental surgeons worked together on an old farm, with Alabama getting the carriage house and Iowa the four horse stalls. "Walking wounded" stood around or sat on wet ground, waiting as the more seriously shot up were helped. Men on stretchers were covered with blankets or raincoats. Doctors operated as medics gave morphine and antitetanus injections, applied splints and bandages, wrote out tags, and moved men on and off the operating table. Trails were muddy and slippery. There were not enough ambulances. Serious cases were given priority to the clearing station and field hospital at Epieds. The chaplain of the 166th (Ohio) was there, though his regiment was not. The 168th chaplain, Roscoe Conklin Hatch, spoke of "'Alabam,' the 167th of beloved memory, which we felt to be both kith and kin."[111]

Major Watts, regimental surgeon of the 167th, later gave a written report:

> Night came on and with it rain, the terribly wounded men staggering along through the deep mud and cold water, stretcher bearers slipping and falling with the mutilated and sometimes lifeless bodies they carried. . . . The wounded accumulated in great numbers, the aid stations were literally full of them, both Americans and Germans. Those who were unable to walk to the rear were made as comfortable as possible. Many of the wounded lay on the wet ground with practically no protection. The Germans had located us and seeing an ever increasing crowd started a heavy shelling, making two direct

hits on the regimental aid post and killing one of the Hospital Corps men while he was in the act of administering morphine to one of his wounded comrades.

The wounded were being brought in during the entire night and were evacuated to the rear as rapidly as possible. The assault battalions advanced about a thousand yards and gained their objective at a cost of approximately one casualty for each yard gained. For when the casualty list was completed the following morning, we sent a list to Regimental Headquarters of over eleven hundred names of wounded who had passed through the aid stations from 5:30 P.M. July 26 to 7:00 A.M. July 27.[112]

One of those wounded men was Will Frazer.[113] During the attack, he crawled into a shell hole after being hit twice in the upper part of his right leg by a 7.92 German machine gun. He remained in that crater in no-man's-land after Bell's and Espy's second assault swept past. Chester Scott, who had been with Will, was still out there somewhere. The attacking Alabamians had drawn even with the French, who had not attacked. Will was in the hole with a French soldier and a dead German. The Frenchman pointed to Will's leg wound and said, "*Bonne blessure.*"[114] Will, relieved that his leg remained unbroken, agreed that it was a good wound. Eventually, the French soldier motioned for Will to stick his head up to see the Germans' location. Will motioned back for the French soldier to do so. He complied and was killed by a single bullet to his head.

After applying a makeshift tourniquet, Will was picked up by a litter party at about eleven that night. He and three other stretcher cases were taken to the regimental aid station, then the clearing station, then to the field hospital in Epieds. On the way to the rear the ambulance slipped off the muddy trail into a ditch near the 167th PC and nearly turned over. Will was happy to eventually be placed on a fine ambulance train bound for Paris.

Another D Company soldier, Montgomery's Corporal George Carter Mastin, wrote his parents from a hospital on July 30:

> Friday afternoon about 3:30 we got orders to advance. We knew it would be hard as we had to face a German machine gun nest—but finally we broke through and drove them back three or four kilometers. We had never realized what war was until our comrades were falling on our side dead and wounded and that caused us to give old Fritz one harder than ever. I got a few, you bet. . . . I never felt better than while that fray lasted—until 9:30 that night when a gas shell exploded a few feet from me. I reached for my gas mask but before I could get it on a high explosive stunned me for a short time and when

I had good sense again, I was awfully sick, never-the-less I put on the gas mask and carried wounded to the aid station—as my platoon had gone on, that is, all who could. . . . Never fear, we will hold up the name of Old Alabama.[115]

Gary Roberts, Abbeville, in a letter home described killing several Germans, then added, "Listen, I want you to put two stars by my picture on the wall and write it down in the Old Account Book where it will not be destroyed or forgotten. . . . Believe me it was some fun as well as exciting. Now I'm sorry I didn't get to kill one for each of you. Perhaps I can get more next time. The first one I got was for Mama and the other one was for myself for the trouble they have given this ole boy."[116] He was awarded a DSC.[117]

The Alabama regiment was racially segregated, but integration prevailed in Base Hospital No. 15.[118] In a July 28, 1918, letter from the hospital to his aunt in Abbeville, Gary A. Roberts wrote, "The negroes are taking a part in the fight, at least the one across the table from me now says they are. We are mixed up here with them eating side by side at the same tables, so long as they stay in their place and help us fight it suits me."[119]

Another hospitalized soldier of the 167th wrote: "Dear folks this leave [sic] me on my way to the hospital. I was slightly wonted [sic] the other day I have been look [sic] after by the U.S. Doctors, and red cross, just fine. I think I will get by very well. So I will write often as I can I also go[t] some gas—not bad I don't think. Hope this will find you all well."[120]

Occasionally the letters showed anxiety. Phipps Kennedy of B Company, Abbeville, wrote his mother from the hospital, assuring her of his safety and lamenting, "There is just a few of the old boys left now."[121]

The high number of casualties was in part due to the lack of American artillery. Bare said, "The fight at Croix Rouge Farm was purely an Infantry action."[122] Once the artillery did start, though, it proved useful. Screws said of the 101st Field Artillery, "I know the fire . . . put down on all roads and avenues of escape for the Germans must have been terrific as the next afternoon, July 27, when we started forward through these roads we picked up over two hundred German prisoners. They came in saying that the fire of the artillery during the night had been too terrific as they started back to Sergy and north of Sergy that their casualties were very heavy. Therefore, they decided they had rather give up."[123]

Captured German orders spelled out the location of defenses on the other side of the Ourcq, to which the 10th Landwehr withdrew. German reports mentioned the demoralizing effect of American artillery fire on the night of July 26.

Their documents said the July 26 assault on Croix Rouge Farm was made by a joint French and American force, but Screws later said the French did not attack that day.[124] The French division was badly shot up and reduced to about thirty men per company, or a total regiment's strength of about 340 men.[125]

Screws's anticipation of the attack order and his planning conferences on the morning of the attack proved critical to his regiment's success. There was no communication through wire, radio, flags, or pyrotechnics. His assault battalions and their companies had been briefed and made ready to jump off using only the watch when the order finally arrived from 84th Brigade and set a time. Otherwise the 167th, like its flanking infantry regiments, the Iowa regiment and the French regiment, would have failed to get off on time.[126]

At Croix Rouge Farm, 162 officers and men from the 167th died.[127] The list included five officers, three platoon leaders, and two company commanders. The officers died leading the attacks. Twenty platoon leaders received wounds that day.[128]

## Reports at Home

A front page headline and story in the July 29 *Montgomery Advertiser* announced, "Allied Troops Enter City Fere en Tardenois—French Guards Have Reached North Bank of the Ourcq River," but it made no mention of the Rainbow, the 167th Infantry, or of bayonets—all of which made those events possible. On August 4 the Montgomery paper reported the Rainbow to be in the thick of the fighting of the Aisne-Marne campaign, but the Alabama regiment was not singled out. The first casualty lists appeared in the August 6 *Montgomery Advertiser*, which announced two killed, Chester R. Vickery and James C. Peak. Nothing was said about the regiment's massive losses or the costly Battle of Croix Rouge Farm.

Finally, nearly a month after the battle, the *New York Times* reported on August 20: "Casualties of a most severe nature were suffered by D Company, the Bessemer, Alabama unit of the 167th Infantry, Rainbow Division, in the fighting which wiped out the Soissons-Rheims salient. That news came in a letter received by the wife of the company commander. Twenty-five members of the company were killed, about a hundred were wounded and several, including Captain Edmundson were gassed. Only about seventy-five men were left in the company."[129]

On his return to Birmingham that summer, Borden Burr wrote newspaper reports about the 167th in combat and gave town-hall-type talks in over forty communities.[130] Burr reported that Alabama and the Rainbow had been among the first American troops to engage the enemy in multiple, large-scale, important, and highly dangerous battles. He told of being in France when Pershing made good his offer of American help for Foch and of witnessing the 167th fighting alongside the French to save Paris during the battle in Champagne. Burr explained Foch's Château-Thierry offensive and told of witnessing the 167th's decisive and costly taking of the Croix Rouge Farm and its crossing the Ourcq and fighting on the east side of it. He explained that the regiment was instrumental in those battles that had done so much to turn the tide of war in France from the Germans to the Allies. Burr's meetings revealed for the first time the extent of the 167th Infantry's accomplishments and suffering. The home folks had not known the full measure of losses in dead and wounded or sacrifice of the regiment until Burr returned to the state to testify as an eyewitness.

Although their recognition in traditional news sources was lacking, the Alabamians attracted notice from Douglas MacArthur. He wrote, "the 167th Alabama assisted by the left of the 168th Iowa had stormed and captured the Croix Rouge Farm in a manner which for its gallantry I do not believe has been surpassed in military history."[131]

# 7

# The Ourcq and
# Brigadier General MacArthur

When dawn broke on July 27, Screws of the 167th looked at the situation. In the distance at La Ventellette—the large woods approximately eight hundred yards east of the farmhouse—French horse cavalry waited with lances and several motorized armored cars.[1] That was the regiment's objective as called for in the attack order the day before. It was supposed to have swept by the Croix Rouge Farm advancing at the rate of two hundred meters in three minutes. That, of course, had not been possible.

Further advance still seemed impossible, but a hot meal, a deep sense of relief, and no incoming artillery helped everyone. The decimated 1st and 3rd Battalions received new allotments of ammunition. Twenty-two German prisoners were taken, and search parties recovered more German and American wounded.[2] The dead of both armies were buried where they fell, and 283 German bodies were counted, many having died from bayonet wounds.[3] Before placing a body into its shallow grave, diggers removed all personal effects. After the war, bodies were disinterred for reburial in official cemeteries or shipment home if the deceased's family desired.[4]

## Reorganization

On the morning of July 27 units were being reorganized all up and down the line.[5] Survivors of the 1st and 3rd Battalions of the 167th were combined into one battalion. Around 2:00 P.M. First Lieutenant Maurice W. Howe assumed command of the remnants of L Company, K Company, and the remaining I Company platoons, a total of 210 men. Captain Ravee Norris commanded another unit consisting of M Company and everybody else standing.[6]

Earlier in the week, Screws had been frustrated when the division was committed piecemeal, but on July 27 he received welcome news: "the rest of the 'Rainbow' were coming into the line."[7] During the night of July 26 the division's fresh 83rd Brigade, consisting of the 165th (New York) Infantry and the 166th (Ohio) Infantry, started relief of the decimated 167th (French) Division north of Croix Rouge Farm. With that, US I Corps was reduced to one division, the 42nd. From then on, any fighting along the Ourcq would be between the Germans and Americans.[8] The French were removed from the sector.

The Germans also made changes on the other side of the Ourcq. On that day, "The 4th Prussian Guard . . . replaced the 10th Landwehr Division near Sergy . . . it was one of the crack divisions of the German army."[9] Another fresh division, the 84th Guard Division, arrived the day after.[10] The 4th Prussian, a storied German unit, evoked a great amount of confusion among Americans, who sometimes used the term "Prussian Guards" to refer to any unidentified German troops. Although several officers, including Screws and Smith, reported facing the 4th Prussian at Croix Rouge Farm, these accounts proved inaccurate.[11] Kurt Gabriel of the 4th Prussian later reported that the unit was not involved there.[12]

It was involved later, on July 28, when Captain Percy A. Lanison of the 168th Infantry led troops across the Ourcq River and took several members of the 4th Prussian Guards prisoner.[13] The captured Germans reported that "the 4th Prussian Guard Division (which was commanded by the Kaiser's son, Prince Eitel Friedrich), the 201st German and 10th Landwehr and 6th Bavarian divisions had orders to hold at all costs."[14] The Germans knew they could not withstand another series of costly losses such as at Champagne and Croix Rouge.

Colonel Screws and his exhausted, shorthanded two battalions could only suspect the Germans' determination, but there was one thing for sure. Captain Everette Jackson's 2nd Battalion would engage the Germans soon, just as they had done with distinction two weeks earlier at Souain. In preparing for the attack, Jackson and his men moved from their support position near the lake up to the farmhouse. At 2:00 P.M. on July 27, the 2nd battalion went to "establish itself on the hills north of the stream," with 1st Battalion in support and 3rd in reserve.[15] Jackson took his battalion northeast on the road from Croix Rouge Farm for about a mile and turned east. After filtering through the woods and fields for a few miles, the unit crossed the Ru de la Taverne, a small branch of the Ourcq.[16] The remaining forces of the 1st and 3rd Battalions, then under First Lieutenant Howe, and Captain Norris followed, stopping for the night behind the 2nd Battalion. Lieutenant Colonel Bare established the regiment's forward PC near the Ourcq.[17] The men received water and hot food. Jackson and his men settled into their first objective, the west side of the Ourcq, at about 8:30 P.M.

The entire Rainbow was by then committed in its usual order of regiments assembled from left to right, the 166th, 165th, 167th, and 168th. Battalion Adjutant Welles said, "During the night, the Germans searched the entire valley of the Rude [sic] de la Taverne with big caliber guns, one of which missed our PC."[18]

With Germans close by, the men of the 167th regiment stretched out and slept for the first time in three days.[19]

## Crossing the Ourcq

On the morning of July 28 Screws established the regiment PC (Post of Command) at L'espérance Farm.[20] His responsibility covered an area ranging from "the wheat fields directly north of l'Esperance Farm," which connected the nearby village of Sergy with the 165th.[21] From that vantage point, the 167th saw the Germans, who occupied carefully planned positions on the two-hundred-foot hills north and east of the Ourcq.[22] The Americans knew they must take the towns in those hills, and the Germans stood ready to defend their positions at all costs.

On July 28 Father Duffy noted that Fère-en-Tardenois was blazing and smoking, having first been shot up by the French during the Germans' occupation, then by the Germans during the French occupation.[23]

Throughout the battle to come, the Rainbow would work together, but each regiment—and the units within it—would pursue a number of individual objectives. They began as one, though, with a general Rainbow Division advancement on July 28. At 9:00 A.M. Jackson led the 167th's 2nd Battalion down the Ru de la Taverne. Turning east, the battalion then waded across the Ourcq while under scattered fire.[24] Although called a river, the Ourcq resembled something smaller. Men described it as "a still water about 30 feet wide," too shallow for swimming.[25]

## Another Battle: July 28

After safely crossing the river, Jackson was ordered to exploit his 2nd Battalion's position. He placed outposts well up the hill, with Meurcy Farm and Seringes on the left and Sergy, which had become the 84th Brigade's principal objective, on the right.[26] German artillery fire, directed from airplanes and observation posts on the rolling hills, started to come down. German machine guns, in excellent

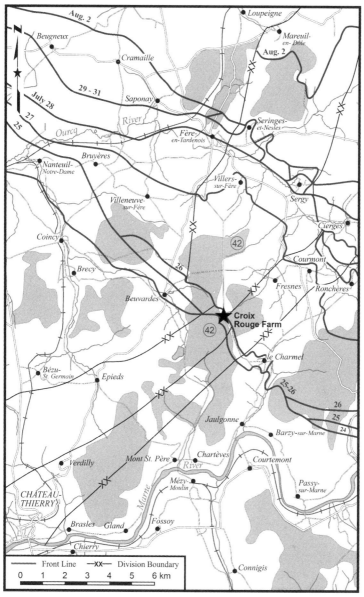

Battle Map 4. Croix Rouge Farm to the heights of the Ourcq River, July 26–
August 2, 1918.

defensive positions, had a labyrinth of well-planned fire lanes lacing the open wheat fields. Flanking fire continued from Sergy and its vicinity.[27]

Held up by the slow advance of the 167th, the 168th struggled to gain the wheat fields on its high ground. Bare reported, "While the men dug in along the sunken road the enemy aero planes flew over and with machine gun fire from the planes killed a great many of our men who were lying flat on the ground."[28]

Major John W. Watts, regimental surgeon, reported terrific hostile artillery fire, which was responsible for a great many casualties. Watts and other medical personnel scrambled to assemble aid stations under difficult conditions. Watts recalled, "On three different occasions in this area, the Aid Stations were so severely shelled that it was necessary to scatter the Medical Department men and wounded so that they could take advantage of the little protection offered by the terrain."[29] Watts finally "located the Regimental Aid Station in an old abandoned site that the Germans had left in such haste that they abandoned a stack of several hundred litters which were soon put to good use."[30]

Challenging times give rise to heroics, and on July 28 Gadsden's F Company rose to the occasion. After its commander, Captain F. L Wyatt, received wounds from a strafing German airplane, command passed to Lieutenant Louis Greet. Greet was then wounded after holding command for only a few minutes. In that time the men made an excellent impression, causing Greet to later boast, "I don't believe there was ever a better infantry company than the one that jumped off that morning from the edge of the woods. I can see them now as they went down the hill under artillery fire. The waves were so well organized as if they were back at Leffonds on the drill field."[31] Even being wounded did not disrupt Greet's confidence in the regiment, as Sergeant Tom Whitworth reports: "I went back where I had seen him fall with a wound in his leg. He was . . . smoking a cigarette. He asked, 'Wonder what the Kaiser thinks of Alabama?'"[32]

But it was a hard day for F Company. Sergeant John D. Brunner of Ashford died on the battlefield. Afterward, his brother Charlie, also in F Company, "did not seem to care anything about himself and would, out of sheer dare-devilitry, stand erect in the open and fire away."[33] When a heavy patrol of Germans threatened the company advance, Jackson sent a squad to protect two machine guns on its left flank. The machine gunners were killed, but two E Company riflemen, Corporal Harry Drysdale, Selma, and Private George Schwend, Montgomery, took over the guns and turned the Germans back. When Drysdale was shot through the bone of his right leg, Schwend carried him to safety.[34]

Not all soldiers had such able comrades to assist them. When F Company fell back Private Julius Grogan, Talladega, was lying prone on the hillside with eight bullet wounds. Upon realizing he would be left by those trying to protect themselves, Grogan "jumped up and away down the hill he ran, crying out before he started: 'all right—damn it! I'll take myself.'"[35]

Another impressive unit—Company G of Ozark, commanded by First Lieutenant Richard B. Kelly Jr.—was in the center of close combat on that first day of battle. At about 10:30 A.M., ninety minutes after jumping off, the leader of its right platoon was killed and the platoon sergeant wounded. Kelly was also wounded, but the fight continued under the exceptional leadership of Corporal Sidney E. Manning, who was born on a farm in Butler County and raised on a farm near Flomaton, Alabama.[36] Kelly said, "Manning took command. . . . Though himself severely wounded he led forward the 35 men remaining in the platoon and finally succeeded in gaining a foothold on the enemy's position, during which time he had received more wounds and all but 7 of his men had fallen [see fig. 18]. Directing the consolidation of the position, he held off a large body of the enemy only 50 yards away by fire from his automatic rifle. He declined to take cover until his line had been entirely consolidated with the line of the platoon on the front when he dragged himself to shelter, suffering from 9 wounds in all parts of the body."[37] He was awarded the Congressional Medal of Honor for this action.

Other G Company standouts included First Lieutenant Peyton V. Deese of Skipperville, who led a platoon in knocking out a machine gun, breaking up a counterattack in which he was wounded, taking German prisoners, and receiving a second wound while taking a fortified position where he died—actions that earned him a Distinguished Service Cross.[38] Although gassed and wounded, Sergeant Bill Brown, Ozark, refused to be evacuated until he had reorganized his platoon and consolidated the position. Brown received a Croix de Guerre with gilt star from the French and a DSC from the United States.[39] Not all 167th soldiers who distinguished themselves that day were from Alabama, not even the United States. Among the G Company men who died on July 27 was a Norwegian, Ole O. Romslo, drafted in South Dakota and sent as a replacement to the 167th before the battle of Champagne.[40]

Fighting continued throughout the day as Germans counterattacked on the hills of the Ourcq, pulling out all stops in hopes of victory. First Lieutenant Isaac Walker, a member of the 151th Georgia Machine Gun Battalion, described his experience supporting the 167th: "We had good shooting. . . . It was our best and largest target. The Germans withdrew running and crawling for cover to the north. Those four Hotchkiss machine guns were certainly worth their weight in

gold. The German counterattack had almost 90 men in two wedge shaped formations. They came across the crest of the hill in an orderly manner. Some wore
French helmets in an attempt at disguise, a replay of attacking Germans in the
Champagne wearing blue French overcoats. The 151st machine gunners with-
held fire until the German helmets and uniforms were recognized at about eight
hundred yards."[41]

The Germans experienced some successes, including the capture of several
American prisoners. Official Prussian Guard reports issued after the battle describe the 42nd Division in positive terms: "The nerves of the Americans are
still unbroken. . . . The individual soldiers are very good. They are healthy, vig-
orous and physically able-bodied men, well developed, in ages ranging from eighteen to twenty-eight years of age, who, at present, lack only necessary training
to make them redoubtable opponents. The troops are fresh and full of straightforward confidence. A remark of one of the prisoners, Lieutenant Vivian Roberts
of the Pennsylvania troops, is indicative of their spirit, 'We kill or get killed.'"[42]

The 1st Battalion fought very hard to clear all snipers and machine guns.[43]
Later Major Smith brought the weakened and combined 1st and 3rd Battalions
to support the 2nd Battalion. Still out of the battle, remains of the depleted 3rd
Battalion received German artillery fire directed by enemy airplanes.[44]

1st Battalion men occupied a front line "gap which existed between the regiment and Iowa."[45] They cleared the area of snipers and machine guns and advanced on the Germans.[46] Two of its platoons reached Sergy "and held it for a few
hours only to be driven out by artillery and lack of protection."[47] A patrol from
the 168th held the village for a short time afterward, but it too was driven out.

That afternoon Major Smith was meeting with Captain Mortimer Jordan on
the heights of the Ourcq when both were wounded.[48] Transported to a field hospital, Jordan received treatment but died on August 2, 1918.[49] Jordan, who received a Distinguished Service Cross for service on July 15 in Champagne, was
cited by the commanding general of the Rainbow Division and by the regimental
commander of the 167th Infantry.[50] This entitled qualified him for two Silver Stars.

Bare attended an afternoon conference at regimental headquarters, leaving
Major Carroll in charge of the advanced regimental PC. A German shell exploded
just outside the entrance to the headquarters shelter, wounding Carroll and killing two others. Captain Ravee Norris, also present, escaped without harm.[51] After
Carroll's wounding, Norris received command of the combined 1st and 3rd Battalions.[52] His men dragged themselves back to the Forêt de Fère to spend the
night of July 28.[53] Groups of worn-out soldiers ate from large insulated galva-

nized cans and drank chlorinated water delivered by carts. Getting food to the regiments at the Ourcq was a challenge, and "on several occasions all of the animals pulling the wagons bringing food supplies were killed."[54] Transport of food and supplies was but one issue among many, and the regiment continued losing officers and men at astonishing rates.

Gas was a problem as the Americans advanced through the low, swampy area approaching the Ourcq River. Hissing came from exploded German artillery rounds that had delivered but not fully released their payloads, the gas formed "curious greenish-yellow clouds [that] moved before light winds, becoming a bluish-white mist, such as is seen over water on a frosty night. Each kind of gas was marked by a distinctive odor. Chlorine smelled like pineapple, phosgene had the stench of putrid fish, and mustard gas had a rich, sweet, almost soapy smell."[55] Men feared mustard gas most, as it caused blindness that could last for months or even become permanent. Decaying carcasses added to the stench, causing one soldier to observe, "The smell of death is almost as disturbing as the sight of it."[56]

First Sergeant Norman L. Summers of M Company, while staying with his unit for two days after being gassed, recalled "fighting a losing fight against the gas that was circulating through me and it finally got a strangle hold on me and I caved in. Everything seemed to go round and round."[57] Summers praised the base hospital, whose staff he called "the best by far"—a bright spot during the bleak time of injury and recovery.

## Soldiering On

Screws liaised with the commander of the 165th regiment earlier in the week, on July 27, but the New York regiment's battalions advanced piecemeal and had offered the 167th little assistance thus far.[58]

Major William T. ("Wild Bill") Donovan, who commanded the "Shamrocks" of the 165th's First Battalion, led it across the Ourcq late on July 28.[59] It had a new objective, Meurcy Farm. After visiting the 167th PC in search of artillery assistance, Donovan recalled, "I thought I should never get back as I went up a little draw that was just singing with machine gun fire and heavy artillery. I had a liaison man from the 167th outfit and I shall never forget him. He knew the best course, the shortest routes and the quickest crossing across the river. He was calm, self contained and cheerful. I would like to see him again."[60] The 167th had arrived only a short time before Donovan, but its men understood the terrain and the importance of guides.

Donovan's man may have been Private Carl W. Dasch, a member of Headquarters Company from Weiser, Idaho, a replacement who served as a messenger for the 167th's 3rd Battalion from July 25 to August 1. Dasch repeatedly distinguished himself, constantly carrying messages between the firing line and regimental headquarters, almost always under fire. Upon returning from the skirmish lines he often transported wounded through the barrages to aid stations, once becoming so badly gassed that he received an order to report to the aid station for treatment.[61]

At about 9:00 A.M. on July 29, the 165th's 3rd Battalion moved forward.[62] Captain Reilley of the New Yorkers said, "We advanced through the open in squad columns under artillery fire. It was a beautiful sunny day. As there was a large amount of open country in front of us we could see everything happening in it. It was the first time that the outfit had ever advanced against artillery fire."[63] The next day they captured Meurcy Farm, prompting K Company's Corporal John J. Casey to call it "the outstanding feat in this advance."[64] The 165th's D Company's Sergeant Richard W. O'Neill received a Medal of Honor for his actions in the fight, the second soldier from the Rainbow and the first of the 165th Infantry to gain that recognition.[65] Casualties remained high, though, as Casey observed: "we were outnumbered and we knew that not many of us would return to tell of the deeds performed by those who we left behind us there. We captured the place, but at what a loss. We lost the cream of the company."[66]

The Alabama regiment also lost a number of key personnel, but it held position east of the Ourcq until the evening of July 29, when "a battalion of the 47th . . . relieved the front line troops."[67] Although the idea of relief sounded good, the circumstances ultimately proved to be very unsatisfactory for the Alabamians.

Circumstances were unorthodox. Corps commander General Hunter Liggett caused the temporary assignment of two battalions of the US 4th Division's 47th Infantry to the 84th Brigade.[68] Its 1st Battalion, supported by the 167th, attacked on July 30 and remained in position until the evening of August 1.[69]

The other borrowed battalion, the 3rd of the 47th, joined the 168th Infantry on July 31 in an attack on Sergy. That battalion was nearly eradicated, leaving it with about forty men and two officers.[70] Its commander had been wounded and evacuated without giving orders to others. MacArthur blamed poor leadership for the debacle, which included an unordered attack on Sergy.[71]

Relief of the battalion assigned to the 167th, the 47th Infantry's 1st Battalion, frustrated many Alabama soldiers. The "borrowed" battalion relieved Captain Everette Jackson's 2nd Battalion at 11:00 PM on July 29. It had been fighting since dawn the previous day.[72] The 167th's combined and spent 1st and 3rd Battalions were to support that loaned 4th Division battalion in its attack at 9:00 A.M. on July 30. The effort of the 4th Division troops—the unit's first time under fire—gained some territory and captured about twenty prisoners and some machine guns before it was stopped with heavy losses.

Relief of that unit, the 1st of the 47th, on August 1 required the exhausted and combined 1st and 3rd Battalions of the 167th to return to action.[73] The Alabama troops, who complained audibly, resented being sent back into battle from the Forêt de Fère without adequate rest. They felt the loaned battalion served too briefly, particularly after the men from the 167th had been so used up. Captain Gardner Greene, who served as temporary commander of the combined 1st and 3rd Battalions, said, "I think what really hurt them [the men of the 167th] more than anything else was the fact that we had been in the offensive you might say from July 5th on the Champagne from up to that time, which was July 31st . . . while being under harassing artillery and machine gun fire at all time without a chance to rest. . . . I think I told Colonel Screws this perhaps, that I believed that my physical stamina was as strong as anyone's in the regiment, that in all my service I had never fallen out or had never given up and never been in the hospital, but I felt that my strength had practically all gone."[74]

After Bare was gassed on July 30 and required hospitalization, Captain Gardner Greene, who had also been gassed, assumed leadership of the combined force of the 1st and 3rd Battalions of the 167th.[75] Speaking via phone on July 31, Greene told Screws that "the men had been gassed for two days, that we were in a ravine . . . and that it was impossible for us to evacuate and get to higher ground, that the night before the first battalion, or what was left of the first battalion had come out of the front line, being relieved by the first battalion of the 47th Infantry; that they had marched back some six or seven kilometers, gotten through breakfast and laid down to rest when they were ordered to the front again." He continued, "the men were completely out and jaded and I felt that making an advance might prove futile to our side."[76]

The 167th's frustration continued. It had been promised artillery support at the start of the battle on the Ourcq, which failed to arrive on time. Screws remained particularly committed to silencing German artillery and said that his "regiment suffered most from [incoming] artillery fire."[77] He carefully investigated the German locations, hoping to convince Americans "to have the heavy artillery do counter battery work" on the places he identified.[78] His plans fell on deaf ears, however, until a German POW captured around August 1 revealed "that his regiment and much of the artillery had gotten back about 10 kilometers on their way to some other sector when they got orders to return to the Ourcq front. He also said their artillery had been reinforced since."[79] Screws then "used every means" possible to coax authorities into accepting his plan, sending copies of the POW's statement to officials and asking some officers to intercede on his behalf.[80] Eventually it worked, and Screws reported that after the American counterbattery fire, "we went forward like a shot."[81]

While it must have been nice to be vindicated, the delay proved costly. The highly respected Major Lloyd D. Ross of the 168th Infantry later concurred, saying, "Had artillery been turned loose on those positions on our first day our artillery would have just walked over Hill 212 and the Germans would never have been able to organize along their next line."[82]

## Relieving Commanders

Troubles ranged beyond the 167th, however. Brigadier General Robert A. Brown, the 84th Brigade commander, was criticized for the problems caused when the 47th Infantry attacked Sergy without orders. MacArthur acknowledged that Brown first learned of the incident after it happened, but in testimony to the inspector general, MacArthur argued that Brown, the officer he would shortly replace, should have maintained closer communication.

Brown responded with reorganization. On July 29 he sacked Colonel Ernest R. Bennett and gave temporary command of the 168th to Major Guy S. Brewer, the regiment's operations officer. The next day he gave Lieutenant Colonel Mathew A. Tinley the permanent position.[83] Then he transferred Major Emory C. Worthington—commander of the 168th's 1st Battalion, who had been in the Iowa regiment for twenty-seven years—to the division military police.

A July 31 telegram from General James W. McAndrew, chief of staff, AEF headquarters, to the commanding general of I Corps, Major General Hunter Liggett, announced Brown's sacking. Major General Charles Menoher, MacArthur's boss, had recommended the relief, and Liggett had approved it. Menoher, who claimed firsthand knowledge of the situation, said Brown had collapsed and was no longer capable of commanding a combat brigade.[84]

Earlier, Pershing's headquarters at Chaumont had ordered Colonel Douglas MacArthur's return to the United States.[85] Now Chaumont issued a new order temporarily approving MacArthur as 84th Brigade commander while the brigade was in action. Brown's removal saved MacArthur from being sent home to a training job and gave him an opportunity at command. Rather than going to Fort Meade, Maryland, to train a new brigade, MacArthur would become the youngest general officer in the army, overseeing a highly regarded combat unit.[86]

The relief of Brown, Bennett, and Worthington from their respective commands emanated from Croix Rouge Farm when Bennett's 168th failed to enter that battle efficiently, effectively, or promptly. Worthington managed his battalion poorly at Croix Rouge Farm, and Brown neglected his oversight of the Iowa regiment along the Ourcq. A fifty-nine-page dossier on Brown's relief and demotion to colonel, the result of an inspector general's investigation made from August 18 to August 23, 1918, quotes MacArthur, then chief of staff of the Rainbow, as ruling Brown unfit for leadership.[87]

This document also contains MacArthur's comments on the location of certain units while the battle at Croix Rouge Farm was being fought. He argued, "The two brigades [the 83rd and 84th] had practically the same hardships, practically the same amount of fighting and practically the same officers. . . . They [the soldiers in the 84th Brigade] had been subjected to exactly the same conditions as the rest of the Division."[88]

The Summary of Operations, 42nd Division, July 25–August 3, 1918, similarly states, "On July 25, the 84th Infantry Brigade relieved the 56th Infantry Brigade of the 28th Division U.S. The remaining elements of the Division were moved into the Epieds Area during the day. . . . On the afternoon of July 26th the 84th Brigade attacked in the direction of Croix Rouge Farm and captured the farm buildings, sustaining heavy losses. . . . During the night the enemy withdrew. . . . On July 27th the entire division took up the pursuit and gained contact along the line of the Ourcq. . . . On the morning of July 28 . . . both Brigades crossed the Ourcq, captured Sergy and established themselves on the northern slope of the stream."[89]

The Rainbow Division history says otherwise: "As the 83rd Brigade was not in action during this time its casualties were fairly light as only due to shells landing in the woods which they occupied."[90] Major Watts, surgeon of the 167th, sent regiment leaders the names of over eleven hundred 84th Brigade wounded who passed through his aid stations between 5:30 P.M. on July 26 and 7:00 A.M. on July 27.[91] Screws also quantified the regiment's losses prior to July 27, stating, "Our casualties were so heavy that . . . when I received orders to proceed to . . . the Ourcq River, I only had one full strength battalion, and two half battalions, making the 167th practically one battalion short all during the fight on the Ourcq."[92]

MacArthur far outranked Screws, but the subordinate Screws stood up to the senior officer, testifying that his unit's situation was unique: "At Croix Rouge Farm we had a particularly hard fight . . . the hardest of any we had . . . the strain naturally made our men much more tired than in any other part of the Division . . . because we were in practically four or five days before the others were in . . . that fight, hand to hand, was bound to tire our troops out, and we had been up practically all night of the 25th . . . on the 27th we moved to the second phase, the Ourcq River, without stopping at the first phase . . . we were subjected to continued shooting and there was no come back."[93]

Soldiers from the 165th reinforced Screws's statement. No less a person than Father Duffy in his July 27, 1918, diary "dateline Courpoil," noted that the New Yorkers were not yet in place and that the 84th Brigade had fought without them on July 26.[94] French evidence concurred, as a July 30 after action report stated that cars transported the 83rd Brigade north of Bézu on July 26.[95] Thus the 83rd Brigade could not have been engaged with the 84th at Croix Rouge Farm on July 26.

Aside from the debate over who was where and when, Liggett and MacArthur received support for their actions from the 42nd Division commander and six Rainbow Division officers.

On the other hand, among those who had been close to combat with Brown were four officers from the 167th, along with three from the 168th and the commander of the 151st Battalion, all of whom testified that they saw nothing unusual or abnormal about Brown's condition, either physical or mental.[96]

Earlier Screws had stood up to Brown when receiving orders to launch the attack at the Croix Rouge Farm without artillery preparation. But Screws later testified in Brown's defense that the brigade's order had been received from 42nd Division impossibly late for proper execution. He said, "I was at Brigade Headquarters when General Brown received his order . . . about 3:25 or 3:30 P.M."[97] Since the order called for a 4:50 P.M. attack, Brown lacked time to summon artillery.

The inspector general prompted Screws to call Brown indecisive and almost invited him to say Brown collapsed mentally and physically on the field of action. Screws stood firm in stating that everyone—including his own men—had been beyond exhaustion, implying that this was also Brown's case.[98]

As the investigation was taking place, things went forward on the battlefield. The Germans began withdrawing on the morning of August 2. Colonel George E. Leach of the 151st Field Artillery received MacArthur's order to "*Advance with audacity.*"[99] Leach's battery used a war-torn Dodge truck to enter Seringes-et-Nesles, where he recorded a bleak scene: "The town is a smoking ruin and the fields covered with dead. There are dead Americans and Germans in every house. I counted 18 German machine guns in one field with the gun squads all dead at their posts. We had to remove the dead from the road before we could progress and picked our way through the shell holes."[100] Another soldier would later describe his feelings at the time, "One cannot believe the misery a person is in when they walk around seeing bodies everywhere and then realizing you may be one of them anytime."[101]

With MacArthur as brigade commander for the first time, the 167th put its least exhausted battalion, the 2nd, on the point of the regiment as it advanced north of the Forêt de Nesles, keeping liaison with the 168th on its right. With scouts out, Jackson's men passed dead Germans and abandoned machine guns and ammunition, and "it became evident that the enemy had made another general retreat."[102] Despite their apparent success, the week of near-constant fighting had worn 2nd Battalion men almost to the breaking point. Most had received only one meal a day.[103] Nervous strain, little or no sleep, and exposure to gas took a toll. Cold and wet at night, hot by day, worn down from the continuous shock of combat, and with many sick from dysentery, the battalion pushed ahead through the rain, reaching the badly shot-up village of Nesles without opposition. There the US 4th Division's 59th and 39th Infantries relieved the Rainbow in about four hours.[104]

When it stopped moving forward the Alabama regiment had traveled about twelve miles from Croix Rouge Farm. The men had expended all their energy and accrued heavy losses in days of hand-to-hand and close combat.[105] They exerted great effort dragging themselves to the Forêt de Fère, which stunk from the smell of dysentery, rotting animals, and mustard and chlorine gas.[106] The entire 167th was a mental and physical wreck. Since the start of the Croix Rouge Farm battle, its strength had fallen from 3,518 to 1,934. The unit suffered 1,785 casualties in action, about 55 percent. Only a small number had been replaced.[107] No other US regiment had been engaged in the entire Aisne-Marne Offensive for as long or had suffered more than the 167th. The Rainbow's casualties from the Ourcq and Croix Rouge Farm totaled 945 killed in action, 269 dead of wounds, and 4,315 wounded—a total of 5,529.[108] The 167th had suffered nearly a third of the 42nd Division casualties in some of the most violent fighting of the war.

Their efforts had succeeded, and the Château-Thierry pocket no longer existed. The salient had been sliced off with the capture of about eighteen thousand Germans. However, shortly after these deeds, Pershing seemed to question his focus on open warfare. On August 7, 1918, he asked chief of staff General James McAndrew "to make a study of the whole question of attack against machine guns and artillery, opining that, 'perhaps, we are losing too many men.'"[109]

## Out of Action: August 2–August 27

When the Rainbow withdrew from the front on August 2, it went out of action for first time since entering the trenches at Baccarat on February 24. Its corps commander, General Hunter Liggett, called it "a first class division in every sense; swift in attack and tenacious in both attack and defense."[110] The division camped in the gas-tainted Forêt de Fère for eight days. Although better than the front, the conditions still proved uncomfortable: "The weather was hot, and the country full of ruined villages, dead, unburied bodies—Boche and American—and thousands of dead horses. The men were dirty; baths were next to impossible."[111] It was probably the last place the men would have expected to encounter a celebrity, or a lovely female one at that. And yet that is exactly what the Rainbow Division received, as Raymond Tompkins notes: "Into the middle of this filthy backyard of war with its sickening smells and sights and its unkempt, lousy men there bounded on a fine afternoon one Elsie Janis—fluffy, beautiful, piquant—not at all unlike a goddess just stepping out of the clouds for a bit to see what it was all about down here below. That's what it seemed like to the Rainbow Division. They hauled a wagon-bed into an open field and made a stage of it, and there Elsie Janis danced and sang before a vast concourse of unwashed doughboys who suddenly remembered that there was such a thing in the world as a pretty American girl—and were somewhat awed and saddened at the remembrance. An aeroplane came whirring overhead while Elsie Janis sang 'Oh, You Dirty Germans!'"[112]

The respite gave the men a moment of normalcy in a chaotic time, and it reminded some old timers of her performance for the Rainbow earlier. Janis recalled it in her memoirs: "I gave my show to one of the finest divisions that ever faced the Germans . . . the name of the particular gang of heroes suggested a lot of colors. . . . The show was in the center of a battlefield where they had fought."[113]

Buoyed by the entertainment, the 167th men departed happily on the morning of August 10 for the two-day march to Château-Thierry.[114] Troops rose be-

fore sunrise to get on the crowded road. Morale improved as the column dis-
tanced itself from the front. They met long convoys of camions bringing up fresh
soldiers. American supply wagons and artillery trains of four mule teams slowly
proceeded with guns, ammunition, and food. The men passed through battlefields
littered with German equipment. Approaching Château-Thierry, the regiment
saw rows of barbed wire on stakes and trenches dug by the French to stop the
recent German drive on Paris. In the midst of the rubble, tenacious French civilians and French army reservists harvested fields of ripe grain. In a letter home,
a Rainbow artillery sergeant reported, "Noticed farming . . . with all American
machinery mostly Deering implements."[115]

The 167th traveled through Château-Thierry, where every building was damaged, and dust rose from pulverized masonry lying in the streets.[116] Buildings
lacked roofs and bell towers lacked bells. Regimental headquarters, Supply Company, Machine Gun Company, and the 1st Battalion continued to Montreuil-aux-
Lions, while 2nd and 3rd Battalions went on to Bézu-le-Guery.[117]

Replacements, many of them draftees, arrived. Until then, draftees were considered members of the National Army, even if serving as a replacement in a National Guard division, Regular Army division, or one of the few National Army
divisions. However, a July 31, 1918, general order consolidated those entities
into one group, the United States Army.[118] Thus the previous distinctions began
fading, though they never entirely disappeared. Many fighters continued to rank
the order of prestige based on who had the most time in combat, the most training, the best reputation, and lastly, who had volunteered for service.

Those volunteers arrived with news from home, and they likely reported how
a by-product of so many men joining the military was the service flag. Families
of servicemen would hang a flag in a front window or on the front door. Usually
about six inches wide and twelve inches tall, it contained a blue star on a white
field with a wide red border and a star for every service member.[119] The star was
gold if the family member had been killed. Such flags helped families back home
feel connected to their servicemen and built morale.

For the soldiers on the road, few satisfactions trumped arriving at a safe rest
area after combat. Everyone in the Rainbow was billeted in homes or barracks
and had a roof overhead for the first time in weeks. The men happily scrubbed
their bodies and boiled clothes to get rid of cooties. There were no work details
or drills, and some officers received leave to Paris.[120]

However, not everyone relaxed into the new routine. John Hayes, a 3rd Battalion company clerk, reflected: "It is a fearful thing to advance into battle over a terrain littered and strewn with the wreckage and debris of military combat, and reeking with the odor of the dead combined with the smell of corrosive mustard and chlorine gas and the penetrating and acrid fumes of bursting shells charges with high explosives—past dead and swollen horses, their legs jutting stiffly in the air, and past human corpses blue and discolored and frozen in the grotesque positions assumed in sudden and violent death."[121] The fear of the days in battle never left some of these soldiers.[122]

People discussed the events of August 8, the day General Ludendorff called the Black Day of the German Army, when Franco-British troops, with Australian, Canadian, and American help, pushed back German units for several miles.[123] Large numbers of Germans, with dwindling morale, stopped fighting and were taken prisoner.

Some French civilians returned to towns around Château-Thierry, starting commercial activities with the Rainbow men as customers. Cafés served wine, and soldiers, who finally received their pay, could purchase bottled wine, champagne, and vermouth. Inexpensive fresh fruit and vegetables offered a welcome change from army rations. By August 14 all units of the division had settled comfortably into the small villages along the Marne not far from La Ferté, which remained the center of activity. The common soldier, who could not reach Paris, turned La Ferté into a miniature version of the City of Light. Almost everyone washed and swam in the river every day, enjoying a sense of relief and thanksgiving.[124]

The enemy started to view the Americans as winners. Pal Kelemer, a Hungarian cavalryman in the Austro-Hungarian army who saw a group of American prisoners in Arlon on the border between France, Luxembourg, and Belgium, noted, "Their amazingly good physical condition, the excellent quality of their uniforms, the heavy leather in their boots, belts and such, the confident look in their eyes even as prisoners, made me realize what four years of fighting had done to our troops."[125]

At least that was the case for some of the enemy. Others felt the Americans had exploited their opponents at their most vulnerable and accused the Rainbow of killing prisoners. German newspapers reported the accusation, and General Menoher ordered an inspector general's official inquiry. It included testimony from twenty-three of Menoher's officers.[126] The investigator asked the recently promoted Major Ravee Norris about any relevant incidents. Norris detailed how the unit had killed attacking Germans in the typical course of duty. He also described a possible source of the accusation: "The second day of the Ourcq I sent a Corporal back with seven or eight prisoners who had just been captured. Sometime later he came back saying that the prisoners had tried to jump him when he was alone with them going to the rear and that to save himself and to prevent their escape he had to shoot them all. This same day at various times nine wounded prisoners were brought to my post of command. They received the same attention as our wounded men, were put on stretchers and carried to the rear, where they were evacuated to a Field Hospital."[127] Norris left the investigator to adjudicate the issue, but the conversation appeared to have ended the investigation.[128]

## Sex and Prostitution

While away from the front lines, soldiers had time and money—a recipe for trouble. AEF regulations forbade them to go to bordellos, which US officials believed to have a high incidence of venereal disease. The large number of men seeking treatment for "the drip" caused Screws to reinstate short arm inspections that substantiated this belief. Despite the risks, many men remained preoccupied with sex and how to get it. Many young Americans arrived in France as virgins, but few departed that way, and "many of them contracted diseases that separated them forever from the conservative, insular communities they left at home."[129]

The French preferred having their own soldiers and the soldiers of the British and American armies go to bordellos. The undesirable alternative was soldiers seeking out young French female family members. American officers discouraged fraternizing with French women, in deference to French concerns about the large numbers of single women due to the war, the weakening of moral values due to a monstrous conflict, and especially the presence of young men away from home and possessing a feeling of financial well-being.[130] An experienced American soldier noted that many sexual exchanges transpired for reasons other than commerce: "The Yank, healthy, amiable, moneyed and with lure of novelty, can have anything he wants. No more surprise at infidelity of wives with husbands au front, maids with thirst for new experience, and old eggs hungry for arms of virile Americans."[131] The men's behavior reflected changing standards.

Many officers' attitudes reflected that as well. Pershing, a fifty-six-year-old widower, said men should practice continence. Tellingly, he made no mention of abstinence. One condition implied control, while the other simply did away with the idea of sex. Pershing's advice suffered from rumors that shortly after arriving in France, he embarked on a relationship with Micheline Resco, an attractive twenty-three-year-old French-Romanian artist.[132]

Prostitution was an issue, but it was always a brief one, as the Rainbow kept heading back to the front.

## On the Road Again

Just when the regiment seemed settled and ready to enjoy more rest along the Marne, the 2nd Battalion and Machine Gun Company received orders to march twenty-one miles to the railhead at Mezy-Moulins. From there they headed east on August 17–18. The remainder of the regiment boarded trains at La Ferté for the trip. The men traveled to Breuvannes, Damblain, and Colombey, not far from Chaumont.[133] The 2nd Battalion stopped about fifty miles from its old hangout at Faverolles, a favorite, the site of its first training in France. Some said the region held a café for every twenty houses, and the village remained unscathed by war. The troops were billeted in modest homes, no one practiced blackouts at night, and the French, who considered the doughboys to be the saviors of France, offered a gracious welcome.[134]

Things seemed too good to be true. Serene weather graced the lush countryside. Some men received leave, and civilian company abounded. Sergeant John D. Brenner of a 151st Machine Gun Company reported: "The French Mademoiselles were not afraid to speak to you in their broken English. The girls would step up to the fellows and ask if they wished to go along."[135]

Although officially in a rest area, the men continued training. The schedule covered a four-week cycle with several all-day and all-night operations for everybody, even the wagon trains. The 167th received replacement ammunition, equipment, and men, but some of those new men were green and unevenly trained. Earlier three hundred Alabama National Guardsmen arrived from Georgia's Camp Wheeler in time to participate in the Château-Thierry push, but many of those coming in later were recruits and draftees sent over with only a few weeks of training. All had to be phased in before the regiment could go into action again. This time Americans rather than French officers conducted the training. Even the new brigade commander got involved: "MacArthur, who spent weeks trying to whip new recruits into shape, was appalled to discover how little they had been taught in the United States before being shipped over. At one point he saw about a hundred troops out of formation, gathered about a sergeant, and was about to issue a reprimand when the sergeant explained: 'Sir, I am teaching them how to load rifles.' MacArthur backed off quickly. 'When an army is in the fix we are,' he said to the sergeant, 'the knowledge of how to load and fire a rifle is rather basic.'"[136]

No rifle ranges existed for target practice, and there was no time to build them. Some replacements did not know simple commands or how to do close order drill at the squad level, and some had no training at all. Replacements reporting to a machine gun officer did not know how to operate a machine gun. They were given jobs as ammunition bearers and teamsters where they might be of some help.[137]

As always, the army used drills to teach new men to respond to any order, even loading rifles and adjusting gas masks. Units conducted open-area maneuvers such as a platoon assaulting a machine gun nest, a company advancing through woods, and a battalion in assault over broken ground.[138] Battle-tested leaders showed newcomers the way. The veterans enjoyed showing off what they knew, and the green troops were eager to learn. All knew they would depend on each other soon.

They practiced blowing a path in barbed wire with Bangalore torpedoes, poles about ten feet long packed with explosives. A soldier on his stomach would shove one underneath wire entanglements, place a fuse, ignite it, and yell, "fire in the hole," giving everyone time to duck before it exploded. The Bangalore torpedo was a new weapon that worked well but required soldiers to expose themselves to great danger in putting them into place.

About a week into the training schedule the regiment received orders to prepare to move.[139] They had rested for nine days, but it was over. They did not know their destination, but the Rainbow men knew they were heading back to the front.[140]

# 8
# From Saint-Mihiel to the Argonne, September 12–October 11, 1918

## Moving Forward

The Rainbow men knew nothing about their next mission for a simple reason: when they began marching to battle on August 28, the French and American generals had not yet finished planning the battle or negotiating which military's officers would lead.

The 167th departed its bases at Colombey, Breuvannes, and Damblain, hiking at night and sleeping during the day to preserve secrecy from enemy aircraft. The weather was hot in the beginning, and the night moves were cooler as well as safer from aircraft observation.

Men made the best of their sleepless nights on the road, filling the darkness with ribald songs "as bawdy as the collective imaginations of 3,000 horny men could conceive."[1] After marching for around forty-five minutes a bugler at the rear of the column sounded "Halt," and the troops flopped to the roadside for fifteen minutes' rest before the bugler called "Forward March." Before dawn the column would scatter under trees to pitch pup tents and wait for the company kitchens.

Marches went well, though men resented not being able to smoke because of the blackout. The regiment stopped at Saint-Paul until September 4. While there it practiced assaulting a fortified farmhouse, just as it had done at Croix Rouge Farm, and seizing a railroad, which it expected to do soon.[2] When the rains set in, men struggled over choppy roads covered with soupy mud that sometimes reached the axles of the trucks, wagons, and artillery pieces. The column made back-to-back night marches in the rain from Saint-Paul to Allain, which was near Uruffe and Gibeaumeix, the 167th's first home in France.[3]

In Allain the regiment held rifle and grenade practice during the day.[4] Preparation for battle made the general climate tense. If, when cleaning his rifle, a

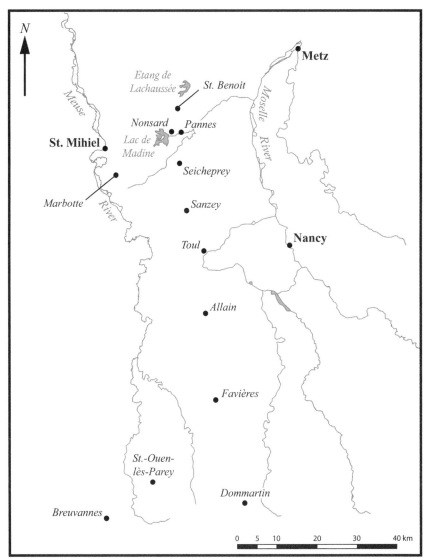

Station Map 3. Saint-Mihiel stations: August 18–October 1, 1918. (1st Battalion Headquarters)

soldier accidentally fired a shot into the ground, men would shout claims to his belongings, implying that someone had shot himself in the foot, choosing a relatively minor, self-inflicted wound rather than risk the Germans doing something worse.[5]

On the night of September 7, the regiment left Allain and arrived at Forêt de la Reine in the predawn hours of September 9.[6] From that mud hole in a forest, where it was almost as dark as night during the daytime, they slogged in driving rain to Toul, an ancient cathedral town.[7] Outside Toul the trucks and mule-drawn cannon congested traffic so much (see fig. 19) that the column repeatedly halted, causing everyone to become restless during the delays.[8] Many marchers slipped and fell in the mud throughout the long and miserable night. They welcomed the chance to drop their rain-soaked packs when finally arriving at the assembly area at 4:15 A.M.[9]

The men pitched shelter half-tents in the dark before wrapping themselves in wet blankets. Toul resembled a swamp. Every road and trail was a bog. French Renault tanks, some manned by Americans, occasionally shimmered through the mist and rain as they made their way to the front, but one Alabamian "was only half-jesting when he drawled that the attack was doomed 'unless the High Command used submarines for tanks, ducks for carrier pigeons and alligators for soldiers.'"[10] The miserable conditions allowed men's minds to wander, turning to anxious thoughts about the battle to come.[11]

## Logistics and Planning

The 1st US Army attack at Saint-Mihiel promised to be the largest American operation the war had yet seen. The attack targeted "a well entrenched position, covered by many bands of barb-wired entanglements" Germany held since "the last ten days of September, 1914, when the Army of the Crown Prince of Bavaria had made this salient."[12] In four years of occupying the salient, the Germans had resisted all Allied attacks.

The Americans at Chaumont included some of the US Army's best minds—including Pershing's plans expert, Lieutenant Colonel George Marshall. Other army command and staff school graduates were familiar with the Saint-Mihiel region. Some planners had studied the 1870 Franco-Prussian battles so thoroughly that they knew the area well enough to sketch maps from memory. It helped substantially in constructing complicated orders. Hugh Drum, 1st US Army chief of staff, and Fox Conner, AEF operations chief, both aided Marshall in the planning. Everyone understood the attack's significance and what victory would mean logistically and in terms of morale. Marshall believed his career depended on the success of this operation, as he understood Pershing did not forgive failure.

The group started working on preliminary plans for Saint-Mihiel in early August, though the exact attack specifications kept changing until the battle actually was fought approximately six weeks later.[13] From the start, planners understood that Saint-Mihiel would be a big battle involving many combat elements. Speed in execution remained essential, as all objectives were to be taken in two days.

There were other constraints. Pershing insisted that the attack be an American-led effort using American troops free from French control. Although he finally succeeded in those demands, the Americans paid a big price in their commitment to future operations. After fighting the battle to seize Saint-Mihiel the army would be nearly doubled in size before starting another battle, this time in the Argonne. There it was to penetrate the forest before attacking the heavily defended Hindenburg/Kriemhilde Line. The Saint-Mihiel and Argonne efforts were part of a larger strategic Allied move, with the British and French first attacking farther north in a major effort to reduce Germany's penetration of France and push them back toward Germany.

This ambitious second battle, coming so quickly after the first, was Pershing's concession to Marshal Foch, who initially resisted the idea of an all-American effort at Saint-Mihiel. Although negotiations grew heated at times, each man ultimately secured something he wanted, finally agreeing to a compromise on September 2.[14]

To say the plan was ambitious is perhaps too generous; Pershing's description makes it sound nearly impossible to execute: "[it] represented a gigantic task, a task involving the execution of the major operation against the St. Mihiel salient and the transfer of certain troops employed in that battle, together with many others, to a new front, and the initiation of the second battle, all in the brief space of two weeks. Plans for this second concentration involved the movement of some 600,000 men and 2,700 guns, more than half of which, would have to be transferred from the battlefield of St. Mihiel by only three roads, almost entirely during the hours of darkness. In other words, we had undertaken to launch, with practically the same army, within the next twenty-four days, two great attacks on battlefields sixty miles apart."[15]

Back at Chaumont, Marshall believed this plan "represented his best contribution to the war."[16] However, success requires more than plans, and Americans lacked adequate numbers of the tools they needed—horses, wagons trucks, ambulances, locomotives, railway cars, and specialty troops to clear and build up the roads, lay telephone and telegraph lines, treat the sick and wounded, and assure supplies of ammunition of all types and sizes.[17]

But that shortage did not stop officers from moving forward with the plans. Pershing began placing corps and divisions at Marshall's disposal for this operation in early August. The Rainbow joined with the 3rd, 4th, and 26th Divisions in a strong grouping that would receive a great deal of responsibility. The commanding general spoke of the four as having "fine morale and considerable experience, as they had fought in the defense about Château-Thierry and in the advance toward the Vesle River."[18]

The Rainbow would enter the battle at Saint-Mihiel between the 1st Division and the 89th Division, regarded by some as the best of the national army, the drafted army. The 3rd Division, now called "The Rock of the Marne" because of its tenacious mid-July stand, was in corps reserve. Marshall's long and detailed attack order treated the Rainbow as special: "The 42nd will attack in the center and will deliver the main blow in the direction of the heights overlooking the Madine River . . . the division will seize its objective of the first phase, first day, without regard to the progress of neighboring divisions."[19]

In the first all-American battle of World War I, the surprise attack at Saint-Mihiel was scheduled for the night of September 11/12.

## The Attack at Saint-Mihiel

Planners made many last-minute changes before the attack launched. The objective was the height overlooking the Madine River. Due to its earlier accomplishments, the Rainbow Division retained a key position in the battle and would "attack in its usual formation of the four infantry regiments abreast, with one battalion of each in the assault line, and one battalion of each in support."[20]

On September 10 the 167th's battalion and company commanders hiked about seven miles through sucking mud to survey the front line. Platoon leaders followed the next day for their first look at the assault position in the trenches the US 89th Division held, which the Rainbow would move through in launching its attack. As its first task the next night, the Rainbow relieved all of the 89th except the observation posts in front of the trenches.[21]

Upon arrival at the front line, division officers saw an elaborate enemy trench system that had withstood two big French attacks. Over four years the Germans had built concrete trenches, deep dugouts, and well-protected fighting positions for rifles and automatic weapons. The system resembled the ones from which the Germans had attacked in Champagne and the ones the Americans faced at Baccarat.[22] Maps showed the first German defense line as two lines of trenches, with connecting communication trenches. The main lines were about two hundred yards apart with heavy barbed wire in front of each. A third line stood behind additional barbed wire about half a mile beyond that. A mile farther back, more

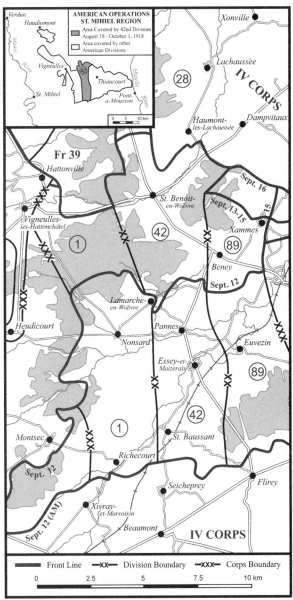

Battle Map 5. The American-led offensive at Saint-Mihiel, September, 12–27, 1918.

wire guarded a fourth line, a support line. It seemed as if the whole countryside was covered with barbed wire. Twenty-three thousand German troops manned defenses five miles deep. Their defense seemed impregnable, but half a million Americans greatly outnumbered the defending Germans.

On the night of the attack, September 11/12, the 167th left packs in the woods. Everyone ate a hot meal of slum, buttered bread, and coffee before marching six miles to the front. Every rifleman carried his rifle and bayonet, a ration of hardtack and corned beef, a canteen of water, one blanket, an aid kit, and the basic load of 250 rounds of ammunition. Some carried small sacks of hand grenades. Automatic rifle teams shouldered an additional burden: bags of metal ammunition clips, each with twenty rounds.

Officers and men had the same equipment to prevent the enemy from being able to recognize and target leaders. The weather also offered cover, as the cold night rain made it so dark that men could hardly see their hands in front of them. Thousands of moving people congested the roads and trails. To keep from losing places, soldiers often held onto the man in front of them. Around midnight, with no incoming artillery, the regiment settled in to its assault positions in the trenches. Slimy duckboard floors contributed to miserable conditions, but at least the Americans remained undetected. American artillery began at 1:00 A.M. As the men had seen at Champagne, "It was most impressive. The Boche flares were going up along the line and the surrounding country and horizon was fairly lit up with explosions of heavy guns of all kinds."[23]

The Germans fired back, but with reduced force. Although the Americans planned a surprise attack, some sources suggest the Germans suspected the assault. Remarkably, the Germans had scheduled a four-night withdrawal from the position at that time, but they had failed to exit completely before the Americans attacked, and some "German troops had to fight while retreating."[24] The German artillery remained in place, however, which substantially aided their efforts. The Alabama soldiers hunkered down until dawn. Some slept through the noise of artillery, but one sleepless soldier described the changing cadences of the German and American guns, saying, "all that time that steady thunder of the guns behind the lines, shelling, shelling, shelling, shelling, all night long, and then toward early morning breaking into drum fire like all hades had broken loose."[25]

The attack occurred close to the town of Seicheprey,[26] an ill-fated name for the Alabamians. Back on April 20, 1918, the Germans, who were engaging American troops for the first time, captured 187 Americans and caused 669 American casualties there. They retained control of Seicheprey up to the time of the Saint-

Mihiel attack. But this time things were different. The Alabamians soon learned "the Germans . . . had taken to their heels at the approach of the Yankees, and their terrific cries, 'Die Amerikaner kommen!' [The Americans are coming!], had echoed and reechoed through the streets. Certainly the great amount of equipment and stores was ample proof of their hurried departure."[27]

After four hours of artillery preparation, "at five o'clock, just as day was breaking, the American infantrymen in the first line climbed out of their trenches and started forward."[28]

Artillery targeted the barbed wire in front of the German line, hoping to weaken it in the time it took the infantry to get there.[29] Montgomery's Major Robert Joerg, after replacing Major Carroll, wounded at the Ourcq River, commanded the assaulting 1st Battalion.[30] Pell City's C Company attacked on the right under Captain Gardner Greene, who was killed.[31] To its left Bessemer's D Company led the jump off at Saint-Mihiel, just as it led at Croix Rouge Farm. Captain Edmundson remained hospitalized after being wounded on the Ourcq River, so the reliable First Lieutenant Shelby V. Gamble led the company. Also wounded at Croix Rouge, Gamble had returned to the unit in time for this operation.

Will Frazer, who had been wounded about the same time as Gamble, also returned in time for Saint-Mihiel. Frazer quickly reunited with his hometown best friend Chester Scott, who avoided hospitalization after being gassed at the Ourcq and remained in good condition. Both men missed Sergeant Worth Lewis, who had taught them a lot about soldiering before he was killed at Croix Rouge.

Men from 1st Battalion's C and D Company assault teams left the trenches first, armed with heavy wire cutters and Bangalore torpedoes. They cut two lanes per company into their own wire, allowing men to travel abreast into no-man's-land. The first men navigated through tangled rows of German barbed wire. Although conventional German doctrine called for covering wire with rifles or machine guns, this did not happen at Saint-Mihiel, and it aided the Rainbow attack substantially.[32] One observer remarked, "It was perfectly astonishing that the men were able to get through at all."[33]

Joerg was wounded on the first day and passed command of 1st Battalion to Captain Bryan Whitehurst. On the second day Whitehurst received wounds, and Captain George A. Glenn of Gadsden, Alabama, replaced him.[34]

The 2nd Battalion served in a support position about a thousand yards back, while the 3rd Battalion stood in reserve another thousand yards behind that. A platoon from Machine Gun Company accompanied each battalion.

On getting through the first rows of wire, "C and D Company assault parties moved down the slope toward the enemy. After the first rush the enemy did not put up much resistance."[35] The first Allied line of attack advanced in two waves, with half of each assault platoon in each wave. Although still dark, the sky quickly glowed with American and German pyrotechnics.[36] After crossing through their own wire, 1st Battalion men fanned out in the light of the flares and spaced themselves for the move forward. The Germans sent up flares from their listening posts and outposts, signaling for their artillery, infantry, and machine guns to shoot everything.

Falling in behind the rolling barrage of American artillery, the 1st Battalion reached the second German trench line, advancing as scheduled at a rate of a hundred yards in three minutes.[37] They were surprised to discover old, rusty, often broken barbed wire throughout the entire defensive system, making it much easier to pass through than anticipated.

Unexpected problems arose, though. Artillery fragments quickly covered the ground, preventing compasses from settling on magnetic north. Allied soldiers checked friendly flares to establish a sense of direction. They took heavy casualties in the first half hour, but the rate dropped substantially as a surprising number of Germans quickly surrendered in groups and singles. The Alabama soldiers had never seen such mass surrender.

In the second assault wave the 2nd Battalion proceeded over the top at 6:00 A.M., an hour after the 1st. It cleaned up behind the 1st and penetrated to the second German trench line on the first day. Although the first wave of troops had the most exposure to the enemy, 2nd Battalion still faced some dangers. While advancing, F Company's Ashad Hawie killed one German and captured another, earning a Distinguished Service Cross.[38]

Surprised and outnumbered, the Germans eased up their artillery. After the failures of July and August, the Germans had less fight in them.[39] Many more surrendered throughout the day. William Langer, a member of the 1st Gas Regiment's E Company, recalled them arriving in great numbers: "Most of them were young and hale in appearance, though there were a few older, war-worn men among them too. I spoke to several of them and invariably they said they were glad to have been captured. One even stated that he was glad that the attack had been made, for he believed it would bring the end nearer."[40]

The attack plan called for a squadron of French Renault tanks, commanded by Major George Patton of the 1st Tank Brigade, to follow both the 167th and the 168th in the assault. High expectations surrounded the tank unit, but it became mired down in the mud, never getting into much of the action. Patton fared little better, as he received a wound while directing the start of operation on foot.[41]

Colonel Billy Mitchell commanded US air cover for the offensive, using the largest number of flights yet seen in the war.[42] Overcast skies and 1,481 French-built American piloted airplanes prevented German attack planes from flying over the 1st US Army at Saint-Mihiel. Mitchell planned for twenty-one balloon companies, seven hundred pursuit planes, 366 observation planes, and a number of bombers. However, the overcast skies, high winds, and driving rains that stalled German aircraft also made Allied aircraft missions virtually impossible.

After clearing the second German trench line, the 1st Battalion, the 167th's first assault wave, crossed through low hills and reached Essey by 11:00 A.M. Its village church steeple and the small mountain behind it, the Butte de Montsec, offered easy reference points for land navigation.[43] After Essey, the land flattened out, and the men saw the Madine River ahead. Despite some resistance the 1st Battalion closed in on Pannes, its objective, at 5:00 P.M. The Americans could not build fires or smoke, and the one blanket each soldier had did not provide much warmth in the chilly air. Not all proved bad, though. The men rejoiced over the fresh German food—fish, bread, cabbage, and beer—discovered in dugouts.

At the end of the day, Lieutenant Bell commanded D Company of 1st Battalion, replacing Lieutenant Gamble, and Lieutenant Wickline commanded C Company, replacing the dead Captain Greene.

On the second morning, September 13, the 2nd Battalion went over the top and captured the Château de Saint-Benoît, a castle that had served as German corps headquarters.[44] Bare (see fig. 20) established the 167th Forward PC (Post of Command) in its basement, while the 1st and 3rd Battalions set up PCs on the grounds. Brigadier General MacArthur located the 84th Brigade PC upstairs. The sites proved temporary, as prisoners warned the Americans that a big gun targeted the castle. The Americans evacuated the building before heavy German artillery destroyed it.[45]

After the successful first day, D Company held three strong points in the new defense system being constructed by the 3rd Battalion. Each fighting position was occupied by half platoon groups, just as they had been in the trenches at Baccarat when the regiment first reached France. The fighting positions were four hundred or five hundred yards apart and had good views of the new German line. The other half platoon groups were positioned along a straight support line about five hundred yards to the rear. Company C was set up in the same way.

Companies A and B of the 1st Battalion no longer had a combat responsibility but were held in reserve three hundred to five hundred yards to the rear of Companies C and D. Everybody dug foxholes and covered them with tin sheets called elephant iron that the Germans had left behind. Some casualties were still being taken. (See fig. 21.)

## After the Battle

On the night of September 27, the Rainbow's 166th Infantry relieved the 167th, which then marched six miles to the rear. Bolstered by the battle's relative ease, the men found going back much easier than coming up. In the thirty-hour assault Pershing's force took 14,000 prisoners, 466 cannon, hundreds of machine guns and mortars, great quantities of small arms, and all sorts of ordinance and matériel. The Rainbow Division lost 234 killed and 667 wounded, a total of 901 casualties.[46] The dramatic success vindicated Pershing's gamble. In taking Saint-Mihiel the Americans succeeded where the French had twice failed.

Pershing wrote, "The striking victory completely demonstrated the wisdom of building up a distinct American army. No form of propaganda could overcome the depressing effect on the enemy's morale of the fact that a new adversary had been able to put a formidable army in the field against him which, in its first offensive, could win such an important engagement. . . . It inspired our troops with unlimited confidence which was to stand them in good stead against the weary days and nights of battle they were to experience later on."[47]

Thus, as the Rainbow Division prepared for the Argonne, Saint-Mihiel ended with a whimper. Private Charles MacArthur described the anticlimactic ending, saying his unit passed "through La Marche, which the doughboys had taken by going 'Boo' at the Germans."[48]

## Enter the Argonne

The glow of success brightened Pershing's forces. The general believed that his army had mastered its logistical, planning, and training problems.[49] Now, it was ready to "break through the enemy's successive fortified zone . . . to insure the fall of the Hindenburg Line."[50] Pershing aimed to cut the railroad carrying half of the German supply and troop moving capacity. The Germans, however, had not yet finished fighting. General von der Marwitz, the German 5th Army's commander, understood the railroad's importance and reinforced the area.[51]

On September 20, Pershing issued orders for an attack to break the Kriemhilde Stellung and take the Côte de Châtillon, an area that united four lines of defense, each line constituting part of the Hindenburg Line and each named for a Wagnerian witch. A historian describes the area's pivotal importance: "If the Americans broke through the Kriemhilde, there would be no time at all to make the next line defensible; the German Army would have to retire again, this time to the other side of the Meuse, and it was uncertain if the river itself could be held against the enemy from the New World."[52]

Nine American divisions attacked in the Argonne on the morning of September 26. Pershing instructed the attackers to move forward "with great vigor," but that did not happen.[53] V Corps, the point of the three attacking corps, had "inexperienced divisions, many of which were seeing their first action of the war."[54] Bolstered by recent successes, many Allied leaders had an inflated sense of ability and "ignored the critical facts that the situation confronting the AEF in the Meuse-Argonne was more complex than anything the inexperienced Americans had encountered before."[55] The green troops failed to meet the expected schedule, and the delay allowed Germany to bring in reinforcements.[56]

The Germans sent four divisions into the fight on September 26. Three days later, those troops witnessed the war's first American retreat. By September 30 six more German divisions had arrived.[57] The combined forces had brought the opening American attack "to a standstill within four or five days."[58] The German 52nd Jaeger Division reported, "Morale brilliant. The troops rejoice to have the Americans in front of them and want to attack for the booty."[59]

Of course, the Germans had not faced the strongest Allied troops. The Rainbow Division, for example, had been given a week's rest after Saint-Mihiel, and several of the other "best AEF divisions" remained noticeably absent from the early Argonne attack.[60] After the American retreat—and seventeen days behind on the battle schedule—Pershing devoted more men to the assault, conducting frontal assaults with a force that ultimately involved twenty-nine American and four French divisions.

The French Army knew that the area's few roads were clogged with material and that American logistics were poor. Many people involved understood the nightmare of traffic caused by moving sixty thousand troops into battle while withdrawing forty-five thousand and taking care not to disrupt the provisions headed to the front lines.[61] Despite this, throughout the weeks of battle, Foch held Pershing accountable for Allied success and continued to ask why the Americans failed to make greater progress.[62]

Most of the Allies believed Pershing had asked for pressure by insisting that his army could win while under American control. Some Allied leaders spoke of reducing Pershing's responsibilities and shifting some of his divisions to French or

British command—a move that would undermine the AEF and President Wilson's role in any peace negotiations.[63] Even French Prime Minister Clemenceau had suggested that Foch ask Wilson to remove Pershing from command.[64]

Aware of the general criticism of him, Pershing reorganized. He launched a second attack on October 4—the same day that German Prince Max von Baden sent Wilson a message asking for an armistice.[65] The German minister for foreign affairs had communicated with the Allies through neutral powers since August 14.[66] However, the Germans kept the pressure on: by October 6 they had put twenty-seven of their best divisions in line and seventeen in reserve. They planned to negotiate the armistice from a position of strength.

All along, Foch's indifference to the substantial German reinforcements infuriated Major General Hunter Liggett, Pershing's I Corps commander.[67] He had just given a good example of what the Americans could accomplish. On October 7 Liggett dangerously committed elements of his reserve, the 328th Infantry of the 82nd Division. The troops crossed a ford in the cold Aire River, got behind the Germans, and turned their flank.[68] Liggett's force cut the vital German north–south road there and on October 8 sent out a historic strong patrol that was stopped by linked machine guns. It was described "as a stroke of imagination in an era of frontal assaults."[69]

The patrol included Acting Corporal Alvin York, a self-effacing conscientious objector who had been drafted from the Tennessee mountains. Although York had been a somewhat rebellious individual who did not choose military service, he took it seriously once conscripted, relinquishing his former life of "drinkin' and fist-fightin'."[70] York excelled in Liggett's renegade operation. Leading sixteen men, he worked his way through the Germans, killing probably twenty-eight and taking 132 as prisoners.[71] His efforts resulted in his promotion to sergeant and receipt of the Medal of Honor. By October 10, three days after the 82nd started its move, the Germans evacuated the Argonne forest. York's achievement contributed to the relief of Major Charles Whittlesey's "Lost Battalion," of which 191 of the original 670 men walked out of their position after having been surrounded from October 2 to 7.[72] Pershing later cited this unit as one that exemplified the "spirit of the rank and file of our great army."[73]

## The 167th Moves to the Battle

The weather was damp, cold, and unpleasant—typical for that time of year in eastern France. Sickness spread through the 1st Army. It diagnosed sixteen thousand new cases of flu during the first week of October.[74] On October 2 Screws was sent to the field hospital with influenza.[75] It was the only time he ever left his post during an operation.

On the afternoon of October 4 the regiment hiked from Bulainville to Parois, twelve miles west of Verdun, and spent a frosty night on a hillside. On October 5 kitchen trucks brought up coffee and a hot breakfast before the unit marched through Avoncourt, where the attack by the US 1st Division had gone over the top on September 26. Rough roads contributed to frequent traffic jams. Thousands of American troops were on the move. Every village was a total ruin. The regiment halted behind the main battle lines at Forêt de Montfaucon. It was far from welcoming: "Craters fifteen feet deep and as wide across, yawned on all sides. All around was a dreary waste of woods, once thick with stately trees and luxuriant undergrowth but now a mere graveyard of broken limbs and splintered stumps."[76] The 167th was placed in overcrowded, shot-up remnants of forests already filled with soldiers moving to battle. That rear area had shell holes so close together that a man could hardly find a level spot to pitch a pup tent. If a wagon or truck got off the road it could not get through. A number of American observation balloons hovered nearby, and German planes attacked them, setting one on fire.[77]

Some American divisions advanced through the area, passing 1st Division soldiers bringing German prisoners to the rear. The prisoners said some of their comrades were ready to quit the fight.[78] The soldiers heard rumors that President Wilson and the German government were in diplomatic discussion.[79]

Despite the weather and rough conditions, many aspects of the stay near Montfaucon were pleasant. A YMCA wagon visited, offering sweets and tobacco. The 167th and 168th bands boosted morale with "frequent concerts of the soul-stirring music which heartens spirits."[80] In such an atmosphere, camping in pup tents and resting would not have been much of a hardship if they had not known they were headed to battle. But the knowledge remained, and it tainted everything.

On October 8, the 167th's Edward R. Wren, a hero from the battle of Croix Rouge Farm, wrote his father, "We have few chances to write or do anything else except move and fight and we are still in the advanced zone waiting, listening to the big guns roar. Expect to move up any minute. I received my commission (from first sergeant to 2nd Lieutenant)." After writing about Captain Whitehurst and Lieutenant Espy, both hospitalized and wounded, he concludes, "I hear that we will be able to continue to push the Germans and make them quit entirely."[81]

The Germans, too, realized that battle was imminent. The German Group of Armies weekly summary for October 9, 1918, noted, "The engagement of the US 42nd Division is to be expected soon. It is in splendid fighting condition, and is counted among the best of American divisions."[82] They anticipated correctly, and on the following day, the 167th received orders to move up that evening to the base of the strong German position that must be penetrated.

Some officers had expressed doubt that MacArthur could take Côte de Châtillon with his brigade alone.[83] MacArthur shared their uncertainty, later admitting that "when General Menoher, the Division Commander, asked me whether or not I could take the Côte de Châtillon I told him as long as we were speaking in strictest confidence that I was not certain."[84] The task was daunting, as the "defenses were virtually impregnable, unless fortune or a wise infantry commander arranged tactics to allow an AEF success."[85] The area boasted strong new wire, concrete bunkers, fixed fire lanes, and strong defenses bolstered by interlocking machine guns. The 167th had a formidable task ahead.

The regiment proceeded west on a line parallel with the front toward Forêt d'Argonne. It took up the combat approach march formation with intervals of five paces for dispersal. On the last night before entering the battle at Côte de Châtillon it camped in a small wood about two miles east of Exermont.[86]

The men faced primitive conditions. A soldier in the 149th artillery observed, "It is most difficult to get rations up to such a place and we subsist on stuff called 'camouflage' because it looks and tastes worse than our camouflage nets would have tasted had we put them in a pot of water and boiled them. It is a combination of solidified vegetables that some 'sharpshooter' back in the States had sold the government and probably made millions on it. It comes in five-gallon containers. It keeps one's bowels in a constant state of uproar and dysentery rages rampant in the outfit."[87]

At 7:00 A.M. on October 11, two officers and two noncommissioned officers from each of the twelve rifle companies joined a contingent from Machine Gun Company in reporting to Lieutenant Colonel Bare. He led the group to the forward slope of Hill 263 for a visual and map recon, passing through dismal hollows filled with gas vapors. All were nearly exhausted when they finally got their first look at the objective through fog and mist.[88] They returned to their units and brought them forward to the edge of the Bois de Romagne, where they relieved the 18th Infantry Regiment of the 1st Division just after dark. They were shelled on the way up but did not take any casualties.[89] The adjutant of the 2nd Battalion of the 167th, Captain S. A. Wells, later wrote, "On relieving the Major commanding the Battalion of the 1st Division, we were very impressed . . . that this fine unit had been through some most severe experiences . . . and also gave us some indication of what we might expect when we took up the advance."[90] The 167th's first assignment—relieving the 18th—was complete, but the real challenges lay ahead.

## The Rainbow Moves Up

The October 4 army-wide offensive appeared stymied. On October 11 the Rainbow moved into position on the front at the Côte de Châtillon, part of Pershing's decision to put experienced fighters into the battle. The Rainbow established its PC at Cierges with artillery and field trains elsewhere. The stage was set for another Allied push, its third of the campaign, to be launched on October 14.

The Rainbow completed its replacement of the spent 1st Division, sometimes called the "Red One" or Pershing's "Praetorian Guard."[91] In the week from October 4 to 11 the 1st Division suffered 7,500 casualties—1,594 killed and 5,834 wounded—the heaviest losses of any division in the Meuse-Argonne campaign.[92] Now that the Rainbow had returned to the front, its men hoped fervently that they could turn the tide of the battle to come.

1. Colonel William P. Screws of Montgomery. (N. T. Frazer Collection. Courtesy Josephine Screws McGowin.)

2. The Mexican Border in downtown Nogales, near the place where the soldiers from Alabama detrained. (Pimería Alta Photo Collection)

*big ridge over camp*
*where I catch my reptiles*

*where other card was taken*
*from I think.*

*reg. street officers row*

N
E
W
S.

3. California National Guard bivouac at Camp Little, which was later occupied by the Alabama unit. (Pimería Alta Photo Collection)

4. Payday in silver on the Mexican border. (Courtesy National Archives, photo no. 111-SC-789 68E)

5. "Valley Forge" march in the snow from Saint-Blin to Faverolles, December 1917. (Courtesy National Archives, photo no. 111-SC-78968)

6. Company at bayonet drill before Colonel Screws, Villiers-sur-Suize, February 4, 1918. (Courtesy MacArthur Memorial Archives, Norfolk, VA, ph 00002400)

7. Major Garrett and Captain Underwood releasing pigeons in the trenches near Sainte-Pôle, May 13, 1918. (Courtesy MacArthur Memorial Archives, Norfolk, VA, ph 00002622)

8. Secretary Baker and General Menoher in Badonviller. (Courtesy MacArthur Memorial Archives, Norfolk, VA, ph 20002400)

9. K Company (Birmingham) and M Company (Oxford) soldiers of the 167th in Vacqueville: Private H. F. Couch, Private J. L. Dismukes, Lieutenant J. L. Cole, Private John B. McCain, May 13, 1918, on the day after a successful patrol killing five Germans. Couch was later killed at Saint-Mihiel. (Courtesy MacArthur Memorial Archives, Norfolk, VA, ph 00002609)

10. The 167th detraining in Vitry-la-Ville on their way to fight the battle of Champagne, June 24, 1918. (Courtesy National Archives, photo no. 111-SC-16783E)

11. Men of Company I from Opelika in front of their pup tents in camouflaged Champagne encampment, July 6, 1918. (Courtesy National Archives, photo no. 111-SC-17107)

12. General Henri E. J. Gouraud with Margaret Patterson Thorington, Laura Mae Hill, Eugenia McGough, and Elizabeth Anderson at the Montgomery Country Club, August 5, 1923, on the occasion of General Gouraud presenting the French Legion of Honor to Colonel William Preston Screws. (N. T. Frazer Collection. Courtesy Margaret Kohn McCall.)

13. For the 167th, the never-ending search for cooties continued. (Courtesy National Archives, photo no. 111-SC-17109)

14. 3rd Battalion signing payroll north of Suippes, July 6, 1918. (MacArthur Memorial Archives Collection, Norfolk, VA, ph 00002768)

15. Camouflage at Suippes, before the July 15 battle, July 6, 1918. (Courtesy MacArthur Memorial Archives, Norfolk, VA, ph 00002769)

16. Supply Company of the 167th cooking behind the front at Beuvardes. (Courtesy MacArthur Memorial Archives, Norfolk, VA, ph 00002778)

17. The Croix Rouge Farm. (Courtesy National Archives, photo no. 111-SC-160048E)

18. American dead of the 167th Infantry and 151st Machine Gun Battalion after the battle of the Ourcq. (Courtesy National Archives, photo no. 111-SC-18812)

19. Americans move to Saint-Mihiel on crowded roads. An ammunition wagon holds up the advance. (Courtesy National Archives, photo no. 111-SC-20902)

20. Captain Chevalier, Brigadier General MacArthur, and Lieutenant Colonel Bare between Beney and Saint-Benoit en Woëvre, September 15, 1918. (Courtesy National Archives)

21. Men of Company H, Alexander City, in dugouts by the road near Bouillonville, September 16, 1918, during the fighting at Saint-Mihiel. Two would be killed by shell fire less than five minutes later. (Courtesy National Archives, photo no. 111-SC-25317E)

22. View of Côte de Châtillon captured by 84th Brigade on October 16, 1918, taken October 20, 1918. (Courtesy MacArthur Memorial Archives, Norfolk, VA, ph 00002848)

23. New German wire in front of Hill 288, Côte de Châtillon. (Courtesy National Archives, photo no. 111-SC-76534E)

24. Officer of the 167th and a liberated family of Bulson near Sedan. (Courtesy MacArthur Memorial Archives, Norfolk, VA, ph 00002867)

25. Commissioned and noncommissioned officers of the 167th in Sinzig, Germany, January 1919. Sergeant Frazer is singled out by the circle in the photograph. (N. T. Frazer Collection)

26. Victory Arch, Commerce Street, a block north of Union Station, Montgomery, Alabama. (Courtesy of the Montgomery County Historical Society)

# 9

# The Côte de Châtillon in the Argonne, October 12–21, 1918

The American Expeditionary Forces changed its command structure just as the Rainbow's battle started at Côte de Châtillon. With a front of more than seventy miles, Pershing separated his army—a highly unorthodox move, but one required by army policy governing size of commands. He created the 1st US Army Group on October 12 to direct his original 1st US Army and the newly formed 2nd US Army. A division was made up of about 25,000 men, a corps 50,000, and an army 150,000. Pershing kept command of it all, a move that put him "on a par with both Haig and Pétain, heads of the British and French Armies. It was a necessary move, possibly overdue."[1]

Many commands changed. Major General Charles Pelot Summerall, nicknamed "Kill 'em All Summerall," was moved from 1st Division commander to V Corps commander.[2] His corps included the Rainbow Division, which he knew from having served as commander of its artillery at Camp Mills, New York.[3]

On the next day, October 13, Foch, supreme commander of the Allied Forces, told Pershing, "No more promises! Results!"[4] Summerall visited MacArthur at the 84th Brigade PC at La Neuve–Forge Farm located in a house behind the Rainbow front.[5] After a brief discussion the corps commander said, "Give me Châtillon, MacArthur, or a list of five thousand casualties." MacArthur replied, "All right, General, we will take it, or my name will head the list."[6] Summerall left without another word.

V Corps' mission was to capture the daunting Kriemhilde Stellung with two of the best divisions in the US Army: the 42nd would take Côte de Châtillon, and the 32nd would take Côte Dame Marie. Both large hills were in rough terrain, and capturing the Kriemhilde Stellung, the German "fourth line of defense," was the most difficult leadership task facing the Americans.[7]

## The 167th into Attack Position

On October 11 the 167th Infantry took over from the 1st Division's 18th Infantry directly in front of the Côte de Châtillon. If that pivot point of the massive German line fell, the Americans would be in a good position to cut off a large salient they had held since 1914. According to Ferrell, "The action at the Côte de Châtillon thus represented a poised moment, with the huge battle seeming to hinge on its success."[8]

Major Corbabon, chief of the French mission with the Rainbow, wrote about changes that had developed on battlefields and doctrine in battle, "the terraine . . . is much more difficult, the position stronger than that on the Ourcq . . . The idea of manoeuvre (rather than rigid adherence to attack formation) . . . . exists . . . It has become less rash and more skillful. . . . Liaison is good."[9]

The atmosphere was tense. Every trail and path in that heavily wooded area of rolling hills was soupy with mud and nearly impassable. German artillery blew out telephone lines almost as fast as they could be spliced together. Narrow ravines were filled with water. There were no roads or trails.[10]

Everything bore signs of the previous week's battle by the 1st Division.[11] Mud-covered and bloated bodies of German and American soldiers were strewn about, and the large proportion of American bodies was unnerving.[12] The green residue of mustard gas marked everything.[13] The few leaves remaining on trees were the only concealment from German artillery observers. Most of the ground was covered with water-filled shell holes, and the oak, beech, fir, and birch trees of the area were shot up and splintered. Clay sucked boots into the mud.

The Côte de Châtillon (Hill of Châtillon) (see fig. 22) looked down on the Rainbow Division. German defenses were the best it ever faced. Multiple bands of new barbed wire, covered day and night with machine gun and rifle fire, were backed by concrete fighting bunkers. There were some machine guns outside the protective wire. The front of the hill was bare, cleared of vegetation to create unobstructed fire lanes, and a narrow gauge railroad served it.[14]

The 167th's regimental PC was a hole in the side of Hill 263 nearly a mile back. That night MacArthur inspected it on a visit with Bare, its new commander, who later wrote, "While we were talking the Germans were . . . shelling the valley with . . . mustard and tear gas . . . neither of us could hardly see nor talk on account of the effect of the fumes."[15]

MacArthur, sometimes called the American d'Artagnan by the French (from *The Three Musketeers*), saw firsthand the dangers and tensions of his front.[16]

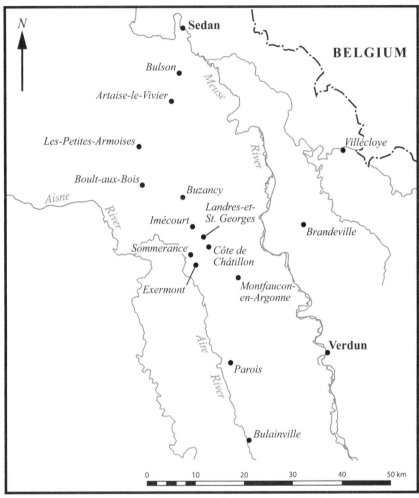

Station Map 4. The final drive: Meuse-Argonne and Sedan Stations: October 1–November 21, 1918. (1st Battalion Headquarters)

The regiment's point battalion, the 3rd, which had not been in the attack at Saint-Mihiel, drew this hard assignment. 2nd Battalion was in the support role on the forward slope of Hill 263 half a mile to the rear, with an OP (Observation Post) giving a good view of the terrain as far north as Landres-et-Saint-Georges.[17] 1st Battalion was in the reserve position on the back slope of Hill 263.

The 151st (Georgia) Machine Gun Battalion was on the forward slope of Hill 263, serving the 167th Infantry in a new way. Its commander, Major Cooper D.

Winn Jr. of Macon, Georgia, advocated machine gun fire accompanying the infantry advance rather than carrying the machine guns themselves forward with infantry in the attack. Reporting directly to MacArthur rather than to the infantry battalion commanders, he fired the first mission of his machine guns at the Côte de Châtillon in the opening attack on October 14 and its second in the attack on October 16.[18]

Winn personally placed his sixty-four Hotchkiss machine guns, which included all spares, on high ground that allowed them to shoot down into all of the Côte de Châtillon. He personally sited target areas with written instructions for each gun as to times and targets.[19] Winn began putting his guns and people in position as soon as Norris's 3rd Battalion took up its position on October 12. It would be four days before the final assault on the Côte de Châtillon, enough time for bringing up more than a million rounds of ammunition.[20]

An infantryman said, "In places, the slain . . . had not been buried. The cold rain to which the battlefields were then exposed had turned the flesh of the corpses to a livid blue or an ashy gray. Before finally being driven back, the Germans had removed the shoes from all dead Germans and Americans."[21]

## October 13: The Rainbow Division Prepares Its Attack

The 168th Infantry was on the right flank of the Rainbow. Patrols sent there by the Alabama regiment on the night of October 12 heard enemy voices but made no contact. On the afternoon of October 13, the 168th received an order to shift its lines to the right for more than a mile and a quarter to accommodate the 32nd Division's fighting at Côte Dame Marie.[22] The 168th followed these orders and failed to notify the 167th. Norris's K Company, under Lieutenant Royal Little, Brookline, Massachusetts, sent patrols to make contact with the 168th, but "the gap was so great that the German patrols filtered in."[23]

On October 13 the division issued its complicated attack order, which relied heavily on the 83rd Brigade's 165th and 166th Regiments. They were to advance with the 82st Division on its left. All four regiments of the Rainbow were to attack on October 14, in parallel with each other but in an irregular line.[24]

The 167th was closest to the Côte de Châtillon and the most advanced of the four regiments. The 168th's jump-off point for the attack was half a mile behind the Alabamians on the right of the dangerous gap. The 165th was on the 167th's immediate left, with the 166th on its far left.

Lieutenant General Robert Lee Bullard, a native of Lee County, Alabama, visited V Corps prior to his taking command of the 2nd US Army. He described the German defenses: "The way out is forward . . . through. . . . Wire tangled devilishly in forests . . . pillboxes, in succession, one covering another . . . no 'fox hole' cover for gunners here, but concrete, masonry, bits of trenches, more wire, defense in depth."[25]

## October 14: The 167th on the First Day of the Attack

The morning was overcast—dark, cold, and misty.[26] The 3rd Battalion of the 167th attacked at 8:30 A.M. from Bois de Romagne. Germans laid down artillery when the attackers advanced from a position three hundred yards south of the German-held La Musarde Farm. The battalion went forward for two hundred yards to a point of woods south of the German-held La Tuilerie Farm. Both farmhouses were near the base of the côte and had to be taken before the hill could be occupied.

The 3rd Battalion attack with four companies was across small fields bordered with hedges. It successfully took a strip outside two bands of new German wire,[27] about twenty-five feet apart (see fig. 23). Riflemen approaching the wire before the attack were kept at bay by machine gun fire.[28] Engineers sent to blow it also failed.

American artillery fire missions were called in, but they were unsuccessful in destroying it, as was usually the case when artillery was used against new wire.[29] Nonetheless, artillery was appreciated. Sergeant Elmer Sherwood, a crewmember, boasted that one of the Alabamians "sang our praises saying how good it felt having us paving the way for them."[30]

The 3rd battalion's advance on the right was led by K Company under Lieutenant Royal Little, a Harvard dropout with a commission from the officers school at Plattsburgh, New York. Its short but significant gain was made with rifle grenades against La Musarde Farm. They were near an opening, a chicane, through German wire immediately south of the Côte de Châtillon. It was cut for the German patrols to pass in and out of defensive positions on the côte before the previous weeks' advances by the 1st Division.

When 3rd Battalion advanced on October 14 the supporting 2nd Battalion moved forward from Hill 263, but it was not yet in the fight. The 1st Battalion, the reserve, was also not yet engaged, but it moved to the forward slope of Hill 263, where Winn's machine gunners were dug in and where they opened mass machine gun fire on that day.[31]

By nightfall, the point battalion of the 167th controlled everything outside German wire in front of the côte except the farmhouses of La Musarde and La Tuilerie. The German-held Tuilerie Farm changed hands for the first of several times as the 168th and the Germans fought over it. The gap between the Alabamians and the Iowans existed all day. Germans filtered into it and fired into the right flank of the 167th.[32] Weather cleared during the day and Germans observation planes came in.[33]

## The 165th Infantry Fights on October 14, the First Day

The New Yorkers jumped off at 8:30 and reached the second objective by 9:30. Renewing the attack at 11:20, it failed to draw even with the Alabamians. Royal Little, commanding the 167th's K Company said, "About noon on the 14th after visiting all my platoons I realized what a serious position we were in as Co. K's failure to advance was really responsible for all of the adjoining units as well."[34]

At 5:00 P.M. the point battalion of the 165th attacked again after an hour-long artillery preparation. It was stopped after a short advance. The Alabamians had not moved forward enough to cover the New Yorkers' right flank. Major "Wild Bill" Donovan, who led the New Yorkers' point battalion and essentially controlled that regiment's fight, recalled, "it did not look as if that regiment (the 167th), despite its wonderful fighting qualities, could get the Côte de Châtillon before we would find ourselves out in the open catching fire from it in our right flank."[35]

## The 168th Infantry on October 14, the First Day

The Iowans were the division's most successful regiment on October 14. Its 1st Battalion crawled up the slope of Hill 288 for four hours with the enemy shooting down at them from strong points.[36] By afternoon, the 168th held all of Hill 288.[37] It took prisoners and seized a mortar, firing it down on the Germans at La Tuilerie Farm. Success came at a cost of more than a hundred casualties, with the wounded being carried out by hand for miles.[38]

## The Night of October 14

The overall failure of the division attack on its first day depressed morale, particularly among the higher-ranking American officers.

The thousand-yard gap between the 167th and the 1st Battalion of the 168th continued to exist.[39] The 167th's point battalion fought to fix it and lost men in the process.

A captured German war diary noted, "according to prisoners brought in, the enemy suffered the severest losses," and added that "the front divisions have now repulsed all attacks." However, another diary admitted "a sense of depression about the future of Germany."[40]

Generals Menoher and MacArthur agreed to try something they had seen the Alabamians do with success at Croix Rouge Farm: send in a big bayonet attack. The plan called for three rifle companies of the 167th and a battalion of the 168th to attack on the next night, October 15, with no firing allowed. The 167th's point battalion commander resisted the order to the point of insubordination, calling it "nothing short of murder."[41] When the Iowans on Hill 288 received a similar bayonet attack order, their commanding officer likewise resisted, saying it was impossible for them to move to the north because of German wire and machine guns and a move to the left would have caused commingling with the 167th.

The bayonet attack order for the Iowans was rescinded that night.[42] However, the order for the 167th remained in place. The rifle company commanders of its 3rd Battalion argued, "Such an attack will never succeed."[43] Norris, their commander, went to the regimental PC that night and objected again, but Bare insisted that orders must be obeyed. During the night Norris was summoned back to regiment for another meeting the following day.

## October 15

Before leaving the front that morning, Norris shook hands with his officers and handed command to the senior captain, I Company's Thomas H. Fallaw, of Opelika. An experienced officer, Fallaw had served as an enlisted man on the Mexican border before receiving a direct commission at Camp Mills.

Norris believed himself to be on the way to reclassification, or SOS (the Service of Supply at Blois, France, or "Bluey," as the soldiers called it), as punishment for protesting the bayonet attack order.[44]

Early that morning, October 15, the 165th Infantry's point battalion commander, "Wild Bill" Donovan, was hit in the knee, causing the battalion and regiment to retreat. He was later to be awarded the Congressional Medal of Honor for having led the advance with vigor as far as it went.

At the end of the day General Summerall relieved the 83rd Brigade commander, Brigadier General Michael J. Lenihan; as well as the 165th Infantry Regiment's commanding officer, Colonel Harry D. Mitchell; his operations officer, Captain Van Santvoord Merrill-Smith; and the adjutant, Lieutenant Harold J. Betty. The withdrawal of the New Yorkers from the attack increased pressure on the other units.[45]

The 167th tried again to advance on October 15, sending out a strong patrol of four platoons. They were turned back.[46]

When Norris reported to Bare that morning he learned the 167th's bayonet attack order was rescinded.[47] Rather than punishment, Norris was given a new responsibility. He recalled, "my spirits went about as far up as they had been down . . . the regiment instead of having an assault which failed with heavy loss on its record, was going to be given their first real chance to capture the Côte de Châtillon."[48]

While all this was happening, the 168th successfully mopped up the remaining German machine guns on Hill 288, and in fighting directly in front of the Côte they took the house and barn at La Tuilerie Farm. They withdrew with heavy losses after which the entire 168th was ordered to help the point battalion. Until then the 168th had not brought its support or reserve battalions into action.

There were no tents for those waiting to go into battle. Miserable from lice, soldiers suffered through the cold, rainy night. They filtered back in small groups to be fed.[49]

Private Thomas S. Neibaur said, "there was no place to get out of the rain except in holes that we dug in the ground . . . we got corrugated iron to put over the top and keep the rain out."[50]

Regimental commanders of the 167th and 168th were given orders on the night of October 15 for the battle to be fought the next day. The front line of the 167th was virtually the same as on the night before.

Everything depended on the 84th Brigade with its 167th and 168th Regiments under MacArthur. They alone were in position to continue the unfolding battle.

Bare knew the attack plan when he said, "everything was in readiness to move forward."[51] He had attended an October 15 meeting with MacArthur, the 168th's Colonel Mathew A. Tinley, the 151st's Machine Gun Battalion's Major Cooper D. Winn Jr., and General Summerall, who participated by telephone. A battalion of the 167th was to attack from the côte's south and a battalion of the 168th was to attack from the east. Summerall wanted the position "taken by 6:00 P.M. (of the following day)."[52] MacArthur endorsed it.[53]

Ravee Norris, who was not at the meeting, later offered a slightly different explanation of how the plan developed—and in his version, the plan originated with him: Baer had gone to see General MacArthur the night of October 14 and

"MacArthur had gotten an airplane photograph made of the Cote de Chatillon and its defenses. This photograph showed one chicane or passage thru the wire a short distance to the right of Musarde farm. This chicane had been left by the Germans to enable reliefs and supplies to reach the men who had been in the woods from which the 1st Division had driven them and which we had taken over from that division."[54] Ravee Norris later continues, "While the overhead machine gun and the artillery concentration were keeping the Germans down I would send about a hundred men . . . along the hedge which ran from the edge of my wood up to the gap in the wire. From this they could reach a hedge which ran parallel to the southeast face of the Cote de Chatillon . . . then when the artillery and machine gun fire lifted and the Germans expecting a frontal attack from the west . . . they would be caught in the flank by my hundred men. . . . This plan was agreed upon."[55]

For the 167th's opening move, Captain Fallaw commanded an attack force of about a hundred men. He received the order to move out at dusk on October 15.[56] Norris was positioned behind the large force responsible for reorganizing stragglers and casuals.

Fallaw's men advanced in the dark toward the open space in the wire, north of La Musarde Farm. They were in the 168th Infantry's sector but the Iowans understood the plan and approved the encroachment. Once through the chicane, Fallaw moved the force back to the left of the gap, in preparation for the assault.[57] Everything was in place for the attack.[58]

According to the present-day owner of the land, a big hole there stored water for the German machine guns.[59] Remains of trenches are visible today from it in the direction of German machine gun positions.

For most of Fallaw's people it was the sixth day of attack. It was cold and they wore summer underwear.[60] Army lore has it that soldiers in combat usually found the danger of death to be less threatening than physical hardships. Many believed death happened to someone else, but the rain, cold, mud, and exhaustion were present and painful. Only those with constitutions of iron could rest.

## The Attack on October 16

At 6:10 A.M. Fallaw put his men in a skirmish line concealed by a hedge.[61] The 168th was ordered to work around Hill 288 to take La Tuilerie Farm, then assault the Côte de Châtillon from the southeast.[62]

Major Winn was set to execute his plan for the 151st Machine Gun Battalion's barrage. It was similar to what he had done on October 14th but heavier.

Shooting over the heads of the attackers directly into the German stronghold at about 2,300 yards, they were close enough and high enough to have clear coverage on all of the entire hill.[63]

Norris said, "About ten . . . the barrage came down."[64] It was stopped after thirty minutes and lifted to fire on the north of the côte for another fifteen minutes. Fallaw's battalion came under German fire and was stopped. The Americans regrouped in "a council of war" and agreed to charge en masse across the open hill after "three blasts of the whistle."[65]

Norris, by then hit in the foot by a shell fragment, described it: "Fallaw's attack cleaned up the machine guns on our side of the hill and then broke out on the left rear of the Germans. Those not killed, wounded or captured promptly ran north . . . they [Fallaw's men] established a line across the northern slope of the Cote de Chatillon. . . . To our right this line was continued by the Iowans."[66] At approximately 1:00 P.M. the attackers from the 168th began to converge on the hill with the Alabama troops.[67]

Sergeant Ralph M. Atkinson of Montgomery's Regimental Mortar Section, with one Stokes mortar and some riflemen, was instrumental in turning back a counterattack by about 250 Germans for which he received a DSC.[68] The attack broke off after fifteen minutes of hard fighting, allowing the 2nd Battalion commanded by Captain Abner Flowers to come up.[69] The point platoon leader of G Company was severely wounded and Sergeant Grady Parrish, of Daleville, took command and continued the advance. He received a DSC.[70]

Lieutenant Royal Little, K Company, had participated in Fallaw's morning attack.[71] In the afternoon, he organized a group of about a hundred men from the northwestern side of the hill and brought them up to join the 3rd and 2nd Battalion of the 167th attacks, which was linking up with the 168th. Little cleared this initiative with the 3rd Battalion before doing it.[72]

A second German counterattack at 3:00 P.M.[73] involved about two hundred Germans reorganized after their retreat through the woods.[74] An automatic rifleman, a replacement in M Company, Private Thomas S. Neibaur, Sugar City, Idaho, was shot three times after his loader and scout were killed. He fired fifty rounds into forty attackers killing many before being cornered. After being taken prisoner for a short time, he recovered a pistol with seven rounds, killed four Germans and captured eleven, all in full view of fellow soldiers.[75] He became the first Mormon ever and the second member of the 167th Infantry to receive the Congressional Medal of Honor.

Norris, wounded and out of the action, learning that the attack had succeeded, laughed with relief, and his eyes filled with tears.[76] He received a DSC.[77]

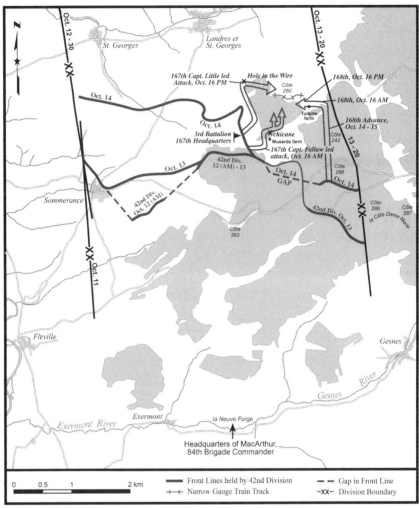

Battle Map 6. Cracking the Hindenburg Line at Côte de Châtillon, October 11–16, 1918.

1st Battalion completed the relief of the 2nd Battalion of the 167th "at 2:00 A.M. on October 17."[78] The battle was over.

## Glory for All

The entire Rainbow shared pride in the victory. It was made possible when the 167th and the 168th cleared Hill 288 and Côte de Châtillon.[79]

Credit for the breakthrough was given to MacArthur, Bare, Norris, and Fallaw of the 167th, and Ross of the 168th. As architect of the massed fire to cover the attack, Winn of the Georgia machine gunners was a major contributor as well.[80] The 167th and 168th equally shared the credits—and both suffered heavy losses. Casualties for the 167th in that fighting were 117 killed or died from wounds and 554 wounded. The 168th had 143 killed or died from wounds and 566 wounded.[81] Despite the big count, there was less resistance and fewer casualties than anticipated.[82] For this success, MacArthur cited the 151st Machine Gun Battalion for honors and recommended Bare, commander of the 167th for the DSC.[83] Winn was promoted and Bare received the Distinguished Service Medal, not the Distinguished Service Cross. Major Lloyd D. Ross of the 168th Infantry received the Distinguished Service Cross and promotion, not the Congressional Medal of Honor for which he was recommended. Captain Fallaw received a DSC.[84]

Summerall was pleased. He later wrote, "Of all things mentioned in the history of the American Army, the most exacting it was ever called on to do was to take the Côte de Châtillon in the Argonne, the key to the Kriemhilde Stellung strong line of defense of the German Army. That the Alabamians did and without that accomplishment the American Army's advance in November would have been utterly impossible. In all things that I have pride in, it is the fact that I was in command of troops who brought about that wonderful feat of arms."[85]

The victories at Côte de Châtillon and Côte Dame Marie gave Pershing continued independence, and the United States gained enhanced power with peace talks approaching.

The men would learn they were critical to the success in the Meuse-Argonne, "the largest battle in American history, in which 1.3 million men took part . . . 26,000 died and tens of thousands were wounded."[86]

# 10

# Final Drive to the Rhine and into Germany

After capturing the Côte de Châtillon the 42nd Division remained in Lieutenant General Hunter Liggett's 1st US Army for the final drive to Sedan.[1] Both Liggett and his V Corps commander, General Summerall, to whom the Rainbow reported, knew the division well.

In the hard weeks of near-constant fighting, supplies had been scarce. Now officers of the 167th arranged for Supply Company to bring "uniforms, underwear, blankets and overcoats to the men who had been living in wet clothes for almost three weeks."[2] Morale soared.

Their German opponents were not so fortunate. Hans Spiess of the Bavarian 2nd Infantry Division updated his family in an October 21 letter: "Right now I am still alive . . . we never have rest anymore, in a few days we had to retreat over 100 km, those who can't run are made prisoners, so don't be worried, it doesn't help, there are no more people here, it can't last much longer."[3] His death the following day, by a shot to the heart, underscores the poignancy of his last missive home.[4]

Screws returned from the field hospital to the regiment on the night of October 21, relieving Bare of command of the 167th at the PC he had occupied since October 16. The exhausted regiment found it "a welcome sight the night of October 21 when the 165th Infantry came to relieve [them]."[5] They slogged out that night through the deep mud to the Bois de Montrebeau between Exermont and Apremont and camped on the southern slope of the hill there until November 2. The regimental PC (Post of Command) was set up on the edge of the woods nearest Exermont, a far cry from an ideal campground but the best place they could find.[6] The 1st Division had badly torn up the site when taking it from the Germans, but the 167th was able to catch up on sleep. The twelve days at Exermont helped restore everyone's mental and physical condition. On October 26 Summerall boosted morale further with a glowing citation, "This Brigade, under the command of Brigadier General Douglas MacArthur, has manifested the highest soldierly qualities and has rendered service of the greatest value during the present operations. With a dash, courage and fighting spirit worthy of the best traditions of the American Army this brigade carried by assault the strongly fortified Hill 288."[7]

Despite being in range of German artillery, YMCA representatives Gertrude Bray of Pawtucket, Rhode Island, and Charles T. Coker of Gadsden, Alabama, visited the regiment with hot chocolate, sweets, and cigarettes.[8] Bray made between 150 and 175 gallons of hot chocolate each day.[9] They also brought word that the YMCA had established a number of rest areas in southeast France and had plans to arrange small rental cars for soldiers to tour the countryside.[10]

Rumors of leave had circulated since the regiment entered the trenches in February, but the Alabamians had always returned to battle without it. Because of intermittent German bombing, fires were prohibited, and in the fourteen hours of darkness that fell each night, rumors gained traction.[11] The cold, damp weather sent people to the field hospital every day. On October 23 Sergeant Will Frazer was evacuated with flu to a hospital near Paris. Despite being struck down by the epidemic, he rejoiced in getting to the French capital and said "he believed [his] war was over."[12]

When the sun finally did emerge, everyone longed to wash, as it had been a month since their last bath at a captured German shower point during the Saint-Mihiel drive. Getting water for boiling cootie-infested clothes also proved difficult. Troops rejoiced when they discovered another German bathhouse several miles from Exermont.[13]

## One More Push

The war wound down slowly and inconclusively as I Corps, III Corps, and V Corps were positioned for a new general offensive. Four American observation balloons were shot down on October 24, though crewmen saved themselves by parachuting from gondolas.

The offensive began with heavy artillery fire on the evening of October 31. By 3:30 A.M. on November 1, it seemed that all the guns in France were firing.[14] The 2nd Division went over the top at 5:30 A.M. near the Alabamians, who did not participate but were under a warning order to be ready to move on short notice.

The three corps chased a defeated foe in full flight toward the border.[15] The drastically weakened German forces, which had "suffered half a million casualties in the five months following the launch of their 1918 offensive," had "few reinforcements left except the overage and the very young, and so the retreat began."[16]

On the morning of November 2 the 167th marched through Fléville, stopping about a mile from Sommerance to camp overnight.[17] They left the next morning at 7:00 A.M. and passed through Sommerance, Landres-et-Saint-Georges, and Imécourt near the Côte de Châtillon. At Imécourt a rumor proclaimed the war over, but the artillery kept firing, and the columns continued marching through fields littered with dead Germans, unburied animals, abandoned equipment, and overlapping shell holes.[18] Three hundred American bombing planes passed over the Rainbow that morning.[19]

On November 4 the 167th continued marching toward the Meuse River, passing through Sivry-lès-Buzancy before stopping at Bar-lès-Buzancy and setting up the PC two miles north of Bar. German artillery fired that afternoon, but there were no casualties. That night German airplanes randomly bombed the restless and nervous Alabama regiment.[20]

On the morning of November 5 the men passed through Fontenoy to Saint-Pierremont. At noon the Rainbow, with regiments abreast, passed through the 78th Division. Keeping the 83rd Brigade on its left, the 167th had the 168th Infantry on its right. MacArthur set up the 84th PC in Bulson, where a happy French civilian greeted him with a five-course, potato-based meal.[21] The 167th regiment moved rapidly through scattered artillery fire before entering Les Grandes Armoises. The countryside had not been fought over or torn by artillery and offered a big change for soldiers unaccustomed to smooth fields and intact buildings.

The Alabamians passed into the Bois du Montdieu, slogging about five miles through mud in the rain. Lieutenant Colonel Bare set up the regiment's advanced PC there in La Grange du Mont, and the battalions camped around it.[22] Traffic slowed as American units advanced and Germans retreated with abandon. An evening storm soaked and chilled everyone. Night skies glowed as the retreating Germans burned material and supplies.

## Diplomatic Crisis

An episode that would become known as the Sedan Affair started on November 5, 1918, and lasted two days. As the 1st US Army's operations officer, Colonel George C. Marshall, prepared orders for both the 1st and 2nd US Armies, which were attacking to the east in the direction of Sedan.[23] Under prompting from Major General Fox Conner, chief of operations of the AEF, Marshall wrote in a November 5 order, "Pershing desires that the honor of entering Sedan should fall to the 1st American Army. He has every confidence that the troops of the I Corps, assisted by the V Corps, will enable him to realize this desire."[24] Pershing's plan ignored Sedan's immense historic importance to the French. In 1870 Prussians had captured Napoleon III there, causing the French to lose the Franco-Prussian War and suffer great humiliation. Consequently the then newly proclaimed German Empire annexed and claimed the provinces of Alsace and Lorraine.[25] Since 1914 the French had fought to retake Alsace and Lorraine and very much wanted the honor of entering Sedan first. Marshall's controversial order caused the American units to race with each other and with the French in attempting to reach Sedan. Contradictory orders caused confusion. Patrolling soldiers from the 1st Division unexpectedly bumped into men from Brigadier General Douglas MacArthur's 84th Brigade. Some overzealous 1st Division men arrested MacArthur.[26] The problem arose because V Corps had been ordered to have its divisions change course by almost ninety degrees, making its route going forward almost perpendicular to that of the other divisions.[27] MacArthur later explained, "The ambiguous and final sentence of the order, 'Boundaries will not be binding' precipitated what narrowly missed being one of the great tragedies of American history."[28]

The infuriated French high command worried about Americans encroaching into their sector with a possible catastrophic friendly fire. General Gouraud protested to Liggett, who quickly instructed Summerall to withdraw V Corps troops.[29] The Sedan Affair ended with the withdrawal of the Americans on November 7 and the beginning of the French move to take the significant city.

## The Collapse of Germany

The end of the war had been approaching for some time. On September 28 German general Ludendorff realized the true impact of the just-launched Allied offensive and made the decision to work toward an armistice.[30] However, Ludendorff refused to accept the Allied terms, and the war continued. Overruled for not accepting those terms, he then resigned on October 26.[31] The Germans continued to work toward an armistice without surrender, but their army was in no shape to fight on. It was believed that "by the first of November, the end was near."[32]

Mutinies took place in Germany during the time of the Sedan Affair. Navy men revolted in Kiel, and revolutionary councils were established in port cities.[33] By November 7–8 the rebellion reached all the big cities, from Berlin to Cologne and Munich.[34] Yet German soldiers displaying "some astonishingly fierce combat" in Sedan seemed not to have gotten that message.[35] All around Sedan and in Sedan itself, they put up a fierce resistance and vigorously defended the approach to their homeland. Rather than practicing a typical retreat, in which they used aggression only when necessary "to stop their pursuer," the Germans "left machine guns in every excellent position from which they could fire on, inflict loss on and hold up their pursuers."[36] The Germans knew they would not win the war, but they would not go quietly.

## The 167th Soldiers On

The 167th was not involved in the Sedan Affair but continued as part in the offensive operation begun on November 1. The regiment pushed through fog and rain on the morning of November 6, with 1st Battalion leading. C and D Companies met sporadic machine gun fire throughout the morning from ranges up to fifteen hundred yards.[37] A and B Companies halted at Artaise-le-Vivier for hot coffee served by French civilians who reported that the last Germans had left town an hour before. Afternoon brought more machine gun fire from the hills near Bulson, where 2nd and 3rd Battalions camped after moving seven miles and crossing swollen streams in muddy going. Corps orders called for a hard advance on the next day, November 7, when the 42nd would "crush and clear up such enemy forces as still remained in its sector, to organize its position, and to push contact patrols across the river Meuse."[38]

On November 7 Captain Abner Flowers ordered his 2nd Battalion forward in the fog at 6:30 A.M. on the Bulson-Thelonne Road. The troops marched in pairs before forming into combat groups when anticipating contact. E and G Companies advanced with F and H Companies in support.[39] They took heavy shell fire before reaching the crest of a hill, where they met machine gun fire. Taking the fire and pushing the Germans back, F and H were in the open when the fog suddenly lifted, exposing them. Corporals Beve G. Sherrill and Oliver O. Skipper were killed, along with Privates Homer J. Lackey, Asa A. McMillion, John Southers, and John Tor.[40] All Flowers's companies—E, F, G, and H—took incoming fire before going into positions for the night. First Lieutenant Ernest T. Bell of Newton, Iowa, was hit that day and died on November 11 from the injuries.[41] He is buried in the Meuse-Argonne Cemetery. First Lieutenants Hugh Hiller and Lew Trayser were wounded.[42] A splinter of a shell hit Flowers.[43] Losses might have been greater but for the shelter of a deep ravine.[44]

In a historic event, 3rd Battalion, then commanded by Captain Fallaw, also moved forward that day and succeeded in driving the Germans out of Thelonne by noon. Patrols from his K and L Companies went out at 1:00 P.M. and reached the Meuse River at 2:15 P.M., becoming the first of the Rainbow to do so.[45] Private Harry E. Rhodes, Selma, of L Company was killed in the advance, and four were wounded.[46] An AEF photographer, Lieutenant Estep, was killed while accompanying a Rainbow patrol.[47] The Germans fought well, firing and falling back with horse-drawn wagons carrying their machine guns from engagement to engagement.

Charles MacArthur wrote, "In the ensuing forty-eight hours before the whistle blew we raced through more slaughter than any other front—useless slaughter. . . . In seven days, we had averaged five meals and less than nine hours sleep, except for an occasional fifteen winks on the march."[48] Luckily, the men did receive a small amount of comfort, as 1st and 2nd Battalion kitchens arrived that afternoon with the men's first hot meals in sixty hours.[49] Screws established regimental headquarters in Bulson (see fig. 24), with the 1st Battalion setting up shelter halves in the rain and the 2nd taking over airplane hangars south of Bulson.[50]

Prattville's Joseph C. Killough, a member of A Company, was hit by a shell fragment near Bulson on November 8. He died in late November.[51] On November 9 the regimental headquarters and other elements moved through Maisoncelle to Artaise-le-Vivier.[52] Private Jessie J. Harwell was killed that day, the last man in the regiment to lose his life on the battlefield.[53]

## Final Things

Meanwhile, Allied ministers in Paris worked on the terms of an armistice some thought so harsh that the Germans would be unlikely to sign. That did not worry Foch. He knew the Germans were beaten. Pershing, however, questioned giving an armistice when the British, French, and Americans stood only a few days from beating the Germans once and for all.[54]

In the German Army's supreme headquarters at Hotel Britannique in Spa, Belgium, Field Marshal von Hindenburg's staff worked around the clock November 6–7 preparing for the Armistice Commission and selecting German representatives for the meeting.[55] The Allies required political representatives and would not meet with the kaiser's representatives or with the German Army. The French agreed to a local cease-fire to allow the German representatives to reach the meeting site, but the overall hostilities continued. Germans sent a message to the French asking where to meet Foch. The French replied with radioed instructions from the new transmitter atop the Eiffel Tower in Paris.

At 3 A.M. on November 8 a German delegation headed by Matthias Erzberger, head of the German Catholic Center Party, left its automobiles at Tergnier, south of Saint-Quentin, and transferred to a French railway coach.[56] Later in the morning near Rethondes in the Forest de Compiègne, forty miles from Paris, the delegates met Foch, who gave them seventy-two hours to obtain their government's consent to Allied terms. No Americans attended the meeting.[57]

On November 9, 1918, the German emperor abdicated. Upon asking the kaiser to leave headquarters, Field Marshal von Hindenburg said, "I cannot assume the responsibility for the Kaiser's being dragged to Berlin by mutinous troops and there handed over as a prisoner to the Revolutionary government."[58]

Parochial US Army matters continued despite the imminent end of the war. A November 10 telegram assigned Brigadier General Douglas MacArthur command of the 42nd Division.[59] Two weeks earlier Pershing had promised Major General Charles Rhodes that command, "effective at such time as operations permitted."[60] On the final morning of the war Rhodes assumed command of the division. But hours later Pershing reassigned him to the 34th Division to make way for MacArthur.[61] When that happened on November 11, Screws and Bare assumed command of the 84th Brigade and 167th Infantry Regiment, respectively. Those orders were then rescinded and they returned to their old commands.[62]

Lieutenant Hart described the night the war ended: "[We] celebrated the end of an era in our lives, an era of adventure and romance such as in our younger days we had never dreamed could only come to pass—filled with memories and friendships which only death itself can take from us."[63]

Despite British and French concerns with the AEF, "the attacks from 1 November to 11 November were carried out with daring and tremendous professional skill. As the Allied offensives continued their steady pressure, Germany began to unravel. Hindenburg later recalled that 'the pressure which the fresh American masses were putting upon our most sensitive point in the region of the Meuse was too strong. . . . The strain had become almost intolerable.'"[64]

On hearing news that the war might end, French general Charles Mangin exclaimed, "No, no, no! . . . We must go right into the heart of Germany, the armistice should be signed there. The Germans will not admit that they are beaten."[65]

Many agreed that letting the Germans avoid an admission of final defeat was an error that would be paid for in the future. Just as those people expected, Wilhelm, Crown Prince of Germany, proclaimed in a November 12 address, "The Army Group has not been defeated by force of arms! Hunger and bitter distress have conquered us! Proudly and with heads erect, my Army Group can leave the soil of France which the best German blood has won."[66]

The 167th rested for two days after the shooting stopped, then moved on to Imécourt, where it requisitioned full equipment for 250 men per company. On November 14 the regiment marched to the valley by Landres-et-Saint-Georges to join the entire Rainbow assembled there. The 31st "Dixie" Division at Camp Wheeler, Georgia, sent the 167th 650 replacements. Many were from Alabama and felt proud to join the famous regiment.[67] With an abundance of excitement and now-unnecessary ammunition, everybody shot off pyrotechnics that night in a celebration of red rockets, green signals, Very lights, six- and ten-star rockets, caterpillars, and white flares.

## The Army of Occupation

Major General Clement Flagler replaced MacArthur as Rainbow Division commander. On November 16 the division marched to Brandeville and received orders for a march to the Rhine to join the new Army of Occupation, the newly created Third US Army.[68] At a former German bathhouse near Brandeville, the men enjoyed showering, working to get rid of lice, and putting on new outfits.[69]

Going into the enemy's home country was a crowning reward, an honor for the Rainbow and the Alabama regiment, but the weather was freezing and winds were high. In order to fully equip Army of Occupation units, "The Army stripped divisions which were not going on into Germany."[70] Rainbow men welcomed new clothes, winter caps, new water carts, kitchens, and wagons.

At Brandeville, Bare was promoted to colonel and transferred from the 167th to command Division Trains. Some of the men felt that Screws should have been made a brigadier general on active duty.[71]

The regiment started its two-hundred-mile trip to Germany with the infantry traveling on foot to Villecloye on November 20.[72] The next day it crossed from France into Belgium for billeting that night at Saint-Mard, a site with no war-damaged houses. Using an orderly billeting process, each unit sent a billeting officer ahead to its next assigned town to coordinate housing with a civilian official.[73] Together they worked out nightly arrangements for the Alabama soldiers, who slept in beds with sheets and heavy comforters. The countryside, untouched by war, supported cattle, chickens, sheep, ducks, and an abundance of good-quality fresh food. Supply Company helped the companies procure fowl, eggs, and fresh milk.

Rainbow Division men, artillery, trucks, wagons, and motorcycles filled the roads. Belgians welcomed them with flowers, garlands, and evergreen arches strung along the roadway. The Americans remembered the 1914 rape of neutral Belgium by the Germans and the subsequent horror stories that helped trigger the United Kingdom's entry into the war. Children sang and flags flew. Local bands played in every village. Cheering and singing people lined the roads. The 167th Infantry band marched at the head of the regimental column and played a selection that included the "Star-Spangled Banner" and "Dixie." Every night's stop was pleasant.[74]

They reached Habergy, Belgium, on November 22.[75] Censorship stopped. The soldiers could write home anything they wanted except "slander against the President of the United States and the YMCA."[76] The next day they passed through Arlon, Belgium, before entering Luxembourg. The regiment stayed at Hobscheid, Luxembourg, until December 1. Cold weather continued, but the mountains were beautiful. Units used the time for drills and practices. B Company's Lieutenant Edward Wren wrote his mother on November 29, 1918: "We are drilling and getting back some of the old spirit that of course active campaigning took away from us. Losing the old men and continuously getting new men to your organizations. Since it is over we sure miss the old boys and especially the ones that were killed in action and we had quite a few to go that way. I think we have about 35 men with us now who came with us."[77] Flagler reviewed the entire division on November 30. Flagler had not been with the Rainbow in combat, which hurt his popularity. His recently imposed drill, ceremony, and having men standing in the cold made him even less popular.[78]

On the afternoon of December 3 the regiment crossed into Germany. The men tramped through hilly, wooded country filled with cliffs and valleys. There the main roads were reserved for artillery, with infantry troops taking the more scenic and difficult routes. After eight days the regiment arrived at Dockweiler, where it spent five days. Many of the French towns in which the regiment served had suffered from the war, but the German towns were unscathed. When the troops reached a community, all they had to do was fall into good German beds and go to sleep. The difference between France and Germany was not lost on the men from Alabama.[79]

Some animosities bubbled over, as in an incident involving men from the 150th Machine Gun Battalion assigned to a small house. They were given a room filled with furniture the German family refused to remove, prompting the soldiers to do it themselves. One soldier recalled, "As I went to remove a large canvas painting of the Kaiser from the wall, the whole family let out a howl, telling us in no uncertain terms that he was the Kaiser. I saw that they would obey the Kaiser if no one else. So I drew my Colt .45 automatic and smashed the glass. Then I took the picture down and put it outside with the rest of the furniture. I then took from my pocket a picture of myself taken in France and hung it on the wall in the same place, telling them, 'Hoch, dat is der Kaiser.'"[80]

Another telling incident occurred on December 5, 1918, when a German-speaking doughboy talked to a man who had been a top sergeant in a German outfit. The American asked "if he was not glad the war was over," to which the reply was "No." The German went on to say, "never did I taste defeat, and then to have the Germans give up at this stage, "[sic] No, I wish they were still fighting."[81]

On December 16 they marched all day down the valleys leading to the Rhine, with the scenery becoming more beautiful as they approached the river. A rainbow appeared over the valley as the unit entered Sinzig. Headquarters Company, 3rd Battalion, Machine Gun Company, and Supply were billeted in town; 2nd Battalion in nearby Westum; and 1st Battalion at Loehndorf. Screws took up residence in a beautiful *Schloss*, or castle.[82]

Men resumed their training schedule, and rifle ranges were opened. On December 18, C Company's Private Amos D. Brenneman wrote his sister, "we are treated better by the German people then I expected," but lamented, "Xmas will soon be here and I sure wish I could be home."[83] While Germany was not home, a sense of routine emerged. Regular company messes served meals. Fraternizing was forbidden but took place anyway. Relationships developed between soldiers and German women. Inflation made German currency nearly worthless, and army pay became more valuable when converted into marks. Soldiers spent money and courted, enjoying wine and women at ridiculously low prices.[84] Aware of such behavior, the army took strong measures to lower the VD rate before soldiers returned home.[85]

Civilians seemed unaware of the political situation throughout Germany. They knew nothing about the short-lived revolution in Berlin led by Spartakists, a communist group that believed Germany ripe for revolution. Demoralized soldiers formed military groups called Freikorps, which organized themselves to fight against the communists and would play a major and unhealthy role during the counterrevolution and against the Weimar Republic. The deteriorating German political situation kept the Army of Occupation on alert. The staff of the 167th continued to put out training schedules and practice plans to cover the event of a German remobilization.[86] An extensive December 27, 1918, order was issued by division headquarters. It covered a battle plan to reengage the Germans.[87]

In the meantime, Will Frazer, hospitalized near Paris, had sufficiently recovered to get his uniform from a hospital locker and go into the city to have his picture taken on November 10, 1918. When released from the hospital he received a letter of passage to rejoin his unit, which he located in the pages of the *Herald Tribune*. Traveling alone or with whatever companions fell in along the way, Will rode trains and trucks where he could and walked through the countryside. He tarried with a companion for several days near Toul, in no hurry to leave France. He enjoyed the adoration of the French, appreciated their lack of inhibition, and would respect them all of his life. Duty did finally call, however, and Will rejoined his friend Scottie in Sinzig, Germany, on Christmas Day.[88]

That holiday for Private Brenneman ended up better than he feared, as he noted in a December 31 letter home: "this was the happy [sic] Xmas ever spent, we did not have know [sic] more then [sic] any other day but to think about the war being over was what made ever body [sic] happy."[89]

The new year brought a number of orders for the 84th Brigade. On January 17, 1919, one instructed the 1st Battalion to put on a demonstration of a battalion in assault. It had a tragic outcome, as "one man was killed and about fifteen were wounded because they used live ammunition."[90] A training schedule calling for a month of field problems was issued on January 31, and regimental maneuvers with artillery were scheduled for February 14.

Still, free time existed, and some men used passes to see the country. Many visited France. A regimental football team suffered a 12–0 defeat from the 150th Machine Gun Battalion. The AEF had introduced boxing to Europe, and the YMCA held boxing matches and showed movies.[91] One veteran wrote home, "Feb. 15, 1919 . . . Went to the theater tonight to see moving pictures of the 42nd Div. in action. Everything from some lousy soldier readying [sic] his shirt to ruined villages. It's a funny sensation to be reminded of things you went thru by pictures. They sure were vivid. Scenes of every front except the last one, the Argonne-Meuse."[92]

On March 8 men met at the Sinzig YMCA to organize a Rainbow Division Association (see fig. 25).[93] The regiment published a newspaper, the *Alabamian*, "an irreverent publication with no respect for rank. In one issue it was reported:

'Chaplain Smith recently returned from a pilgrimage to Cologne, where he worshipped at the cathedral. He said the beer there is excellent.'"[94] As part of his chaplain duties at the front, Smith had buried soldiers, acted as a censor, organized entertainment when in garrison, and written letters for the illiterate.[95]

For three months the soldiers did little but train and travel for pleasure. Then on March 16 Pershing reviewed the entire 42nd Division—some thirty thousand men— between Kriip and Remagen.[96] He also presented awards, including Corporal Sidney Manning's Congressional Medal of Honor and Lieutenant Wren's Distinguished Service Cross.[97] A few days later, Pershing wrote a letter to the division addressed to Flagler commending all of the Rainbow's accomplishments in France.[98]

Before leaving Germany the 42nd Division issued an important announcement to all other units in the US Army, asserting that it spent more days in the trenches in the face of the enemy, gained more ground against the enemy, and marched farther in its operations than any other AEF Division. It had been opposed by the best German Army divisions and made its record at their expense. Its fighting power had been officially mentioned by the American, French, and German commands, and its order and discipline had elicited the admiration of the Germans in its area of occupation.[99]

Then the most coveted news arrived. The 167th would leave Germany by train about April 6. The division would move about 4,500 men a day, with forty-five men assigned to each of the boxcars outfitted with wooden bunks. For the sixty-hour trip to the Atlantic, officers rode in ordinary passenger cars with wooden seats. The 167th went to Camp Pontanezen outside of Brest, France, before boarding US Navy warships. Companies M and L boarded the *Minnesota*; Companies E, F, G, H, L, K, and Machine Gun Company boarded the *Montana*; and Screws, Supply Company, Headquarters Company, the Sanitary Detachment, and 1st Battalion with Companies A, B, C, and D boarded the *North Carolina*. Although the men had long awaited the departure, sadness was in the air. Corporal John B. Hayes of Company I, 167th, reflected that only fifty men who had come with him to France would be on the return voyage: "Many of the 50 had been wounded. During its combat operations, Co. I received 800 replacements to keep its war strength at 250 men."[100] The Alabama men had served tenaciously and fiercely, and they had forged deep bonds in the process. The transition to domestic life back home, while welcome, also raised anxieties. The men had seen—and in many estimates, even saved—the world. Now they would return to their lives in Alabama, which seemed, to some, sedate by comparison.

# 11
# Return of the Immortals,
# May 7–13, 1919

Few family members met the returning heroes in New York, but two women from Greenville were there. Although D Company's Sergeant Worth Lewis had been killed in the bayonet attack at Croix Rouge Farm on July 26, 1918, his mother and sister welcomed the debarking regiment on April 25, 1919.[1] The two ladies had visited Camp Mills in 1917 to see the unit off to France, and this welcoming closed the circle. The Lewis family greeted D Company as family members, and the men loved them for it.[2]

Alabama governor Thomas E. Kilby sent official representatives at state expense to greet the regiment, which had lost almost three-fourths of all Alabama soldiers killed in the war. Kilby assigned Lieutenant Governor Herman Miller to lead a thirty-five-person reception committee greeting the regiment from a tugboat in New York Harbor, then to visit it in Hoboken, New Jersey, and in its temporary home at Camp Merritt, New Jersey. The delegation met with Screws's staff to plan the 167th's return to Alabama and to connect it with local welcoming committees in Huntsville, Albany-Decatur, Anniston, Birmingham, Montgomery, and Mobile.[3]

The waiting period from April 25 to May 7 passed quickly at Camp Merritt. Officials oversaw administration, assigning units to barracks and trains, processing soldiers, and issuing army orders for travel, pay, and discharge. The regiment processed fifty-one officers and about fourteen hundred men for return to the state and discharge at Camp Shelby, Mississippi.[4] Those individuals not from Alabama were mustered out at Camp Merritt if they wished, although they were invited to travel to Alabama for the celebrations.[5] Hospitalized veterans and discharged casuals also received invitations.

Large numbers of Alabama soldiers visited New York City, where they were welcomed with open arms. "Wild Bill" Donovan, national hero and darling of the New Yorkers, in singling out the Alabamians for praise had described them as "a wild bunch, not knowing fear."[6] It was a high compliment from the man who later established the Office of Strategic Services—a precursor to the Central Intelligence Agency—in World War II and who, at the time of his death, was the most decorated man in America.[7]

No other American division was as well known in New York as the Rainbow. Of the forty-one divisions in France at the end of the war, the 1st, 2nd, 42nd, and 89th had proven themselves the best.[8] The 42nd, the only National Guard division among them, suffered casualties of 2,950 killed and 13,292 wounded—a total greater than half the division's authorized strength of 28,000. The division incurred one-sixteenth of all casualties in the AEF. New York City honored all its regiments—the 165th, 166th, 167th, and 168th—and all of its support troops.

The camaraderie was mutual, and the Alabamians were happy when the beloved Father Duffy was honored with a large statue in Times Square funded by donations. They came from many, including "many men of the Rainbow from all over the country."[9] He had risen to the senior chaplain of the 42nd Division, but, more than that, he was beloved and respected by all of the division's men and the nation.[10]

W. T. Sheehan, editor of the *Montgomery Advertiser*, traveled to New York and sent home stories about the regiment's time at Camp Merritt.[11] Various welcoming committees exchanged flurries of telegrams with the House Committee on Military Affairs in Washington. The *Montgomery Advertiser* and other newspapers throughout the state carried information about events, and all reception committees prepared to activate their plans on forty-eight to sixty hours' notice.

Eventually, the men were released, and three troop trains of top-of-the-line, all steel, luxurious Pullman cars with a sleeping berth for every soldier left Camp Merritt on May 7. The soldiers had never traveled first class before, and they reveled in the luxury as they turned south toward home and glory.[12]

## The Journey through Alabama

En route to their mustering-out site in Mississippi, the men would travel through much of Alabama and various communities on their way to planned celebrations. The men entered Alabama on May 9 to a wide range of fanfare.

The fifteen-car train carrying D and E Companies and their many Huntsville men stopped in Madison County, where pretty girls bombarded the soldiers with flowers. The *Huntsville Daily Times* reported that thousands of citizens met the soldiers at the train station.[13]

After leaving Huntsville, that train stopped at 3:00 P.M. in Albany-Decatur (later renamed Decatur), home of E Company, where it and other soldiers paraded through town in battle gear, delighting thousands of schoolchildren who pelted them with flowers. The Morgan County Red Cross fed the troops, who departed for Birmingham at 9:00 P.M. When the train pulled out of town, the twin cities of Albany and Decatur blew every whistle and rang all bells.[14]

Colonel Bare, the original organizer of Gadsden's F Company, called that city home, so the train carrying him stopped there in his honor. He, Screws, the regimental band, and F Company paraded through town, joined by all other troops from their train. The *Gadsden Times-News* reported that more than ten thousand visitors lined the streets, and citizens held a dinner in Screws's honor.[15]

Meanwhile, the train carrying Anniston's and Oxford's Company M stopped in Anniston at 7:15 P.M. Here, as in most towns, soldiers received food and flowers. Led by Anniston's Major Ravee Norris, the contingent paraded in full battle gear before their trains left for Birmingham.

The entire regiment participated in the parade and celebration in Birmingham, where crowds besieged Terminal Station long before the first train arrived at 8:37 P.M. on May 9.[16] Roars greeted Screws as he jumped onto the platform. By midnight all units had arrived, and happy parties filled the streets until very late.[17] Screws was put up in the Tutwiler Hotel.

People came from all over the state for the next day's honors, and it was called "the biggest day in Birmingham history."[18] The front page praised "Alabama's Immortal Heroes of the 167th Infantry."[19] Other papers used the same reference, calling the regiment's men "The Immortals." Mr. Bernard, window trimmer at the Louis Saks Clothing Company, designed a beautiful memorial arch for soldiers to pass through at the conclusion of the triumphal parade in Wilson Park.

On Saturday morning the Terminal Station was lined with tables draped in white. Early risers found coffee, tobacco, and chocolate.[20] Red Cross workers reached the station at 4:00 A.M. to prepare a bountiful breakfast of chicken hash, bacon, eggs, hot rolls, and bananas. After breakfast and a complimentary film at the Lyric Theatre, the troops marched to 17th Street between 6th and 8th Avenues, where they stacked arms and waited.[21]

John T. Yeatman oversaw parade arrangements, and Borden Burr, the Birmingham lawyer who came to serve the regiment as a YMCA representative in

Champagne and Croix Rouge Farm, was chairman of the general committee.[22] The parade started at 11:00 A.M. behind a US Navy band. Nine other bands occupied various places on the parade route.[23] The roars and cheers of the crowd—estimated to be a hundred thousand people—surged above the martial music.[24] The regimental band preceded the soldiers, who marched behind a tall, uniformed ex-soldier of the Union Army carrying an American flag and flanked by Confederate veterans in gray. The 167th wore full battle array as it marched through streets filled with cheering, crying, singing, and shouting people. Hundreds of thousands of flowers showered the soldiers.[25]

The *Birmingham News* editorialized: "There is no full-grown red blooded American on the streets of Birmingham but who would not be proud and glad to swap his piping, peaceful liberty as a civilian for the privilege of swinging down the avenues with those hardened heroes from overseas. They mixed in with great game. . . . They were the Crusaders. We who stayed were their servants."[26]

An army plane flew overhead, crossing back and forth as the soldiers marched. The balcony of the Tutwiler Hotel, overlooking 20th Street, served as the parade reviewing stand. The 21st Street viaduct had just been completed, and the doughboys from the 167th were the first to cross it in a parade.

The exclusive South Highlands neighborhood transformed into a welcome home carnival, with a block assigned to every company for its people to receive visitors when the parade ended. The finest automobiles in Birmingham gave free tours of the city to any soldier who desired. That evening about a thousand cars moved from downtown to West 20th Street, where a street dance lasted into the night.[27]

After such extravagance, the men rested into the morning, and the three troop trains pulled out of Birmingham in the late afternoon on May 11. Birmingham offered a lovely welcome, but grand parades and receptions awaited the men in Montgomery and Mobile.[28]

## Triumphant Return to Montgomery

Thousands gathered in Montgomery as the first troop train pulled into the cavernous Union Station at 8:00 P.M. on Sunday.[29] Screws, cigar in the corner of his mouth, stepped off to the ground first. Swept up by a surging mass of people, he and the officers and men of F, H, and L Companies were embraced and cheered by the happy and proud crowd.[30] The other two trains pulled in at 9:30 and 10:15 P.M. Soldiers and civilians swarmed through the Victorian terminal and into the city for much of the night. The troop trains remained open, and the men were not required to check in until 6:00 A.M.[31]

Monday, May 12, dawned bright to become "the day of all days," declared by the *Montgomery Advertiser* to be the greatest in the city's history.[32] The regiment had first mobilized and come together there nearly three years earlier, in June 1916, for deployment to the Mexican border.[33] These returning veterans were those remaining of the 167th's 3,677 officers and men who began their journey to France from this very same railroad station eighteen months earlier.

As recruits in 1916 and as an untested regiment in 1917, the men of the 167th had paraded before many of these same citizens. This time, though, they were victorious veterans, a vital part of the Rainbow Division's success. The Alabamians were known all over France as "Alabama Wildcats" and the "Alabama Wildmen."[34] Friend and enemy alike saw these men as different, a special breed, willing to fight, and showing little fear. James Hopper, correspondent for *Collier's Weekly* in Europe from 1914 until the end of the war, wrote of the Alabama boys that they had acquired, "a name for ferocity in battle and turbulence when at rest."[35] Father Duffy said, "No regiment, indeed, has a higher reputation throughout the United States than the wild bunch that was Alabama's contribution to the Rainbow Division."[36]

Montgomery's official welcome home ceremony took place at the intersection of Water and Commerce Streets at 8:30 A.M. People crowded in to be seen with the parade marshal, Judge Charles R. Bricken of the Alabama Supreme Court, and assistant parade marshal William C. Oates Jr., son of a Civil War hero and former governor. The parade started at 10:30 A.M.[37] The smartly turned out troops responded with "spit and polish" precision for their triumphal parade. Taking rifles from stacked arms, men raced to fall into ranks at the position of order arms, with metal rifle butts clanging as they slammed into the brick street. Senior officers bellowed commands that echoed down the line for battalion and company commanders to repeat. They shouted orders for "inspection arms," and rifle bolts clashed open as metal hit metal. At the command of "right shoulder arms," men placed their rifles on their shoulders as their hands slapped the rifle's wooden parts and leather slings. The slings' metal fixtures rattled up and down the lines as they hit wooden parts of the rifle. Airplanes droned overhead. There were shouts and tears everywhere, as Montgomery had "never had such a celebration or such a crowd in all her history."[38]

Thousands of Montgomerians and visitors, "drunk with joy," spilled into downtown.[39] The mass of cheering, excited black and white men, women, and children extended from Union Station to the capitol, almost a mile.[40] People "dressed in style for the occasion," showing off their finest Sunday clothes.[41]

A platoon of mounted police cleared the parade route. A hundred young ladies in full-length flowing white gowns followed, scattering roses as they went. Walking in eight files in front of the soldiers, they approached the four-story-high triumphal arch called the Rainbow Arch (see fig. 26), built across the street in the second block of Commerce.[42] A beautiful woman posed atop of it as the Goddess of Liberty, with boy scouts at her side. Children dressed as cupids scattered roses before the arch. Governor Kilby, Chief Justice John C. Anderson, Mayor W. T. Robertson, and other dignitaries in automobiles followed the advancing files of young ladies. The last open car carried sponsors of the parade, Misses Thorington, LeGrande, Thigpen, Anderson, and McGough, daughters of prominent citizens.[43]

Screws and Bare led the parade on foot in steel helmets, web equipment, gas masks, and pistols, marching behind the national and regimental colors flanked by armed guards.[44] Screws, a professional soldier and native of Alabama, had trained and led these volunteers, ordinary people, into combat.

A catafalque—the kind used to carry the bodies of fallen warriors or royalty—followed the colors. The shouting crowd turned silent at the catafalque's appearance, and the band played Chopin's Funeral March.[45] Mounted on poles, it was carried in sedan chair fashion by eight soldiers wearing steel helmets and carrying backpacks with bayonet holsters attached. They wore ammunition belts with leather-holstered automatic pistols, canvas-covered canteens, and first-aid kits. Eight other soldiers in full battle gear held ribbons extending to flowers on the catafalque. The casket bore the numerals 616, made of gold stars and symbolizing the regiment's men killed or missing in action in France. Heads bowed as the catafalque and escort passed.

The regimental staff and the band followed the catafalque as it passed under the arch of victory. Frantic cheering and shouting grew louder when the troops appeared and as locals and families recognized individual units and loved ones.[46] The soldiers marched in wave after wave, unsmiling, following the band in traditional order—1st Battalion, then 2nd, then 3rd—each led by its staff and each with four rifle companies led by its officers. Then came a battalion formation made up of special troops, the Machine Gun Company, Supply Company, and the Sanitary Department, each led by its officers on foot.[47] Montgomery had never had such a triumphant parade, nor has it seen such a thing since.[48] They approached the fountain at Court Square, called the Fountain of Roses, decorated with garlands of evergreens and roses.[49]

As they neared the capitol at the head of Dexter Avenue, troops passed under a high, white wooden bridge. Dripping with flowers and ribbons it made a living rainbow, and on it stood the hundred young ladies in flowing dresses who had preceded the soldiers in the parade. The ladies threw thousands of flowers on the marchers passing underneath, then descended and mixed with the crowd after the long column passed.

The regiment turned south off Dexter, passed in front of the capitol on Bainbridge, and marched to Washington Avenue. There it passed through a surging crowd before massing in ranks on the south grounds of the capitol.[50]

The band from the Alabama Polytechnic Institute, called the Auburn Band, played for the ceremonies, which included seventeen speeches, songs, and responses.[51] At 1:00 P.M. soldiers lunched in the city auditorium. Court Square was the scene of a street festival from 3:00 to 6:00 P.M., with music by the 167th Infantry Band and the Shriners Band. A reception at the Murphy House on Madison Avenue, then used as the Elks Club, preceded a reception and military ball at the nearby city auditorium from 7:30 to 11:00 P.M. An open air festival on Perry Street lasted from 5:00 to 11:00 P.M.[52]

Also on Perry Street, the grandest homes in town opened as public reception centers for the regiment in the afternoon and evening. Each served as headquarters for a specific company, a place for its officers and soldiers to receive families and friends in an elegant atmosphere.[53]

The troop trains pulled out of Montgomery for Mobile after midnight. The men had come back to the place where they started, but their journey had not yet ended.

## Onward to Camp Shelby

On May 13 the regiment's three trains loaded with "Alabama's Husky Heroes" arrived in Mobile between 8:30 and 9:30 A.M. Thousands lined the tracks and cheered.[54] Starting at 10:00 A.M., troops marched four abreast in platoons of about fifty men behind the regimental staff and the band in a parade equal to the Montgomery parade. Crowds were fifteen people deep and lined both sides of the streets. Starting at the depot, the regiment marched in full combat gear through Government, Royal, Saint Francis, Conception, and Water Streets before countermarching and returning to the depot for the stacking of arms. The *Mobile News-Item* reported, "Their entry into Mobile was marked by probably the most remarkable demonstration this city has ever witnessed. Thousands of visitors, added to practically the entire population of Mobile and surrounding territory, lined Government Street where the soldiers marched in triumph and from the moment that the soldier lads started from the L & N depot great cheers rent the air."[55]

The newspaper highlighted the air of revelry, stating that it exceeded the crowds and excitement of Mardi Gras. It remarked on the solemnity interspersed among the jubilant celebrations, "Seeing them march. . . . Their stern young faces bedewed with sweat under the heavy helmets wore a look that choked the cheers in the throats of some of those who watched. The wound stripes on so unbelievably many arms, the scars on the brown cheeks were the price of a thousand blessings."[56]

Screws accepted the gift of a flag from Rabbi A. G. Moses. Every officer and soldier received a bronze medal in an impressive ceremony in the municipal shed after the parade. All of the clubs and halls of the city held afternoon receptions. It was the largest homecoming ever staged in Mobile. Crowds gathered in Bienville Square at 5:30 P.M. for the public dance to be held under the municipal shed at 8:00 P.M.[57] The heroes were cheered, fed, feted, decorated, and promenaded.[58]

In large red letters the headline of the evening newspaper proclaimed, "ALABAMA VETERANS HOLD CITY CAPTIVE; LEAVE FOR CAMP SHELBY LATE TONIGHT."[59]

The regiment's trains pulled out after midnight for Camp Shelby in Hattiesburg, Mississippi, to officially conclude their long tour of duty. Most would return to Alabama and resume their everyday lives. But they would never forget the welcome their state gave them when they returned home from the Great War. And, of course, memories of the war itself—the friendships, the ghosts, the cooties and mud—stayed with the men throughout their lives. No longer just citizens of a state, the men of the 167th were forever part of the great "Alabam'."

# Epilogue

People remember the Great War mostly for having saved Europe from Imperial Germany. For some Americans who were involved, it offered tough schooling for a successful life in business, government, and the military. But that was not always the case. Many in the 167th could never escape the fear that accompanied their first patrols in the no-man's-land of the Lorraine. They could not shake the terror of seeing a mass of German infantry running toward them in Champagne, or of trying to dodge German machine gun fire and facing bayonets in the assault at Croix Rouge Farm, or of being told to "soldier on" with a unit at half strength, physically and mentally exhausted on the heights of the Ourcq. Those who survived those battles participated in the attack at Saint-Mihiel before being called on to fight the Rainbow's toughest battle of the war, breaking the Hindenburg Line at the Côte de Châtillon.

After such feats, adjusting to everyday life proved challenging for some. Many of those trials wrought destruction on personal lives. Some never recovered, and many succumbed to alcoholism. That is what happened to the two men who loomed so large in my childhood experience: my father, William Johnson Frazer, and his best friend Chester Kirk Scott.

After the war, Will Frazer married Margaret Thompson, nicknamed "Chinkie," from Montgomery, Alabama. Young, attractive, and smitten with hero worship, she had been featured as a beauty in the Auburn University yearbook. Will took her to Greenville, where he owned the town's first laundry and dry cleaning business. He became first lieutenant in the local National Guard Cavalry Troop and completed the company officers school at Fort Riley, Kansas. He served as a Boy Scout leader for a time and was a charter member of the Greenville Country Club. Chinkie organized the American Legion Women's Auxiliary and helped with the business. Will's National Guard commission ended when he was deemed not to have enough education to be promoted. His alcoholism undoubt-edly contributed to that. Will was too proud to accept being passed over. There were two sons, more drinking, separation, reconciliation, and a divorce in 1937. Chinkie left Greenville, taking the boys.

A second wife, Carolyn Bryan, and her family pulled Will out of alcoholism in later years, but it was too late to put together what had once been a promis-ing life. Will told his sons, both of whom held graduate degrees from Ivy League universities, that he had not passed a day for fifty years without regretting his lack of education.

Chester Scott returned to Greenville and married Gertrude "Trudie" Pride of Uniontown, Alabama. A pretty and vivacious graduate of the University of Ala-bama, she was a good catch, as they said in those days. Trudie played the piano and had acted in lead roles in college dramatics with the Blackfriars, the univer-sity theater troop. They made their home in a comfortable frame house and were on the guest lists for many dances and fashionable parties throughout south Ala-bama. They also had two sons. Scottie drank heavily and became alcoholic, keep-ing a jug of corn whiskey under the bed and his army issue 1903 Springfield rifle over the fireplace. His .45 automatic pistol, the one he carried in France, stayed on the night table, always loaded and in full view. His small business faltered. Late on the night of December 16, 1937, he telephoned Will Frazer and said he was going to kill himself. Will arrived too late. Scottie had taken his life with the .45. His grave stands by itself in Greenville's Magnolia Cemetery and is marked by a government headstone placed there by friends in the American Legion.

To all of those whose story of heroism and sacrifice remains untold, I dedi-cate this book.

# Appendix A:
# World War I Chronology

Timeline of Events Relevant to the 167th Alabama and Its Participation in the Great War

## 1914

| Date | World War I | United States and World War I | 167th Alabama |
|---|---|---|---|
| June 28 | Assassination of Archduke Franz Ferdinand in Sarajevo | | |
| July 28 | Austria-Hungary declares war on Serbia | | |
| August 1 | Germany declares war on Russia; general mobilization in France and Germany | | |
| August 3 | Germany declares war on France | | |
| August 4 | Germany invades Belgium; Great Britain declares war on Germany | | |
| August 14 | Battle of the frontiers begins | | |
| August 15 | | US government deems loans to belligerent countries inconsistent with spirit of neutrality | |
| August 19 | | President Wilson's Declaration of Neutrality | |
| August 26–31 | German Army defeats Russian Army at Tannenberg; Austria-Hungary invades Russian Poland (Galicia) | | |
| August 23 | Japan declares war on Germany | | |

| Date | World War I | United States and World War I | 167th Alabama |
|---|---|---|---|
| Sept. 2 | Paris is evacuated | | |
| Sept. 6–9 | First battle of the Marne; German advance is stopped; trench warfare begins | | |
| Sept. 9–14 | Russia is defeated at the first battle of the Masurian Lakes | | |
| Oct.–Nov. | Race to the sea. Western front is stabilized from English channel to Switzerland | | |
| November 1 | Ottoman Empire enters the war on the side of Central Powers | | |
| November 7 | Japanese take over; German concession of Qingdao | | |
| November 23 | | US troops withdraw from Veracruz | |

## 1915

| Date | World War I | United States and World War I | 167th Alabama |
|---|---|---|---|
| Jan.–March | Allied offensives in Artois and Champagne; major losses; inconclusive results. German Zeppelins bomb England and Paris | | |
| Jan. 28 | | US Coast Guard designated as a branch of US military | |
| Jan. 31 | First use of poison gas by German Army against Russian troops | | |

| | |
|---|---|
| Feb.–April | Second Russian defeat at Masurian Lakes; Russia counterattacks successfully against Austria-Hungary in Galicia |
| Feb.–August | Allied assault on the Dardanelles and Gallipoli; British, ANZAC (Australia/New Zealand), and French troops besieged by Turkey; worst disaster in British military history |
| April 22 | First use of poison gas by German Army on the western front at the battle of Ypres |
| April–May | Beginning of Armenian massacre in Turkey |
| May 7 | German U boats sink *Lusitania*. Loss of American lives on *Lusitania*. US-German diplomatic crisis |
| May 23 | Italy declares war on Austria-Hungary |
| June 23–Dec. 2 | Austria-Hungary battles Italy on Isonzo River (1st to 4th battles); costly and indecisive |
| July 9–Aug. 4 | South Africans complete conquest of German SW Africa |
| July 28 | US occupation of Haiti begins |
| Sept. 25–Nov. 6 | Allies launch second Artois and Champagne offensives; huge losses, few results |
| Oct. 5 | Bulgaria enters the war on the side of Central Powers |

| Date | World War I | United States and World War I | 167th Alabama |
|---|---|---|---|
| Oct.–Nov. | Invasion of Serbia by Austro-Hungarian, German, and Bulgarian forces; Serbian Army driven out of its own country; survivors evacuated to Corfu by French and Italian ships | | |
| September | | US government authorizes loans to belligerent countries | |
| December | | United States addresses a protest to Great Britain against maritime warfare | |

## 1916

| Date | World War I | United States and World War I | 167th Alabama |
|---|---|---|---|
| January | Last Allied troops evacuated from Dardanelles | | |
| Feb. 3 | Draft established in Great Britain | | |
| Feb. 18 | French and British troops complete conquest of German Cameroon | | |
| Feb. 21–Dec. 18 | Battle of Verdun: *Ils ne passeront pas* (They will not pass) | | |
| March 8–9 | | Pancho Villa raids Columbus, New Mexico, and other US border towns with 1,500 troops | |
| March 16 | | General Pershing enters Mexico | |

| | | |
|---|---|---|
| March 11–Nov. 14 | 5th–9th battles on the Isonzo; very costly for both Austria-Hungary and Italy and still indecisive | |
| April | In Mesopotamia British forces advance on Baghdad | |
| May 4 | | Sussex pledge: Germany accepts US terms and conditions to stop submarine warfare |
| May 7 | | US troops land in Santo Domingo for fear of German use of the island against the United States |
| May 16 | With Sykes-Picot agreement, Britain and France share in advance the spoils of the Ottoman Empire | |
| May 31 | Battle of Jutland; while a German success, Britain remains mistress of the seas | |
| June 10 | Start of Arab revolt against Turks led by Sharif Hussein in Hejaz | |
| June–Aug. June 19 | Russians defeat Turks in Caucasus | |
| June 4–Sept. 30 | Russia Brusilov offensive scores a major victory against Austria-Hungary | National Guard mobilization |

| Date | World War I | United States and World War I | |
|---|---|---|---|
| July 30 | | German agents destroy the Black Tom ammunition depot in Jersey City; seven people killed | |
| July 1– Nov. 18 | Franco-British troops launch Battle of the Somme, a blood bath. Britain uses tanks successfully for the first time | | 4th Alabama begins training in Montgomery |
| July 4– Oct. 21 | | | |
| August 7 | Portugal joins the Allies | | |
| Aug.–Dec. | Romania overrun by German Army after joining Allied side | | |
| Oct. 29– March 15, 1917 | | | 4th Alabama on the Mexican border |
| November 7 | | Woodrow Wilson reelected president | |

**1917**

| Date | World War I | United States and World War I | 167th Alabama |
|---|---|---|---|
| January 11 | | German saboteurs set off explosion in Kingsland, New Jersey | |
| January 22 | | Wilson calls for "Peace without Victory" in Europe | |

## 1917

| | |
|---|---|
| January 30 | United States announces the end of its search for Pancho Villa, and Pershing's troops start withdrawing back to United States |
| January 31 | Germany proclaims unrestricted submarine warfare |
| February 5 | United States severs diplomatic relations with Germany |
| March 1 | Publication in the United States of the Zimmerman telegram in which Germany offered Mexico military alliance to recover Texas, Arizona, and New Mexico |
| March 11 | Baghdad falls to British forces |
| March 15 | Abdication of Russian Czar Nicholas II |
| April 6 | United States recognizes government of elected Mexican president Carranza |
| April 9–20 | French offensive at the Chemin des Dames; massive costly failure |
| May 15 | General Pétain named head of French Army |
| May 18 | United States declares war on Germany |
| May–June | Mutinies in French army |
| | Selective Service Act |

|  |  | |
| --- | --- | --- |
| May 12–October 24 | 10th–12th battles of the Isonzo; at Caporetto, rebellious Italian Army is nearly destroyed | |
| June 3 | Russian troops refuse to follow General Brusilov | |
| June 5 | Conscription begins | 4th Alabama becomes 167th Alabama Infantry Regiment |
| June 13 | Pershing, commander of the AEF, arrives in France | |
| June 15 | Espionage Act | |
| June 28 | First US troops arrive in France | |
| June 29 | Greece enters war on Allied side | |
| June–July | British battles of Paschendaele and Cambrai | |
| Aug. 1 | Pope Benedict XV calls for peace without conquest or annexations | |
| Aug. 14 | China declares war on Germany | |
| Aug. 15 | | 167th part of US 42nd Division, the Rainbow Division |
| Sept. 1–Oct. 18 | | Shipment to France |
| Oct. 26 | Brazil declares war against Central Powers | |
| Nov. 2 | Balfour Declaration for the establishment of a Jewish homeland in Palestine | |

## 1917

| Date | World War I | United States and World War I | 167th Alabama |
|---|---|---|---|
| Nov. 6 | October Revolution in Russia. Lenin and the Bolsheviks take over | | |
| Nov. 28–Feb. 18, 1918 | | | Training in Lorraine |
| Dec. 7 | | United States declares war on Austria-Hungary | |
| Dec. 9 | Jerusalem falls to British forces | | |
| Dec. 15 | Bolsheviks concludes a separate armistice with Germany and Austria-Hungary | | |

## 1918

| Date | World War I | United States and World War I | 167th Alabama |
|---|---|---|---|
| January 8 | | State of the Union: Wilson defines his 14 points plan for peace | |
| Feb. 21–March 21 | | | In trenches with French troops in the Baccarat sector |
| March 13 | Russia signs peace treaty at Brest-Litovsk | | |
| March 21 | German offensive in Picardie; British front collapses | | |

|  | | | |
|---|---|---|---|
| March 23 | Long range German cannon starts bombing Paris | | |
| March 30 | | Pershing puts US forces at Foch's disposal | |
| March 31–June 31 | | | Responsibility for trenches in the Baccarat sector |
| April 9 | German offensive in Flanders | | |
| April 14 | Allies create unified command on western front under General Foch | | |
| April 20 | | 136 soldiers from 26th Division taken prisoners in a German raid at Seicheprey | |
| April 27 | German offensive on the Chemin des Dames; French front collapses | | |
| May 16 | | Sedition Act | |
| May 28 | | Battle of Cantigny, first major US action (28th Regiment, 1st US Division) | |
| June 6 | | US 3rd Division captures southern part of Belleau Woods | |
| July 3–July 18 | German offensive in Champagne: the Friedensturm, the drive for peace; for the Allies, it is the beginning of the Second Battle of the Marne | | Champagne offensive |
| July 6 | | Wilson agrees to US intervention in Siberia | |

|  |  | |
|---|---|---|
| July 17 | Assassination of Czar Nicholas II and his family | |
| July 27–28 | | Croix Rouge Farm battle (Aisne-Marne) |
| July 28–Aug. 2 | | Battle of the Ourcq (Aisne-Marne offensive) |
| August | Spanish flu becomes pandemic | |
| Aug. 8 | Franco-British troops attack in Mondidier; black day for Germany | |
| Sept. 12–27 | | Saint-Mihiel offensive |
| Sept. 15–29 | Army of the Orient (Serb, Czech, Italian, French, British) under General Franchet d'Esperey overruns Bulgarian forces; armistice with Bulgaria on the 29th | |
| Sept. 26–Nov. 11 | Meuse-Argonne offensive under Foch leadership | |
| Sept. 30 | General Allenby (with Lawrence of Arabia and Faysal) enters Damascus | |
| October | Franchet d'Esperey and the Army of the Orient march toward Hungary | |
| Oct. 4 | German chancellor Max von Baden asks President Wilson for an armistice | |

|  |  |  |
| --- | --- | --- |
| October 5 | German public informed for the first time of the dismal German situation | |
| Oct. 5–10 | | Argonne Forest |
| October 8 | Corporal Alvin York single-handedly kills 25 and captures 132 Germans in the Argonne Forest | |
| Oct. 11–21 | | Côte de Châtillon |
| Oct. 28 | The German Reichstag formally accepts the October Reforms, transforming Germany in a constitutional monarchy | |
| Oct. 30 | Armistice with Turkey | |
| Nov. 2–9 | | Sedan Drive |
| Nov. 3 | Armistice with Austria-Hungary | |
| Nov. 9 | German Emperor Wilhelm II abdicates | |
| November 11 | Armistice with Germany | |
| Nov. 16–April 15, 1919 | | Army of Occupation in Germany |
| Nov. 23 | German general Lettow-Vorbeck surrenders his undefeated German army in East Africa | |
| Dec. 18 | Wilson arrives in France | |

| Date | | World War I |
|---|---|---|
| **1919** | | |
| January 18 | | Peace conference opens in Paris |
| April 29 | Camp Merritt, NJ | |
| May 7–13 | Return to Alabama | |
| May 15 | | The Treaty of Versailles is drafted and signed with Germany |
| May 7–June 28 | Mustered out at Camp Shelby, Miss. | |
| Sept. 10 | | The Treaty of Saint-Germain-en-Laye is signed with Austria |
| Sept. 27 | | The Treaty of Neuilly-sur-Seine is signed with Bulgaria |
| Oct. 2 | Wilson is left debilitated by a stroke | |
| **1920** | | |
| Date | | World War I |
| March 19 | US Senate refuses to ratify the Treaty of Versailles and to participate in the League of Nations | |
| June 4 | | The Treaty of Trianon is signed with Hungary |
| Aug. 10 | | The Treaty of Sevres is signed with Turkey |

# Appendix B:
# Organization of the 42nd Division

As recorded in the *Journal des Marches et Opérations*, Novembre 1917–Janvier 1919, 42$^e$ DIUS Mission Française, SHD/DAT.

## RECRUITMENT IN CAMP MILLS

### 83rd Infantry Brigade

165th Infantry Regiment (New York)
166th Infantry Regiment (Ohio)
150th Machine Gun Battalion (Wisconsin)

### 84th Infantry Brigade

167th Infantry Regiment (Alabama)
168th Infantry Regiment (Iowa)
151st Machine Gun Battalion (Georgia)

### 67th Field Artillery Brigade

149th Field Artillery Regiment: 75 mm guns (Illinois)
150th Field Artillery Regiment: 155 mm howitzers (Indiana)
151th Field Artillery Regiment: 75 mm guns (Minnesota)
117th Trench-Mortar Battery (Maryland)

### Divisional Troops

149th Machine Gun Battalion (Pennsylvania)
117th Field Signal Battalion (Missouri)
117th Engineer Regiment (South Carolina and California)
Headquarters Troop (Louisiana)

### Trains

117th Headquarters Train and Military Police (Virginia)

117th Sanitary Train (New Jersey, District of Columbia, Michigan, Nebraska, Colorado, Oregon, Oklahoma)
117th Engineer Train (North Carolina and Tennessee)
117th Ammunition Train (Kansas)
117th Supply Train (Texas)

Commanding Officers and Field Officers
upon Arrival in Vaucouleurs (France)

Division Commander: Major General William A. Mann
Chief of Staff: Colonel Douglas MacArthur

67th Field Artillery Brigade: Brigadier General Summerall
149th Field Artillery Regiment: Colonel Reilly
150th Field Artillery Regiment: Colonel Tyndall
151th Field Artillery Regiment: Colonel Leach

83rd Brigade: Brigadier General Lenihan
165th Infantry Regiment: Colonel Hine
166th Infantry Regiment: Colonel Hough

84th Infantry Brigade: Brigadier General Brown
167th Infantry Regiment: Colonel Screws
168th Infantry Regiment: Colonel Bennett

# Appendix C:
# Organization of the
# 167th Infantry at Camp Mills

As recorded in Amerine.

## REGIMENTAL FIELD OFFICERS

Colonel William P. Screws
Lieutenant Colonel Walter E. Bare

## FIRST BATTALION

Major John W. Carroll

Company A, Montgomery
Company B, Abbeville
Company C, Pell City
Company D, Bessemer

## SECOND BATTALION

Major Hartley A. Moon

Company E, Decatur
Company F, Gadsden
Company G, Ozark
Company H, Alexander City

## THIRD BATTALION

Major Dallas B. Smith

Company I, Opelika
Company K, Birmingham
Company L, Alabama City
Company M, Oxford

SUPPORT BATTALION

Headquarters Company, Montgomery
Supply Company, Montgomery
Machine Gun Company, Montgomery
Sanitary Detachment, Birmingham

# Appendix D:
# Remembering the Members of the 167th Alabama Infantry Regiment Who Died in France during World War I

The soldiers of the regiment who died on the battlefields of France were often, at first, buried where they fell.[1] After the war, bodies were located and reburied in consolidated locations before they could find a permanent resting place in France or be repatriated to the United States depending of the decision of their next of kin.

In France, the US government established six cemeteries after World War I.[2] All have a nonsectarian chapel built on the site. Today they hold the bodies of over thirty thousand US soldiers who died in combat or from wounds. In each of these cemeteries are graves of the soldiers or a wall of the missing, and the sites are beautifully maintained by the American Battle Monuments Commission (ABMC).[3]

The ABMC was established in 1923 by an act of Congress at the request of General John Pershing to commemorate the service, achievements, and sacrifice of US armed forces since they served overseas in 1917. Since 1934 it has been responsible for the eight cemeteries and eight memorials or markers commemorating World War I, and for cemeteries and memorials from subsequent wars. An excellent database allows families to look for their relatives (www.abmc.gov). In 1930 the War Department of the United States, having compiled a list of mothers and widows of deceased soldiers, sailors, and marines killed in World War I, offered to send them to visit the resting places of their loved ones. Many of those entitled to the pilgrimage chose to take it.[4] Lisa Budreau's book *Bodies of War: World War I and the Politics of Commemoration in America, 1919–1933* covers this subject in masterful fashion.[5]

Two hundred eighty soldiers of the 167th Alabama Infantry Regiment are buried on French soil.[6] Their names are listed on the Croix Rouge Farm Memorial Foundation website according to the cemetery where they are buried.[7] They, and all their comrades in the Rainbow Division they were all so proud to belong to, are honored by a memorial at the site of the Battle of Croix Rouge Farm. The name of the Croix Rouge Farm battle is also inscribed on the entablature of the American monument overlooking the Marne River and the city of Château-Thierry. This costly victory of the Alabama regiment, on July 26, 1918, made it possible for the division to cross the Ourcq River the next day and push the Germans back.

The state of Alabama honored its World War I dead by the construction of the World War Memorial Building. In 1901 Thomas Owen created the Alabama Department of Archives and History (ADAH), the first state historical department in the nation. In 1918 he conceived the idea of a new archives building on the block across from the Capitol as a living memorial to the Alabamians who sacrificed their lives in service to the nation in World War I. After his death his wife, Mary Bankhead Owen, continued his effort to secure a new archives building and secured the funding through the Works Progress Administration of the New Deal. Since her effort was a resurrection of her husband's dream of a World War I memorial, the words "Alabama World War Memorial" appear over the south entrance.

The ADAH houses the extensive correspondence Dr. Owen had with World War I soldiers while they were on the front.[8] It also houses the Gold Star collection donated by families of World War I soldiers and memorializes the lives of those men who served in the AEF and died in service of their country.[9]

The city of Birmingham named a viaduct in honor of the Rainbow Division. It installed plaques at the bridge's center, listing those Jefferson County men killed in action with the regiment.[10] Mortimer Jordan is memorialized by a monument in front of the VA Medical Center in Birmingham, and a public school is named for him.

Other cities across the state put up plaques or monuments commemorating the World War I dead from their respective communities. Etowah County's Rainbow City takes its name from the Rainbow Division.

# Appendix E:
# November 1917 Roster of Alabamians in the 167th Alabama Infantry Regiment When It Left Camps Mills (NY) for France

This list of Alabamians in the 167th Infantry Regiment was drawn from the full roster of the regiment published by W. Amerine (*Alabama's Own*) in 1919. In some cases, the spelling of communities has been corrected, but last names have been left as they were in the original listing even if the author recognized obvious misspellings.

### REGIMENTAL STAFF AND FIELD OFFICERS

Colonel William P. Screws, Montgomery
Lieut.-Colonel Walter E. Bare, Gadsden
Major Dallas H. Smith, Opelika
Major John W. Carroll, Ozark
Major Hartley A. Moon, Birmingham
1st Lieut. Herbert B. May, Montgomery
1st Lieut. John H. Powell, Opelika

### MEDICAL CORPS

Major John W. Watts, Birmingham
Captain Isham Kimbell, Auburn
Captain James Y. Hamil, Troy
Captain Robert A. Burns, Alabama City
Captain William M. Peters, Centerville
Captain William W. Long, Birmingham
1st Lieut. Albert G. Sims, Talladega
1st Lieut. D. C. Malcolm G. Dabney, Birmingham
1st Lieut. Emmett P. Smith, Auburn
2nd Lieut. George F. Spann, Autaugaville
Arant, Winston, Pvt., Mt. Creek

Baxley, Grover, Pvt., Dothan
Beasley, Eugene T., Pvt., Birmingham
Bruce, Odus, Pvt., Attalla
Burns, Lawson, Pvt., Piedmont
Busby, Milton, Pvt., Pittsview
Calhoun, Curtis T., Pvt., Grove Hill
Carr, Oscar J., Pvt., Moulton
Carter, Harry L., Pvt., Albany
Chism, Leon T., Pvt., North Port
Cowling, Alex E., Pvt., Benton
Duke, Willie, Pvt., Pritchard
Ellis, Jesse E., Pvt., Marbury
Ernest, George F., Pvt., Benton
Forbes, William C., Pvt., Birmingham
Forwood, Frank P., Pvt., Monroeville
Frankenberger, Irvin, Pvt., Birmingham
Freeman, Otis C., Pvt., Phoenix,
Fullington, Lawrence T., Pvt., Gadsden
Goodrich, Charles S., Sgt., Birmingham
Hall, Claude E., Pvt., Atmore
Hill, Erskin R., Pvt., Birmingham
Hornsby, Joseph A., Pvt., Dothan
Langford, Henry L., Pvt., Montgomery
Lee, Bishop M., Pvt., Birmingham
Lessley, Melvin, Pvt., Green Station

McDade, Joe W., Pvt., Montgomery
Nelson, Louis, Pvt., Birmingham
Otwell, Joseph M., Sgt., Ensley
Parker, William O., Sgt., New Castle
Peak, James C., Pvt., Montgomery
Phillips, Harry, Pvt., Alabama City
Pruitt, Walter, Pvt., Ensley
Richard, Leslie J., Pvt., Mobile
Saunders, Cabell C., Pvt., Birmingham
Sherman, Clarence, Pvt., Montgomery
Sims, Edward C., Pvt., Jemison
Sykes, Leslie B., Pvt., Birmingham
Van Aller, Godfrey H., Pvt., Mobile
Warren, Morrell S., Pvt., Tallassee
Whitt, Ernest T., Pvt., Alabama City

## HEADQUARTERS COMPANY

1st Lieut. William I. Cole, Birmingham
2d Lieut. Ben Moore, Birmingham
Agerton, Silas, Pvt., Atmore
Alley, Louis B., Pvt., Montgomery
Atchison, Dan J., Pvt., Maplesville
Atkinson, Percy L., Pvt., Birmingham
Atkinson, Ralph, Sgt., Camden
Austin, John C., Pvt., Sylacauga
Bachman, William L., Pvt., Birmingham
Bailey, Forest, Pvt., Sycamore
Barksdale, Elton L., Pvt., Athens
Beasley, Charles B., Sgt., Ozark
Becker, Joseph, Pvt., Mobile
Bell, Charles A., Pvt., Range
Bennett, George F., Pvt., Birmingham
Bentley, Homer J., Musician, Phoenix
  City
Bergwall, Carl, Pvt., Willington
Bidez, Paul R., Band Leader, Auburn
Bittle, Johnnie, Pvt., Anniston
Bixler, Henry E., Pvt., Bay Minette
Blackenship, Eugene, Birmingham
Blackwood, Ben G., Pvt., Gadsden
Bohannan, William H., Pvt., Mobile
Brewer, Charles M., Pvt., Florence

Britt, John M., Musician, Eufaula
Brock, James A., Pvt., Sylacauga
Brown, Arthur C., Pvt., Fairfield
Bruce, Robert D., Pvt., Wellington
Bruce, Roy, Pvt., Clanton
Buchannon, Frederick H., Sylacauga
Burrell, Arthur C., Pvt., Alexander
Carey, Clinton W., Pvt., Centerville
Carroll, Willie, Pvt., Sycamore
Carter, Allen M., Pvt., Marion
Cartledge, Graves, Pvt., Jacksonville
Cartwright, Chipley, Pvt., Jay
Chambers, William R., Birmingham
Clark, Jewell M., Pvt., Gadsden
Cochran, Oscar, Pvt., Alabama City
Cogburn, Frank, Corp., Notasluga
Corley, John R., Pvt., Whistler
Courtney, Hugh E., Pvt., Centerville
Covin, Charles V., Pvt., Oakman
Cox, Clarence W., Pvt., Birmingham
Cox, Harvey H., Pvt., Fairfield
Crawson, William, Pvt., Calera
Cropper, Ben, Pvt., Gadsden
Crosby, Clarence, Pvt., Atmore
Crosthwaite, Marion G., Musician, Bir-
  mingham
Culuris, Apostal, Cook, Montgomery
Daniels, LeRoy, Pvt., Lanet
Davis, Archie B., Pvt., Oxford
Davis, Charles J., Pvt., Mobile
Davis, Homer A., Pvt., Eufaula
Davis, Joe A., Pvt., Montgomery
Dean, George D., Musician, Anton
Dees, Mace, Pvt., Montgomery
Dickinson, Sterling L., Pvt., Hurtsburo
Dodd, Arnold W., Pvt., Mobile
Drysdale, George, Pvt., Pratt City
Dunson, Henry, Pvt., Canoe
Dunson, Walker, Pvt., Canoe
Eddings, Bailey C., Pvt., Piper
Ellenburg, Ross W., Pvt., Montevallo
Elliot, Howard C., Bn. Sgt.-Maj., Opelika
Elliot, Luther D., Cook, Mobile

Emmal, Thomas M., Pvt., Ensley
Emmons, Jesse, Pvt., Flomaton
Ferguson, Arvel, Pvt., Anniston
Foster, Ware, Musician, Montgomery
Fox, Jerome A., Pvt., Birmingham
Foxworth, Charles E., Pvt., Selma
Fulcher, Frank F., Pvt., Enterprise
Gardener, John H., Pvt., Talladega
Glenn, Edward H., Pvt., Anniston
Gless, Harvey, Pvt., Maplesville
Golden, Ross L., Pvt., Enterprise
Goodman, William O., Pvt., Eclectic
Goree, Harper, Pvt., Opelika
Gothard, Bennett W., Pvt., Randolph
Guy, Ralph, Pvt., Montgomery
Harmon, John S., Pvt., Birmingham
Harvey, Walter, Pvt., Alabama City
Hayden, William W., Corp., Huntsville
Haynie, Charles R., Pvt., Jacksonville
Heath, Luther Z., Pvt., Birmingham
Hendrick, Horace E., Pvt., Birmingham
Hensley, Frank C., Pvt., Sheffield
Higdon, Frank, Pvt., Evergreen
Hill, Hugh H., Pvt., Gadsden
Hill, John R., Musician, East Lake
Hinton, Graham S., Pvt., Carrolton
Hinton, Hayes R., Pvt., Carrolton
Holderfield, Tommy G., Pvt., Fairfield
Holderitch, Ben, Pvt., Eoline
Holliday, Claude A., Reg. Sgt.-Major,
   Montgomery
Holloway, David, Musician, Lanett
Holmes, Henry G., Pvt., Birmingham
Holsenback, Floyd, Pvt., Anniston
Howard, Emmet, Pvt., Acmar
Howell, Frank L., Mechanic, Birmingham
Hubbard, Henry, Pvt., Grandville
Hughes, William R., Huntsville
Hunt, Alfred M., Pvt., Birmingham
Hutto, John B., Pvt., Birmingham
Hutton, George, Pvt., Spring Hill
Jarrett, Manuel, Pvt., Ensley
Jellison, John R., Pvt., Birmingham
Jenkins, Percy, Pvt., Montgomery
Johnson, Claude T., Pvt., Cullman
Johnson, Howard M., Musician, Girard
Jones, Chas C., Pvt., Centerville
Jones, Edgar M., Bn., Sgt.-Major, Bufton
Jones, Henry E., Pvt., Centerville
Jones, Richard A., Pvt., Centerville
Jones, Sidney, Pvt., Blocton
Keener, Will J., Pvt., Sylacauga
Kelley, Duke, Pvt., Evergreen
Kelley, Leon C., Band Corp., Alabama City
Kennedy, Paul A., Color Sgt., Gadsden
King, William A., Pvt., Porter
Lee, Cecil H., Pvt., Eutaw
Levens, Carl T., Pvt., Mobile
Lewis, Joseph L., Sgt., Gadsden
Lewis, Thomas M., Pvt., Florence
Longshore, William, Pvt., Montgomery
Mabry, Olly B., Pvt., Birmingham
Maddog, Efford, Pvt., Boaz
Maddox, Sidney, Pvt., Dothan
Martin, Frank M., Pvt., Mobile
Martin, John T., Pvt., Fayetteville
Martin, Melvin, Pvt., Munford
Mayfield, Hugh, Pvt., Sycamore
Mayfield, Jasper, Pvt., Talladega
McCarty, Everett, Pvt., Anniston
McCombes, Andrew, Pvt., O'Hatchie
McConnell, William, Pvt., Birmingham
McCool, Roland, Pvt., Blocton
McCord, Charles E., Musician, Bir-
   mingham
McGraw, Robert E., Mess Sgt., Mont-
   gomery
McInnis, Ernest, Pvt., Mobile
McIntyre, Tollie E., Pvt., Chilton
McPherson, Scott, Musician, McKenzie
Meeks, George A., Pvt., Andalusia
Merritt, Charles, Pvt., Alabama City
Miller, Henry, Pvt., Mobile
Miller, William H., Pvt., Carbon Hill
Mizzelle, Clifton, Pvt., Sylacauga
Monk, James D., Sgt., Eufaula

Morrison, Ollie, Pvt., Anniston
Mullin, William, Musician, Bessemer
Munghall, Douglass, Pvt., Pell City
Newell, John T., Pvt., Samson
Norwood, David, Sgt., Birmingham
Nunn, Mitchell, Color Sgt., Birmingham
Odiorne, Charles, Pvt., Birmingham
O'Rear, Clide, Pvt., Montgomery
O'Rear, Ralph, Pvt., Montgomery
O'Shields, Leonard, Pvt., Anniston
Parnell, Leighton C., Pvt., Maplesville
Patton, Joe J., Battles Wharf
Patton, Robert L., Pvt., Kaulton
Patton, Willie J., Pvt., Battles Wharf
Peek, Joe, Pvt., Talladega
Pippin, Robert R., Sgt., Ozark
Pitts, Willie, Pvt., Piper
Prescott, Thomas L., Corp., Ensley
Pugh, Archie C., Pvt., Wylam
Rabblais, Leo L., Cook, Birmingham
Ragsdale, Charlton, Sgt., Birmingham
Ramser, Dozier B., Pvt., Eufaula
Rappaport, Eugene, Pvt., Birmingham
Ray, Wheeler B., Pvt., Pratt City
Reynolds, Ruben L., Pvt., Birmingham
Roberts, Guy H., Pvt., Clanton
Robertson, John E., Musician, Mont-
  gomery
Ross, Fred, Bn. Sgt.-Major, Bessemer
Salter, George H., Pvt., Skinnerton
Scarbrough, Abb, Band Corp.,
  Chocolocco
Schell, Harry H., Band Sgt., Jacksonville
Schell, Herschell M., Band Sgt., Jacksonville
Scott, Hollis R., Pvt., Gadsden
Seigal, Charles, 1st Sgt., Birmingham
Shaner, Eugene, Pvt., Talladega
Sheldon, John G., Corp., Ensley
Sheppard, John, Pvt., Anniston
Shierling, Menzo, Pvt., Talladega
Shirah, Silas, Dothan
Shoults, Bush, Pvt., Lawley
Smith, Anthony A., Pvt., Birmingham

Smith, Avery R., S., Pvt., Maplesville
Smith, Claude, Pvt., Florence
Smith, Henry A., Pvt., Munford
Smith, James M., Pvt., West Blocton
Smith, William, Pvt., Talladega
Smitherman, Thomas, Pvt., Maplesville
Snyder, Charles, Pvt., Montgomery
Stephens, Dee, Pvt., Newton
Suther, William B., Pvt., Centerville
Taylor, Francis M., Band Corp., Auburn
Taylor, Owen L., Pvt., Pratt City
Teal, Russell A., Pvt., Maplesville
Thomas, Gordon M., Pvt., Renfroe
Thomas, Otis L., Pvt., Sycamore
Thompson, Emmerson, Pvt., Calvert
Thompson, Oscar M., Pvt., Gadsden
Thompson, Willie H, Corp., Gadsden
Tillmon, Mont, Musician, Girard
Tooel, William D., Pvt., Blue Mountain
  City
Tucker, Percy R., Pvt., Heighberger
Tucker, Wesley O., Pvt., Maplesville
Tuggle, Greeley W., Pvt., Short Creek
Vaughn, James F., Pvt., Mobile
Vickers, Richard C., Pvt., Mobile
Vickery, John W., Pvt., Atmore
Walden, John H., Pvt., Alabama City
Wall, Dove, Sgt., Ozark
Wallace, Claude J., Pvt., Randolph
Walls, James L., Pvt., Birmingham
Weller, Charles K., Pvt., Talladega
West, Lee A., Pvt., Uniontown
White, Oscar, Pvt., O'Hatchie
Williams, David, Musician, Birmingham
Wilson, Ruel H., Pvt., Mobile
Wingard, Dick, Pvt., Eclectic
Wolf, Joseph J., Pvt., Montgomery
Wood, Claud W., Pvt., Florence
Worley, John W., Sgt., Decatur
Wright, Eugene, Pvt., Birmingham
Yarborough, James L., Pvt., Dadeville
Yeates, Thomas M., Musician, Gadsden
Young, Edward, Pvt., Florence

## MACHINE GUN COMPANY

Captain Newman Smith, Montgomery
1st Lieut. Julien M. Strassburger, Montgomery
2d Lieut. Harry Porter, Montgomery
2d Lieut. Oscar Crenshaw, Montgomery
Alexander, Eugene, Sgt., Montgomery
Alford, James R., Pvt., Montgomery
Amos, Dewey, Pvt., Abertville
Barfield, Richard S., Pvt., Anniston
Barr, Sam, Corp., Bessemer
Bates, Sidney H., Pvt., Putnam
Bice, Lawson, Pvt., Anniston
Boone, Herman, Pvt., Selma
Bowlin, Russell, Pvt., Ashville
Boyd, Bevie L., Pvt., Albertville
Brady, Andrew J., Pvt., Potters Station
Broach, Franklin, Pvt., Montgomery
Brodie, John E., Pvt., Searight
Brown, Coley, Pvt., Clanton
Brown, Leon M., Pvt., Birmingham
Brown, Max, Pvt., McKenzie
Burger, Lewis A., Pvt., Birmingham
Burgess, Chester, Pvt., Edwardsville
Burkett, William H., Pvt., Pansey
Burt, George W., Corp., Montgomery
Camp, John S., Sgt., Silgo
Campbell, Amby, Pvt., Albertville
Clark, Charles J., Pvt., Aliceville
Clark, Franklin A., Pvt., Andalusia
Clayton, Clayton C., Pvt., Dawson
Coker, Charlie, Pvt., Alabama City
Collins, James S., Pvt., Opelika
Cox, Joe, Pvt., Uriah
Crenshaw, Ed, Pvt., Georgiana
Culver, Jesse G., Pvt., Ashford
Davis, Fitzhugh L., Pvt., Chunchula
Davis, Frank S., Pvt., Mobile
Dawsey, Aubrey, Pvt., Montgomery
Dees, Marion F., Pvt., Matthews Station
Deloit, Ellis B., Pvt., Deatville
Dickson, Eddie G., Pvt., Albertville
Dickson, Grover Y., Pvt., Thomaston
Dickson, Malcolm P., Pvt., Thomaston
Digmon, Eslie W., Pvt., Freemanville
Dobbs, Russell, Pvt., Maplesville
Dooley, Clate M., Corp., Boaz
Duff, William D., Pvt., Birmingham
Dunn, Albert, Pvt., Uriah
Dunn, David S., Pvt., Uriah
Dupree, Irma D., Sgt., Shady Grove
Durham, Samuel A., Pvt., Fort Payne
Eakens, Aubrey L., Corp., Ensley
Elliott, James H., Pvt., Birmingham
Fallin, Fay W., Pvt., Montgomery
Farmer, James D., Pvt., New Decatur
Ford, Walter E., Pvt., Sprotts
Foster, Walter E., Pvt., Braggs
Free, Isaac N., Pvt., Lanette
Gay, Margie, Pvt., Gadsden
Gaynor, Leo H., Pvt., Jackson
Gibson, Dan H., Pvt., Enterprise
Gilliland, Mac, Pvt., Equalitu
Gordon, Mitchell C., Pvt., Glenville
Green, William C., Pvt., Huntsville
Griffin, Travis, Pvt., Dutton
Hanks, Henry, Pvt., Atmore
Harris, Duncan D., Pvt., Glenwood
Harrison, Gladden, Sgt., Montgomery
Hart, Lewis E., Pvt., Camden
Hassey, Wesley L., Pvt., Montgomery
Heilperj, Bert H., Pvt., Montgomery
Hendrix, James E., Corp., Roy
Higdon, Eugene, Pvt., Repton
Hill, Dave, Pvt., Holt
Holder, Lee, Pvt., Uriah
Houston, Newell, Pvt., Statesville
Howell, William D., Pvt., Geneva
Hudson, John, Pvt., Chapman
Hughes, Hubbard E., Pvt., Marion
Hughes, Walter, Pvt., Montgomery
Hughes, William S., Pvt., Marion
Hughley, James W., Pvt., Bessemer
Hunt, Joy, Pvt., Quin
King, James E., Pvt., Onnento

Kissinger, Joseph E., Pvt., Gadsden
Lambert, Gray, Sgt., Lascar
Langham, John S., Pvt., Atmore
Ledbetter, Rubin F., Pvt., Matthews Station
Lee, David S., Corp., Midland City
Lee, Theodore, Pvt., Midland City
Lee, Therman E., Pvt., Midland City
Lobell, William H., Pvt., Birmingham
Malcomb, James M., Corp., Andalusia
Mancil, James H., Pvt., Foshee
Mathers, Charles S., Pvt., Jackson
Matthieu, George E., Pvt., Ensley
McCloud, Clint, Pvt., Wallace
McElhany, Bowen, Stable Sgt., Atmore
McElhany, Woody L., Pvt., Atmore
McKinley, Ishan, Corp., Tunnle Springs
Megginson, Edward, Pvt., Thomasville
Monsky, Soll, Sgt., Montgomery
Morgan, Grover C., Pvt., Pine Hill
Morris, Jack, Pvt., Gadsden
Morris, Roy, Pvt., Gadsden
Nichols, Harry, Pvt., Albertville
Nichols, Walter R., Corp., Selma
Nichols, William O, Pvt., Selma
Owen, Arthur D., Corp., Bay Minette
Parker, Calvin D., Pvt., Lanette
Piechowski, Sidney, Pvt., Mobile
Pierce, George D., Pvt., Opp
Pittman, Arthur G., Corp., Polin
Pledger, Huey, Pvt., Pelham
Price, Bryant, Pvt., McKenzie
Puckett, John T., Pvt., Carrolton
Puckett, William C., Pvt., Opelika
Rachel, James, Pvt., New Brockton
Rainey, Bill, Pvt., Bessemer
Ray, James H., Pvt., Albertville
Rhodes, Russell F. A., Pvt., Opp
Scollick, Joseph E., Pvt., Mobile
Shaw, Nathaniel M., Pvt., Pratt City
Shine, Emmett, Pvt., Opp
Sims, Arthur W., Mess Sgt., Montgomery
Skinner, John H., Pvt., Birmingham
Slaughter, Macon R., Pvt., Luverne

Smalley, Cleveland L., Pvt., Mobile
Smith, John F., Pvt., Montgomery
Snell, Arthur J., Pvt., Opp
Sparks, Mose E., Pvt., Union Grove
Spencer, Lucien, Pvt., Bessemer
Stephens, James D., Pvt., Albertville
Stewart, Oscar, Pvt., Opp
Stokes, Lee, Pvt., Slocomb
Story, Elmore J., Sgt., Auburn
Story, Walter C., Sgt., Auburn
Stowers, Joseph H., Sgt., Matthews Station
Strickland, Roy P., Pvt., Surginer
Tennimon, James F., Corp., Selma
Totherow, Charlie, Pvt., Albertville
Tucker, Robert M., Pvt., Albertville
Tuggle, Joseph G., Pvt., Birmingham
Vaughan, William P., Pvt., Polin
Vernon, Lewis E., Corp., Clanton
Waldrop, Perry, Pvt., Anniston
Walker, James H., Pvt., Birmingham
Walker, Muthey D., Pvt., Bessemer
Wallace, Victor D., Pvt., Sprotts
Watson, James G., Pvt., Section
Webb, Ernest, Pvt., Scottsboro
Westmoreland, James D., Pvt., Center
Whitmore, Charles D., Pvt., Attalla
Wilhite, Henry C., Pvt., Natural Bridge
Williams, Edward A., Supply Sgt., Montgomery
Williams, Ernest, Pvt., Dozier
Wilson, Joseph T., Pvt., Birmingham
Winn, Roland W., Pvt., Birmingham
Wolcott, Edward H., Pvt., Mobile
Woodham, William J., Pvt., Sanford.
Wynn, Rush P., Pvt., Montgomery
Zaner, Sam, Pvt., Anniston
Zimmerman, Horace J., Sgt., Burnsville

### SUPPLY COMPANY

Capt. John M. Smith, Montgomery
Lieut. Joseph M. Dickerson, Montgomery
Andrade, Albert P., Pvt., Mobile

Antley, Asa, Pvt., Webb

Avant, William F., Wag., Skipperville

Bailey, Howard M., Pvt., Florala

Batson, James H., Pvt., Sylacauga

Bell, Fred, Pvt., Hopewell

Blackmon, Noonie, Pvt., Mobile

Boatright, John, Pvt., Florence

Brassell, C. M., Wag., Montgomery

Brightwell, T. C., Wag., Auburn

Briscoe, Arthur, Pvt., Cullman

Browder, Tim J., Pvt., Montgomery

Brown, Dave E., Pvt., Birmingham

Brown, Ed, Pvt., Alexander City

Bullock, Charlie, Pvt., Gordon

Bullock, C. D., Pvt., Eufaula

Burt, Charles W., Pvt., Montgomery

Busby, Jessie, Pvt., Calera

Caldwell, Fred, Pvt., Talladega

Calloway, Oliver, Wag., Sylacauga

Childs, Bernice, Pvt., Harford

Chronis, John A., Pvt., Prichard

Clanton, Samuel, Pvt., Cloverdale

Clifton, Onie R., Pvt., Ensley

Coleman, Herman, Pvt., Enterprise

Condry, Alonzo, Pvt., Ariton

Condry, Daniel, Pvt., Ariton

Crawford, Angus, Pvt., Ozark

Cruise, Mulkey D., Wag. Plantersville

Dandridge, Curry, Pvt., Florala

Davis, Joseph E., Pvt., Highland Home

Daw, Deneley, Pvt., Mobile

Dean, John E., Pvt., Mt. Meigs

Dement, Levon, Pvt., Birmingham

Demouy, Edward, Pvt., Mobile

Dent, George H., Sgt., Eufaula

Dolive, Dillon S., Pvt., Mobile

Dunn, William, Wag., Montgomery

Edins, James L., Pvt., Oxmore

Finley, Lonnie A., Pvt., Jasper

Fleming, Albert, Pvt., Geneva County

Foshee, Sie, Saddler, Montgomery

Fuller, Ira, Pvt., Dothan

Galatas, Jules J., Wag., Montgomery

Gary, John, Pvt., Clanton

Glass, Taylor, Pvt., Tallassee

Glover, Tom, Pvt., Brookside

Gray, Lamar E., Pvt., Brent

Haygood, Douglas D., Wag., Montgomery

Henderson, Ollie, Wag., Luverne

Herring, John C., Wag., Gadsden

Herrington, Charlie, Pvt., Dothan

Herrington, Henry, Pvt., Dothan

Heustess, Arthur, Wag., Montgomery

Hines, Clarence, Pvt., New Brockton

Hitt, Ropice L., Pvt., Cuba

Hogan, Paul J., Sgt., Montgomery

Holland, Eli, Pvt., Dothan

Houston, Joe M., Wag., Carland

Hughes, Iroy, Pvt., Dothan

Hulsey, Frank L., Wag., Anniston

Jackson, Curry, Wag., Bessemer

Joiner, Louis A., Pvt., Ashford

Jones, Boyd, Pvt., Mobile

Jones, Charlie, Pvt., Cragford

Jones, James H., Pvt., Chandles Springs

Jones, Joe E., Pvt., Harpersville

Jones, Will A., Pvt., Calera

Jones, William N., Pvt., Enterprise

Kahn, Nathan M., Sgt., Montgomery

Keith, Frank T., Pvt., Gants Quarry

Kelly, John P., Pvt., Talladega

Kelly, William A., Pvt., Talladega

Kinsaw, Talmage, Pvt., Hartford

Kirkland, Dan R., Pvt., Birmingham

Lawrence, Loyt A., Pvt., Vernon

Lewis, Frank A., Pvt., Tallassee

Little, George E., Wag., Alabama City

Malasanos, John B., Pvt., Montgomery

Martin, Paul, Pvt., Mobile

May, Albert W., Pvt., Greensboro

McCormick, Eldridge, Pvt., Goshen

McCullough, J. C., Pvt., Pell City

McCullough, L. L., Corp., Pell City

McMahan, William C., Wag., Heflin

Mitchell, Robert A., Pvt., Florence

Moseley, John, Pvt., Hartford

Murphy, William N., Pvt., Camden

Murrell, Q. Oliver, Wag., Montgomery
Nabors, Jasper H., Pvt., Calera
Neuert, Phil, Sgt., Montgomery
Neville, James, Wag., Fayette
Patterson, James L., Pvt., Talladega
Peagler, John, Pvt., Mobile
Pilgreen, Ira, Pvt., Calera
Powell, Thomas, Pvt., Opp
Price, Edgar W., Pvt., Albertville
Ranshaw, James, Pvt., Harperville
Riley, Boyce, Pvt., Dreway
Ringlestein, Homer, Pvt., Florence
Rogers, Charles L., Pvt., Citronelle
Searcy, Harvard, Pvt., Florala
Sharp, Willie O., Montgomery
Shinholster, Floyd, Pvt., Gordon
Shinholster, Louis, Pvt., Gordon
Simpson, Joseph, Wag., Montgomery
Smith, Andrew, Pvt., Cottonwood
Stokes, Roy, Pvt., Coffee Springs
Stone, William F., Pvt., Kilpatrick
Stough, James, Pvt., Montgomery
Sudduth, Charles R., Pvt, Birmingham
Suggs, Monroe, Pvt., Anniston
Sutton, George S., Pvt., Bangor
Tallent, Roy L., Birmingham
Taylor, James, Wag., Montgomery
Taylor, William C., Pvt., Dothan
Temple, Peter E., Sgt., Montgomery
Thaxton, Charlie, Pvt., Carrollton
Thompson, Claud, Pvt., Russellville
Thompson, Oscar, Wag., Montgomery
Thornton, Leslie, Pvt., Jasper
Tiller, Ben, Pvt., Headland
Walker, Louis A., Citronville
Weaver, Lasca, Wag., Lineville
Webb, Cecil, Pvt., Columbia
Welch, Howard, Pvt., Dothan
Wesson, Luke, Sgt., Alexander City
White, T. Ray, Wag., Danville
Wiggs, Grady L., Wag., Gadsden
Wilkinson, Oscar, Pvt., Columbia
Wilson, Harbert, Pvt., New Brockton

Wynn, Henry, Wag., Phoenix City
Yeatman, Roy O., Wag., Anniston

## COMPANY A

1st Lieut. Edgar Collins, Montgomery
2d Lieut. Robert W. Smith, Montgomery
Allen, John G., Pvt., Eufaula
Andrews, Robert C., Pvt., Montgomery
Armstrong, Cecil, Pvt., Clanton
Baldwin, Fufas A., Pvt., Roanoke
Barbor, Daniel, Pvt., Coden
Barfield, Charles A., Pvt., Mount Union
Barfield, Willie, Pvt., Mount Union
Barnett, Henry P., Pvt., Mount Vernon
Barnett, Malcolm, Pvt., Montgomery
Barry, John O., Sgt., Montgomery
Berry, Bailey J., Corp., Colbran
Bethune, Wilbur H., Pvt., Union Springs
Blauvelt, Clifton O., Pvt., Maplesville
Boozer, Samuel J., Pvt., Sweetwater
Bowen, Carl, Pvt., Attalla
Buhring, James H., Pvt., Coden
Burdin, Howard L., Corp., Montgomery
Busby, Jim, Pvt., Theodore
Bush, John W., Pvt., Plateau
Byrd, Monte M., Pvt., Montgomery
Cabler, Joseph E., Pvt., Prichard
Carpenter, Aurelius M., Pvt., Carpenter
Carter, John W., Corp., Prattville
Castleberry, Oswald, Pvt., Boaz
Chambless, D. S., Pvt., Booth
Chestang, Leo J., Pvt., Toulmanville
Clark, Wilton, Pvt., Greenville
Clayton Luther, Pvt., Petrey
Clements, Homer T., Pvt., Montgomery
Clifton, Herbert L., Corp., Eufaula
Cobb, Sam B., Pvt., Milbrook
Cofield, Owen L., Pvt., Delta
Collins, Arthur, Pvt.
Conner, Harold H., Pvt., Montgomery
Cox, William C., Pvt., Montgomery
Crane, Cleveland, Pvt., Prichard

Creeswell, Eraly W., Union Springs

Cummings, Percy N., Pvt, Mobile

Curry, John H., Sgt., Mobile

Curtis, Joseph E., Sgt., Montgomery

Danelly, James, Pvt., Atmore

Daniels, Benjamin F., Pvt.

Davis, Grady W., Pvt., Tuskeegee

Davis, Jefferson, Pvt., Greenville

Davis, William A., Pvt., Cherokee

Day, William A., Corp., Wellington

Dean, Samuel J., Jr., Montgomery

Deramus, Charles M., Pvt., Maplesville

Dial, Oliver L., Corp., Anniston

Dismuke, Homer, Mechanic, Anniston

Dobson, Willie D., Pvt., Choccolocco

Driggers, Dazzie, Corp., Eufaula

Driggers, Eley, Pvt., Eufaula

Drye, William H., Corp., Roy

Duett, John T., Pvt., Tallassee

Durden, Lester, Pvt., Prattville

Elliott, Terry, Pvt., La Pine

Elmore, Loid, Pvt., Headland

Fallen, James, Pvt., Prattville

Fassman, Lawrence J., Pvt., Montgomery

Fisher, Milton E., Pvt., Prattville

Forster, Walter, Pvt., Prattville

Galatas, Sidney E., Pvt., Montgomery

Gann, William R., Pvt., Sellers

Gardner, Vernon, Sgt., Grady

Garrett, Will E., Pvt., Marbury

George, Raymond, Pvt., Plateau

George, Willie, Pvt., Mobile

Gilmore, Wade M., Pvt., Montgomery

Graham, Robert E., Pvt., Coden

Griffith, James T., Pvt., Prichard

Hall, Joseph W., Pvt., Montgomery

Hall, William F., Sgt., Montgomery

Ham, John C., Pvt., Montgomery

Hamilton, Joe, Pvt., Prichard

Hammonds, Louis L., Pvt., Eufaula

Hanks, Fred N., Pvt., Roy

Hardy, Richard O., Pvt., Montgomery

Harless, John G., Pvt., Maplesville

Harris, Ezra F., Pvt., Montgomery

Harwell, Claude C., Sgt., Montgomery

Harwell, Jessie J., Pvt., Mobile

Havron, Richard, Corp., Crichton

Headley, Marvin W., Pvt., Clanton

Hellebusch, Charles, Corp., Montgomery

Henderson, Charlie, Pvt., Mt. Creek

Hendrix, William R., Sgt., Roy

Hewett, William F., Pvt., Oxford

Hines, Jesse F., Pvt., Prattville

Holbrook, Lawson H., Pvt., Greensboro

Holland, Bryan, Pvt., Deatsville

Holley, Nathaniel, Pvt., Prattville

Howell, Dan, Sgt., Montgomery

Huff, Lidell, Corp., Gadsden

Jackson, Jim, Pvt., Prattville

Jenson, Otten, Pvt., Mobile

Jordon, William T., Pvt., Montgomery

Kahle, Albert R., Supply Sgt., Selma

Keenum, Hugh R., Pvt., Prichard

Killett, Ben E., Pvt., Prattville

Killough, Joseph C., Pvt., Prattville

Kilpatrick, John J., Corp., Brantley

King, James T., Pvt., Lower Peachtree

King, Percy G., Pvt., Montgomery

Kruse, John D., Pvt., Mobile

La Fargue, Cleve A., Pvt., Tolmanville

Lambert, Andrew M., Pvt., Plateau

Lambert, George H., Cook, Heflin

Lawrence, Henry, Pvt.

Lee, Arthur, Pvt., Prichard

Lee, Eddie W., Pvt., Black Rock

Lee, William C., Pvt., Forche

Leonard, Roy L., Corp., Sylacauga

Levins, Clanton O., Pvt., Titus

Locke, Wallace B., Brewton

Logan, Arthur, Pvt., Prattville

Lucas, Joseph, Pvt., Prattville

Ludlow, Steve, Pvt., Montgomery

Macon, Preston A., Pvt., Wetumpka

Malone, James H., Pvt., Mobile

Manly, William A., Pvt., Birmingham

Marcus, Harold, Mechanic, Montgomery

Marcus, William S., Corp., Montgomery
Massey, Harry P., Pvt., Chunchula
Matthews, Herbert D., Pvt., Whistler
Maxey, Pearson, Bugler, Montgomery
McBurnett, Sam E., Corp., Lincoln
McCoy, Jet, Pvt., Titus
McDonald, Eugene, Pvt., Montgomery
McGlamry, James G., Pvt., Deatsville
McKinney, Leo D., Pvt., Prattville
Mickle, Henry F., Pvt., Roanoke
Miller, Daniel M., Cook, Montgomery
Miller, Julius R., Pvt., Pine Hill
Milton, Hilliard, Pvt., Prattville
Milton, Lester, Pvt., Prattville
Milton, Marvin M., Pvt., Prattville
Moody, Clarence, Pvt., Theodore
Moore, Linwood P., Pvt., Mobile
Morrill, Robert E., Pvt., Montgomery
Morris, John, Pvt., Atmore
Morrison, Thomas L., Mechanic, Heflin
Moses, George, Corp., Montgomery
Mumme, Fred W., Pvt., Mobile
Nelson, John D., Mechanic, Thomasville
Newell, James N., Pvt., Mobile
Nowell, Thomas J., Pvt., Ashford
O'Leary, Joseph A., Mess Sgt., Montgomery
Overstreet, Commiele, Pvt., Prichard
Owen, Odis, Corp., Edwardsville
Owens, Ernest S., Pvt., Montgomery
Patrick, Thomas J., Pvt., Parrish
Pearce, Grover, Corp., Gadsden
Perkins, Dee M., Pvt., Heflin
Perkins, Jesse, Heflin
Petrey, George D., Pvt., Petrey
Petrey, Willie, Pvt., Petrey
Platts, Earl P., Pvt., Northport
Plier, Porter M., Pvt., Clanton
Poole, Ernest, Pvt., Gordo
Powell, Arze, Corp., Columbia
Powell, John, Corp., Columbia
Powers, Brady, Pvt., Anniston
Prim, James C., Pvt., Randolph

Pritchett, Ernest W., Pvt., Union Springs
Puckett, William J., Pvt., Mobile
Purcell, Fletcher, Pvt., Prattville
Raspberry, Deece, Corp., Mobile
Ray, Charlie H., Pvt., Centerville
Reese, Roy A., Pvt., Cullman
Roberts, Leonard E., Pvt., Montgomery
Robinson, George, Pvt., Plateau
Robinson, Peter, Pvt., Plateau
Ross, Calvin, Cook, Prattville
Ross, George L., Pvt., Prichard
Roy, Wesley, Pvt., Prattville
Rutledge, Jodie F., Pvt., Anniston
Sawyer, Ben F., Corp., Roy
Sawyer, Bernie M., Pvt., Monroeville
Seamon, Clifton, Pvt., Prattville
Sellars, Carl E., Pvt., Ashford
Shreve, Rex R., Pvt., Crichton
Shumake, John McD., Pvt., Prattville
Singleton, Emmett R., Corp., Iron City
Smith, Ernest C., Sgt., Montgomery
Smith, Floyd C., Corp., Montgomery
Stanfield, Charles D., Longdale
Stanford, Harold, Pvt., Montgomery
Starke, Grady, Corp., Prattville
Stephen, Jule, Pvt., Union Springs
Stephens, Charlie R., Montgomery
Stewart, Henry E., Pvt., Mobile
Stewart, Jimmie J., Pvt., Old Spring Hill
Stroud, Fitzhugh L., Pvt., Canoe
Stubbs, Ocie O., Pvt., Birmingham
Swain, Eddie, Pvt., Mobile
Sweester, Leslie, Pvt., Spring Hill
Tarver, Willie C., Pvt., Montgomery
Thigpen, James B., Sgt., Montgomery
Thornton, Harry L., Pvt., Montgomery
Thompson, James T., Pvt., Roanoke
Tobias, John M., Pvt., Hope Hull
Tolbert, Joseph, Pvt., Montgomery
Toole, John, Pvt., Eufaula
Toole, John T., Pvt., Eufaula
Trehern, Leoder, Pvt., Irvington
Treutel, Allen O., Pvt., Mobile

Veasey, Jesse L., Pvt., Andalusia
Verneuille, Daniel H., Pvt., Mobile
Waits, Leo, Pvt., Wellington
Wakeford, Charles H., Pvt., Mobile
Watson, Dave G., Eufaula
Wiggins, Heurd, Pvt., Montgomery
Wilson, James O., Pvt., Magazine Point
Wilson, Willard B., Pvt., Mobile
Wood, Berry, Pvt., Wetumpka
Wood, Henry C., Corp., Leesburg
Woodcock, Lawrence, Pvt., Mobile
Zarko, Robert J., Pvt.

### COMPANY B

Captain Bryan Whiteburst, Clopton
1st Lieut. George A. Glenn, Gadsden
Acree, Arthur, Pvt., Andalusia
Adams, Sam, Pvt., Clayton
Agerton, Thomas R., Pvt., Atmore
Andrews, Bud, Pvt., Elba
Armstrong, Benn F., Pvt., Millry
Atwell, Jim W., Pvt., Brundidge
Ayres, Orin P., Corp., Headland
Barnhill, Hugh A., Pvt., Enterprise
Bell, Fred, Pvt., Clayton
Beverley, George S., Pvt., Greenville
Beverley, Grover C., Pvt., Greenville
Blair, Mack, Pvt., Brewton
Blair, Sam, 1st Sgt., Eden
Booth, Wilbur F., Pvt., Prattville
Bradford, Thomas C., Pvt., Birmingham
Bradley, William E., Pvt., Abbeville
Brannon, Robert W., Sgt., Eufaula
Broughton, Dan, Corp., Hurricane
Brown, Sherman K., Pvt., Creola
Bryars, Joseph W., Pvt., Abbeville
Bush, Henry L., Pvt., Abbeville
Bush, Jesse, Corp., Cotton Hill
Bush, Richard H., Corp., Carpenters
Byrd, William E., Pvt., Bay Minette
Byrne, George T., Sgt., Bay Minette
Cain, Kramer G., Sgt., Birmingham

Chaudron, Norwell L., Pvt., Flomaton
Churchwell, Oscar, Pvt., Skipperville
Clark, Alvin W., Pvt., Stapleton
Cogdell, James F., Pvt., Union Springs
Cook, Malcolm, Pvt., Skipperville
Cook, Melvin O., Pvt., Enterprise
Cox, Jesse E., Pvt., Bay Minette
Crockett, James E., Pvt., Headland
Crockett, Joe, Pvt., Headland
Cummings, William H., Pvt., Webb
Dabney, Albert C., Pvt., Ensley
Danzey, Luther L., Pvt., Abbeville
Davis, Albert C., Pvt., Abbeville
Davis, Tom W., Pvt., Headland
Davidson, William T., Pvt., McKenzie
Davison, Leslie, Pvt., Canoe
Dolive, Harvey L., Pvt., Hurricane
Drew, William E., Pvt., Lottie
Duck, Robert S., Pvt., Brady
Dunn, Frank, Pvt., Elamville
Dunn, Sam, Pvt., Elisha
Durant, Little Ed, Pvt., Brimley
Durham, Albert E., Pvt., Chavis
Edward, Raymond S., Pvt., Eclectic
Edwards, James A., Pvt., Shorterville
Ethridge, Ralph L., Pvt., Columbia
Farmer, Watson, Pvt., Kinston
Faulk, John, Pvt., Dyas
Faulk, Vander, Pvt., Haleburg
Felice, Mike, Pvt., Birmingham
Flowers, Lorenzo C., Pvt., Brundidge
Floyd, Frank, Bugler, Clayton
Franklin, Otto B., Pvt., Red Level
Frederick, Altie A., Pvt., Adamsville
Frederick, John D., Pvt., Adamsville
French, Cyril G., Pvt., Brundidge
Fretwell, Henry H., Pvt., Perdido
Gamble, James R., Pvt., Abbeville
Garrard, Alfred S., Pvt., Montgomery
Gates, Ance M., Pvt., Atmore
George, Curtis W., Pvt., Foshee
Gilmore, Ernest E., Pvt., Clayton
Graham, Thomas J., Pvt., Atmore

Grant, George, Pvt., Greenville
Gray, Harry H., Pvt., Edgewater
Greene, Cecil E., Pvt., Selma
Grimes, Daniel M., Pvt., Daphne
Grimsley, Brenton A., Pvt., Haleburg
Gunter, Carlie G., Corp., Brundidge
Hall, Dempsey W., Pvt., Nakomis
Hammock, George, Pvt., Bay Minette
Hardwick, Roy M., Pvt., Hardwicksburg
Harris, Edward T., Corp., Bay Minette
Hasselvander, Peter P., Pvt., Ackerville
Haywood, Zebedee, Pvt., Talladega
Hodges, Lester, Pvt., Texasville
Holmes, Origen S., Pvt., Foley
Houston, Wallace, Pvt., Clayton
Howard, Harry J., Pvt., Union Springs
Huff, Walter A., Pvt., Foley
Hughes, Joseph H., Sgt., Mobile
Jackson, Perry, Pvt., Haleburg
Jackson, Stewart M., Pvt., Birmingham
James, James C., Sgt. Q. M., Eufaula
Johnson, Joe O., Pvt., Atmore
Johnson, Oliver, Pvt., Nokomis
Kennedy, John C., Pvt., Clayton
Kennedy, Phipps, Pvt., Abbeville
Kervin, Tyson, Pvt., Red Level
Land, Frank, Pvt., Rome
Laney, Henry C., Abbeville
Langford, Albert, Sgt., Columbia
Lee, John, Pvt., Brooks
Lewis, Ulysses, Pvt., Birmingham
Lint, Frank H., Pvt., Birmingham
Lockhart, Dan, Pvt., Clanton
Lott, Henry, Pvt., Abbeville
Loyd, Alexander, Pvt., Eliska
Luker, William L., Pvt., Atmore
Maddox, Hobson, Pvt., Stapleton
Maddox, Horace S., Pvt., Abbeville
Maddox, Lonnie, Pvt., New Brockton
Martin, John J., Pvt., Clayton
Martin, Sterling B., Pvt., Clayton
Mason, William A., Pvt., Atmore
Mathison, Bertram, Pvt., Abbeville

Mathison, Woodie B., Sgt., Abbeville
Matson, Howard H., Pvt., Talladega
McCain, Ulysses, Pvt., Clay County
McCann, William B., Pvt., Sylacauga
McGhee, Noah, Pvt., Atmore
McGhee, Riley, Pvt., Atmore
McGriff, Harry Lee, Pvt., Columbia
McLain, James W., Pvt., Lottie
McLain, Leon H., Pvt., Red Level
Mezick, Otis, Corp., Ashland
Ming, J. H., Pvt., Newton
Mills, Samuel A., Pvt., Branch
Milstead, Homer B., Pvt., Atmore
Milsted, Corie L., Pvt., Atmore
Milton, Lee, Pvt., Oakystreak
Money, William H., Pvt., Abbeville
Monk, Everett, Pvt., Shorters
Moring, Benjamin, Pvt., Abbeville
Morrison, Grover, Pvt., Clayton
Morrison, Lester, Pvt., Clayton
Noble, Ralph, Pvt., Birmingham
Nolan, Busey, Pvt., Bratt
Northrup, Albert F., Pvt., East Lake
Norton, Robert, Pvt., Clayton
Odom, Ernest B., Pvt., Atmore
Owens, Burl, Pvt., Edwin
Parker, Clyde, Pvt., Perdido
Parker, Samuel, Pvt., Perdido
Patterson, Bob, Pvt., Black
Payne, John W., Pvt., Attala
Penuel, Luther, Pvt., Abbeville
Perdue, Jake, Pvt., Opp
Pratt, John E., Pvt., Birmingham
Quillen, Jeff, Pvt., Clayton
Quisenberry, William Y., Pvt., Pine Apple
Ray, Aubrey C., Pvt., Bay Minette
Reynolds, Henry, Pvt., Abbeville
Rhodes, Carl, Corp., Capps
Richardson, Sibley B., Pvt., Stockton
Roberts, Gary A., Corp., Bay Minette
Roberts, Greil, Pvt., Bay Minette
Roberts, Thomas, Pvt., Capps
Roy, John J., Pvt., Millry

Scott, Ben H., Pvt., Bay Minette
Scroggins, Rufus, Corp., Louisville
Searcy, Samuel R., Pvt., Skipperville
Shirley, Loyd, Sgt., Abbeville
Sims, Coy V., Pvt., Sycamore
Smith, Ernest M., Pvt., Stapleton
Smith, Ernest T., Pvt., Prattsville
Snellings, Willie I., Pvt., Gurley
Starnes, Orr, Pvt., Pell City
Steadhams, Orie D., Pvt., Daphne
Taylor, Alexander G., Corp., Silas
Taylor, Douglas M., Pvt., Bay Minette
Taylor, Henry F., Corp., Gilberton
Taylor, John T., Pvt., Bay Minette
Taylor, Perry A., Pvt., Bay Minette
Thompson, Gideon P., Pvt., Clayton
Thompson, Robert, Pvt., Stockton
Tiller, Benjamin L., Sgt., Headland
Toiler, Fletcher C., Pvt., Carpenters
Turner, Newman, Mech. Pvt., Collinsville
Ward, Frank D., Pvt., Birmingham
Watson, Clyde, Pvt., Clayton
Weekley, Buford, Pvt., Perdido
Wells, Arthur, Pvt., Albertville
West, Cullen, Corp., Baker Hill
Whatley, Harvey, Pvt., Headland
White, Frank B., Pvt., Bay Minette
White, Kinnon R., Pvt., Muscogee
White, Loyd R., Pvt., Bay Minette
White, Marshall N., Pvt., Bay Minette
Whitehurst, Alto L., Sgt., Clopton
Williams, C. B., Pvt., Clayton
Williams, James, Pvt., Bay Minette
Wilson, Walter E., Pvt., Jackson
Wilson, William H., Pvt., Cullonburg
Woodham, Terrel C., Cook, Pvt., Capps
Wren, Edward R., Sgt., Talladega

## COMPANY C

Capt. Gardener Green, Pell City
1st Lieut. Richard Kelly, Jr., Birmingham

2d Lieut. Stephen W. Harris, Huntsville
Acklen, Raymond, Pvt., Huntsville
Adams, Joseph, Corp., Pell City
Aldredge, Evert A., Pvt., Guntersville
Arnold, Frank B., Pvt., Falkville
Autrey, Oscar L., Pvt., Pine Hill
Banister, John M., Pvt., Gwin
Barnard, Harry, Pvt., Samson
Bean, Elmer, Pvt., Easonville
Bearden, Alvin C., Pvt., Birmingham
Bearden, John T., Pvt., Birmingham
Beck, Cecil C., Pvt., Fort Payne
Bell, Lois, Pvt., Geneva
Bowdin, Guy, Pvt., Eden
Brown, Henry W., Pvt., Geneva
Brown, Ollis C., Corp., Eden
Brown, Preston, Pvt., Coffee Springs
Brown, Ruben O., Corp., Pell City
Burnett, Caulia, Pvt., Ocampo
Burton, Will H., Pvt., Daviston
Butler, Cleve, Pvt., Pell City
Butler, Covoso, Pvt., Cordova
Calahan, Sam, Pvt.
Cale, Robert W., Corp., Pratt City
Callahan, Edgar, Pvt., Pell City
Cameron, Frank H., Pvt., West Grun
Cantrell, Herman, Pvt., Huntsville
Carter, Lester, Pvt., Hawk
Cash, Samuel R., Pvt., Winfield
Caudle, Bert, Pvt., Gwin
Causey, George, Pvt., Pell City
Causey, James H., Pvt., Pell City
Chambers, Frank, Pvt., Pell City
Coats, Britt, Pvt., Newtonville
Conger, Charles C., Pvt., Ensley
Cornett, Joseph C., Sgt., Talladega
Croft, Lewis, Pvt., Dawson
Crunk, Percy, Pvt., Florence
Currence, Gilbert, Pvt., Cuba
Davenport, Oliver C., Pvt., Woodward
Davidson, Marcus, Corp., Lincoln
Day, Claude, Pvt., Birmingham
Deaux, Walter D., Pvt., Poarch

DeGaris, Julien S., Sgt., Pell City
Derrick, WM. H., Corp., Birmingham
Derting, Lillard B., Pvt., Huntsville
Dopson, Richard F., Pvt., Wetumpka
Dotson, Walter L., Pvt., Carbon Hill
Drake, Adolphus, Pvt., Wadley
Drake, James L., Pvt., Birmingham
Dunn, Jessie, Pvt., Black
Dunn, Leonard, Pvt., Black
Dunn, Marvin, Pvt., Black
Dupay, Joseph T., Corp., Birmingham
Dye, James A., Corp., Pell City
Fant, George, Sgt., Eden
Foreman, Edgar E., Pvt., Geneva
Forman, Grady D., Pvt., Springville
Fought, Lester, Pvt., Carbon Hill
Gentry, Herman D., Pvt., Huntsville
Gibbons, Marrell, Pvt., Red Level
Gillette, Richard W., Pvt., Ensley
Glasgow, Jack E., Pvt., Birmingham
Gold, Clyde O., Pvt., Chase
Gore, Preston, Corp., Hurtsboro
Goza, Calvin W., Pvt., Fyffe
Graham, Grady, Pvt., Pell City
Griffith, Ralph, Pvt., Pell City
Haney, Owen C., Pvt., Winfield
Hanner, Eugene, Pvt., Elkwood
Harmon, Wasson, Sgt., Pell City
Hassell, John T., Pvt., Andalusia
Hathcox, Wallace, Pvt., Ragland
Haywood, Sterling, Pvt., Daleville
Heflin, Fred, Pvt., Moulton
Helton, Sam, Pvt., Huntsville
Hesterly, Bruton, Pvt., Pell City
Hibbs, Jesse B., Pvt., Birmingham
Hicks, Shelly S., Pvt., White City
Higginbothan, George, Pvt., Pell City
Hill, Floyd J., Pvt., Moulton
Holcomb, James L., Pvt., Kansas
Hollis, Kelcie, Pvt., Brilliant
Holman, Sam, Pvt., Huntsville
Homer, Art, Pvt., Brilliant
Homer, Floyd, Pvt., Brilliant

Howard, Claude S., Cropwell
Hudson, Audrey, Pvt., Thomasville
Hutchinson, Everett H., Pvt., Salies
Hutto, Allan, Pvt., Hartford
Jarrett, Oscar, Corp., Easonville
Johnson, Robert H., Pvt., Brilliant
Johnson, Robert S., Pvt., Kimberly
Johnston, Henry P., Pvt., Luverne
Johnston, Jeff, Pvt., McIntosh
Jone, Fred, Pvt., Walkers Crossing
Jones, Claude W., Pvt., Cowper
Kernodle, George E., Pvt., Birmingham
Kilgore, Randall, Corp., Pell City
Killingsworth, Hayden H., Pvt., Calere
Knowlton, Gilbert R., Pvt., Birmingham
Koonce, Oscar H., Corp., Huntsville
Lacey, Phillip, Pvt., Gardendale
Lambert, William C., Pvt., Jasper
Land, Columbus C., Pvt., Dixonville
Laurell, Ralph, Pvt., Birmingham
Leggett, Melvin, Pvt., Hartford
Linam, Abner, Pvt., Daleville
Longcrier, Paul J., Pvt., Sulligent
Luker, Thomas, Pvt., Lacey Springs
Manning, Berto, Pvt., Majestic
Marsh, Charlie M., Pvt., Mt. Pinson
Mathis, John, Pvt., Dora
Matthews, George M., Pvt., Mathews
Mattinson, Charley, Pvt., Birmingham
McDaniel, James D., Pvt., Springville
McGee, George W., Pvt., Fyffe
McGowan, Early, Pvt., Hartford
McKinnon, Wallace, Pvt., Geneva
Merrill, Jim, Pvt., Warrior
Mitchell, Ernest V., Pvt., Pell City
Mize, Leonidas, Mech., Odenville
Moncrief, Tillman H., Pvt., Gardendale
Moncrief, William F., Pvt., Gardendale
Moore, Dwight, Pvt., Leeds
Morgan, Acie, Pvt., Edgewater
Morrison, Harvey, Sgt., Pell City
Morton, Robert I., Pvt., Birmingham
Mowery, Paul, Pvt., Eden

North, Harwell, Sgt., Lathrop
O'Brien, Thomas E., Pvt., Birmingham
O'Neal, Daniel H., Pvt., Ensley
O'Neal, John D., Pvt., Ensley
Osburn, Charlie, Pvt., Darrington
Parker, John H., Pvt., East Gadsden
Partain, George T., Corp., Birmingham
Patterson, Carlyle W., Corp., Huntsville
Patterson, Fred, Cook, Cropwell
Patterson, William A., Pvt., Pell City
Pitts, Joe, Pvt., Union Springs
Pritchett, Henry G., Pvt., Dozier
Ray, Fred, Pvt., Bell Mills
Rayborn, Elmore, Pvt., Thomasville
Rhea, Raymond, Pvt., Somerville
Riley, Allen, Pvt., Florala
Roberson, James, Corp., Pell City
Sanders, Finus, Corp., Huntsville
Sanders, James, Corp., Pell City
Schell, William M., Pvt., Pell City
Schmidt, George M., Pvt., Birmingham
Scoggins, Jesse T., Sgt., Pell City
Scrimscher, Wilbur, Pvt., Birmingham
Seals, Charlie, Bugler, Pell City
Searcy, Larry P., Pvt., Birmingham
Self, Fred H., Pvt., Mt. Pinson
Shaw, John F., Pvt., Blocton
Sheets, William C., Pvt., McCullough
Sims, Theodore E., Corp., Birmingham
Snell, Edward, Pvt., Lewisburg
Smith, Charles C., Pvt., Jasper
Smith, Leroy, Pvt., Pell City
Smith, Robert S., Pvt., Birmingham
Smith, Sam, Pvt., Birmingham
Smith, Willie, Pvt., Hartford
Somerset, Henry B., Pvt., Geneva
Spradley, Mannon T., Bugler, Pell City
Stephens, James, Pvt., Daviston
Stephens, Oscar D., Corp., Lincoln
Stewart, Lee, Pvt., Cullman
Stubblefield, John W., Pvt., Columbus City
Sullivan, Berry, Pvt., Echola

Sullivan, Mit M., Sgt., Echola
Swan, John D., Pvt., Wellington
Talley, William E., Cook, Torey
Tenney, Roston, Pvt., Coalmont
Thompson, David, Pvt., Chavies
Thunderburk, George W., Pvt., Sulligent
Trotter, Fred B., Pvt., Warrior
Wade, Harrison C., Pvt., Cropwell
Wade, Robert L., Pvt., Huntsville
Walker, Houston E., Pvt., Springville
Walker, Robert B., Pvt., Cropwell
Walker, Willie, Pvt., Huntsville
Watson, Bert, Corp., Eden
Weems, Jesse J., Pvt., Courtland
Williams, George, Pvt., Wilsonville
Williams, Simon J., Pvt., Birmingham
Williamson, Abner, Cook, Odenville
Williamson, Howard, Sgt., Pell City
Willingham, George H., Pvt., Cropwell
Willingham, James B., Cook, Pell City
Willingham, Ran, Corp., Cropwell
Wilson, Benjamin F., Pvt., Ardell
Wilson, Oscar E., Geneva
Windham, Cuthbert T., Pvt., Black
Wolf, Claude, Pvt., Oakman
Wolf, Joe, Pvt., Dora
Wolf, Sim, Pvt., Dora
Wright, Jeff D., Pvt., Ozark
Wright, Will N., Pvt., Geneva
Wyatt, Willie S., Pvt., Birmingham
Young, Cliff, Pvt., Birmingham

## COMPANY D

Capt. Lacey Edmunson, Bessemer
1st Lieut. William A, Jeffery, Andalusia
2d Lieut. Ernest E. Bell, Bessemer
Aaron, Loyd, Pvt., Bessemer
Aloms, Henry, Pvt., Ft. Deposit
Alverson, Benjamin F., Pvt., Huntsville
Ardoyno, John E., Pvt., Mobile
Arnold, Jim, Mech. Huntsville
Atchison, John W., Pvt., Bay Minette

Bailey, Andrew, Sgt., Bessemer
Baker, McCleveland, Pvt., Canoe
Barron, Oran, Sgt., Bessemer
Bell, Joseph, Pvt., Oak Grove
Bethany, Roger H., Pvt., Albany
Birch, Will, Pvt., Red Star
Booth, Lonnie, Pvt., McCullough
Boyington, Colbert W., Pvt., Robertsdale
Bradley, Rufus G., Mech. Chapman
Brightman, Willey T., Pvt., Hayneville
Brightwell, Arthur, Pvt., Sellars
Brumley, James S., Pvt., Harvest
Bullard, Rex, Pvt., Bessemer
Burgin, Joseph A., Pvt., Bessemer
Burnett, Henry I., Pvt., Bessemer
Burnett, Usry, Corp., Bessemer
Burt, Albert, Pvt., Greenville
Burt, Henry O., Pvt., Greenville
Burt, Herbert, Pvt., Greenville
Bush, Amos, Pvt., Greenville
Campbell, William E., Pvt., Talladega
Canoles, Carl, Pvt., Bessemer
Capps, Elijah, Pvt., Bessemer
Casey, Herbert, Pvt., Ozark
Chavis, Marvin, Pvt., Black
Cheatham, William T., Pvt., Greenville
Childress, Reuben, Pvt., Chapman
Chism, Carl, Pvt., Calera
Cochran, Stewart H., Pvt., Bessemer
Coffee, Carl, Pvt., Yolande
Coker, Eugene, Pvt., Greenville
Cone, Clayton, Pvt., Lagrange
Copeland, Roy N., Pvt., Mulberry
Cottingham, Charles J., Pvt., Ramer
Coulter, George D., Pvt., Huntsville
Cowart, Virgil, Pvt., Huntsville
Crosby, Willis J., Pvt., Atmore
Cross, Dan, Pvt., Letohachee
Cross, Isaac, Pvt., Bessemer
Davis, Dewey, Pvt., Bessemer
Davis, Newton J., Pvt., Adger
Davis, Paul W., Pvt., Bessemer
Davis, Samuel H., Pvt., Adger

Day, Carl C., Pvt., Lagrange
Dean, Raymond, Sgt., Bessemer
Deitz, Ross, Sgt., Bessemer
DeVaughan, Sanford, Pvt., Clayton
Dixon, Joseph G., Pvt., Bromley
Dockery, Will, Pvt., Brockwood
Doughtry, Columbus, Pvt., Georgiana
Douglass, John, Sgt., Bessemer
Edwards, William H., Pvt., Flomaton
Evans, John, Pvt., Mobile
Fitzpatrick, Deloach, Pvt., Ensley
Flippo, John E., Pvt., Corona
Forshee, Barney, Pvt., Clanton
Fowlkes, Robert, Pvt., Bessemer
Franklin, Johnnie, Pvt., Greenville
Frazer, William J., Pvt., Greenville
Fredick, Paul, Pvt., Mobile
Freeman, E. H., Corp., Montevalo
Freeman, John I., Corp., Bessemer
Gafford, Stephen F., Pratt City
Gaston, Clyde L., Pvt., Birmingham
Gault, William C., Pvt., Huntsville
Glaze, Columbus C., Pvt., Bessemer
Glover, Othel, Pvt., Jonesboro
Godfrey, Andrew J., Pvt., Ashford
Goodwin, Charlie, Pvt., Palmyra
Gray, Fred, Pvt., Flomaton
Gray, Harold J., Pvt., Albany
Gray, Jesse S., Pvt., Range
Greenlee, Sam, Pvt., Epps
Grubbs, McThias L., Pvt., Black
Grumbles, David, Pvt., Lownsboro
Hall, Varner, Sgt., Birmingham
Hardy, Adrien F., Pvt., Brewton
Harper, James, Pvt., Columniana
Harrison, Thomas L., Pvt., Slocomb
Hatcher, Clyde, Pvt., Bessemer
Haynes, Pugh, Pvt., Sandy Ridge
Henderick, James C., Pvt., Montevalo
Hill, Rufus W., Pvt., Honoraville
Hires, Emmit M., Pvt., Beatrice
Hires, Homer R., Pvt., Beatrice
Holland, Will, Pvt., Sirees

Holley, Alfred, Pvt., Clanton
Hollowell, Luther V., Pvt., Bessemer
Hope, Ben, Pvt., Huntsville
Howell, Ruel E., Pvt., Bay Minette
Howton, Iven, Pvt., Yolande
Hubbard, William F., Pvt., Thompson
Huey, Telman, Pvt., Quinton
Hughes, Clarence M., Corp., Bessemer
Hurst, Frank D., Corp., Bessemer
Jackson, Jefferson R., Pvt., Clanton
Johns, Albert L., Pvt., Brantley
Jones, Carl, Pvt., Bessemer
Jones, Clifton V., Pvt., Johns
Jones, Henry W., Pvt., Greenville
Jones, Robert, Cook, Jemison
Kiker, Henry, Pvt., Browns Station
King, Fred L., Pvt., McCalla
Knight, LeRoy, Pvt., Dyas
Knight, Walter, Corp., Polas
Kyser, Percy, Pvt., Canoe
Lane, Sam E., Pvt., Bessemer
Laney, Ernest, Pvt., Ensley
Lantrip, Herman E., Pvt., Bessemer
League, Will, Pvt., Huntsville
Lee, Joseph, Pvt., Bay Minette
Lee, Sam, Corp., Bessemer
Lewis, Jimmie O., Pvt., Sweetwater
Lewis, Worth, Sgt., Bessemer
Livingston, William Grady, Pvt., Bessemer
Lockhart, John T., Pvt., Clanton
Lockhart, Zeb, Pvt., Clanton
Loyd, Roy W., Corp., Eusley
Manning, Malachi, Mech., Foley
Mariani, Jake G., Pvt., Birmingham
Marlar, Herbert, Pvt., Georgiana
Martin, Phillip, Pvt., Huntsville
Marvin, Charles O., Pvt., Cullman
Mason, James T., Sgt., Huntsville
Mastin, George C., Pvt., Fort Deposit
Matthews, Hardy E., Pvt., Geneva
Mayes, Turner, Pvt., Huntsville
Mays, Henry, Pvt., Bessemer
McAnally, Ernest G., Pvt., Atmore

McCorkle, John A., Pvt., Columbia
McCreary, Ernest R., Pvt., Beatrice
McDaniel, James W., Pvt., Bessemer
McGill, John H., Pvt., Flomaton
McGuire, Fred, Corp., Bessemer
McKinney, John, Pvt., Coopers
McLane, Jim W., Mech., Ensley
Merritt, Warren L., Bugler, Bessemer
Miller, Guy, Pvt., Enterprise
Miller, Isom, Pvt., Plevna
Mitchell, Clarence, Pvt., New Decatur
Mitchell, Leonard, Pvt., Robertsdale
Moorer, John W., Cook, Bay Minette
Moorer, Minter M., Pvt., Bay Minette
Morgan, Thomas, Pvt., Montgomery
Morris, Joe, Pvt., Alabama City
Morrison, John, Corp., Bessemer
Mott, William D., Pvt., Selma
Murray, Ernest, Pvt., Camp Hill
Naylor, Wilbur C., Pvt., Bessemer
Naylor, William Clyde, Pvt., Bessemer
Nerren, Frank, Pvt., Huntsville
Nerren, Sam, Pvt., Huntsville
Newton, Roy, Pvt., Decatur
Nicholson, Harve, Pvt., Hopewell
Niles, Wilfred, Sgt., Bessemer
Norris, Claude M., Sgt., Honoraville
Oglesby, Jim, Pvt., Bessemer
O'Neal, Morris, Pvt., Huntsville
Overton, Homer B., Pvt., Huntsville
Overton, Vernon D., Pvt., Huntsville
Parker, Sloan, Pvt., Clanton
Parsons, Cee, Cook, Johns
Peteete, Oakley, Pvt., Tyson
Peterson, Charles C., Pvt., Greenville
Petty, Paul, Pvt., Andalusia
Pickel, Robert, Pvt., Bessemer
Posey, Seab, Pvt., Bessemer
Pounds, Willis E., Pvt., Clanton
Powell, Frank A., Sgt., Bessemer
Price, James W., Pvt., Huntsville
Reynolds, Wallace, Corp., Bessemer
Ridner, Ben C., Pvt., Huntsville

Rigsby, Horace, Pvt., Georgiana
Roberts, Opal H., Pvt., Huntsville
Rogers, Fred, Sgt., Ensley
Rogers, Robert, Ensley
Rollan, C. C., Pvt., Clanton
Romano, Joe, Pvt., Bessemer
Roper, Jerry, Pvt., Ft. Deposit
Roper, Johnsy O., Pvt., Honoraville
Roy, Newton W., Pvt., Bessemer
Roy, Will, Sgt., Morgan
Ruff, Austin, Corp., Ensley
Russell, Barney, Pvt., Yolande
Russell, S. T., Pvt., Kimbrough
Sampley, James L., Pvt., Honoraville
Satifield, Albert, Pvt., Bessemer
Satifield, Kirk, Pvt., Huntsville
Sawyer, Robert D., Pvt., Bessemer
Scott, Chester K., Pvt., Greenville
Shinglebar, Henry E., Pvt., Albany
Shirley, Alonzo S., Pvt., Clanton
Slinker, Jesse, Pvt., Bessemer
Smith, Harry, Pvt., Bessemer
Speakes, Bernice, Pvt., Bessemer
Spence, Leonard, Pvt., Brewton
Staggs, Robert, Pvt., Maxine
Sullivan, James C., Pvt., Mt. Vernon
Sullivan, John L., Pvt., Huntsville
Syphurs, Herman G., Pvt., Bessemer
Tatum, Ernest F., Pvt., Deatsville
Teske, Amos, Pvt., Coal Valley
Thomley, Joseph W., Pvt., Perdido
Throwyer, Lawrence, Pvt., Flomaton
Tidwell, Gideon, Pvt., Bessemer
Turner, Isaac J., Pvt., Red Level
Turner, Robert J., Pvt., Billingsly
Turner, Rufus, Pvt., Billingsly
Vann, Robert, Pvt., Huntsville
Waller, Tom, Pvt., Honoraville
Watson, Mitchell, Pvt., Jonesburo
Weir, Willie, Pvt., Bessemer
Wheeler, Willie F., Pvt., Bessemer
Whited, Homer, Pvt., Bessemer
Whitehead, Sam, Pvt., Bessemer

Wilcox, Curtis P., Pvt., Mobile
Willbanks, Rolgier, Pvt., Walnut
Windham, Samuel C., Pvt., Oakland
Woodruff, Alto, Pvt., Mt. Willing
Woods, Oscar L., Pvt., Coal Valley
Wooley, Knox E., Pvt., Montevalo
Yansey, Claud, Cook, Huntsville
Young, John O., Sgt., Birmingham

## COMPANY E

Capt. Everette H. Jackson, Montgomery
1st Lieut. Raymond R. Brown, Decatur
Adams, Frank, Pvt., Mobile
Adcock, Jim, Pvt., Andalusia
Albes, John H., Pvt., Decatur
Bailey, Charlie W., Pvt., Butte
Barber, Dewey, Pvt., Athens
Barber, Gaines A., Pvt., Silas
Barnes, Charlie A., Pvt., Opp
Bennett, William J., Pvt, Montgomery
Biggs, Olen D., Pvt., Andalusia
Black, Sam, Pvt., Albany
Blackwell, Sam H., Corp., Albany
Blasingame, Sidney, Pvt, Montgomery
Booker, Guy, Cook, Evergreen
Brandenberg, Henry L., Pvt., Mt. Vernon
Brewer, William R., Pvt., Brooklyn
Bunch, Richard, Pvt., Albany
Burson, Herbert I., Pvt., Montgomery
Buxton, Earlie V., Pvt., Selma
Byford, Andrew W., Sgt., Albany
Byrd, Lawrence Y., Pvt., Birmingham
Camp, John S., Cook, Decatur
Campbell, Smith, Pvt., Ardmore
Clardy, Ben J., Pvt., Moulton
Clark, Jack B., Pvt., Dees Park
Clements, Hugh, Pvt., Hartselle
Coate, Lester L., Pvt., Grove Hill
Cobb, Rufus F., Pvt., Brooklyn
Coesens, Frederick, Pvt., Foley
Coker, James W., Pvt., Prichard
Cole, Kirby, Pvt., Harvest

Conway, Clarence W., Pvt., Cartwright
Crook, David W., Corp., Albany
Dameron, Alex L., Pvt., Mobile
Davis, Ira W., Pvt., Mobile
Dennis, Dolphus R., Pvt., Florala
Derrick, Ira B., Pvt., Gurley
Desmond, Nick J., Pvt., Mobile
DeWinter, Ellis C., Mobile
Dill, Turner, Pvt., Mobile
Dixon, Jessie, Pvt., Mobile
Donel, Corbett R., Pvt., Decatur
Downs, Evans, Pvt., Clanton
Drake, Leslie E., Pvt., Albany
Driver, Letus V., Pvt., Cullman
Drysdale, Harry H., Pvt., Selma
Dubose, William G., Pvt., Florala
Dunn, Ira L., Pvt., Pine Hill
Dunning, James N., Pvt., Thomasville
Dutto, Bryan M., Pvt., Huntsville
Eager, Christian C., Corp., Birmingham
Easterwood, Clarence, Sgt., Huntsville
Eaton, Herbert, Pvt., Moulton
Eley, Clayton, Pvt., Montgomery
Erwin, Frank B., 1st Sgt., Albany
Feeney, Michael P., Pvt., Mobile
Fenn, Ollie R., Pvt., Hartselle
Fletcher, Herndon, Pvt., Mobile
Franklin, Millard N., Pvt., Lockhart
Free, John E., Florala
Free, Joseph J., Pvt., Florala
Gannon, Tillmon, Pvt., Huntsville
Garrett, Bully, Opp
Garrett, Jasper C., Pvt., Lockhart
Gaskin, James A., Pvt., Laurel Hill
Gebhardt, Edward, Pvt., Mobile
Gebhardt, Ward, Pvt., Mobile
Glover, Leo M., Pvt., Mobile
Goldberg, Harry, Pvt., Montgomery
Goodman, Allen J., Pvt., Florala
Goodman, Charlie B., Pvt., Florala
Gover, Jessie, Pvt., Falkville
Grady, Howard J., Pvt., Decatur
Green, Vinton R., Pvt., Silas

Gregory, James R., Pvt., Whalley
Grimes, Grady B., Pvt., Florala
Gwin, Robert E., Pvt., Walker Springs
Hadaway, Richard D., Pvt., Lanett
Haggenmacker, Luther, Pvt., Athens
Hambrick, William M., Corp., Huntsville
Harding, Scott W., Pvt., Mobile
Hardy, Thomas A., Pvt., Montgomery
Harris, Flave F., Pvt., Arlington
Harris, Walter H., Pvt., Mobile
Hearn, Andrew J., Pvt., Prichard
Hearn, Henry T., Pvt., Prichard
Heine, Robert L., Pvt., Cottage Hill
Hendrix, Herbert H., Pvt., Mobile
Hendrix, Lester E., Pvt., Whistler
Hethcoat, Jessie, Pvt., Decatur
Holesapple, Cole F., Pvt., Albany
Howell, Ralph, Pvt., Evergreen
Hunt, Edward L., Pvt., Florala
Hurst, Walter R., Pvt., Albany
Hyland, Dennis, Pvt., Mobile
Jaggers, William R., Pvt., Cullman
Jarvis, William G., Pvt., Allen
Jones, Daniel R., Pvt., Montgomery
Jones, John R., Pvt., Montgomery
Jones, Laurie T., Pvt., Huntsville
Jones, Lemmie C., Pvt., Corona
Jones, McClusky M., Pvt., Montgomery
Jones, Rufus, Pvt., Montgomery
Jones, William E., Pvt., Prichard
Jowers, Jack, Pvt., Florala
Kelly, Nick A., Sgt., Toney
Kirkland, Ralph, Pvt., Opp
Kratzer, Kit C., Pvt., Lamison
Lane, James A., Pvt., Huntsville
Lazenby, Joseph, Pvt., Thomas Station
Lee, George, Pvt., Mobile
Lewis, Clarence S., Pvt., Florala
Lewis, John L., Pvt., Decatur
Lott, George M., Pvt., Mobile
Lucus, John F., Pvt., Whatley
Mahoney, James F., Pvt., Mobile
Main, Curtis, Pvt., Montgomery

Malone, James T., Pvt., Athens
Marlin, Watson C., Pvt., Toney
Marsal, Marcelino, Pvt., Mobile
Maxwell, William M., Pvt., Albany
Mayton, James, Pvt., Thomasville
Mayton, Thomas K., Pvt., Thomasville
McCoy, Aubrey, Pvt., Silas
McCrory, Joseph M., Pvt., Albany
McDonald, Edward H., Pvt., Mobile
McFarland, Pvt., Grove Hill
McGregor, William R., Pvt., Decatur
McMullen, William R., Sgt., Huntsville
McNab, Albert H., Pvt., Cullman
McNerney, Robert, Pvt., Mobile
McNerney, Thomas W., Pvt., Mobile
McSween, John, Pvt., Florala
Means, Willie D., Pvt., Decatur
Mims, Arthur L., Pvt., Florala
Mitchell, Corbet, Pvt., Bellemina
Mott, Roy A., Pvt., Selma
Mullen, Johnnie, Pvt., Mobile
Negus, Graham R., Pvt., Mobile
Newbold, William H., Pvt., Mobile
Nichols, Edwin P., Pvt., Mooresville
Norsworthy, Allen B., Pvt., Brewton
Olsen, John E., Pvt., Mobile
Pate, Stephen N., Pvt., Birmingham
Penland, David A., Pvt., Triana
Philliphs, Douglas L., Pvt., Talladega
Pollenitz, Julius I., Pvt., Rembert
Pool, Milton W., Pvt., Mobile
Porterfield, Clyde F., Pvt., Thomasville
Powell, William B., Pvt., Bayou La Batre
Prestwood, Louis M., Pvt., Andalusia
Pugh, Johnnie, Pvt., Grove Hill
Rabby, Henry T., Pvt., Mobile
Ragsdale, Joe T., Mechanic, Albany
Raubon, Albert G., Pvt., Thomasville
Raugesdale, Ernest C., Sgt, Albany
Rollings, Walter, Pvt., Dothan
Ross, Philip C., Pvt., Albany
Sanderson, Jimmie, Pvt., Athens
Schaffer, John F., Pvt., Mobile

Schwend, George, Montgomery
Scott, Tade, Pvt., Huntsville
Shanholtzer, George L., Pvt., Deer Park
Sharer, Guy C., Cook, Brooksville
Sherrill, Beve B., Pvt., Moulton
Singleton, Joseph T. Pvt., Grove Hill
Singleton, Wit W., Pvt., Wetumpka
Smith, Charles L., Sgt., Albany
Smith, John W., Pvt., Grove Hill
Smith, Lee, Pvt., Heartselle
Snell, Clifford J., Pvt., Grove Hill
Snell, William C., Pvt., Grove Hill
Snow, James T., Pvt., Brewton
Snyder, Edward, Pvt., Selma
Southern, William B., Pvt., Albany
Spencer, Edward, Pvt., Mobile
Spooner, William E., Pvt., Mobile
Stockton, Frank R., Pvt., Albany
Stucky, William C., Pvt., Garland
Swan, Clifton, Pvt., Silas
Tackett, Louie Pvt., Decatur
Tardy, Edwin, Pvt., Mobile
Taube, Samuel, Pvt., Mobile
Taylor, Amos R., Pvt., Tibbie
Taylor, Clay Pvt., Huntsville
Taylor, Frank J., Pvt., Mobile
Tew, Charles E., Pvt., Mobile
Tew, Henry H., Mobile,
Thrower, Chalmers, Pvt., Mobile
Tisdale, Henry I., Pvt., Opp
Tolbert, Perry, Pvt., Evergreen
Troupe, Lee Pvt., Huntsville
Trudeau, Adrian, Pvt., Herbert
Upshaw, Ruel, Pvt., Cullman
Vantreese, Eugene C., Albany
Walker, Harvey C., Pvt., Samson
Walker, Sam, Pvt., Roanoke
Walters, Lorenzo D., Pvt., Montgomery
Warren, Dott A., Corp., Evergreen
Watkins, James A., Pvt., Athens
Watkins, John R., Pvt., Selma
Weir, William A., Pvt., Prattville
White, John J., Pvt., Mobile

Wideman, Roscoe H., Pvt., Central
Wilkinson, John D., Pvt., Mobile
Williams, Thomas E., Pvt., Decatur
Willingham, Albert L., Danville
Winchester, George, Pvt., Mobile
Worley, Earl C., Corp., Decatur
Wright, Gerald O., Pvt., Albany
Yarbrough, Clarence M. Pvt., Selma
Yates, Clarence E., Pvt., Albany

### COMPANY F

Captain Frederick L. Wyatt, Gadsden
1st Lieut. Louis Greet, Gadsden
2nd Lieut James A. Webb, Birmingham
Ables, Crawford Z., Pvt., Gadsden
Adams, Halbert, Pvt., Nauvoo
Adams, Joe F., Pvt., Lanett
Aiken, Chester E., Pvt., Cordova
Allen, Loyd, Pvt., Lanett
Alley, Carl G., Cook, Attalla
Andrews, J. C., Pvt., Lanett
Arrington, William D., Pvt., Murry Cross
Autrey, Evans, Pvt., Flatwood
Bailey, John W., Corp., Gadsden
Baker, Robert H., Pvt., Gadsden
Barnett, Homer, Pvt., Gadsden
Batchelor, Harry H., Pvt., Lanett
Bates, Johnnie C., Mech., Keener
Beckham, Thomas V., Pvt., Dothan
Benton, Edwin J., Bugler, Gadsden
Binion, Eugene M., Pvt., Selma
Blackwood, Champion R., Gadsden
Boone, C. C., Pvt., Sylacauga
Branton, William T., Pvt., Dothan
Brewer, George, Pvt., Russellville
Brown, Walter, L., Pvt., Florala
Bruner, Charlie C., Pvt., Ashford
Bruner, John D., Pvt., Ashford
Bullis, Clayton, R., Pvt., Gadsden
Campbell, Harry, Pvt., Gadsden
Cargill, Olando G., Pvt., Eufaula
Carroll, Alvin C., Pvt., Florala

Chapman, William H., Pvt., Ensley
Christopher, Walter, Pvt., Gadsden
Clem, Johnson, Pvt., Glass
Clements, Dan J., Pvt., Florala
Clements, Sylvester, Pvt., Geneva
Cleveland, Presley, Corp., Selma
Cocke, Henry Y., Pvt., Birmingham
Coker, John T., Pvt., Leesburg
Cooper, Howard G., Sgt., Gadsden
Cooper, William J., Pvt., Alabama City
Cork, Jessie, Pvt., Tuscaloosa
Cox, Ashburn F., Pvt., Lanett
Crowder, Lester D., Pvt., Lanett
Dailey, Claud L., Pvt., Vance
Dale, John R., Pvt., Gadsden
Dandridge, W. B., Pvt., Florala
Davis, George S., Pvt., Birmingham
Davis, William F., Pvt., Lockhart
Dill, Beland, Pvt., Cordova
Dodd, Jasper A., Pvt., Russellville
Donaldson, Thomas, J., Pvt., Opp
Doughtie, Porter R., Pvt., Opp
Drake, John C., Cook, Attalla
Duke, Joseph W., Pvt., Cullman
Elmore, Henry, Pvt., Dothan
Englebert, Charles S., Pvt., Holt
Epps, James G., Pvt., Oneaniah
Essary, Marvin S., Pvt., Greensboro
Essary, Silas G., Pvt., Greensboro
Evans, John, Pvt., Brewton
Everett, Mallie L., Pvt., Florala
Farley, James C., Pvt., Northport
Faulk, Grover E., Pvt., Dothan
Faulk, Plez. C., Pvt., Dothan
Ferguson, Thomas E., Pvt., Attalla
Floyd, Mathews, Pvt., Lineville
Foster, Frank L., Pvt., East Thomas
Foster, Westley, B., Pvt., Lanett
Frazier, Thomas M., Pvt., Union Springs
Freeman, Irvin, Pvt., Lanett
Gafford, Zeak R., Pvt., Holt
Gammon, Charlie, Pvt., Cordova
Garrett, Dan P., Corp., Gadsden

George, Henry H., Pvt., Tuscaloosa
Gertsel, Henry, Pvt., Birmingham
Gilbreath, Junious, Pvt., Sylvania
Glen, Perry A., Pvt., Florala
Goode, Frank, Pvt., Lipscomb
Goss, James W., Pvt., Piedmont
Gramling, John, Pvt., Gadsden
Grammar, Earl, Pvt., Brookwood
Gray, Cue G., Pvt., Hockaday
Gray, Tolbert, H., Pvt., Lanett
Green, Johnnie, Pvt., Guntersville
Griffin, Carl H., Sgt., Gadsden
Grogan, Julius, Pvt., Talladega
Gulledge, Henry M., Pvt., Center
Gwin, Paul L., Corp., Gadsden
Hamaker, Otto, Pvt., Benait
Hammett, Julius, Pvt., Jacksonville
Hammett, Walter, Pvt., Pallas
Harkins, Lonnie, Pvt., Rogers Mill
Harless, Lee D., Sgt., Gadsden
Harrington, James C., Pvt., Lineville
Harris, Miller, Cook, Gadsden
Harrison, John, Pvt., Ft. Deposit
Hatcher, Clayton, A., Pvt., Headland
Hawie, Ashad G., Pvt., Mobile
Hayes, Hubert, Pvt., Dothan
Heath, Robert, Pvt., Marbury
Herring, Shannon C., Pvt., Lanett
Hicks, Othema, Pvt., Gadsden
Hill, Brock, Pvt., Attalla
Hockaday, Andrew, Pvt., Birmingham
Hodge, Walter, Pvt., Florala
Holley, Grover C., Pvt., Lawley
Holloway, Willie, Pvt., Shelby
Huggins, John H., Pvt., Mountain Creek
Hunt, B. H., Sgt., Gadsden
Jackson, Millard F., Corp., Pine Apple
Jackson, Willie, Pvt., Ashford
Jarvis, John B., Pvt., Kincey
Johnson, Ernest, Pvt., Enterprise
Jones, Burl, Pvt., Lineville
Jones, Richard A., Lockhart
Jones, Walter, L., Pvt., Florala

Keene, Taylor, Pvt., Tuscaloosa
Kemp, Clinton, Pvt., Tuscaloosa
Kennedy, Arthur J., Pvt., Bradford
Knight, Joseph L., Pvt., Ensley
Land, Robert, R., Pvt., Birmingham
Largin, James C., Pvt., Vance
Leach, Giles, Pvt., Montgomery
Lee, William L., Pvt., Georgiana
Logan, Walter, J., Pvt., Gadsden
Maas, Charles, S., Pvt., Selma
MacDonald, Gerald, Pvt., Gadsen
Maddox, Cleveland C., Pvt., Dothan
Marchand, Henry, Pvt., Nyland
Marler, Claudie J., Pvt., Lockhart
Marquess, Luther H., Corp., Gadsden
Martin, Peter, T., Pvt., Greensboro
Mathews, William G., Pvt., Crosville
Mathis, Raymond, Pvt., Marbury
May, Chester, D., Pvt., Lanett
Mayes, Robert H., Pvt., Hokes Bluff
McAlileiy, Roy S., Pvt., Clinton
Mcdoanld, Sam, Pvt., Daleville
McDougle, Nathaniel C., Pvt., Sampson
Meeks, Lonnie, Pvt., Gadsden
Meeks, Wiliam H., Pvt., Gadsden
Messer, Lee, Pvt., Dothan
Morgan, Judge T., Pvt., Holt
Moses, Jim Pvt., Brookwood
Moss, Dewey, Pvt., Boyles
Mouchette, Robert W., Pvt., Aliceville
Murdock, Larkin, C., Pvt., Sampson
Murphy, Christopher, Pvt., Ashford
Nails, Robert N., Pvt., Murry Cross
Nevins, Chester, Pvt., Moundville
Newby, Edeard C., Pvt., Lanett
Newsom, Marcus, F., Pvt., Florala
Norred, Jason, Pvt., Talladega
Norwood, Hosea, Pvt., Natural Bridge
O'Bar, Ellihue, Pvt., Piedmont
Otts, Olija Pl, Pvt., Addison
Peacock, Calvin C., Pvt., Dothan
Potter, Rutledge M., Pvt., Birmingham
Prickett, Florence D., Pvt., Jacksonville

Pruett, James A., Pvt., Round Mount
Quinn, Bob, Pvt., 1st class, Hobbs City
Quinn, Jeff D., Corp., Hobbs City
Robertson, Dewey, Pvt., Gadsden
Robinson, Arthus H., Pvt., Birmingham
Roby, John O., Pvt., Tuscaloosa
Rowan, Richard D., Pvt., Selma
Ryan, Joe E., Pvt., Tuscaloosa
Ryan, Leon M., Pvt., Tuscaloosa
Salmon, Joe, Pvt., Dothan
Sanders, Ellie, G., Pvt., Lawley
Santoroa, John, Pvt., Birmingham
Satterfield, Grover C., Pvt., Fort Payne
Scott, Jim K., Pvt., Dothan
Seay, Royal, Pvt., Tuscaloosa
Seymore, Tarleton, T., Pvt., Dothan
Shirley, Bernie L., Pvt., Headland
Short, Shirley, Pvt., Daubee Springs
Sigler, Roy, E., Pvt., Tuscaloosa
Simpson, Luther H., Pvt., Alabama City
Sims, James C., Pvt., Lanett
Sitz, Bob, Pvt., Attalla
Skipper, Hazy L., Pvt., Grimes
Smith, Albert R., Pvt., Tuscaloosa
Smith, Clarence J., Pvt., Eutaw
Smith, Eddie, C., Pvt., Florala
Smith, Edward G., Sgt, Gadsden, Ala
Smith, Jack, Pvt., Piedmont
Smith, Joe, Pvt., Lanett
Smith, Martin L., Pvt., Enterprise
Smith, William E., Pvt., Oakman
Soots, George, Pvt., Cordova
Southers, John A., Pvt., Peechburg
Spratlan, Mason, H., Pvt., Hardaway
Squires, William, J., Pvt., Peterson
Stephens, Murphy, Pvt., Greensboro
Strickland, Wilbur C., Pvt., Eutaw
Sutton, Will R., Bugler, Gadsden
Sykes, Henry P., Pvt., Birmingham
Tatum, Ammon, Pvt., Florala
Thomas, Edward B., Pvt., Weighton
Thomas, Ray, Pvt., Gadsden
Thomaston, Thomas, Pvt., Lanett

Thompson, Horace, Cook, Attalla
Thompson, James O., Pvt., Birmingham
Thorp, Hugh H., Pvt., Millville
Tierce, Robert C., Pvt., Northport
Tierce, Willie A., Pvt., Northport
Trim, Hiram B., Pvt., Dothan
Vickery, Chester, R., Pvt., Dothan
Vickery, Earl W., Corp., Gadsden
Vinson, Luther, Pvt., Montgomery
Vinyard, Lester, Pvt., Sayreton
Walker, Joseph G., Corp., Gadsden
Wallace, Walter, Pvt., Garland
Walters, John B., Pvt., Gadsden
Ward, James, Pvt., Lanett
Ware, Leon, Pvt., Talladega
Waters, Joe, Pvt., Florala
Watson, John C., Corp., Pine Apple
Webb, Frank, Corp., Gadsden
West, James H., Sgt., Hokes Bluff
West, Lee, Pvt., Cullman
Whitehurst, Emory J., Pvt., Florala
Whitehurst, Marion A., Pvt., Florala
Whitworth, Thomas J., Pvt., Gadsden
Williams, Frank W., Pvt., Mobile
Williams, Jessie V., Pvt., Lanett
Williams, Patton, N., Pvt., Coker
Williams, Robert, Pvt., Lanett
Wilson, David F., Pvt., Florala
Wilson, Emmett C., Pvt., Gadsden
Wood, Edwin M., Corp., Selma
Woodall, James T., Pvt., Florala
Yeats, Joe J., Sgt., Gadsden
Young, Grover V., Pvt., Gadsden

## COMPANY G

Captain Oscar C. Speight, Eufaula
1st Lieut. Abner Flowers, Ozark
2nd Lieut. Peyton Deese, Skipperville
Adams, Joe L., Pvt., Troy
Adams, Lewie H., Pvt., Midland City
Adams, Walter M., Pvt., Troy
Adcock, Len K., Pvt., Newton

Ammons, Thomas, J., Pvt., Ozark
Ammons, William T., Corp., Ozark
Anderson, John W., Pvt., Pineapple
Andrews, Pres H., Pvt., Midland City
Avant, Lester, Corp., Midland City
Baggett, Nick, Pvt., Vellie
Baldwin, Schafnerr M., Corp., Midland City
Ballard, Ewell F., Pvt., Troy
Bedgood, Ira, Pvt., Brewton
Bettress, Fred D., Sgt., Newton
Blackman, Clarence, Pvt., Flomaton
Blackman, John, Pvt., Foshee
Blowers, Marshall, Pvt., Malvern
Brooks, Hiram B., Pvt., Ozark
Brown, Bill, Corp., Ozark
Brown, Charlie, Corp., Brewton
Brown, Everett H., Pvt., Brewton
Bryan, John T., Pvt., Crenshaw
Burnett, Henry G., Pvt., Brewton
Cain, Colie, Pvt., Ozark
Canter, Moses E., Pvt., Coffee Springs
Capps, Joe L., Pvt., Ozark
Carr, Henry, Corp., Eufaula
Carroll, Arthur A., Pvt., Ozark
Carroll, Edward W., Pvt., Ozark
Carter, Oscar J., Pvt., Ariton
Casey, Lemuel A., Sgt., Ozark
Cason, Brannon, Pvt., Ozark
Chandler, William, Pvt., Ozark
Chesser, Frank M., Pvt., Atmore
Clark, Joseph S., Pvt., Ozark
Coe, Daniel A., Mech., Dothan
Corey, John A., Corp., Evergreen
Coskery, Horace C., Pvt., Troy
Cotton, Samuel, Mess. Sgt., Ozark
Cotton, Willie W., Pvt., Ozark
Cowart, Eugene A., Pvt., Troy
Cowart, William J., Pvt., Troy
Cox, Samuel L., Pvt., Local
Crawford, Luther C., Pvt., Ozark
Cutts, Ernest E., Corp., Brewton
Davis, Willie N., Pvt., Pollard

Dean, Barnie J., Pvt., Ozark
Dean, Tullie M., Pvt., Ozark
Deese, William A., Jr., Sgt., Ozark
Dick, Leslie L., Pvt., Midland City
Digman, Kevil, Pvt., Greenville
Dixon, Cullie, Pvt., Brewton
Dixon, Harry B., Pvt., Brewton
Dixon, Hubert, Pvt., Daleville
Dixon, John P., Pvt., Brewton
Downing, Jessie Pvt., Wallace
Edwards, James I., Pvt., Flomaton
Ellis, Roy G., Sgt., Ozark
Entrekin, Joe L., Pvt., Canoe
Ezelle, Clayton, Pvt., Ozark
Ezelle, Henry I., Corp., Ozark
Findley, Albert L., Pvt., Brewton
Franklin, Emery B., Pvt., Dothan
Freeman, John H., Pvt., Brewton
Fuller, Edmond, Pvt., Brewton
Gatwood, Houston, Pvt., Pollard
Gatwood, Millard F., Pvt., Brewton
Gatwood, Ollie, Pvt., Pollard
Godwin, Barney C., Pvt., Daleville
Goff, Hansel M., Bugler, Ozark
Griffin, David A., Pvt., Atmore
Hammac, Carey, Pvt., Brewton
Hammock, Hiram, Pvt., Daleville
Harper, Freeman L., Pvt., Atmore
Haveard, Charlie L., Pvt., Roberts
Hawkins, Glen H., Corp., Ariton
Helms, Albert W., Corp., Ozark
Herndon, William H., Corp., Troy
Hicks, William T., Pvt., Ozark
Holladay, Ess B., Pvt., Brewton
Holladay, Henry E., Pvt., Brewton
Holladay, Kena, Pvt., Brewton
Holland, Chester L., Pvt., Castleberry
Jerkins, Rayvonie, Pvt., Columbia
Johnson, Louis D., Sgt., Ozark
Jones, Calloway, Pvt., Newton
Jones, Clayton, Pvt., Mount Willing
Jones, Gus, Pvt., Brewton
Jones, Jule M., Sgt., Ozark

Jordan, Ben F., Pvt., Brewton
Jordan, Foy D., Corp., Daleville
Judah, Richard H., Cook, Daleville
Kennedy, Barnie, Pvt., Foshee
Killingsworth, Easby, Pvt., Pollard
King, Early, Pvt., Ariton
Kirkland, Alexander, Pvt., Midland City
Kirkland, Bryant, Pvt., Castleberry
Kirkland, Samuel, Corp., Midland City
Lambert, Henry S., Pvt., Dothan
Lamberth, Charlie W., Pvt., Pollard
Leroy, Hughie, Pvt., Midland City
Lowery, Donnie D., Corp., Atmore
Lynn, John T., Pvt., Brewton
Malone, Halcomb H., Supply Sgt., Brew-
ton,
Mancil, Jake, Pvt., Dixie
Mann, William P., Corp., Midland City
Manning, James J., Pvt., Brewton
Manning, Louis A., Corp., Brewton
Manning, Mathew G., Pvt., Pollard
Manning, Sidney E., Pvt., Flomaton
Martin, William A., Pvt., Brewton
Massingill, Isadorre, Pvt., Brewton
Massingill, Parker, Pvt., Kirkland
McArthur, Robert G., Pvt., Brewton
McCollum, John C., 1st Sgt., Bessemer
McGee, Jessie, G., Pvt., Enterprise
McKay, John C., Pvt., Skipperville
McLain, Dan J., Pvt., Nakomis
McLain, Hosea G., Pvt., Ozark
McLain, John, Pvt., Dothan
McLain, Max, Sgt., Dothan
McLain, Wesley M., Pvt., Nakomis
McRee, John G., Pvt., Ozark
Melton, Lonnie, Sgt., Ozark
Metcalf, William F., Mech., Ozark
Middlebrooks, Clyde, Pvt., Midland City
Middlebrooks, Thomas B., Pvt., Mid-
land City
Miller, Green L., Pvt., Ozark
Ming, Eddie C., Pvt., Newton
Ming, Ernest J., Pvt., Newton

Mooneyham, Erie N., Pvt., Clio
Mooneyham, Lester, Corp., Clio
Mooneyham, Nealie, Pvt., Clio
Morris, Charlie, Pvt., Atmore
Morris, Dave, Pvt., Atmore
Morris, Jim H., Pvt., Roberts
Morris, Marvin, Pvt., Roberts
Morris, Pitt R., Pvt., Daleville
Morris, William, Pvt., Ozark
Morrow, Charles T., Corp., Ozark
Myhand, Hobson P., Pvt., Auburn
Nichols, Marvin, Pvt., Brewton
Nelson, Claude M., Sgt., Newton
Newsome, Richard C., Corp., Ozark
Pace, Albert C., Mech., Florala
Palmer, James A., Pvt., Midland City
Parker, Bruce A., Pvt., Brewton
Parker, Bode S., Sgt., Brewton
Parker, Stewart, Corp., Brewton
Parrish, Grady, Corp., Daleville
Parrish, Zack, Pvt., Pollard
Patterson, Travis B., Pvt., Ozark
Pennington, Joseph H., Pvt., Troy
Peters, Benjamin F., Pvt., Ozark
Pilcher, Robert R., Corp., Ozark
Poole, William C., Pvt., Sellers
Powell, Charles A., Pvt., Bay Minette
Pullen, Harry M., Pvt., Dothan
Reneau, Lonnie, Dothan
Riley, Hurley, T., Bugler, Ozark
Riley, John L., Mech., Ozark
Riley, Major D., Pvt., Ozark
Ruggs, Judge A., Pvt., Dothan
Saliba, Gabriel, Pvt., Ozark
Sasser, Wiley D., Pvt., Atmore
Saunders, Curtis, Pvt., Echo
Shirah, Angus M., Corp., Ozark
Shiver, Louis A., Pvt., Tennville
Simmons, Grover C., Pvt., Daleville
Skipper, James O., Pvt., Slocomb
Skipper, Olive O., Corp., Ozark
Skipper, Sidney M., Pvt., Ozark
Smart, Victor L., Pvt., Troy

Smith, Horace, Pvt., Brewton
Smith, James I., Pvt., Brewton
Snell, John D., Pvt., Brewton
Snellgrove, Charlie, Pvt., New Brockton
Spurlock, Hillary, Pvt., Ozark
Steele, Walter, Pvt., Foshee
Stevens, Perry H., Pvt., Midland City
Strickland, Edgar B., Corp., Ozark
Tatum, Frederick D., Pvt., Banks
Tatum, William P., Pvt., Newton
Thames, Edward E., Pvt., Manster
Thomas, Dee C., Pvt., Newton
Thomas, Jay H., Pvt., Newton
Thornton, Orlin, Pvt., Route B, Newton
Thweatt, Henry, Pvt., Newton
Tillman, Arnold, Pvt., Clio
Trammell, William, Pvt., Dothan
Trawick, Haywood J., Corp., Newton
Veal, Franklin D., Pvt., Troy
Walker, Henry C., Pvt., Ozark
Walker, John L., Pvt., Webb
Walker, Leon G., Pvt., Atmore
Walker, Willie R., Corp., Atmore
Watson, Thomas G., Pvt., Enterprise
Weaver, Elton P., Pvt., Brewton
Weaver, Levi P., Pvt., Brewton
Weaver, Walter C., Pvt., Flomaton
Webb, Jeptha A., Pvt., Columbia
Weeks, Samuel E., Pvt., Kinston
White, James F., Pvt., Brewton
White, Loran, Pvt., Brewton
Whittle, John B., Pvt., Ozark
Wiggins, Cilby, Pvt., Brewton
Williams, Ernest W., Pvt., Dothan
Williams, Thomas, Corp., Midland City
Woodall, John L., Cook, Ozark
Wright, Mallie C., Corp., Ozark
Yarbrough, Fred L., Corp., Dothan

## COMPANY H

Captain Herman W. Thompson,
  Alexander City

Abernathy, John F., Pvt., Hollins
Adams, Sanford N., Pvt., Dadeville
Allen, William E., Pvt., Troy
Anderson, Robert C., Pvt., Selma
Andrews, Walter C., Pvt., Enterprise
Arant, Charlie O., Pvt., Selma
Armstrong, James D., Pvt., Sanford
Atchison, George E., Mech., Bigbee
Baker, A. A., Pvt.
Baker, William H., Pvt., Doris
Barley, Lum, Pvt., Coffee Springs
Batchelor, Henry L., Pvt., Enterprise
Bates, Joe H., Pvt., Belmont
Beck, George A., Pvt., Brundidge
Benson, Robert L., Pvt., Alexander City
Billingsley, Hezzie, Pvt., Goodwater
Blair, Lonnie W., Pvt., Brooklyn
Blair, Sidney, Pvt., Andalusia
Boddie, Henry C., Pvt., Tallassee
Bouyden, George M., Pvt., Talladega
Boyette, Pleas R., Pvt., Enterprise
Boyles, Howard H., Pvt., Mobile
Brantley, Alphus, Pvt., Troy
Bridges, James F., Pvt., Fairfax
Brown, Davis, Pvt., Columbiana
Brown, Homer, Pvt., Alexander City
Brown, Virgil, Pvt., Stevenson
Brunson, Joseph F., Pvt., Selma
Bryan, Gus J., Pvt., Elba
Bryant, James F., Pvt., Leeds
Bullard, Alto L., Pvt., Elba
Bumpers, Earl, Pvt., Selma
Bumpers, Leon, Pvt., Selma
Bunkley, Frank K., Sgt., Montgomery
Burns, Edward J., Pvt., Clintonville
Buxton, Samuel E., Pvt., Selma
Buxton, William B., Pvt., Enterprise
Byrd, Acrel A., Pvt., Enterprise
Byrd, Joe Tom, Pvt., Enterprise
Caldwell, Thomas F., Pvt., Dadeville
Carlton, George R., Pvt., Alexander City
Carroll, Jacob E., Pvt., Andalusia
Carroll, Martin E., Pvt., Enterprise

Cassels, Marion, Pvt., Sylacauga
Catchings, Euell, Pvt., Tallassee
Champion, James, Pvt., Munford
Clark, William B., Cook, Tallassee
Clowd, Guss, Pvt., Stevenson
Collins, Edward, Pvt., Dawes
Collins, George, Pvt., Georgiana
Collins, James C., Pvt., Selma
Commander, H. H., Pvt., Enterprise
Conville, David H., Mech., Sylacauga
Cope, Eldridge, Pvt., Inverrniss
Cordle, Lehman C., Pvt., New Brocton
Cotheran, Henry C., Pvt., Deatsville
Culbreth, Arthur F., Pvt., Cotton Wood
Culver, Clarence L., Pvt., Elber
Dabbs, Henry L., Sgt., Anniston
Dabbs, Pattie P., Pvt., Munford
Daniel, Roy, Pvt., Ensley
Dassinger, Edgar, Pvt., Inverniss
Daugherty, Walter, Pvt, Gadsden
Davidson, Daniel C., Pvt., Oakman
Davis, Charles, Supply Sgt, Birmingham
Davis, Curtis F., Pvt., Kensie
Dial, Bob, Pvt., Long Island
Dial, Frank, Pvt., Long Island
Dillard, Jessie M., Pvt., Notasulga
Dixon, Nelo M., Pvt., Cusseta
Donaldson, James W., Pvt., Red Level
Duke, Ary A., Pvt., Dosie
Duke, Cletus T., Mess. Sgt., Alexander
  City
Dunn, Aubrey, Pvt., Tallassee
Dunn, Aubrey, Pvt., North Port
Dupree, Henry B., Sgt., Dadeville
Edward, Carmen E., Pvt., Selma
Elliot, Harvey Lee, Corp., Aberden
Emmons, Abraham, Pvt., Brewton
Faircloth, Legal, Pvt., Tennille
Fillingim, Lanie G., Cook, Tennille
Fincher, William R., Sgt., Alexander City
Franklin, Dock J., Pvt., Andalusia
Franklin, Earl S., Corp., Goodwater
Free, William H., Pvt., Enterprise

Fulcher, Tom, Newton
Fuller, John T., 1st Sgt., Alexander City
Gillis, James, Pvt., Troy
Golden, Henry M., Pvt., Enterprise
Graham, Renial, Pvt., Eclectic
Greagory, James M., Pvt., Goshen
Green, Leonard R., Pvt., East Tallassee
Grey, Edgar D., Pvt., Hacoda
Grimsley, Arnold B., Pvt., Enterprise
Grimsley, Joseph H., Pvt., New Brocton
Hamilton, Robert, Sgt., Alexander City
Hancock, James O., Pvt., Alexander City
Harper, Charles H., Pvt., Selma
Harris, Ivon N., Pvt., Enterprise
Harris, John L., Pvt., Banks
Head, Arthur, Pvt., Linwood
Helm, Willie, Pvt., Selma
Hicks, Leon, Pvt., Andalusia
Hill, Robert W., Pvt., Napoleon
Holland, George, Pvt., New Brockton
Holloway, Willie, Pvt., Enterprise
Hoomes, Louis J., Pvt., Brooklyn
Hornsby, Jasper L., Pvt., Sylacauga
Huges, Ellis, Pvt., Selma
Hughes, Euart C., Pvt., Enterprise
Hutchison, Roscoe R., Pvt., Enterprise
Hysmith, Louis J., Pvt., Elba
Jackson, Ernest, Pvt., Selma
Jarrett, Marshall H., Pvt., Childersburg
Johnson, Carl, Pvt., China Grove
Jones, Donald G., Pvt., Toot
Jones, Frank P., Sgt., Lanett
Jones, John A., Corp., Sylacauga
Jones, Lester, Pvt., Wetumpka
Jowers, Carley J., Pvt., Enterprise
Keefe, Robert, Pvt., Andalusia
King, Rupert W., Pvt., Troy
Lawhorne, Clarence M., Pvt., Shawmut
Lightsey, Fred H., Corp., Childersburg
Lindley, William H., Bugler, Abbeville
Logan, Lehman H., Pvt., Enterprise
Lyerly, Charlie M., Pvt., Wetumpka
Lyerly, Willie V., Wetumpka

Mangrum, Willie P., Pvt., Shawmut
McCaskill, Haley, Pvt., Troy
McCluskey, James, Pvt., Tallassee
McCormick, Burgie, Pvt., Pigeon Creek
McDaniel, Guydie, Cook, Alexander City
McGlon, James, Pvt., Lanett
McInstosh, William D., Pvt., Chancellor
McLaney, James W., Pvt., Louisville
McLeod, James A., Pvt., Opp
McMurphy, Oscar H., Pvt., Breadenburg
Melton, William H., Pvt., Tallassee
Merrill, James O., Pvt., Andalusia
Miller, Will, Pvt., Enterprise
Milner, Jack W., Pvt., Alexander City
Milstead, Graham, Pvt., Calera
Milstead, John, Pvt., Ridersville
Milstead, Russell, Pvt., Calera
Mitcham, Otho L., Pvt., Kellyton
Moore, Shelly D., Pvt., Enterprise
Morgan, Hughie F., Pvt., Sylacauga
Morris, James L., Pvt., Shawmut
Morrison, Odis, Pvt., Alexander City
Murdock, Charlie, Pvt., Enterprise
Niblett, Doil F., Sgt., Kellyton
Nichols, Talmadge R., Pvt., Chancellor
Nugent, Laney E., Pvt., Columbus
Odom, Leonard R., Pvt., Enterprise
Oliver, Leonard R., Pvt., Lanett
Orr, Archie D., Pvt., Tallassee
Orr, Roland, Pvt., Tallassee
Owens, Eston, Pvt., Eufaula
Owens, Robert E., Pvt., Tallassee
Parker, Tom, Pvt., Alexander City
Parrish, Otto, Pvt., Ozark
Pittman, Vergie B., Pvt., Fackler
Pitts, David F., Grantville
Plant, Allen L., Pvt., East Tallassee
Powell, Lacey E., Pvt., Troy
Powell, Robert E., Pvt., Notasulga
Rachaels, Daniel N., Pvt., New Broston
Rain, Sam G., Pvt., Selma
Rainey, Marvin, Pvt., Troy
Raley, Millard A., Pvt., Andalusia

Riley, Dock, Pvt., Enterprise
Roberson, George, Pvt., Andalusia
Roberson, Neusom, Pvt., Andalusia
Roberson, Tom, Pvt., Sycamore
Robinson, John, Sgt., Tallassee
Russell, Walter F., Pvt., Anniston
Sandlin, Richard T., Sgt., Alexander City
Sargent, Lord, Pvt., East Tallassee
Scott, William G., Corp., Summerville
Senn, Clifford, Pvt., Troy
Sharp, General G., Pvt., Troy
Shows, Daniel E., Pvt., McKinsie
Sikes, Willie J., Pvt., Troy
Sims, Henry, Pvt., Sylacauga
Smith, Benjamin, Pvt., Quenton
Smith, Crumpton, Pvt., Andalusia
Smith, John A., Pvt., Red Level
Smith, Robie V., Pvt., East Tallassee
Smith, William G., Pvt., Eclectic
Stewart, Percy M., Pvt., Andalusia
Stuckey, Charlie F., Pvt., Andalusia
Tant, Orbie, Pvt., Tallassee
Taylor, James C., Pvt., Phoenix City
Thames, Jesse, Pvt., Andalusia
Thompson, James H., Pvt., Enterprise
Tidwell, Cleveland M., Pvt., Florala
Tillery, John, Pvt., Andalusia
Tomblin, Cook E., Pvt., Enterprise
Tucker, Joe, Pvt., Selma
Vaughn, William L., Pvt., Troy
Vines, Erbie G., Pvt., McKensie
Wadsworth, Lee A., Pvt., Mulberry
Walker, Grady E., Pvt., Rome
Walker, Joe B., Pvt., West Point
Ward, Will, Mech., Andalusia
Whatley, Wesley J., Pvt., Birmingham
Whidby, Nelo, Corp., Troy
Williams, Canyoun, Corp., Springville
Williams, John B., Pvt., Tallassee
Williams, Madison J., Pvt., Selma
Willis, Joe, Pvt., Chancellor
Wilson, James, Pvt., Chancellor
Windham, James B., Pvt., Daleville

Windham, John M., Corp., Elba
Yarbrough, Cumby, Pvt., Dadeville
Yates, Robert, Pvt., Anniston

## COMPANY I

Captain Robert A. Dobbins
1st Lieut. George R. Newbegin
1st Lieut. George W. Erwin
2nd Lieut. Harry R. Young
2nd Lieut. Henry L. Griggs
2nd Lieut. James C. Blaney
2nd Lieut. James H. Donough
Aarons, Joe C., Pvt., Owassa
Aarons, Mark A., Pvt., Evergreen
Aarons, Nick, Pvt., Owassa
Abernathy, Floyd, Pvt., McCall
Acreman, Clarence J., Pvt., Georgiana
Andrews, James L., Pvt., Repton
Ardis, John, Pvt.
Arnold, Oscar, Pvt., Malvern
Atkins, Jesse D., Pvt., LaGrange
Baggett, Lee, Pvt., Castleberry
Barnes, Jesse C., Mech., Shawmut
Batley, William C., Pvt., Frankville
Beeder, Owen, Cook
Berry, Bryant, Pvt., Notasulga
Bolen, John R., Pvt., Jackson
Booker, Dewey, Pvt., Smith Station
Boutwell, Charlie, Pvt., Evergreen
Boyd, William T., Sgt., LaFayette
Braxton, Edward J., Pvt., Evergreen
Brown, Clyde, Pvt., Phoenix
Brown, Esbie C., Pvt., Lightwood
Bryant, Wallace J., Pvt., Bluffton
Burkett, Walter J., Pvt., Castleberry
Cain, Sam E., Pvt., Phoenix
Champion, John W., Pvt., Clayton
Cheeks, Wiley H., Pvt., Girard
Cheney, Prather, Pvt., Phoenix
Chestian, Hilliard S., Pvt., Jackson
Clements, John M., Pvt., Opelika
Cline, Henry E., Pvt., Wedowee

Coker, Jay C., Pvt., Evergreen
Coleman, Charles A., Pvt., Creola
Crawford, John E., Mobile
Crenshaw, Clarence W., Pvt., Leroy
Crim, Luther J., Pvt., Calera
Crosby, William, Corp., Phoenix
Cumbie, Elmer C., Pvt., Dothan
Cunningham, Clifford, Pvt., Atmore
Currie, Jabe, Corp., Alexander
Curry, Joe D., Pvt., River Falls
Dalton, John I., Pvt., Detroit
Davis, Roy, Pvt., Castleberry
Digby, Roy, Pvt., 1st class, Girard
Donovan, Dan J., Pvt., Montgomery
Doyle, Marshall N., Pvt., Mobile
Duke, James L., 1st Sgt., Opelika
Dunn, Claude M., Pvt., Salitpa
Eastburn, Eugene B., Pvt., Delchamps
Edwards, Robin, Pvt., Phoenix
Eldridge, Columbus, Pvt., Dothan
Elliott, Grandville, Sgt., Opelika
Ellis, James C., Pvt., Darlington
Ellison, Talbert C., Pvt., Creola
Ethredge, Marion D., Pvt., Samson
Ewing, John L., Pvt., Gardendale
Fallin, Courtney B., Corp., Montgomery
Fletcher, Jasper N., Pvt., Estell Springs
Fletcher, Robert, Pvt., Girard
Fore, Dewitt, Pvt., Monroeville
Franklin, Oscar, Pvt., Montgomery
Friddle, Alver, Pvt., Thomasville
Fuller, Archie, Pvt., Wadley
Fullerton, Omer M., Pvt., Phoenix
Gates, Monroe J., Pvt., Thomasville
Gay, Eldridge, Sgt., Tallassee
Gay, Joseph W., Pvt., Central
Giles, Dewey, Pvt., Ensley
Gilmore, Henry L., Pvt., Phoenix
Glasscock, James, Pvt., Wetumpka
Golden, Henry, Cook, Phoenix
Goode, James C., Pvt., Lipscomb
Green, Lewis, Pvt., Castleberry
Greene, William E., Corp., Wedowee

Griffin, Bowen, Pvt., Greenwood
Griggs, Charlie, Pvt., Girard
Griggs, Ocie O., Pvt., Girard
Griggs, Royal A., Pvt., Girard
Hall, Hartridge, Pvt., Malvern
Hall, Jesse A., Pvt., Malvern
Hall, Wilmer P., Corp., Geneva
Hammac, William E., Pvt., Wallace
Hardin, Leo, Mechanic, Girard
Harrell, John H., Pvt., Castleberry
Harris, Robert P., Corp., Tallassee
Hayes, Ernest H., Pvt., Columbus
Hayes, John B., Pvt., Notasulga
Hendrix, Milton, Pvt., Wylom
Hestley, Daniel M., Bugler, Shawnut
Higgins, Charles R., Pvt., Birmingham
Hodge, Joe, Pvt., Phoenix
Holeman, Charlie R., Pvt., Cottondale
Holley, Marion, Pvt., Wetumpka
Hood, Gurvis, Pvt., Smith Station
Howard, Cullin, Pvt., Gardendale
Huckaby, Crawford L., Corp., Lineville
Huff, Wylie C., Pvt., Shawmut
Hughes, Grover C., Corp., Slocomb
Hughes, Jess, Pvt., Warrior
Hutchins, David, Pvt., Notasulga
Ingram, Robert L., Pvt., Brewton
Jernigan, William H., Pvt., Wallace
Johnson, Ernest L., Pvt., Benoit
Johnson, Joe H., Pvt., Auburn
Johnson, John S., Corp., Evergreen
Johnson, Rander, Corp., Samson
Jones, Brady, Pvt., Clanton
Kelly, Henry G., Pvt., Eldridge
Kelly, Otis H., Mechanic, Girard
Kines, Horace, Sgt., Center
Lavender, John R., Pvt., Grove Hill
Lipford, Omie, Pvt., Girard
Loosen, Otto H., Supply Sgt., Opelika
Loyless, James C., Pvt., Hilton
Lyons, Jesse, Mechanic, Shawmut
Maiden, Walter G., Pvt., Castleberry
Martin, Alma M., Girard

Mathews, Frank, Pvt., Montgomery
McCarley, Willis F., Pvt., Shawmut
McCartney, Joe F., Corp., Samson
McCollister, William T., Pvt., Phoenix
McDonald, Sam A., Pvt., Jackson
McDurmont, Leaman, Corp., Coffee Springs
McGee, Will C., Pvt., Roba
McGraw, Pete, Sgt., Opelika
McGuire, Henry V., Pvt., Phoenix
McGuire, John W., Pvt., Notasulga
McInish, Paul J., Pvt., Eclectic
McVey, Curtis, Pvt., McVey
Meadows, Floyd, Pvt., Birmingham
Miller, Calvin G., Corp., Samson
Miller, Charles H., Pvt., Jasper
Millican, Virgil C., Corp., Fabius
Milstead, Albert R., Pvt., Jackson
Mitchell, Collis W., Corp., Seale
Moonk, Elvin C., Pvt., Suggsville
Mullin, Joseph L., Pvt., Phoenix
Neese, Oscar, Pvt., Whistler
Neese, Otto, Pvt., Whistler
Newsome, Chester, Pvt., Girard
Newton, John G., Sgt., Slocomb
Nicholas, Thomas H., Pvt., Evergreen
O'Hara, Ben, Pvt., Opelika
Oliver, Archie C., Pvt., Tallassee
Parker, Edward B., Corp., Wedowee
Patterson, Byron, Pvt., Opelika
Patterson, Harvey R., Pvt., Opelika
Payne, Sydnie A., Pvt., Grove Hill
Peagler, Frank, Pvt., Evergreen
Peavy, Joe N., Pvt., Bellville
Pierson, Paul W., Pvt., Birmingham
Powell, George A., Pvt., Carson
Pratt, John W., Pvt., Salem
Priester, Henry D., Pvt., Samson
Putman, Clyde, Pvt., Phoenix
Ratliff, Edgar, Sgt., Girard
Ray, Lee, Corp., Phoenix
Renfro, Clarence M., Mess Sgt., Opelika
Rice, Irvin F., Pvt., Opelika

Richardson, Oscar T., Pvt., Wetumpka
Rinfroe, John, Corp., Samson
Salter, Joe W., Pvt., Opelika
Seay, Early, Pvt., Clintonville
Shelton, Ernest, Pvt., Moulton
Sikes, Herbert C., Pvt., Wedowee
Smith, Bascom W., Sgt., Slocomb
Smith, Lloyd, Pvt., Moreland
Smith, Ryx I., Pvt., Evergreen
Stevenson, Koe, Pvt., Ashland
Stitt, Jim W., Corp., LaGrange
Strickland, John W., Pvt., Birmingham
Tallie, John, Pvt., Arondale
Taylor, Juel, Pvt., LaGrange
Terrell, Clarence T., Bugler, Shawmut
Thames, Riley H., Pvt., Andalusia
Thomas, Wiley M., Pvt., Herbert
Thompson, Robert H., Corp., Hartford
Thornton, John T., Pvt., Centerville
Thornton, Robert M., Pvt., Central
Tindell, Sam, Pvt., Silocomb
Troulis, Albert, Pvt., Adamsville
Truitt, Louis R., Pvt., Pratt City
Turner, Frank T., Pvt., Phoenix
Walker, Lee E., Pvt., Cullman, Ala,
Walker, William P., Cook, Cullman
Wallace, Hugh M., Sgt., Cusseta
Watts, George O., Pvt.
Whatley, Albert B., Corp., Opelika
White, Tom, Corp., Gadsden
Whittington, William, Pvt., Sylacauga
Wilkerson, Enoch H., Corp., Cuthbert
Williams, Harry P., Pvt., Birmingham
Williams, Herbert H., Pvt., Brooklyn
Williams, Inge W., Pvt., Birmingham
Williamson, Erwin, Pvt., Clanton
Wilson, Herbert, Pvt., Birmingham
Winters, Eddie, Pvt., Phoenix
Woodley, Jasper N., Pvt., Jasper
Word, Claude G., Sgt., Wedowee
Worley, Lonnie, Pvt., Acipco
Wrigght, Andrew, Pvt., Girard
Wyche, Thomas A., Pvt., LaFayette

York, Louis W., Pvt., Birmingham
Young, John W., Pvt., Phoenix

## COMPANY K

Captain Mortimer Jordan, Birmingham
1st Lieut. Alan M. Smith, Birmingham
1st Lieut. Hugh W. Lester, Birmingham
Allen, Arden R., Cook, Cooper
Allison, Archie B., Pvt., Birmingham
Anderson, Vayden L., Pvt., Sunny South
Ardoyno, Charlie, Pvt., Mobile
Atwood, Joseph I., Corp., Birmingham
Autrey, Henry M., Pvt., Sunny South
Avery, Jesse, Pvt., Black
Barber, Willie E., Pvt., Milbry
Barrett, William C., Corp., Birmingham
Barton, John W., Pvt., Samson
Bass, James, Pvt., Montgomery
Bell, Glenn A., Pvt., Birmingham
Black, James A., Pvt., Beatrice
Blackman, Stinson B., Sgt., Birmingham
Bolin, Paul L., Bugler, Birmingham
Bonner, Hamilton H., Pvt., Mobile
Boswell, James B., Pvt., Hartford
Boulet, Louis T., Pvt., Mobile
Brannon, Malcom, Pvt., Hartford
Brinson, William T., Pvt., Montgomery
Burch, William, Pvt., Black
Burch, Willie, Pvt., Daleville
Burrage, Herbert D., Pvt., Axis
Byrd, Arthur, Pvt., Sampson
Byrd, Jim F., Pvt., Birmingham
Calloway, Walter, Pvt., Deatsville
Cammander, Thomas D., Pvt., Hartford
Canady, Hoyt A., Pvt., Dothan
Casey, Carse M., Corp., Silocomb
Chambliss, Malcom G., Bugler, Mont-
  gomery
Cheshire, Ross M., Cook, Silocomb
Chestang, John P., Pvt., Citronelle
Clenner, Early W., Pvt., Coopers
Cobb, Alto, Pvt., Dothan

Cochran, Buford F., Pvt., Lowell
Cook, Gustavo L., Pvt., Birmingham
Cooley, Charlie M., Pvt., Brookside
Cornelius, Fred, Pvt., Oneonta
Cothran, Cabot, Pvt., Deatsville
Couch, Harry P., Sgt., Birmingham
Couch, Sam G., Pvt., Anniston
Craft, James C., Pvt., Mobile
Crowder, Wilber, Pvt., Birmingham
Cullen, Lester M., Sgt., Birmingham
Davis, George W., Pvt., Atmore
Davis, John P., 1st Sgt., Birmingham
Dawson, James A., Mech., Birmingham
Day, Chap P., Pvt., Argo
Denmark, James, Mech., Birmingham
Dennis, Richard, Pvt., Mountain Creek
Dickinson, Fate, Pvt., Citronelle
Downey, Daniel, Pvt., Natural Bridge
Drewery, George H., Sgt., Garrnsey
Duffy, John H., Jr., Pvt., Mobile
Dunn, William E., Pvt., Camden
Dunson, Willie, Pvt., Samson
Dykes, Leonard V., Pvt., Tibbie
Edwards, Joe, Pvt., Roberts
Elkins, Stephen B., Sgt., Birmingham
Ellas, Roy S., Pvt., Birmingham
Englet, Clarence A., Pvt., Sunny South
Ethridge, George W., Pvt., Dickson Mill
Evatt, Carl E., Pvt., Wadsworth
Farley, Mose, Pvt., Morris
Faulkner, Hugh L., Pvt., Birmingham
Ferguson, Earley O., Pvt., Aquilla
Flemming, James S., Pvt., Birmingham
Foster, Hughlet S., Corp., Birmingham
Frye, John C., Pvt., Claiborne
Gaffney, William F., Cook, Birmingham
Gardener, Samuel, Pvt., Vinegar Bend
Geney, Porter C., Pvt., Mobile
Gidley, Dewitt, Corp., Dolomite
Glass, James B., Pvt., Jemison
Glass, William L., Pvt., Birmingham
Golden, Herbert D., Pvt., Hanceville
Goodman, Leslie C., Corp., Mobile

Grace, Morris L., Pvt., Calvert
Green, John A., Jr., Pvt., Ararat
Greer, Neil, Pvt., Lightwood
Grimes, Willie T., Pvt., Keonton
Hamilton, Eugene P., Pvt., Prichard
Hanks, Henry A., Jr., Pvt., Mobile
Hansberger, Brunce N., Pvt., Ardilla
Hardwick, Herman, Pvt., Ardilla
Harmon, John A., Corp., Lewisville
Harrison, Frank, Supply Sgt., Edgewater
Hartley, Thomas F., Pvt., Hartford
Harville, Braxton B., Corp., Edgewater
Hawkins, Charlie B., Pvt., Wylam
Hayes, Elmus J., Pvt., Adamsville
Henckell, Emile, Corp., Birmingham
Hendricks, Frank, Corp., Pratt City
Hendricks, R. P., Pvt., Greenville
Hendricks, Winston, Pvt., Greenville
Hennigan, Oscar R., Pvt., Birmingham
Henson, Carey, Pvt., Hawthorne
Henson, Ray, Corp., Hawthorne
Henson, Wilber B., Pvt., Alemedia
Hodges, Arthur J., Pvt., Birmingham
Hollan, Dewey L., Pvt., Hartford
Homer, Andrew W., Pvt., Mobile
Hougesen, Harry J., Pvt., Vinegar Bend
Howard, Hovey C., Pvt., Birmingham
Hunter, Carl J., Pvt., Clanton
Hurst, Robert, Pvt., Dothan
Hyatt, James G., Pvt., Tibbie
Johnson, Lawrence, Pvt., Birmingham
Jolly, Ernest C., Mech., Birmingham
Jones, Lonnie M., Pvt., Lomax
Kelley, Maxwell J., Pvt., Fairford
Kelley, Richmond H., Pvt., Fairford
Mason, Arrel V., Pvt., Birmingham
Mayes, Edward B., Pvt., Crichton
Millard, Leslie, Mess Sgt., Birmingham
Mills, Claude, Pvt., Geneva
Mimms, Robert L., Pvt., Escatawpa
Mitchell, Charlie, Pvt., Mobile
Moore, Ernest, Pvt., Rendalia
Moore, Lee, Pvt., Winterboro

Moore, Spurgeon, Pvt., Talladega
Moore, Walter D., Sgt., Bradford
Murphy, Purse, Pvt., Malvern
Onderdonk, Henry A., Pvt., Chatom
Owens, George K., Pvt., Citronelle
Parrish, James J., Pvt., Irondale
Pate, Amer N., Pvt., Ozark
Patjans, William H., Pvt., Cullman
Patrick, Buck H., Pvt., Cullman
Paulk, John, Pvt., Cottonwood
Pearson, Henry, Jr., Pvt., Sunny South
Pettus, Northern, Pvt., Hanceville
Platt, Kerry H., Pvt., Escatawpa
Posey, John W., Pvt., Dothan
Pratt, Robert, Corp., Birmingham
Rhodes, Percey H., Pvt., Saville
Roberts, Wesley, Pvt., Mobile
Robinson, Arguness, Pvt., Clanton
Robinson, J. P., Pvt., Birmingham
Rosser, Thomas, Pvt., Bessemer
Rudd, Malt, Corp., New Castle
Rylant, Rivers H., Pvt., Birmingham
Sanders, Joseph A., Pvt., Slocomb
Scarborough, James L., Pvt., Sunny South
Schreiner, Ernest H., Pvt., Mobile
Seals, Mitchell J., Sgt., Birmingham
Seay, Talbert F., Pvt., Sampson
Sheehan, William E., Pvt., Cox Heath
Sherrell, John B., Sgt., Birmingham
Shivers, Kenoth, Pvt., Hartford
Shouse, John, Pvt., Montgomery
Skipper, Hosea, Pvt., Dothan
Smith, Euclid J., Pvt., Birmingham
Smith, Hannis R., Pvt., Mobile
Smith, J. C., Pvt., Altoona
Spinks, Samuel L., Pvt., Thomasville
Stewart, John L., Pvt., Hartford
Swann, Ross B., Pvt., Garden City
Thames, Thomas M., Pvt., Citronelle
Thomas, Dewitt, Corp., Hartford
Thomas, Oscar B., Corp., Warrior
Thompson, Ernest, Pvt., Montgomery
Thompson, Lewis, S., Pvt., Chatom

Trainor, Everett T., Pvt., Birmingham
Trainor, James T., Sgt., Birmingham
Vann, James M., Pvt., Deatsville
Vermillion, John E., Mech., Edgewater
Vogel, Bertram J., Corp., Mobile
Waters, Leo, Pvt., Mobile
Watford, Leander, Pvt., Slocomb
Webb, Fletcher, Pvt., Seaboard
Welborn, Floyd C., Corp., Birmingham
Whidby, George T., Pvt., Calrent
Wingender, Henry, Corp., Bon Secour
Wilkinson, Albert C., Pvt., Calvert
Williams, Daniel C., Pvt., St. Stephens
Willman, Charlie G., Pvt., Citronell
Wilson, Henry W., Pvt., Stapleton
Wolfe, Dewey H., Pvt., Camden
Wood, Wiley H., Corp., Tallassee
Woodall, Mabry W., Corp., Birmingham
Woodruff, Rupert, Pvt., Dawson Springs
Wooten, John B., Pvt., Anniston
Wren, Harmon E., Mech., Birmingham
Wright, Roy C., Pvt., Birmingham

## COMPANY L

Captain Joe P. Esslinger, Alabama City
2nd Lieut. Thomas H. Fallaw, Opelika
Aaron, John, Pvt., Arley
Aaron, Virgil E., Pvt., Arley
Alexander, Houston, Pvt., Kennedy
Alexander, Talmage, Pvt., Union Grove
Anthony, Pope A., Pvt., Ensely
Armstrong, Acton, Pvt., Gadsden
Austin, Edward, Pvt., Bear Creek
Baird, Lem G., Pvt., Guin
Baswell, Preston, Sgt., Wellington
Baugh, Edward, Pvt., Guntersville
Benton, Luther J., Pvt., Coosada
Berry, Dewey, Pvt., Guntersville
Berry, Hurshell, Pvt., Guntersville
Black, Welcome H., Sgt., Guntersville
Blackwell, Henry W., Pvt., Selma
Bolding, Calvin, Cook, Guntersville

Boswell, Thomas M., Pvt., Clanton

Boyett, Howard, Pvt., Hamilton

Brown, Carl. Pvt., Hamilton

Brown, Henry P., Corp., Montgomery

Brown, Hewett A., Pvt., Gardo

Brown, James L., Pvt., Kansas

Brown, Robert, Pvt., Oakman

Campbell, Ernest S., Pvt., Selma

Campbell, Patrick F., Pvt., Yolande

Carpenter, Bernice, Pvt., Hamilton

Carroll, William O., Corp., Plantersville

Chambers, William, Pvt., Birmingham

Chancey, Claud, Pvt., Enterprise

Chism, Archie, Corp., Tuscaloosa

Chism, Reynolds, Pvt., Calera

Christenberry, Curn, Pvt., Landersville

Christian, Sam, Pvt., Tuscaloosa

Clark, Jack, Pvt., Gadsden

Cleveland, Arnold B., Mess Sgt., Walnut Grove

Coffman, Thomas, W. E., Pvt., Ensley

Coleman, David B., Pvt., Greensboro

Coley, Oscar F., Pvt., Fort Payne

Collier, Robert L., Pvt., Selma

Conn, Zeke, Pvt., Birmingham

Cook, Claude E., Pvt., Selma

Cook, Henry L., Pvt., Selma

Cox, Roscoe, Cook, Anniston

Crabbe, James C., Pvt., Tuscaloosa

Crane, Harry A., Pvt., Birmingham

Creel, Ivan, Pvt., Boaz

Crews, John T., Pvt., Union Town

Crocker, William L., Sgt., Attalla

Crockett, James D., Pvt., Birmingham

Cruse, Henry F., Corp., Huntsville

Cruse, Jim, Pvt., Henrysville

Cummings, John, Pvt., Guntersville

Dailey, Christopher C., Pvt., Selma

Delffs, Newton, Pvt., Florence

DeYampert, Robert, Pvt., Uniontown

Eastes, Allen, Pvt., Brighton

Eeds, James P., Pvt., Etheiville

Eerwin, George W., Pvt., Gadsden

Eddings, Oscar, Pvt., Pineapple

Edmonds, Lawrence C., Pvt., Coatapa

Evans, Jake, Pvt., Calera

Everett, Walter, Pvt., Acton

Farris, William, Pvt., Tuscaloosa

Favor, Joseph H., Pvt., Drain

Fielding, John, Corp., Guntersville

Flanegan, Thomas, Bugler, Anniston

Fletcher, Colonel, Pvt., Guntersville

Fletcher, Newman, Pvt., Guntersville

Flynn, Lester, Pvt., Beaverton

Forf, Neil, Pvt., Hamilton

Fuller, Joe, Pvt., Johns

Gable, Bee, Pvt., Oneonta

Gardner, John, Pvt., Chandler Springs

Garner, Dewey, Corp., Anniston

Garner, Jack, Pvt., Anniston

George, Frank, Pvt., Blockton

Gibson, Willis, Corp., Vinegar Bend

Giles, Noble, Pvt., Haleyville

Gofford, Richard, Pvt., Valleyhead

Golden, Lonnie, Pvt., Scottsboro

Gosa, Ernest, Pvt., Utaw

Graham, F. M., Pvt., Birmingham

Grant, Grover, Pvt., Guntersville

Gray, J. C., Pvt., Longview

Gregg, Lano, Pvt., Cordova

Grodon, Claud D., Corp., Anniston

Guthrie, Houston, Pvt., Sipsey

Haggard, Bert, Pvt., Birmingham

Hall, Herman W., Pvt., Gadsden

Hamil, Burley, Corp., Guntersville

Hammock, Willis J., Pvt., Union Grove

Hanna, EBA, Corp., Choccolocco

Harrison, Homer, Pvt., Anniston

Heaton, John W., Pvt., Wylam

Henderson, Alfred, Pvt., Alabama City

Henderson, Ernest, Pvt., Albertville

Hester, Henry, Pvt., Guntersville

Hice, Ernest A., Mechanic, Ensley

Hill, Dock, Corp., Huntsville

Hill, William, Pvt., Yolande

Hines, Frank C., Pvt., Alabama City

Hinton, William S., Pvt., Reform
Hitt, D. C., Pvt., Alabama City
Holcomb, Lonnie E., Pvt., Cordova
Holder, Mathew A., Corp., Gadsden
Holiday, Luddie J., Pvt., Sulligent
Holland, Tom, Pvt., Valleyhead
Hollis, Hugh L., Corp., Selma
Holtz, William H., Corp., Wylam
Howell, Wade E., Pvt., Union Grove
Hudgins, Willie S., Pvt., Union Grove
Hulsey, Robert T., Pvt., Gadsden
Hurshell, Conn, Sgt., Attalla
Huskey, Walter, Mechanic, Huntsville
Hutto, Sterling, Sgt., Plantersville
Jaquess, General, Corp., Inland
Jaquess, James, Pvt., Inland
Jenkins, Lonnie, Pvt., Guntersville
Jones, Homer S., Pvt., Coatapa
Kelly, Charles P., Corp., Blackton
Kolodner, Charlie, Pvt., Calera
Kornegay, Dewey, Pvt., Centerville
Kornegay, Reuben C., Pvt., Centerville
Lancaster, Marvin, Pvt., Reef
Laycock, Anders, Pvt., Northport
Ledlow, Dalton, Pvt., Echola
Leverett, Starling, Pvt., Alabama City
Levy, Cedric, Mechanic, Birmingham
Lindsey, Walter, Pvt., Anniston
Lipscomb, Ben, Pvt., Gadsden
Littlepage, Connie T., Pvt., Union Town
Logan, Robert N., Pvt., Moulton
Logan, Walter, B., Pvt., Union Town
Luck, John, J., Pvt., Birmingham
Lutes, Arthur, Sgt., Attalla
Lyles, Austin B., Pvt., Uniontown
Malone, Frank, Corp., Mobile
Mason, James A., Pvt., Cullman
Massingill, S. N., Supply Sgt., Alabama City
Maxwell, Lawrence, Pvt., Manchester
Mayton, Thomas, J., Pvt., Uniontown
McAteer, Lester, Pvt., Gordo
McClendon, Robert, Pvt., Guntersville

McCrary, Sidney S., Pvt., Selma
McDonald, James K., Pvt., Gadsden
McGinnis, George W., Birmingham
McGregor, Russell, Corp., Citronelle
McKee, Emmett, Corp., Clanton
McKinstry, George S., Corp., Mobile
McWilliam, John M., Pvt., McWilliams
Merrett, Alvis M., Bugler, Alabama City
Meyers, Oscar, Corp., Edgewater
Milner, James P., Pvt., Columbiana
Milstead, James R., Pvt., Acton
Mitchell, Luke, Mechanic, Guntersville
Moore, Carl, Pvt., Jasper
Morrow, Pettus, Pvt., Summerfield
Murphey, Nelson, Pvt., Eodin
Neely, Robert E., Pvt., Birmingham
Newman, Clifford, Corp., Mobile
Nichols, James P., Pvt., Thomaston
Nix, Charles, S., Pvt., Guntersville
Nunnally, James R., Pvt., Ashville
Ogletree, Willie T., Pvt., Blockton
Otwell, Emmett D., Pvt., Tuscaloosa
Palmer, Ernest D., Pvt., Gadsden
Parker, Ernest L., Pvt., Huntsville
Perdue, John W., Pvt., Tuscaloosa
Perry, Allen G., Pvt., Boaz
Phillips, Robert H., Pvt., Thomaston
Pierce, William, E., Pvt., McWilliams
Porter, James E., Pvt., Huntsville
Posey, Reuben S., Pvt., Greensboro
Prince, Calvin L., Corp., Oxford
Pritchett, Thomas M., Pvt., Uniontown
Ray, Jesse P., Corp., Birmingham
Reece, Dewey, Pvt., Valleyhead
Reese, John T., Cook, Alabama City
Reid, William G., Pvt., Anniston
Rhodes, Cecil W., Selma
Richter, Charles A., Pvt., Birmingham
Riggins, William, Pvt., Diamond
Robert, Marion, Pvt., Jasper
Robertson, Ike A., Pvt., Tuscaloosa
Robinson, Dee, Pvt., Cordova
Robinson, William M., Pvt., Jasper

Rogers, Thomas, C., Pvt., Selma
Romine, Titus, Pvt., Oakman
Russ, Tommie, Pvt., Rockford
Sample, John, Pvt., Albertville
Sanders, John, Pvt., Akron
Sandin, Claud G., Pvt., Carbon Hill
Scott, Curtis, L., Pvt., Reform
Shafter, Otts, Pvt., Beaverton
Sharpton, L. C., Sgt., Alabama City
Silvey, George E., Pvt., Gadsden
Sims, Albert J., Pvt., Mobile
Sizemore, Jessie, Pvt., Valleyhead
Skinner, Frank H., Pvt., Uniontown
Smart, Roy W., Pvt., Alabama City
Smith, Andrew J., Pvt., Blockton
Smith, Clarence T. Pvt., Fayette
Smith, Cleveland, Pvt., Northport
Smith, Ellotte, Corp., Georgiana
Smith, Jack, 1st Sgt., Gadsden
Smith, John Hollis, Pvt., Jamestown
Smith, John R., Sgt., Alabama City
Smith, Roy C., Corp., Huntsville
Snider, Clarence, Pvt., Gamble Mines
Sortor, Phocion, Corp., Guntersville
Stephens, Glenn W., Pvt., Tuscaloosa
Stephens, Willie, Corp., Alabama City
Stewart, Andrew J., Pvt., Elba
Sullivan, Thomas, J., Pvt., McConell
Swendle, Clyde, Pvt., Oakman
Taylor, Clarence, Sgt., Oakman
Thacker, Joseph E., Corp., Alabama City
Thomas, Robert D., Pvt., Rewbert
Trapenski, Alex, Pvt., Blockton
Traylor, Deleware, Pvt., Guntersville
Turner, James, Pvt., Guntersville
Walston, Roy D., Pvt., Birmingham
Ward, Joseph, Pvt., Yolande
Webster, David L., Corp., Alabama City
Whitehead, Solon, Pvt., Winfield
Wight, Jim, Pvt., Empire State
Williams, John, Pvt., Red Hill
Woodham, Esker, Pvt., Norma
Yeatman, John C., Pvt., Anniston

## COMPANY M

Captain Ravee Norris, Birmingham
1st Lieut. Otho W. Humphries, Oxford
2nd Lieut. James W. Drive, Anniston
Abney, Wilson, G., Pvt., Albertville
Alberson, Lewie, Pvt., Enterprise
Allen, Carl R., Pvt., Birmingham
Allen, Jim, Pvt., Anniston
Andrews, John M., Pvt., LaFayette
Angle, Newt, Pvt., Anniston
Baggett, Leroy C., Roy
Baker, Percy C., Pvt., Birmingham
Baldwin, Charles E., Corp., Birmingham
Barksdale, Robert, Mechanic, Birmingham
Barlow, Clarence, Pvt., Manafly
Bates, Harvey T., Pvt., Alexander City
Bearden, Homer A., Pvt., Birmingham
Beasley, Tom, Pvt., Anniston
Bice, Ellis, Pvt., Alexander City
Bice, Marvin, M., Corp., Anniston
Bird, Jesse E., Pvt., Montgomery
Blythe, Eugene, Pvt., Talladega
Bolling, Will, Pvt., Butler Springs
Bowen, John A., Sgt., Anniston
Bradshaw, Claude F., Pvt., Ashville
Brown, Oscar, Pvt., Anniston
Buchanan, Thomas F., Pvt., Ensley
Butler, Ed H., Pvt., Cullman
Buzbee, Andrew V., Pvt., Bessemer
Carson, William W., Pvt., Bessemer
Champion, Lonnie, Pvt., Bynum
Champion, William, Pvt., Bessemer
Clark, Alex C., Pvt., Birmingham
Clark, John, Pvt., Munsford
Clark, William D., Pvt., Pyrton
Clay, Hugh G., Pvt., Piedmont
Cleckler, Joseph B., Corp., Oxford
Clements, Edwin, E., Supply Sgt., Montgomery
Clepper, Frank, Pvt., Garland
Cochran, Grady, Pvt., Alabama City

Coffman, George S., Pvt., Alabama City
Collins, Ervin, Pvt., Anniston
Comer, Alvin F., Pvt., Birmingham
Connelly, George M., Pvt., Gadsden
Cook, Lamar A., Pvt., Gerard
Cotton, Pete, Sgt., DeArmanville
Crosby, Lattrell, Pvt., Centry
Daniels, George E., Pvt., Caldwell
Daniels, Samuel D., Pvt., Billington
Davis, Calvin D., Pvt., Bolling
Davis, William H., Pvt., Hanceville
Dickerson, Daniel, Pvt., Anniston
Dismukes, John, Jr., Pvt., Birmingham
Dorsey, James C., Corp., Birmingham
Doss, Elbert, Cook, Anniston
Dreyspring, Ernest J., Pvt., Birmingham
Duckworth, Zack, O., Pvt., Reform
Edwards, James W., Pvt., Blue Mountain
Eichelberger, Augustus, Pvt., Anniston
Eichelberger, Rufas A., Sgt., Anniston
Evans, Ira, Pvt., Prattville
Everett, Grover L., Pvt., Elkmont
Falls, Ben O. F., Pvt., Tuscaloosa
Ferrell, Cecil D., Mechanic, Anniston
Floyd, Charlie, Pvt., Jacksonville
Galloway, Palmer, Pvt., Alexander City
Garner, Walter, Cook, Cullman
Gay, Will, Pvt., Ashland
Gilmore, Rupert, Pvt., Montgomery
Givins, Roscoe, Pvt., Birmingham
Glasscock, Oscar, Pvt., Birmingham
Gooden, Paul S., Pvt., Talladega
Goram, Wilton, Pvt., Georgiana
Gordon, Robert C., Pvt., Anniston
Gredy, Laurent, Pvt., Montgomery
Hall, Edgar W., Pvt., Chapman
Hall, Ross, Pvt., Chapman
Hamby, B., Bryant, Pvt., Tuscaloosa
Harper, Edward Winston, Pvt., Bessemer
Harrison, Arthur, Jr., Bugler, Oxford
Harwell, Jim H., Pvt., Anniston
Hawkins, Earl, Sgt., Anniston
Hawkins, John, Pvt., Luverne

Hawkins, Lewis S., Sgt., St. Clair
Hayes, Thomas O., Pvt., Anniston
Haynes, Burl, 1st Sgt., Anniston
Haynes, Dewey, Corp., Anniston
Haynes, Lester, Pvt., Anniston
Haynie, A. W., Pvt., Equality
Helton, Lee R., Pvt., Birmingham
Herring, Lon, Pvt., Greenville
Higdon, James C., Pvt., Rickey
Hill, James H., Pvt., Anniston
Hilliard, Eddie L., Pvt., Montgomery
Holland, Willie T., Pvt., Patsburg
Holleman, Hinton W., Pvt., Eufaula
Holsenback, Alexander, Pvt., Anniston
Hoomes, Charles L., Pvt., Chapman
Hopkins, Henry L., Sgt., Oxford
Hughes, Arthur, G., Pvt., Anniston
Jacobs, Brady, Pvt., Black
James, Edwin, B., Pvt., Birmingham
James, Homer L., Pvt., Anniston
Johnson, Joe C., Pvt., Blountville
Jones, Charles R., Pvt., Montgomery
Jones, Grady, Pvt., Anniston
Jones, Marion, Pvt., Chandler Springs
Jones, Shelby L. Pvt., Troy
Jones, William W., Pvt., Anniston
Kelley, Ashford L., Pvt., Black
Kelsoe, Dan, Pvt., Pigeon Creek
Kent, Maston, Pvt., Asbury
Kettles, Carl C., Pvt., Anniston
Knight, Willam S., Pvt., Troy
Kuykendall, J. W., Pvt., Anniston
Leslie, Arthur C., Pvt., Birmingham
Liggon, Claude A., Pvt., Wetumpka
Loaard, Holsen K., Pvt., Montgomery
Lybrand, Willie O., Pvt., Anniston
Mackey, Parker, Pvt., Tuscaloosa
Mantione, Jasper, Pvt., Birmingham
Martin, Reuben L., Pvt., Troy
McCombs, Roy, Pvt., Oxford
McCombs, Sam D., Pvt., Oxford
McCourry, Thomas A., Corp., Anniston
McCrarey, Hugh, Pvt., Prattville

McGill, William A., Pvt., Shorter
McInvale, Polie, Pvt., Delter
McLendon, Robert Z., Pvt., Tennette
Merk, James E., Pvt., E. Birmingham
Messer, David, Bugler, Alexander City
Moates, Horace A., Pvt., Lewisville
Moody, Henry, Pvt., Anniston
Mooney, Fred R., Pvt., Birmingham
Mooren, Weston, Pvt., Birmingham
Morrison, Telas, Pvt., Anniston
Newman, Julius N., Pvt., Gerard
Nolan, Robert Bruve, Pvt., Pipscourt
Nolen, Edward W., Sgt., Anniston
Norton, Robert W., Pvt., Anniston
Nowlin, William G., Corp., Jacksonville
O'Dell, Cubie, Pvt., Oxford
Odom, James, Corp., Anniston
Osborne, Edwin V., Pvt., Birmingham
Owen, Ozie W., Pvt., Calhoun
Owens, James, R., Pvt., Greenville
Parkman, Harry E., Pvt., Jackson
Parsons, Vernon, Corp., Bessemer
Patterson, Ira P., Pvt., Shelby
Payne, Henry C., Pvt., Albertville
Phelps, Julius F., Pvt., Honoreville
Pickron, Coleman, Pvt., Montgomery
Pike, Charlie F., Pvt., Carbon Hill
Pitts, James F., Pvt., Barfield
Pitts, William A., Pvt., Anniston
Presley, Fred, Pvt., Anniston
Putman, Leon G., Pvt., Birmingham
Ray, Jimmie, Pvt., Anniston
Reaves, Belton, Pvt., Oxford
Rice, Paul L., Pvt., Ft. Payne
Robbins, John M., Pvt., Birmingham
Roberts, William T., Pvt., Gadsden
Robertson, Dudley, Corp., Anniston
Robertson, James W., Pvt., Brundidge
Robertson, Shirley, Corp., Greenville
Rogers, Grady T., Pvt., Red Level
Rosser, Dolly C., Pvt., Bessemer
Russell, Grover G., Pvt., Mornee
Salvo, Herman, Pvt., Alexander City

Sanderson, David D., Pvt., Eutaw
Sanford, Dallas M., Pvt., Montgomery
Schultz, Heber, Pvt., Brundidge
Shears, Mont, Pvt., Oxford
Shears, Samuel G., Pvt., Oxford
Shields, John C., Pvt., Lincoln
Shortnacey, Lee, Mechanic, Anniston
Sikes, James D., Pvt., Montgomery
Sims, Rufas J., Pvt., Birmingham
Smallwood, Willie, Pvt., Roanoke
Smith, Albert, Pvt., Montgomery
Smith, Bennie D., Pvt., Montgomery
Smith, Douglass P., Pvt., Mull
Smith, Henry, Corp., Lineville
Smith, Joe, Pvt., Bessemer
Smith, John C., Cook, Anniston
Smith, Joseph E., Sgt., Choccolocco
Sparks, Allsie G., Pvt., DeArmandville
Sparks, Emerson, Pvt., DeArmandville
Stanley, Warwick G., Sgt., Anniston
Stewart, John, Mess Sgt., Birmingham
Summers, Norman L., Corp., Anniston
Swindle, Clarence, Pvt., Birmingham
Tarver, William J., Pvt., Anniston
Taylor, James T., Pvt., Anniston
Thames, Thomas F., Pvt., Bolling
Thigpen, Otho Y., Pvt., Greensboro
Thompson, Dewey, Pvt., Anniston
Thornton, Brown M., Pvt., Birmingham
Thorpe, Horace L., Pvt., Adger
Thurmann, Matt, Mechanic, Oxford
Tillery, Chester, Pvt., Searcy
Tillery, Oscar, Pvt., Chapman
Tucker, Samuel F., Pvt., Bayview
Turner, Shirley, Cook, Birmingham
Upchurch, Buren, Pvt., Lynville
Urquhart, Henry E., Pvt., Montgomery
Usry, John H., Pvt., Anniston
Vann, Frank, Pvt., Anniston
Vann, John D., Corp., Alexander City
Veitch, Henry L., Pvt., Ensley
Vines, Reuel, Pvt., Bessemer
Walker, Bailey J., Pvt., Birmingham

Walker, Henry L., Pvt., Clayton
Ward, Rufas J., Corp., Oxford
Weeks, James W., Corp., Oxford
Weeks, Samuel, Corp., Anniston
Wesley, Charles E., Pvt., Red Level
Whaley, Basil, Pvt., Cullman
White, Leon K., Corp., Anniston
White, Truman E., Pvt., Jacksonville

Wilkerson, Harvie, Pvt., Talladega
William, James H., Pvt., Birmingham
Williams, Frank, Pvt., Lipscomb
Wilson, Jacob B., Pvt., Jacksonville
Wingo, Lorenzo, Pvt., McFall
Winningham, John H., Pvt., Hull
Woodard, Coleman B., Pvt., Anniston

# Notes

## Preface

1. William H. Amerine, *Alabama's Own in France* (New York: Eaton and Gettinger, 1919). Hereafter cited as *Alabama's Own*.

2. *Alabama's Own*, 163.

3. As quoted in Lise M. Pommois, with Charles Fowler, *In Search of Rainbow Memorials* (Bedford, PA: Aberjona Press, 2003), 45.

4. *Alabama's Own*, appendixes C and F, 340–405, 410–16.

5. Ruth Smith Truss, "Military Participation at Home and Abroad," in *The Great War in the Heart of Dixie*, ed. Martin T. Olliff (Tuscaloosa: University of Alabama Press, 2008), 40.

6. Douglas MacArthur, Personal Correspondence, Folder 10, October 23–31, 1950, Letter dated October 27, 1950, MAMA, RG 10, Box 21.

7. Clark Lee and Richard Henschel, *Douglas MacArthur* (New York: Henry Holt, 1952), 33.

8. *Rainbow Reveille*, 1923, 2.

9. As an example in Historical Branch, War Plans Division, General Staff, *Brief Histories of Divisions, U.S. Army, 1917–1918* (Washington, DC: GPO, June 1921).

10. "Papers of the 42nd Infantry Division/National Archives," MAMA, RG 15, Box 78, Folder 1. The full summary of operations of the 42nd Division in the World War was published in 1944: *42nd Division, Summary of Operations in the World War* (Washington, DC: GPO, 1944).

11. Robert H. Tyndall Collections, Indiana Historical Society, Manuscripts and Archives Department, #M0280, Box 1, Folder 3.

12. John H. Taber, *The Story of the 168th Infantry*, 2 vols. (Iowa City: State Historical Society of Iowa, 1925).

13. Henry J. Reilly, *Americans All: The Rainbow at War; Official History of the 42nd Rainbow Division in the World War*. Columbus, OH: F. J. Heer, 1936. The Digital Bookshelf, 1998. Hereafter cited as *Americans All*.

14. Created in 1919 in Bad Neuenahr, Germany, the "Rainbow Division Veterans" orga-

nization held its first National Convention in Birmingham, Alabama, in July 1920. For a list of reunions and presidents between 1919 and 1936, see *Americans All*, 883–84. Their newspaper was named the *Rainbow Reveille*.

15. *Alabama's Own*, vi, 1.

16. Ibid., 3.

# Chapter 1

1. *Montgomery Advertiser,* June 19, 1916, 1.

2. Ruth Smith Truss, "The Alabama National Guard" (PhD diss., University of Alabama, 1992), 13.

3. *Alabama's Own*, 30.

4. John K. Mahon, *History of the Militia and the National Guard* (New York: Macmillan, 1983), 148.

5. *Americans All*, 18.

6. Ibid., 22.

7. Gary Mead, *The Doughboys: America and the First World War* (Woodstock, NY: Overlook Press, 2002), 69.

8. John S. D. Eisenhower, *Intervention! The United States and the Mexican Revolution, 1913–1917* (New York: W. W. Norton, 1993), xi.

9. John S. D. Eisenhower, *Yanks: The Epic Story of the American Army in World War I* (New York: Free Press, 2001), 8.

10. Eisenhower, *Intervention*, 216.

11. Ibid., 217.

12. Ibid.

13. Mead, *Doughboys*, 117.

14. Eisenhower, *Yanks*, 5.

15. Mead, *Doughboys*, 118.

16. Eisenhower, *Intervention*, 234.

17. Mead, *Doughboys*, 118.

18. Eisenhower, *Intervention*, 240.

19. *Alabama's Own*, 30.

20. Ibid.

21. "Old Fourth Is Being Rushed to Full War Strength by Screws," *Montgomery Advertiser*, August 19, 1917.

22. Thomas McAdory Owen, *History of Alabama and Dictionary of Alabama Biography*, vol. 1 (Chicago: S. J. Clarke, 1921). 29.

23. Jordan, *Letters*, Birmingham Public Library, Birmingham, AL, June 27, 1916. Jordan's letters typically included a full date but occasionally noted only the month and year. The notes include the most complete information available.

24. Truss, "Military Participation at Home and Abroad," 39.

25. Jordan, *Letters*, June 19 and June 27, 1916.

26. "Troops Move for Camp on Friday, Next," *Montgomery Advertiser*, June 21, 1916.

27. Jordan, *Letters*, June 27, 1916.

28. Ibid., June 29, 1916.

29. Mahon, *History of the Militia and the National Guard*, 151.

30. Wesley P. Newton, "Tenting Tonight on the Old Camp Grounds," in *The Great War in the Heart of Dixie*, ed. Martin T. Olliff (Tuscaloosa: University of Alabama Press, 2008), 43.

31. *Americans All*, 22.

32. Truss, "Military Participation at Home and Abroad," 39.

33. Ibid., 25.

34. Robert Sanders Jr., "World War I, Catalyst for Social Change in Alabama," in *The Great War in the Heart of Dixie*, ed. Martin T. Olliff (Tuscaloosa: University of Alabama Press, 2008), 187.

35. Truss, "Military Participation at Home and Abroad," 25.

36. *Alabama's Own*, 26.

37. Truss, "Military Participation at Home and Abroad," 24.

38. "South's Birthplace Celebrate Fourth in Patriotic Way," *Montgomery Advertiser*, July 5, 1916.

39. "Great Crowd Sees Soldier Boys on Parade," *Montgomery Journal*, July 5, 1916.

40. *Alabama's Own*, 25.

41. Francis P. Duffy, "Colonel Bill," *Rainbow Reveille*, October 1928, 2.

42. Jordan, *Letters*, October 1916.

43. Ibid., January 13, 1917.

44. "Old Fourth Is Being Rushed to Full War Strength by Screws," *Montgomery Journal*, August 19, 1917.

45. Reported by the author's father, who served under him from 1916 to 1919.

46. *Gadsden Evening Journal*, May 9, 1919.

47. Jordan, *Letters*, July 24, 1916.

48. Ibid., June 11, 1916.

49. *Alabama's Own*, 27.

50. George Browne, *An American Soldier in World War I*, ed. David L. Snead (Lincoln: University of Nebraska Press, 2006), 44.

51. Allan M. Brandt, *No Magic Bullets: A Social History of Venereal Diseases in the United States since 1880* (New York: Oxford University Press, 1987), 111.

52. Ibid., 45.

53. "Big Parade Is Reviewed by Governor," *Montgomery Advertiser*, September 21, 1916.

54. *Alabama's Own*, 35–36.

55. Jordan, *Letters*, September 13, 1916.

56. *Greenville Advocate*, anniversary edition, October 6, 1916, 39.

57. Captain Jordan believed the European conflict had direct links to the National Guard's mustering. He later wrote repeatedly of this belief to his family members, asserting, "You will remember that all along I said that my return to the National Guard was because of my belief that we were sure to get mixed up with a big war. I never regarded this Mexican affair as nothing more than an excuse to get in training." (*Letters*, February 4, 1917).

58. *Alabama's Own*, 40.

59. Jordan, *Letters*, October 1916.

## Chapter 2

1. *Alabama's Own*, 35.

2. Ibid., 37.

3. Jordan, *Letters*, October 1916.

4. *Alabama's Own*, 38.

5. Jordan, *Letters*, November 3, 1916.

6. Ibid.

7. Jordan, *Letters*, October 29, 1916.

8. Mead, *Doughboys*, 116.

9. Byron Farwell, *Over There: The United States in the Great War* (New York: W. W. Norton, 1999), 39.

10. David M. Kennedy, *Over Here: The First World War and American Society* (Oxford: Oxford University Press, 2004), 171.

11. Donald Smythe, *Guerrilla Warrior: The Early Life of John J. Pershing* (New York: Scribners, 1973), 58.

12. Mead, *Doughboys*, 117.

13. Eisenhower, *Yanks*, 28.

14. The jump arose from a regulatory quirk. A US president could not promote a captain to major, but he could promote one to brigadier general. Pershing later commanded many of those passed-over officers (Eisenhower, *Yanks*, 28).

15. Smythe, *Guerrilla Warrior*, 262.

16. Ibid., 262–63.

17. Eisenhower, *Yanks*, 28.

18. Eisenhower, *Intervention*, 235–36. Elsewhere Eisenhower records how Pershing's subsequent World War I service continued to aid in this manner. See *Yanks*, 28–29.

19. Eisenhower, *Intervention*, 323.

20. Herbert Molloy Mason Jr., *The Great Pursuit* (New York: Random House, 1970), 76, and picture between 130–31.

21. Martin Gilbert, *A History of the Twentieth Century: 1900–1933*, vol. 1 (New York: Avon Books, 1998), 261.

22. Thomas Boghardt, *The Zimmerman Telegram: Intelligence, Diplomacy, and America's Entry into World War I* (Annapolis, MD: Naval Institute Press, 2012), 33.

23. Gilbert, *A History of the Twentieth Century*, 296.

24. Ibid., 299.

25. Mason, *The Great Pursuit*, 39–41.

26. Boghardt, *The Zimmerman Telegram*, 38.

27. *Alabama's Own*, 40.

28. Daniel Vann, Letters (Courtesy of James Vann, Macon, GA), November 13, 1916.

29. Alma Ready, *Open Range and Hidden Silver: Arizona Santa Crux County* (Nogales, AZ: Pimeria Alta Historical Society, 1973), 87.

30. Alma Ready, ed., *Nogales, Arizona, 1880–1990, Centennial Anniversary* (Nogales, AZ: 1990), 67.

31. Ibid.

32. Jordan, *Letters*, October 29, 1916.

33. Governor Charles Henderson of Alabama was quoted at the time of the guard's return to Alabama as saying that the total force was 4,955 men. *Nogales Daily Herald*, January 18, 1917.

34. Jordan, *Letters*, October 29, 1916. The area is still known as Camp Little in contemporary times.

35. Ibid., November 2, 1916.

36. Ibid.

37. Vann, *Letters*, October 29, 1916. The author's visit to the site in 2010 reveals no changes in the border.

38. Jordan, *Letters*, November 9, 1916.

39. Ibid., December 2, 1916.

40. Ibid., November 2, 1916.

41. Ibid., October 29, 1916.

42. *Alabama's Own*, 44.

43. Jordan, *Letters*, November 2, 1916.

44. Roger G. Miller, *Preliminary to War: The First Aero Squadron and the Mexican Punitive Expedition of 1916* (Bolling AFB, DC: Air Force Historical Studies Office, 2003), 51.

45. The author's uncle, Nimrod W. L. Thompson Jr., was first sergeant in an Alabama National Guard Signal Corps company on the border. William H. Amerine, author of *Alabama's Own in France*, also served on the border in the Signal Corps.

46. Everything in this paragraph and much more is included in NARA Special Media Archives Services Division, Mexican Punitive Expedition, SC-111.

47. The Santa Cruz is a subterranean river with a strong flow of water underneath the surface of the riverbed. The riverbed itself fills with water only during times of rainfall and water runoff.

48. Jordan, *Letters*, November 11, 1916.

49. The firm sold over four thousand portable chlorination units, some mounted on trucks, to Allied armies and the Red Cross before World War I concluded. It still exists and is credited with the elimination of waterborne diseases.

50. NARA, Mexican Punitive Expedition, SC-111.

51. Vince O. Armstrong, ed., *World War One Soldiers: Training, Trenches, and Weapons* (Web-Word, LLC, 2009), 87; NARA 111-SC: photographs of practice training.

52. *Alabama's Own*, 44.

53. Ibid., 43.

54. *Infantry Drill Regulations (Provisional)*, part 1 (Paris: Imprimerie E. Desfossés, 1918), 71. Smith's unit later constructed a similar defensive position to secure the Saint-Mihiel perimeter in France.

55. *Alabama's Own*, 43–45. At Baccarat in France, the regiment made its first patrols against the Germans from similar positions.

56. A detailed program of training can be found in Truss, "The Alabama National Guard," chapter 7.

57. Jordan, *Letters*, November 13, 1916.

58. *Alabama's Own*, 42.

59. Ibid.

60. Ibid.

61. Jordan, *Letters*, November 29, 1916.

62. Ibid.

63. *Infantry Drill Regulations*, 104.

64. Jordan, *Letters*, November 29, 1916.

65. Ibid., December 2, 1916.

66. Cavalry units were troops and squadrons, not companies and battalions as was the case with infantry.

67. Eisenhower, *Yanks*, 28.

68. *Alabama's Own*, 44–45.

69. Jordan, *Letters*, February 10, 1917.

70. Vann, *Letters*, November 13, 1916.

71. Truss, "The Alabama National Guard," 269.

72. Vann, *Letters*, November 13, 1916.

73. Truss, "The Alabama National Guard," 287.

74. Jordan, *Letters*, October 1916. Calculations made in 2009 by J. C. Flowers and Company, New York.

75. Vann, *Letters*, November 13, 1916.

76. Jordan, *Letters*, February 3, 1917.

77. Ibid., December 23, 1916.

78. Ibid., December 26, 1916.

79. *Nogales Daily Herald*, January 12, 1917.

80. Jordan, *Letters*, January 13, 1917.

81. *Greenville Advocate*, January 3, 1917.

82. Ibid. Jordan reports that on their return to Alabama, they learned that three officers and fifteen enlisted men had died on the border. Jordan, *Letters*, January 6, 1917.

83. Jordan, *Letters*, January 6, 1917.

84. *Montgomery Advertiser*, January 16, 1917.

85. Truss, "The Alabama National Guard," 246.

86. Eisenhower, *Intervention*, 305–7.

87. Mead, *Doughboys*, 118.

88. Smythe, *Guerrilla Warrior*, 280. Smythe reports that in choosing Funston's replacement, President Wilson and Secretary of War Baker considered the likelihood that American troops would soon be involved in the European war. Upon hearing Pershing's name mentioned for the position, Wilson reportedly said, "It would be a good choice."

89. Eisenhower, *Yanks*, 318–24.

90. Gary Mead reports 15,000 regular troops and 156,000 men from all other services in *Doughboys*, 117.

91. *Montgomery Advertiser*, March 15, 1917.

92. *Alabama's Own*, 47.

93. Jordan, *Letters*, March 15, 1917.

94. "First Alabama Calvary Spends Two Hours Here Last Saturday," *Greenville Advocate*, March 28, 1917.

95. Commander of Camp Sheridan, Steiner would then command the 62nd Brigade of the 31st Division. "Military record of Robert E. Steiner, 1933," PISF, SG017093, ADAH. The 31st Division, unlike the 42nd Division, spent most of the war at Camp Wheeler. It was sent to France in late October 1918, as "a depot division whose members filled individual vacancies in other organizations" (see Truss, "The Alabama National Guard," 338).

96. *Alabama's Own*, 47.

97. "State Pays Honor to Her Soldiers from the Border," *Montgomery Advertiser*, March 28, 1917.

98. Jordan, *Letters*, March 28, 1917.

99. *Americans All*, 23.

100. Mead, *Doughboys*, 24.

101. The *Lusitania* was a British passenger ship that went down with 128 Americans on board. The United States had objected and Germany apologized. Martin Gilbert, *The First World War* (1994; reprint, New York: Holt Paperbacks, 2004), 157.

102. Mead, *Doughboys*, 59.

103. Gerhard Hirschfeld, Gerd Krumeich, and Irina Renz, eds., *Enzyklopädie Erster Weltkrieg* (Paderborn: Verlag Ferdinand Schöning, 2009), s.v. "Seekrieg," 830–31.

104. Barbara Tuchman, *The Zimmerman Telegram* (1958; reprint, New York: Ballantine Books, 1994), 146.

105. Mead, *Doughboys*, 8.

106. Eisenhower, *Yanks*, 8–9.

107. Nancy Gentile Ford, *The Great War and America: Civil-Military Relations during World War I* (Westport, CT: Praeger Security International, 2008), 15.

108. Ibid., 23.

109. Mead, *Doughboys*, 72.

110. David Fromkin, *In the Time of the Americans: FDR, Truman, Eisenhower, Marshall, MacArthur—The Generation That Changed America's Role in the World* (London: Macmillan, 1995), 83.

111. Farwell, *Over There*, 50.

112. Nancy Gentile Ford, *Americans All! Foreign-Born Soldiers in World War I* (College Station: Texas A&M University Press, 2001), 44.

113. Eisenhower, *Yanks*, 9.

114. Mead, *Doughboys*, 54.

115. Kennedy, *Over Here*, 14.

116. Mead, *Doughboys*, 16.

117. Gilbert, *First World War*, 334.

118. Eisenhower, *Yanks*, 14.

119. Farwell, *Over There*, 37.

120. The name, meaning "the hairy ones," arose from the beard or moustache most of the men wore. It was a national term of affection, originated in the nineteenth century to designate a courageous soldier.

121. Fromkin, *In the Time of the Americans*, 142.

122. John J. Pershing, *Final Report* (Washington, DC: GPO, 1920), 7–8.

123. Built by Louis XIV in 1670 as a hospital for wounded veterans, the Hôtel des Invalides became the national Army Museum in 1905.

124. Farwell, *Over There*, 89.

125. Told to the author by his father in a conversation during the Korean War.

126. *Alabama's Own*, 49.

127. Mead, *Doughboys*, 70.

128. Thomas Fleming, *The Illusion of Victory: America in World War I* (New York: Basic Books, 2004), 87.

129. Kennedy, *Over Here*, 149.

130. Sanders, "World War I, Catalyst for Social Change in Alabama," 187.

131. Jennifer D. Keene, *Doughboys: The Great War, and the Remaking of America* (Baltimore: Johns Hopkins University Press, 2001), 213.

132. From May 1917 on, the army controlled such promotions.

133. Jordan, *Letters*, May 17, 1917.

134. *Alabama's Own*, 50.

135. *Illustrated Review Fourth Alabama Infantry, United States Army* (Montgomery, AL: Service Engraving and Paragon Press, 1917), n.p.

136. *Montgomery Advertiser*, August 3, 1917.

137. Senator John Bankhead was elected as member of the US House of Representatives in March 1917 and served until September 1940, the last four years as speaker of the House.

138. *Montgomery Journal*, August 2, 1917.

# Chapter 3

1. *Illustrated Review Fourth Alabama Infantry, United States Army*, n.p.

2. His pay was $4,000 a year, $86,400 in 2009 money. Calculation made by J. C. Flowers and Company, New York.

3. *Alabama's Own*, 52–53. For a full list of the regiment's members, see *Alabama's Own*, 340–405.

4. Truss, "Military Participation at Home and Abroad," 37.

5. Jordan, *Letters*, August 22, 1917.

6. *Montgomery Advertiser*, August 15, 1917.

7. *Americans All*, 26.

8. In contrast to the selection process used for the men, the army selected senior commanders from its regular establishment. The army appointed the brigade and division commanders and regimental commanders. The National Guard appointed all personnel junior to these ranks.

9. *Americans All*, 27.

10. Ibid., 28.

11. Eisenhower, *Yanks*, 62.

12. *Americans All*, 24.

13. Ibid., 25.

14. Ibid., 28.

15. Ibid., 41–43.

16. During my childhood my father would identify families with slackers from World War I and later from World War II. It seemed perfectly normal to me. Those were men who were not ready to do their duty, to fulfill their political obligations. Their presence on the home front caused widespread support for draft enforcement (Christopher Capozzola, *Uncle Sam Wants You: World War I and the Making of the Modern American Citizen* [2008; reprint, New York: Oxford University Press, 2010], 30).

17. Jordan, *Letters*, May 2, 1918.

18. Ibid., August 22, 1917.

19. *Americans All*, 33.

20. Ibid., 34.

21. *Alabama's Own*, 53.

22. *Montgomery Advertiser*, November 19, 1917.

23. *Alabama's Own*, 30.

24. Ruth Smith Truss, "The Alabama National Guard's 167th Infantry Regiment in World War I," *Alabama Review* (January 2003): 12.

25. Franklin Ashton Clark, Collection, *Diary*, Special Collections and Archives, Auburn University, AL, August 27, 1917.

26. *Alabama's Own*, 54.

27. As told to the author by Joe L. Coleman from Lowndes County in a conversation in the 1960s. Coleman witnessed this event.

28. Clark, *Diary*, August 31, 1917.

29. Ibid.

30. Ibid.

31. Pommois, *In Search of Rainbow Memorials*, 11.

32. Jordan, *Letters*, October 3, 1917.

33. John Coulter, Papers, *Scrap Book. Forty Second Division (Rainbow Division) Camp Mills, 1917*, 2: 8, MAMA. Coulter was General Mann's aide-de-camp.

34. Sherman L. Fleek, *Place the Headstones Where They Belong: Thomas Neibaur, WWI Soldier* (Logan: Utah State University Press, 2008), 65.

35. *Montgomery Advertiser*, September 18, 1917.

36. Jordan, *Letters*, September 1917.

37. *Alabama's Own*, 57.

38. AMHI, World War I Veterans Survey, 42nd Division, 167th Infantry Regiment, John M. Donaldson, Lieutenant, Company B (Rhode Island, diary covering Plattsburgh and Camp Mills).

39. Ibid.

40. Jordan, *Letters*, September 1917.

41. According to the official site of the present 42nd Division, http://dmna.ny.gov/arng/42div/42id.php?id=patch (accessed July 26, 2013), the military eventually standardized the insignia, which it authorized on May 22, 1918; Dan Joyce, "42nd Division Shoulder Sleeve Insignia, A.E.F.," *Military Collector and Historian,* 59 (Summer 2007): 149–51.

42. Jordan, *Letters*, February 10, 1917.

43. John B. Hayes, *Heroes among the Brave: A Story of East Alabama's Own Co. 1 and the Famous Rainbow Division of World War I* (Loachapoka, AL: Lee County Historical Society, 1973), 119.

44. Fleek, *Place the Headstones*, 63.

45. James Hopper, *Medals of Honor* (New York: John Day, 1929), 211.

46. *Americans All*, 41.

47. *Alabama's Own*, 56. Members of the 167th typically spoke of the "Alabam," omitting the final "a." Other units adopted the practice.

48. *New York Times*, October 28, 1917.

49. Jordan, *Letters*, September 1917: Farwell, *Over There*, 97.

50. *Brooklyn Eagle,* October 15, 1917; *New York Age,* October 18, 1917.

51. Jordan, *Letters*, January 30, 1918.

52. Nancy K. Bristow, *Making Men Moral: Social Engineering during the Great War* (New York: New York University Press, 1996), xvii.

53. Ibid., xviii, 53.

54. *Americans All*, 32.

55. Gary Roberts, *Letters*, October 11, 1917, "Soldiers' Letters," PISF, SG017101, ADAH.

56. Franklin Ashton Clark, Collection, *Letters*, Special Collections and Archives, Auburn University, AL, October 14, 1917.

57. Clark, *Diary*, August 30, 1917.

58. Bristow, *Making Men Moral*, 37.

59. Clark, *Diary*, September 27, 1917.

60. Jordan, *Letters*, September 1917.

61. His son and namesake, a captain, would later join the regiment as a 3rd Battalion staff officer.

62. His son, Captain Julian M. Strassburger, a highly intelligent and precocious lawyer who graduated in law from the University of Alabama as a teenager, was among the 167th's soldiers training at Camp Mills.

63. Coulter, *Scrap Book*, 2, 19.

64. Ibid., 2, 15.

65. Ibid., 2, 17.

66. William P. Screws, *Family Scrapbooks*, LPR260, Box 1, ADAH. E.P.S. from Hempstead, Long Island, NY, September 24, 1917, unnamed newspaper.

67. Jordan, *Letters*, September 26, 1917.

68. Clark, *Diary*, September 23, 1917.

69. As told to the author by his father, an Alabama veteran who served for two years alongside the Iowans.

70. AMHI, World War I Veterans Survey, 42nd Division, 167th Infantry Regiment, Robert D. Pickel, Private, Company D.

71. Coulter, *Scrap Book*, 2, 55.

72. *Montgomery Advertiser*, November 12, 1917.

73. Coulter, *Scrap Book*, 2, 75.

74. World War I strength of a division was set at 28,105 officers and men, or 16,193 rifles.

75. Eisenhower, *Yanks*, 56.

76. Jordan, *Letters*, October 11, 1917.

77. James Sullivan, ed., *The History of New York State, XI: New York in Seven Wars* (New York: Lewis Historical Publishing, 1927), 7. Modern-day historians continue to debate about which was the best regiment in the division. Cooke ranks the 84th Brigade and the 167th Infantry as the best outfits in the Rainbow (James J. Cooke, *The Rainbow Division in the Great War, 1917–1919* [Westport, CT: Praeger, 1994], 61 and 134–35), while Mahon, using a matrix weighting significant achievements, awards for valor and battlefield casualties, ranks Alabama and New York at the same level (21 points), followed by Iowa (19 points) and Ohio (15 points) (John Mahon, *New York's Fighting Sixty-Ninth: A Regimental History of Service in the Civil War's Irish Brigade and the Great War's Rainbow Division* [Jefferson, NC: McFarland, 2004], 233–37).

78. Colonel de Chambrun and Captain de Marenches, *The American Army in the European Conflict* (New York: Macmillan, 1919; reprint, La Vergne, TN: Kessinger Publishing, 2009), 333.

79. Edward M. Coffman, *The War to End All Wars: The American Military Experience in World War I* (Lexington: University Press of Kentucky, 1998), 228. Some claim that no US troop transports were sunk during the war, but the *Covington* and two others were sunk on return voyages to the States. The *Covington* went down on its fifth trip, but no troops were aboard. For more information, see Reilly, *Americans All*, 68.

80. *Americans All*, 65.

81. *Alabama's Own*, 60.

82. Ibid., 63.

83. Joseph J. Patton is buried at Brookwood American Cemetery in Surrey, England.

84. James H. Hallas, *Doughboy War: The American Expeditionary Force in World War I* (2000; reprint, Mechanicsburg, PA: Stackpole Books, 2009), 37.

85. James J. Cooke, *Pershing and His Generals* (Westport, CT: Praeger, 1977), 20–21.

86. *Americans All*, 111.

87. Donald Smythe, *Pershing: General of the Armies* (Bloomington: Indiana University Press, 2007), 68.

88. Eisenhower, *Yanks*, 87.

89. *Montgomery Advertiser*, December 29, 1917.

90. *Alabama's Own*, 70.

91. Hayes, *Heroes among the Brave*, 9–10.

92. As late as October 1918, when the US First Army held its own sector of the front and was heavily engaged in the Meuse-Argonne, the BEF commander Field Marshal Haig bemoaned the "ignorance" of American officers and equated their professional abilities with those of the Belgian army, a comparison intended as an insult to both parties. For more information, see Robert E. Bruce, *A Fraternity of Arms: America and France in the Great War* (Lawrence: University Press of Kansas, 2003), 225.

93. Chambrun and Marenches, *American Army*, 333.

94. Winston S. Churchill, *Never Give In! The Best of Winston Churchill's Speeches* (New York: Hyperion Books, 2003), 75.

95. *Alabama's Own*, 72.

96. Joseph E. Persico, *Eleventh Month, Eleventh Day, Eleventh Hour, Armistice Day 1918: World War I and Its Violent Climax* (New York: Random House, 2004), 178.

97. Eisenhower, *Yanks*, 56–57.

98. Joël Mangin, *Les Américains en France, 1917–1919: La Fayette, Nous Voici!* (Saint-Cyr-sur-Loire: Alan Sutton, 2006), 136.

99. SHD, 17 N 125. Letter from November 26, 1917, from officer interpreter de La Mettrie, assigned to the 42nd US Division, to the general head of the French Military Mission to the US Army.

100. *Alabama's Own*, 81.

101. Ibid., 80.

102. Jordan, *Letters*, December 29, 1917.

103. John Wade Watts, *Memoir of Work with the Rainbow Division*, circa 1920, SPR571, ADAH, 8.

104. Jordan, *Letters*, December 6, 1917.

105. R. M. Cheseldine, *Ohio in the Rainbow, Official Story of the 166th Infantry 42nd Division in the World War* (Columbus, OH: F. J. Heer Printing, 1924), 76.

106. Robert Lee Bullard, *Personalities and Reminiscences of the War* (Garden City, NY: Doubleday, 1925), 54.

107. Jordan, *Letters*, New Years Day, 1918.

108. *Alabama's Own*, 81.

109. Ibid.

110. Ibid.

111. Ibid.

112. Joan of Arc and Domrémy held such symbolic significance that even Secretary of War Baker visited the village while on a trip to AEF Headquarters in Chaumont three months later.

113. *Alabama's Own*, 82.

114. Ibid., 81.

115. Jordan, *Letters*, January 11, 1918.

116. Amos D. Brenneman, C Company, 167th (Alabama) Infantry, *Letters*, Crawfordsville District Public Library, Indiana, RL 929.2 and RL 940.3. We are very grateful to Librarian Jodie Wilson for providing a copy of the file on Amos Brenneman and Harley Barton who served in the 150th Indiana Field Artillery http://www.cdpl.lib.in.us/lh-ww1letters.php (accessed September 2, 2013)

117. Jordan, *Letters*, December 16, 1917.

118. *Alabama's Own*, 82.

119. SHD, 17 N 125, General Orders Number 22, Headquarters 42nd Division, December 22, 1917.

120. *Americans All*, 101.

121. *Alabama's Own*, 84.

122. Taber, *The Story of the 168th Infantry*, 1: 49.

123. NARA, RG 120, World War I Organization Records, Entry 1241, 42nd Division Historical Record, 84th Infantry Brigade, Misc. March Reports and Correspondence, 56.2–65.1.

124. *Americans All*, 101.

125. AMHI, World War I Veterans Survey, 42nd Division, 151st Machine Gun Battalion. Isaac G. Walker, Lieutenant, Company A.

126. *Americans All*, 102.

127. Cheseldine, *Ohio in the Rainbow*, 98.

128. SHD, 17 N 125, General Orders Number 22, Headquarters 42nd Division, December 22, 1917.

129. Between fifty and fifty-five km (thirty-one and thirty-four miles) depending on where the units were billeted. Amerine (*Alabama's Own*, 83) notes the distance covered by the different battalions.

130. Francis P. Duffy, *Father Duffy's Story* (Garden City, NY: George H. Doran, Country Life Press, 1919), 48, 51.

131. *Alabama's Own*, 84.

132. *Americans All*, 102.

133. Jordan, *Letters*, January 30, 1918.

134. *Alabama's Own*, 84.

135. Hugh S. Thompson, *Trench Knives and Mustard Gas: With the 42nd Rainbow Division in France*, ed. Robert H. Ferrell (College Station: Texas A&M University Press, 2004), 62.

136. Jordan, *Letters*, January 20, 1918. They would have been called "Les Amis," which was pronounced by the French as "Les Samis."

137. Mead, *Doughboys*, 185.

138. John J. Pershing, *Final Report* (Washington, DC: GPO, 1920), 18.

139. Until then, the AEF was without power and organization. All combat decisions were made under the French. Upon establishment of the 1st US Army, the AEF organizational structure evolved and started moving toward an all-American army.

140. Major John W. Watts, the regimental surgeon of the 167th, undertook a course of instruction with them. Watts, *Memoir*, 8, 21.

141. Allan R. Millett, *The General, Robert L. Bullard and Officership in the United States Army, 1881–1925* (Westport, CT: Greenwood Press, 1975), 318.

142. *Alabama's Own*, 86.

143. Ibid.

144. Jordan, *Letters*, February 27, 1918.

145. Ibid., March 15, 1918.

146. *Alabama's Own*, 86.

147. Cooke, *Pershing*, 21.

148. Jordan, *Letters*, January 20, 1918.

149. *Alabama's Own*, 86.

150. Ben Allender, Company G, 168th (Iowa) Infantry, *Diary of World War I*, MAMA RG 123.

151. *Alabama's Own*, 87–88.

152. Ibid., 89.

153. Jordan, *Letters*, January 25, 1918.

154. *Infantry Drill Regulations*, 1, 25.

155. Taber, *The Story of the 168th Infantry*, 1: 57.

156. Edward M. Coffman, *The War to End All Wars: The American Military Experience in World War I* (Lexington: University Press of Kentucky, 1998), 31; and A. Lincoln Lavine, *Circuits of Victory* (Garden City, NY: Country Life Press, 1921), 182.

157. Lavine, *Circuits of Victory*, 571–74.

158. *Alabama's Own*, 89.

159. George E. Leach, *War Diary* (Minneapolis, MN: Pioneer Printers, 1923), 35. Leach had a celebrated career, rising to the rank of major general and receiving such honors as the Distinguished Service Cross, the Distinguished Service Medal, and the Purple Heart.

## Chapter 4

1. *Alabama's Own*, 92.

2. Hayes, *Destiny of a Soldier*, SPR91, ADAH, 130.

3. André Thirion, *Revolutionaries without Revolution* (New York: Macmillan, 1972), 36.

4. A plaque on the present-day town's city hall memorializes the destruction.

5. Thirion, *Revolutionaries*, 40.

6. *Alabama's Own*, 94.

7. Hunter Liggett, *AEF, Ten Years Ago in France* (New York: Dodd, Mead, 1928), 29; and E. J. Sadler, ed., *California Rainbow Memories: A Pictorial Review of the Activities of the 2nd Battalion, 117th Engineers during the World War*, 1925, n.p. Ronald Schaffer quotes Major Hugh W. Ogden, judge advocate for the 42nd Division: "We don't bomb their headquarters, and they don't bomb ours. . . . In other words, we fight like gentlemen up here in this part of the country and everyone is happy." Ronald Schaffer, *America in the Great War: The Rise of the War Welfare State* (New York: Oxford University Press, 1991), 153.

8. Thirion, *Revolutionaries*, 43.

9. Lawrence O. Stewart, *Rainbow Bright* (Philadelphia: Dorrance, 1923), 34.

10. Allender, *Diary*.

11. Thirion, *Revolutionaries*, 43.

12. Jas. A. Webb, "Painting the Rainbow," *Army and Navy Record* (April 1920): 34.

13. Walter B. Wolf, *A Brief Story of the Rainbow Division* (New York: Rand McNally, 1919), 11.

14. SHD 18N392 (Groupe d'Armées de l'Est).

15. *Alabama's Own*, map between 90 and 91.

16. Wolf, *Brief Story*, 11.

17. Ibid.

18. *Americans All*, 123. The French 167th Regiment (http://167e.regiment) was part of the 128th French Division, the "Division des Loups," the Wolves division, a nickname given to them for their ferocity against the Germans in the 1915 fight in Bois le Prêtre. The 167th FR regiment medal shows a head of a wolf with the inscription: "Les Loups de Bois le Prêtre, 167 RI," which translates as "the wolves of Bois le Prêtre, 167 Infantry Regiment." Léon Groc, *La Division des Loups*, Collection Patrie, 17 (Paris: Rouff, 1919), 4.

19. Louis L. Collins, *History of the 151st Field Artillery Rainbow Division*, ed. Wayne E. Stevens, vol. 1 (St. Paul: Minnesota War Records Commission, 1924), 36.

20. *Americans All*, 135; Miller G. White and Arthur H. Peavy, *The 151st Machine Gun Battalion, 42d (Rainbow) Division: A Battalion History and Citations of the Rainbow, August 13, 1917, to April 26, 1919* (Macon, GA: J. W. Burke), 6.

21. Stewart, *Rainbow Bright*, 47.

22. Cheseldine, *Ohio in the Rainbow*, 113.

23. Charles MacArthur, *War Bugs* (New York: Grosset and Dunlap, 1929), 57.

24. Hayes, *Heroes among the Brave*, 35.

25. Armstrong, *World War One Soldiers: Training, Trenches, and Weapons*, 177.

26. Watts, *Memoir*, 8.

27. *Alabama's Own*, 100.

28. Cheseldine, *Ohio in the Rainbow*, 113.

29. André Kaspi, *Le temps des Américains, 1917–1918* (Paris: Publications de la Sorbonne, 1976), 5.

30. Raphaëlle Autric, "La rivalité franco-américaine: L'instruction des soldats américains en France (1917–1918)," *Revue Historique des Armées* 246 (2007): 22–32.

31. Eisenhower, *Yanks*, 79, 52.

32. *Americans All*, 123.

33. MacArthur's participation was reported in a letter on February 25, 1918 (SHD, 17 N 125) by Captain de Roulet, liaison officer, to the French general of the French mission to the American Army. He concluded by suggesting that a citation of MacArthur would be good politics and would have an enormous morale impact on the US Division.

34. SHD, 26 N 706/3, *Journal de Marche* du 167e *Régiment*, 21 Mars 1918.

35. Cheseldine, *Ohio in the Rainbow*, 107.

36. Bruce, *Fraternity of Arms*, 198.

37. George Sylvester Viereck, *As They Saw Us: Foch, Ludendorff, and Other Leaders Write Our War History* (Garden City, NY: Doubleday, Doran, 1929), 50.

38. *Alabama's Own*, 93.

39. Ibid.

40. Ibid., 93–94.

41. Ibid., 95.

42. Webb, "Painting the Rainbow," 38.

43. Watts, *Memoir*, 9.

44. *Alabama's Own*, 94.

45. Ibid., 96–97.

46. Ibid., 104.

47. Cooke, *The Rainbow Division*, 64.

48. Ibid.

49. Raymond S. Tompkins, *The Story of the Rainbow Division* (New York: Boni and Liveright, 1919), 12.

50. Cooke, *The Rainbow Division*, 80.

51. Donovan to his wife, May 13, 1918, in the William J. Donovan Papers, AMHI, quoted in Cooke, *The Rainbow Division*, 80.

52. Cooke, *The Rainbow Division*, 63.

53. SHD, 17 N 125, Mission Française près l'Armée Américaine, 27 Février 1918. Quotation translated from the original French.

54. *Americans All*, 125.

55. *Alabama's Own*, 97–98.

56. Taber, *The Story of the 168th Infantry*, 1: 88–111.

57. Ibid., 109–10.

58. *Americans All*, 168.

59. Ibid., 172.

60. Cooke, *Pershing*, 20–21.

61. *Americans All*, 179.

62. Ibid., 133.

63. Ibid., 210. Kilmer died on July 29, 1918, near the Ourcq River. His body lies in the Oise-Aisne American Cemetery near where he fell.

64. http://www.archives.state.al.us/goldstar/images/other/Gentry_HermanD.pdf, accessed July 27, 2013.

65. Albert M. Ettinger and A. Churchill Ettinger, *A Doughboy with the Fighting 69th* (New York: Pocket Books, 1993), 88.

66. Taber, *The Story of the 168th Infantry*, 1: 131.

67. Webb, "Painting the Rainbow," 38.

68. Thirion, *Revolutionaries*, 45.

69. *New York Times*, March 21, 1918.

70. James G. Harbord, *Leaves from a War Diary* (New York: Dodd, Mead, 1925), 243–44.

71. Chambrun and Marenches, *American Army*, 130.

72. SHD 17 N126, Intelligence, 2ᵉ bureau, liaisons, 30 Avril 1918.

73. Jordan, *Letters*, March 19, 1918.

74. Harbord, *Leaves from a War Diary*, 243–44.

75. John J. Pershing, *My Experiences in the World War* (New York: Frederick A. Stokes, 1931), 1: 342. This award was authorized on July 8, 1918. Its name was changed to the Silver Star in 1932.

76. They continued to garner recognition for years to come. On June 29, 1919, the city of Verdun, France, authorized issue of the Médaille de Verdun to members of the Rainbow who fought in the Argonne in 1918. On February 22, 1931, Congress created the Purple Heart for those wounded or killed in action, making its award retroactive to those killed or wounded in World War I. This was the two hundredth anniversary of the birth of George Washington, who had established the original Purple Heart medal at Newburg, New York, on August 7, 1782. That original medal was later phased out in favor of a wound stripe on the uniform sleeve.

77. *Alabama's Own*, 100.

78. *Americans All*, 169.

79. AMHI, World War I Veterans Survey, 42nd Division, 167th Infantry Regiment, Lieutenant Duncan Campbell.

80. Thompson, *Trench Knives and Mustard Gas*, 86.

81. AMHI, Einar Paterson, Papers, the Infantry, US 42nd Division, Box 15. E. Paterson was former president of 42nd Division Association.

82. Around that time the French had decorated several senior officers in the Rainbow with the Croix de Guerre. They included Colonel MacArthur, chief of staff of the 42nd Division, Colonel Barker, commanding the 165th (New York), Colonel Hough, commanding the 166th (Ohio) and Lieutenant Colonel Matthew Tinley, from the 168th (Iowa), as well as Battalion Commander "Wild Bill" Donovan from the 165th (New York), as mentioned in SHD, *Journal de Marches et Opérations* de la 42$^e$ DIUS, 15 Février–21 Mars 1918. Colonel Screws, commanding the 167th (Alabama) was the only regimental commander not among the recipients.

83. *Alabama's Own*, 101.

84. "Album de la Guerre," *L'Illustration*, vol. 2 (Paris, 1929), 853.

85. Gilbert, *First World War*, 406.

86. Ibid., 406–7.

87. Davis Wade, *Into the Silence* (New York: Alfred A. Knopf, 2011), 196.

88. Gilbert, *First World War*, 413.

89. Bernd Ulrich and Benjamin Ziemann, *Frontalltag im Ersten Weltkrieg* (Essen: Klartex Verlag, 2008), 137. Quotation translated from the original German.

90. SHD, 26 N 706/3, *Journal de Marche* du 167e *Régiment*, 21 Mars 1918.

91. *Order of Battle of the United States Land Forces in the World War. American Expeditionary Forces: Divisions, 42nd Division (NG)*, vol. 2 (Washington, DC: Center of Military History, United States Army, 1988), 277.

92. Robert H. Ferrell, *America's Deadliest Battle: Meuse-Argonne, 1918* (Lawrence: University Press of Kansas, 2007), 21.

93. Mead, *Doughboys*, 213.

94. Ibid., 215.

95. John Keegan, *The First World War* (New York: Vintage Books, 2000), 405.

96. Repeated disagreements between Pétain and Haig had rendered the situation increasingly tense, especially considering the magnitude of the crisis. The British and the French leadership decided to give Foch "the coordination of the military operations of the Allied Armies on the Western Front" (Smythe, *Pershing*, 99–100).

97. Mead, *Doughboys*, 215.

98. Pershing, *My Experiences in the World War*, 1: 365.

99. Elmer Frank Straub, *A Sergeant's Diary in the World War: The Diary of an Enlisted Member*

*of the 150th Field Artillery, October 27, 1917 to August 7, 1919* (Indiana Historical Commission, 1923), 57.

100. Pershing, *My Experiences in theWorldWar*, 1: 375.

101. Smythe, *Pershing*, 115.

102. "Papers of 42nd Infantry Division/National Archives", 4, MAMA, RG 15, Box 78. Folder 1.

103. *Order of Battle, AEF: 42nd Division*, 277.

104. These are personal comments from having visited all the places where the soldiers of the 167th stayed in France, and looked at photographs and postcards of them during the war.

105. NARA, RG 120, World War I Organizational Records, Entry 1241, 42nd Division Historical Record, 167th Infantry Regiment, 32.13–66.1.

106. On March 20, the Rainbow had received orders to receive further training in the Rolampont area (*Americans All*, 192). The previous page quotes MacArthur explaining how the Rainbow had been the first division to find its way into German trenches.

107. NARA, RG 120, World War I Organizational Records, Entry 1241, 42nd Division Historical Record, 167th Infantry Regiment, 32.13–66.1.

108. Ibid.

109. *Alabama's Own*, 105.

110. Tompkins, *Story of the Rainbow Division*, 15; and Reilly, *Americans All*, 196. Breeding, a full-blooded Indian, evoked awe in the men, who associated Native Americans with fierceness.

111. NARA, RG 120, World War I Organizational Records, Entry 1241, 42nd Division Historical Record, 167th Infantry Regiment, 32.13–66.1. Others whose names regularly appeared on the patrol reports were Lieutenants Ernest J. Bell, Henry L. Griggs, Alton P. Woods, Frank. D. Scotten Jr., James W. Driver, Stephen W. Harris, C. F. O'Dougherty, Clyde D. Wesson, Emmanuel Meslasky, Richard M. Hersey, Royal Little, Joseph M. Murphy, Asbury Hall, Harry R. Young, Herman A. Lorenz, M. A. Matthews, Duncan Campbell, and John M. Donalson.

112. Ibid.

113. *Alabama's Own*, 105.

114. Such raids are described in Douglas MacArthur, *Reminiscences* (1964; reprint, Annapolis, MD: Naval Institute Press, 2001), 54–55.

115. Cooke, *The Rainbow Division*, 86.

116. *Alabama's Own*, 106.

117. The Red Cross, in a letter to the family, wrote that his last words had been to take care of the lieutenant and that he would manage. Several of his fellow soldiers—listed in the Red Cross letter as Private Eugene Benion, Private Robert Nails, and Captain John R. Dale, although F Company records listed Benton and Nails—provided information to aid in searching for his body. Nails said there were two patrols, one led by Lieutenant Woods and

one by Walters. They were hit by machine gun fire and both leaders were hit. Walters said, "Carry the lieutenant back. I ain't bad and can crawl." Despite the men's information, Walters's body was never found. He received a DSC for his action on the patrol. Courtesy of his nephew John Walters of Gadsden, who kept all letters and medals from his uncle and shared them with the author. They are now at the ADAH in Montgomery.

118. Tompkins, *Story of the Rainbow Division*, 15.

119. http://militarytimes.com/citations-medals-awards/recipient.php?recipientid=10863, accessed July 27, 2013. He was also cited by the commander general of the Rainbow Division and by the regional commander, Colonel W. P. Screws, in *Alabama's Own*, 336, 338. Breeding was killed in action on July 28, 1918, and his DSC was awarded posthumously.

120. Allender, *Diary*.

121. J. Douglas Brown, provost emeritus at Princeton University, served in the Rainbow Division and describes a spit bath: "There are few satisfactions greater than arriving at a rest area after a protracted period of combat . . . one could remove one's clothes and take a 'spit bath' with water heated in a pail over an open fire." J. Douglas Brown, "In Action with the Rainbow Division, 1918–19," *Military Review* (January 1978): 40.

122. Taber, *The Story of the 168th Infantry*, 1: 222–28.

123. *Alabama's Own*, 106.

124. Keegan, *First World War*, 329; Liggett, *AEF*, 73.

125. Harbord, *Leaves from a War Diary*, 288.

126. Roberts, *Letters*, PISF, SG017101, ADAH, June 3, 1918. ADAH Digital Archives Q9512–9515.

127. Edward R. Wren Collection, *Letters*, Special Collections and Archives, Auburn University, Alabama, May 29, 1918.

128. Jordan, *Letters*, June 15, 1918.

129. Elsie Janis, *The Big Show: My Six Months with the American Expeditionary Forces* (New York: Cosmopolitan Book, 1919), 111.

130. Ettinger and Ettinger, *A Doughboy with the Fighting 69th*, 105.

131. Mike Wallach, *"Farmer: Have You a Daughter Fair?"* (New York: Vanguard Press, 1929), 25.

132. Leslie Langille, *Men of the Rainbow* (Chicago: O'Sullivan Publishing House, 1933), 61–62.

133. MacArthur, *War Bugs*, 30.

134. Coffman, *War to End All Wars*, 133.

135. Cooke, *The Rainbow Division*, 68.

136. Bristow, *Making Men Moral*, 7.

137. *Americans All*, 227–28.

138. Duffy, *Father Duffy's Story*, 102–3.

139. NARA, RG 120, World War I Organization Records, Entry 1241, 42nd Division Historical Record, File 242-338, 33.1–33.8.

140. They were relieved by the 307th US Infantry: *Alabama's Own*, 107.

141. Mark Ethan Grotelueschen, *The AEF Way of War: The American Army and Combat in World War I* (New York: Cambridge University Press, 2007), 206–7.

142. Jordan, *Letters*, June 12, 1918.

143. *Americans All*, 225.

144. Ibid., 228.

145. Pershing, *My Experiences in the World War*, 2: 96.

146. Henri J. E. Gouraud, "My Memories of the Rainbow Division," *American Legion* (November 1933): 56.

147. Davis, *Into the Silence*, 196.

148. *Rainbow Reveille*, January 1923, 2.

## Chapter 5

1. The town of Châlons-sur-Marne was renamed Châlons-en-Champagne in 1998. After the war, 119 of these demarcation stones were erected in France and Belgium along the six hundred miles of the German advance of 1918.

2. *Alabama's Own*, 107.

3. Ibid.

4. Descriptions stem from the author's 2010 visit and from investigations of extensive postcard and photograph collections, particularly the Signal Corps photographs at NARA, 111-SC.

5. *Alabama's Own*, 115.

6. *Americans All*, 225.

7. William Manchester, *American Caesar: Douglas MacArthur, 1880–1964* (1978; reprint, New York: Back Bay Books, 2008), 92.

8. *Alabama's Own*, 115.

9. Manchester, *American Caesar*, 92.

10. *Alabama's Own*, 116.

11. Ibid., 117.

12. Ibid., 116.

13. Ibid., 118.

14. NARA, RG 120, World War I Organizational Records, Entry 1241, 42nd Division Historical Record, 167th Infantry Regiment, 32.13–66.1.

15. *Alabama's Own*, 108.

16. Bruce, *Fraternity of Arms*, 228.

17. *Americans All*, 247.

18. Eisenhower, *Yanks*, 103.

19. Bruce, *Fraternity of Arms*, 222.

20. http://www.ecpad.fr/wp-content/uploads/2010/06/1918-07.pdf, accessed July 27, 2013.

21. *Alabama's Own*, 110.

22. Bruce, *Fraternity of Arms*, 223.

23. Ibid., 220.

24. MacArthur, *Reminiscences*, 57.

25. *Americans All*, 236.

26. AMHI, World War I, 42nd Division, Box 17, *The Battle of the 15th of July, 1918*, explained by General Hug, Former Chief of the Bureau of Operations of the 4th Army, upon the Occasion of the Twentieth Anniversary of the Battle of Champagne.

27. Duffy, *Father Duffy's Story*, 120.

28. *Alabama's Own*, 121.

29. H. L. Carter, "Story of B. C. Dunlop: 'The Apostle of Sunshine,'" *Army and Navy Record* (April 1920): 28.

30. Borden Burr, *Diary*, LPR262, Box 1, ADAH, July 1, 1918.

31. Winfred E. Robb, *The Price of Our Heritage: In Memory of the Heroic Dead of the 168th Infantry* (Des Moines, IA: Kessinger, 1919), 105.

32. *Alabama's Own*, 109.

33. Ibid., 118.

34. NARA, RG 117, Records of the American Battle Monuments Commission, Entry A1 49, American Battle Monuments Commission, Summary of Operations in the Champagne, July 4–17, 1918, Meeting Minutes and Agenda 1923, Letter Written by Douglas MacArthur on September 15, 1925, from Headquarters Third Corps Area, Baltimore, Maryland.

35. SHD, 26 N 680/5, 109e Régiment d'Infanterie.

36. *Alabama's Own*, 118.

37. *Americans All*, 269.

38. *Alabama's Own*, 121–122

39. Ibid., 118.

40. http://chtimiste.com/regiments/citationsinfanterie100-176.htm#_109ème_Régiment_d'Infanterie (accessed August 30, 2013)

41. *Americans All*, 270.

42. *Alabama's Own*, 124.

43. NARA, RG 117, Correspondence with former Divisions officers, Entry A1 31, File 714.2-E/DO Summary of Operations in the Champagne.

44. "Papers of the 42nd Infantry Division/National Archives," MAMA, RG 15, B 78, Folder 1.

45. Clarence W. Cox, "Private Clarence W. Cox, Hquarters [*sic*] Company, Relates His Most Exciting Experiences," *Army and Navy Record* (1920): 32.

46. The author's father said in conversation in the 1950s that they got a lot of rest.

47. David Homsher, "Was the 'Rainbow' Tarnished by Its Behavior on the Battlefield?" *Military Collector and Historian* 58 (Fall 2006): 158.

48. *Alabama's Own*, 120.

49. Wallach, "*Farmer: Have You a Daughter Fair?,*" 87–88.

50. Stewart, *Rainbow Bright*, 69.

51. Robb, *The Price of Our Heritage*, 106.

52. SHD, 26 N 588/4, *Journal de Marche du 17eRégimentd'Infanterie*, 14 Juillet 1918. Quotation translated from the original French.

53. NARA, RG 117, Records of the American Battle Monuments Commission, Entry A1 31, Correspondence with Former Division Officers, 42nd Division, File 714.2-E/DO.

54. *Americans All*, 242.

55. Leach, *War Diary*, 78.

56. *Alabama's Own*, 121.

57. *Americans All*, 253.

58. Ibid.

59. *Alabama's Own*, 123.

60. Thomas Neibaur, "How Private Neibaur Won the Congressional Medal of Honor, A Thrilling and Wonderful War Story, Told in His Own Words," *Improvement Era* 22 (1919): 784–85.

61. *Americans All*, 253.

62. Ibid., 254.

63. Leach, *War Diary*, 86.

64. SHD, 26N 680/5, 109e Régiment d'Infanterie.

65. Gilbert, *Twentieth Century*, 1, 503.

66. *Alabama's Own*, 125.

67. Taber, *The Story of the 168th Infantry*, 1: 283.

68. *Order of Battle, AEF: 42nd Division*, 279.

69. *Americans All*, 254.

70. Stewart, *Rainbow Bright*, 69.

71. Neibaur, "How Private Neibaur Won the Congressional Medal of Honor," 785.

72. *Alabama's Own*, 127; appendix F reports that for this action, Hughes was cited by the 167th Infantry, which entitled him to a Silver Star, and the French decorated him with a Croix de Guerre.

73. Tompkins, *Story of the Rainbow Division*, 21.

74. "Album de la Guerre," 1: 429.

75. Gaston Esnault, *Le poilu tel qu'il se parle* (Paris: Editions Bossard, 1919), 439. Will Frazer received his medal of Verdun for the fiftieth anniversary of the battle.

76. *Americans All*, 268–69.

77. Chambrun and Marenches, *American Army*, 163.

78. Ibid.

79. *Alabama's Own*, 126–27.

80. *Alabama's Own*, 125.

81. Ibid.

82. NARA, RG 120, Organizational Records, Entry 1241, 42nd Division, 167th Infantry Regiment, 32.13–66.1, 242-32-15.

83. *Alabama's Own*, 128–29.

84. *Americans All*, 271.

85. Sullivan, *The History of New York State, XI*, 1309. Sullivan add that "it was the first time in the history of the Western Front that a rifleman on the ground had done so and that it had to be an Alabamian, this triggered the harangue from the Colonel to do as well as the Alabamians," another example of the friendly competition that existed between the regiments.

86. *Americans All*, 272.

87. NARA, RG 117, Records of the American Battle Monuments Commission, Entry A1 31, Correspondence with Former Division Officers, 42nd Division, File 714, American Battle Monuments Commission Summary of Operations in the Champagne, July 4–17, 1918, 2-E/DO #7.

88. Straub, *A Sergeant's Diary*, 126. Eighty-eight km is about fifty-five miles.

89. Duffy, *Father Duffy's Story*, 137.

90. *Americans All*, 271.

91. *Alabama's Own*, 131.

92. NARA, RG 117, Records of the American Battle Monuments Commission, Entry A1 31, Correspondence with Former Division Officers, 42nd Division, File 714, American Battle Monuments Commission Summary of Operations in the Champagne, July 4–17, 1918, 2-E/DO #7.

93. Taber, *The Story of the 168th Infantry*, 1: 301.

94. Herbert George, *The Challenge of War* (New York, Vantage Press, 1966), 76.

95. Lawrence Sondhaus, *World War I: The Global Revolution* (New York: Cambridge University Press, 2011), 414.

96. Jordan, *Letters*, July 23, 1918.

97. US Adjutant General's Office, *Congressional Medal of Honor, the Distinguished Service Cross, and The Distinguished Service Medal Issued by the War Department since April 6, 1917, up to and Including General Orders, No. 126, War Department, November 11, 1919* (Washington DC: GPO, 1920), 43.

98. SHD, 17 N126, Archives, 23 Juillet1918. Quotation translated from the original French.

99. SHD, 26 N 680/6, 109e Régiment d'Infanterie

100. Mahon, *New York's Fighting Sixty-Ninth*, 234.

101. American Battle Monuments Commission (ABMC), *American Armies and Battlefields in Europe* (Washington, DC: GPO, 1938), 514.

102. SDH, 17 N 125, *Rapport sur les journées des 15 et 16 Juillet, 1918*, 3ème Bureau. Quotation translated from the original French.

103. SHD, 26 N 819/7, *Journal de Marche* du 10e *Bataillon de Chasseurs à Pieds*, 15 Juillet 1918. Quotation translated from the original French.

104. Chambrun and Marenches, *American Army*, 163.

105. SDH, 17 N 125, *Rapport sur les journées des 15 et 16 Juillet, 1918*, 3ème Bureau. Quotation translated from the original French.

106. Teilhard de Chardin later became a Jesuit and one of France's most famous philosophers and ethnographers. Pierre Teilhard de Chardin, *Genèse d'une pensée: Lettres, 1914–1919* (Paris: Bernard Grasset, 1961), 284. Quotation translated from the original French. Italics original.

107. Jordan, *Letters*, July 23, 1918.

108. Van Dolsen, letter to his aunt, in Cooke, *The Rainbow Division*, 80.

109. Gustave Babin, "Sur le champ de bataille de Champagne: La victorieuse défense de Chalons," *L'Illustration* (July 27, 1918): 95. Quotation translated from the original French.

110. *Americans All*, 302.

111. Ibid.

112. Ibid., 315.

113. MacArthur, *War Bugs*, 95.

114. Elmer E. Sherwood, *A Soldier in World War I: Diary of a Rainbow Veteran, Written at the Front* (1929; reprint, ed. Robert E. Ferrell, [Indianapolis: Indiana Historical Society Press, 2004], 58.)

115. MacArthur, *War Bugs*, 96.

116. Family papers of Josephine Screws McGowin, newspaper clipping without date or name for the paper.

117. Borden Burr, *Scrapbook*, LPR262, Box 3, ADAH, 1–11.

118. Soldiers of the 4th Army received a typed letter, later published in a handwritten form with a photograph of General Gouraud stating, "C'est un coup dur pour l'ennemi. C'est une belle journée pour la France." UNLA, *Rainbow Division Veterans Association Papers, 1917–2000*, Spec MS #104 RDVA Records World War I, Box 88 File 5.

119. Jordan, *Letters*, July 23, 1918.

120. Mead, *Doughboys*, 264.

121. Pershing, *My Experiences in the World War*, 2: 162.

122. Crown Prince Wilhelm, *Memoirs of the Crown Prince of Germany* (1919; reprint, Uckfield, East Sussex: Naval and Military Press, 2005), 195.

123. NARA, RG 117, Records of the American Battle Monuments Commission, Entry A1 49, American Battle Monuments Commission, Summary of Operations in the Champagne, July 4–17, 1918, Meeting Minutes and Agenda 1923, Letter Written by Douglas MacArthur on September 15, 1925 from Headquarters Third Corps Area, Baltimore, Maryland.

124. The First Battle of the Marne had been fought by the French and the British in early September 1914.

125. Bruce, *Fraternity of Arms*, 249–50.

# Chapter 6

1. Salient, meaning a "portion of the line forming an angle," Collins, *151st Field Artillery*, 41. During World War II, the use of *salient* would be eclipsed by the term *bulge*.

2. Cheseldine, *Ohio in the Rainbow*, 191.

3. MacArthur, *War Bugs*, 123.

4. Michael S. Neiberg, *The Second Battle of the Marne* (Bloomington: Indiana University Press, 2008), 85.

5. Hervey Allen, *Toward the Flame: A Memoir of World War I* (1926; reprint, Lincoln: University of Nebraska Press, 2003), 131. From the Marne to the Vesle the Americans were part of the French army.

6. Robert H. Ferrell, *The Question of MacArthur's Reputation: Côte de Châtillon, October 14–16, 1918* (Columbia: University of Missouri Press, 2008), 45.

7. Allen, *Toward the Flame*, 131.

8. *Alabama's Own*, 142.

9. NARA, RG 117, Records of the American Battle Monuments Commission, Entry A1 31, Correspondence with Former Division Officers, 42nd Division, File 714.2-G/AM #8.

10. *Alabama's Own*, 143–44.

11. This failure eventually caused Pershing to relieve Edwards on October 22. Edward M. Coffman details how General Edwards's relief "became a *cause célèbre*" and controversy over the dismissal went on for a decade. Coffman, *War to End All Wars*, 251–52.

12. Coffman, *War to End All Wars*, 253.

13. This 167th French Division is not to be confused with the 167th French Regiment that was part of the French 128th Division and with which the 167th (Alabama) had served in Lorraine.

14. NARA, RG 120, World War I Organization Records, Entry 1241, 42nd Division Historical Record, Folder 242-32.7.

15. *Americans All*, 311.

16. *United States Army in the World War, 1917–1919, Military Expeditions of the American Expeditionary Forces*, vol. 5 (Washington, DC: Center of Military History, United States Army, 1989), 516.

17. NARA, RG 117, Box 230, Correspondence with Former Division Officers, 42nd Division, File 714.2-G/AM.

18. Neiberg, *Second Battle of the Marne*, 154.

19. *Alabama's Own*, 144.

20. Hayes, *Heroes among the Brave*, 22.

21. *Americans All*, 355.

22. Ibid., 344.

23. White and Peavy, *The 151st Machine Gun Battalion*, 10.

24. *Alabama's Own*, 145.

25. Ibid., 144–45.

26. Allen, *Toward the Flame*, 155–56.

27. *Americans All*, 346.

28. Ibid.

29. *Alabama's Own*, 146.

30. Ibid.

31. Hayes, *Heroes among the Brave*, 22.

32. Edmund F. Hackett, First Lieutenant, *The Fight at Croix Rouge Farm*. Public Information Subject Files—Alabamians at War, "Battles and Histories: Reminiscences of 167th Infantry Member," SG017102, ADAH.

33. Stewart, *Rainbow Bright*, 79.

34. Hayes, *Heroes among the Brave*, 22. See also Croix Rouge Farm Battle Map.

35. Hayes, *Heroes among the Brave*, 22.

36. *Alabama's Own*, 145.

37. UNLA, *Rainbow Division Veterans Association Papers*, Box 1, Folder 6, 42nd Division AEF Intelligence Report, July 25–July 26, 8 P.M. to 8 P.M., by command of General Menoher, signed by Douglas MacArthur, chief of staff.

38. *Americans All*, 356.

39. Ibid., 357.

40. Taber, *The Story of the 168th Infantry*, 1: 334.

41. NARA RG 117, Records of the American Battle Monuments Commission, Entry A1 31, Correspondence with Former Division Officers, 714.2-G/AM #8, Summary of Operation 42nd Division (plus 47th Infantry) Aisne-Marne, July 25–August 2, 1918.

42. The battle of Croix Rouge Farm is not mentioned in the book on the Rainbow Division written by a soldier in the 3rd Battalion of the 168th, Private Hoffman, I Company, 168th Regiment, upon his return from the war. W. M. R. Hoffman, *The Famous 42nd "Rainbow" Division Who Helped Close the Lid of Hell* (Plattsmouth, NE: Hoffman and Steinhauer, 1919).

43. NARA, RG 165, Records of the War Department General and Special Staffs, War College Division and Special Staffs Division, German Military Records Relating to World War I, 1917–1919, Entry 320, 10th Landwehr Division, Entry 320, File 632-33.5 CHM #322 Division Operation Champagne-Marne, Aisne-Marne, July 15–August 6, 1918.

44. Neiberg, *Second Battle of the Marne*, 158.

45. NARA, RG 165, Records of the War Department General and Special Staffs, War College Division and Special Staffs Division, German Military Records Relating to World War I, 1917–1919, Entry 320, 10th Landwehr Division, Entry 320, File 632-33.5 J.P.R. #39.1936, Division Operation Champagne-Marne, Aisne-Marne, July 15–August 6, 1918.

46. Hayes, *Heroes among the Brave*, 22.

47. Ibid. Although Hayes speaks only of white lines, Hackett mentions red lines, while

Reilly refers to both white and red: "On a great many of the trees they had painted on the side facing them aiming markers of white and red bands. These markers gave the machine gunners the aiming point for traversing machine gun fire" (*Americans All*, 348).

48. Hackett, *Fight at Croix Rouge Farm*, SG017102, ADAH.

49. Douglas MacArthur, Personal Correspondence, "Reminiscences Manuscript," MAMA, RG 10, Box 193a.

50. *Alabama's Own*, 146.

51. http://www.archives.alabama.gov/goldstar/images/Ford_Neil/bioform.pdf, accessed July 27, 2013.

52. *Alabama's Own*, 146.

53. As told by his father in a 1954 conversation.

54. *Americans All*, 347.

55. Ibid., 349–50.

56. Hayes, *Heroes among the Brave*, 22–23.

57. *Alabama's Own*, 146.

58. As told by his father in a 1954 conversation. Corporal Will Frazer also spoke of lying behind a log that morning and seeing Colonel MacArthur. No other accounts record MacArthur paying such a visit to the D Company position, but Will described it. He said, "It was raining at about eleven o'clock in the morning. I looked to the rear and MacArthur was there behind a slight rise in the ground. He did not stay long." This conversation about senior officer visits to the front lines took place between the author and his father in 1953 or 1954 after the Korean War had ended. Frazier Hunt in *The Untold Story of Douglas MacArthur* (New York: Devin-Adair, 1954), 80, refers to MacArthur who, that morning, "walked the deadly woods and studied the fields of slaughter. He realized the terrible mistake: the Germans were no longer rapidly retreating."

59. Watts, *Memoir*, 14.

60. Although the 26th Division's field artillery officers attended the meeting, Ferrell reports that they did not receive the order to fire. Ferrell, *The Question of MacArthur's Reputation*, 49.

61. *Americans All*, 345.

62. Ibid.

63. Ibid, 348.

64. Taber, *The Story of the 168th Infantry*, 1: 322.

65. Hackett, *Fight at Croix Rouge Farm*, SG017102, ADAH.

66. Burr, *Diary*, July 26, 1918.

67. *Alabama's Own*, 147.

68. Ibid.

69. Burr, *Diary*, July 26, 1918.

70. *Alabama's Own*, 149.

71. NARA, RG 165, Records of the War Department General and Special Staffs, War

College Division and Special Staffs Division, German Military Records Relating to World War I, 1917–1919, Entry 320, 10th Landwehr Division, Entry 320, Division Operation Champagne-Marne, Aisne-Marne, July 15–August 6, 1918, File 632-33.5 J.P.R. #39.1936. American sources state that the site was quiet by 8:00 P.M.

72. *Alabama's Own*, 335. From citation awarding him a Distinguished Service Cross for service on July 26, 1918. US Adjutant General's Office, *Congressional Medal of Honor*, 42. Hope had received a citation by Colonel Screws for bravery in the Champagne battle on July 15: http://www.archives.state.al.us/goldstar/images/Hope_Ben/letter3.pdf, accessed July 27, 2013.

73. http://www.archives.state.al.us/goldstar/images/card/Burnett_Usry.pdf, accessed July 27, 2013.

74. http://www.archives.state.al.us/goldstar/images/Canoles_Carl/bioform.pdf, accessed July 27, 2013.

75. *Alabama's Own*, 149.

76. http://www.archives.state.al.us/goldstar/images/other/Bowlin_Russell.pdf, accessed July 27, 2013.

77. http://www.archives.state.al.us/goldstar/images/Houston_NewelS/information.pdf, accessed July 27, 2013.

78. http://www.archives.state.al.us/goldstar/images/Hughes_WilliamS/bioform.pdf, accessed July 27, 2013.

79. NARA, RG 117, Records of the American Battle Monuments Commission, Entry A1 31, Correspondence with Former Division Officers, 42nd Division, File 714.2-G/AM #8.

80. Taber, *The Story of the 168th Infantry*, 1: 331.

81. Burr, *Diary*, July 26, 1918.

82. NARA, RG 117, Records of the American Battle Monuments Commission, Entry A1 31, Correspondence with Former Division Officers, 42nd Division, File 714.2-G/AM.

83. AMHI, World War I Veterans Survey, 42nd Division, 167th Infantry Regiment, Diary of Norman L. Summers, First Sergeant, M Company.

84. Hayes, *Destiny of a Soldier*, 157.

85. *Americans All*, 353.

86. Ibid., 352.

87. NARA, RG 165, Records of the War Department General and Special Staffs, War College Division and Special Staffs Division, German Military Records Relating to World War I, 1917–1919, Entry 320, 10th Landwehr Division, Entry 320, Division Operation Champagne-Marne, Aisne-Marne, July 15–August 6, 1918, File 632-33.5 J.P.R. #39.1936. American sources state that the site was quiet by 8:00 P.M.

88. *Alabama's Own*, 151.

89. Hackett, *Fight at Croix Rouge Farm*, SG017102, ADAH.

90. *Alabama's Own*, 151. In addition to sharing in the honor of leading the successful second attack, Espy also led the strong patrol sent by Colonel Screws to protect the 167th left

flank. He also received the DSC. For details, see US Adjutant General's Office, *Congressional Medal of Honor*, 40.

91. *Americans All*, 349.

92. *Alabama's Own*, 151.

93. *Americans All*, 345–46.

94. *Alabama's Own*, 334.

95. Ibid., 151.

96. Hackett, *Fight at Croix Rouge Farm*, SG017102, ADAH.

97. Carroll received a regimental citation for his leadership and conduct (*Alabama's Own*, 338).

98. *Birmingham News*, May 10, 1919, 2.

99. Hayes, *Heroes among the Brave*, 23.

100. Hayes, *Destiny of a Soldier*, 156. Wren, previously promoted from corporal to sergeant and later commissioned, was personally decorated with a DSC by Pershing following a 42nd Division review in Remagen, Germany. He also received the French Croix de Guerre for other services. Wren, *Letters*, March 31, 1919, and *Alabama's Own*, 310.

101. Hayes, *Heroes among the Brave*, 23.

102. *Alabama's Own*, 151.

103. Ibid., 152.

104. *Americans All,* 360.

105. Ibid.

106. Taber, *The Story of the 168th Infantry*, 1: 336.

107. NARA, RG 117, Records of the American Battle Monuments Commission, Entry A1 31, Correspondence with Former Division Officers, 42nd Division, File 714.2-G/ AM #8.

108. *Americans All*, 352.

109. Ibid., 350–51.

110. AMHI, World War I Veterans Survey, 42nd Division, 167th Infantry Regiment, J. Douglas Brown, Private, 1st Battalion Medical Detachment.

111. *Americans All*, 368.

112. Watts, *Memoir*, 16.

113. The author's father.

114. Recorded in postwar notes by Will's first wife, Margaret Thompson Frazer, and later mentioned in conversation between Will and the author.

115. Family papers of Josephine Screws McGowin, newspaper clipping without date or name for the paper.

116. Roberts, *Letters*, July 28, 1918.

117. *Alabama's Own*, 335.

118. African American units were the only troops amalgamated with the French, therefore seeing combat before most white Americans. The first Americans to receive the French

Croix de Guerre for gallantry were two black Americans, Henry Johnson and Robert Need-ham. They belonged to the all-black US 93rd Division, and its four regiments served with the French. General Pershing would comment later (Pershing, *My Experiences in the World War*, 1: 291): "Very much to my regret these regiments never served with us, but it was gratifying later to hear of them being highly commended by the French."

119. Roberts, *Letters*, July 28, 1918.

120. Brenneman, *Letters*, August 6, 1918.

121. Phipps Kennedy, *Letters*, August 9, 1918. Courtesy of James Vann, Macon, GA.

122. *Americans All*, 349.

123. Ibid., 346.

124. NARA, RG 165, Records of the War Department General and Special Staffs, War College Division and Special Staffs Division, German Military Records Relating to World War I, 1917–1919, Entry 320, 10th Landwehr Division, Entry 320, File 632-33.5 J.P.R. #39.1936, p. 81: Gefechsbeutel II/378 Division Operation Champagne-Marne, Aisne-Marne, July 15–August 6, 1918; *Americans All*, 345.

125. *Alabama's Own*, 145.

126. *Infantry in Battle* reports that proper anticipation, planning, and strict adherence to orders by relying on the watch was memorialized in 1930 by George C. Marshall when he was a colonel and commandant of the Infantry School at Fort Benning, Georgia. The school published a monograph of lessons to be learned from World War I and referenced Colonel Screws as setting the example of getting an attack off on time despite breakdowns in communication. *Infantry in Battle* (Washington, DC: The Infantry Journal, 1939), 142–46.

127. See appendix D.

128. *Alabama's Own*, 408–9.

129. *New York Times*, August 21, 1918.

130. Burr, *Diary*, 60–63.

131. *Americans All*, 317–18.

# Chapter 7

1. *Alabama's Own*, 155.

2. Ibid.

3. *Americans All*, 346.

4. According to Neil Hanson, "Seven out of ten American next of kin remained immune to all arguments for burial overseas and ultimately opted to have their dead returned home." Neil Hanson, *Unknown Soldiers: The Story of the Missing of the First World War* (New York: First Vintage Books, 2006), 243.

5. *Alabama's Own*, 155–56.

6. NARA, RG 117, Records of the American Battle Monuments Commission, Entry A1 31, Correspondence with Former Division Officers, 42nd Division, File 714.2-G/AM.

7. Ibid.

8. *Alabama's Own*, 158.

9. Collins, *151st Field Artillery*, 93. The small village of Sergy had and would change hands a number of times during the combats.

10. SHD 17 N 125, Rapport sur les opérations du 25 au 29 Juillet 1918, 30 Juillet, 1918.

11. *Americans All*, 346, 353.

12. Gabriel continues with this highly unusual description: "The Americans attacked our lines in heavy columns, with officers on horseback, and this unusual sight bluffed us completely. Soon our machine gun fire and the impact of our artillery had dispersed the heavy columns of the enemy. It became again a one man to one man fight." This remains an isolated account of US officers charging on horseback during World War I. Kurt Gabriel, *Die 4 Garde Infanterie Division, Der Ruhmesweg einer bewährten Kampftruppe durch den Weltkrieg* (Berlin: Verlag Klafing, 1921), 152–53. Quotation translated from the original German.

13. *Americans All*, 364.

14. Wolf, *Brief Story*, 33.

15. *Alabama's Own*, 156.

16. Ibid., 157.

17. Ibid.

18. NARA, RG 117, Records of the American Battle Monuments Commission, Entry A1 31, Correspondence with Former Division Officers, 42nd Division, File 714, American Battle Monuments Commission Summary of Operations in the Champagne, July 4–17, 1918, 2-E/DO.

19. *Alabama's Own*, 157.

20. Ibid.

21. *Americans All*, 369–70.

22. Ibid.; *Alabama's Own*, 157.

23. Duffy, *Father Duffy's Story*, 158.

24. *Alabama's Own*, 158.

25. *Americans All*, 386.

26. *Alabama's Own*, 158.

27. Ibid., 158–59.

28. *Americans All*, 372.

29. Watts, *Memoir*, 17.

30. Ibid.

31. Greet refers to Leffonds, in the Haute-Marne, where they trained in January and February 1918. *Americans All*, 375.

32. *Americans All*, 377.

33. *Alabama's Own*, 157.

34. *Americans All*, 377.

35. *Alabama's Own*, 159.

36. Richard B. Kelly, "Bravery of Sidney E. Manning," *Army and Navy Record* (April 1920): 68.

37. Manning's action was the first in the Rainbow Division and the first in the 167th Infantry to result in the award of the Congressional Medal of Honor.

Citation: Rank and organization: Corporal, U.S. Army Company G, 167th Infantry, 42d Division. Place and date: Near Breuvannes, France, 28 July 1918. Entering service at: Flomaton, Ala. Born: July 17, 1892, Butler County, Ala. G.O. No.: 44, W.D., 1919. http://www.history.army.mil/html/moh/worldwari.html, accessed July 29, 2013.

Four enlisted men and one officer of the Rainbow Division, two in the 167th and three in the 165th, were awarded the Medal of Honor listed here in order of their action date: Manning, O'Neill, Donaldson, Donovan, and Neibaur.

38. http://www.archives.state.al.us/goldstar/images/card/Deese_PeytonV.pdf, accessed July 29, 2013.

39. *Alabama's Own*, appendix B, 334; and http://www.archives.state.al.us/goldstar/images/card/Brown_Bill.pdf, accessed July 29, 2013.

40. Romslo, who received campaign clasps for service in defensive sector, Champagne-Marne and Aisne-Marne, was first buried in France. His body was later returned to Norway at the request of his family. According to family records provided by his great-nephew Roald Sjursen, two American officers traveled to Norway to bring back the body for burial there. As soon as the United States instituted the draft, citizens and immigrants had been asked to register. While many citizens of neutral countries, including Norwegians, were eager to serve to demonstrate their loyalty to the United States, neutral countries protested the drafting of their citizens and only those, like Romslo, who stated their intention to ask for naturalization on their draft card, would be sent to France (*Americans All*, 44, 52.).

41. AMHI, World War I Veterans Survey, Walker. The International Convention at Geneva would later deny prisoner of war protection to soldiers captured out of their own national uniform.

42. George, *Challenge of War*, 89.

43. *Alabama's Own*, 156.

44. Ibid.

45. Ibid.

46. Ibid.

47. Ibid.

48. *Americans All*, 373.

49. Jordan died and as Smith's name no longer appears in the story of the regiment in France, we assume that he spent the rest of the war in a hospital. After the war he contributed to *Americans All*.

50. Jordan is buried in Arlington National Cemetery. US Adjutant General's Office, *Congressional Medal of Honor*, 43.

51. *Americans All*, 372.

52. *Alabama's Own*, 160.

53. Ibid.

54. *Americans All*, 372–73.

55. Hanson, *Unknown Soldiers*, 210–11.

56. Holmes, *Acts of War*, 177.

57. AMHI, World War I Veterans Survey, 42nd Division, 167th Infantry Regiment, Norman L. Summers, First Sergeant, Company M.

58. *Alabama's Own*, 156.

59. *Americans All*, 390.

60. Ibid., 390–91.

61. Dasch received a DSC for his exemplary service. General Orders No. 102, W. D., 1918, http://www.homeofheroes.com/members/02_DSC/citatons/01_wwi_dsc/dsc_05wwi_Army_DE.html, Accessed July 29, 2013.

62. *Americans All*, 396.

63. Ibid.

64. Ibid., 398.

65. Ibid., 397.

66. Ibid., 398.

67. *Alabama's Own*, 159.

68. Coffman, *War to End All Wars*, 253.

69. NARA RG 117, Records of the American Battle Monuments Commission, Entry A1 31, Correspondence with former division officers, 714.2-G/AM #8, Summary of Operation 42nd Division (plus 47th Infantry) Aisne-Marne, July 25–August 2, 1918.

70. Ibid.

71. NARA, RG 200, Index and Case Files relating to Reclassification and Reassignment of Officers, Reclassification of Regular Army Brigadier generals and major generals, Entry NM 1022, Relief History of Brigadier General R. A. Brown, 130-84-2-5, August 21, 1918, 22.

72. *Alabama's Own*, 159–60.

73. Ibid., 161–62.

74. NARA, RG 200, Index and Case Files relating to Reclassification and Reassignment of Officers, Reclassification of Regular Army Brigadier generals and major generals, Entry NM 1022, Relief History of Brigadier General R. A. Brown, 130-84-2-5, August 24, 1918, 36.

75. *Alabama's Own*, 162.

76. NARA, RG 200, Index and Case Files relating to Reclassification and Reassignment of Officers, Reclassification of Regular Army Brigadier generals and major generals, Entry NM 1022, Relief History of Brigadier General R. A. Brown, 130-84-2-5, August 24, 1918, 36.

77. *Americans All*, 370.

78. Ibid.

79. Ibid.

80. Ibid.

81. Ibid.

82. Ibid., 516–18.

83. Taber, *The Story of the 168th Infantry*, 2: 21.

84. NARA, RG 200, Index and Case Files relating to Reclassification and Reassignment of Officers, Reclassification of Regular Army Brigadier generals and major generals, Entry NM 1022, Relief History of Brigadier General R. A. Brown, 130-84-2-5, August 21, 1918, 24.

85. NARA, Microcopy number T-900, Roll number 17, Index to correspondence of the Office of the Commander-in-Chief, AEF, 1917–1919. Author's note: MacArthur's return to the United States was announced in a *New York Times* article on August 3, 1918.

86. Ferrell, *The Question of MacArthur's Reputation*, 83.

87. NARA, RG 200, Index and Case Files relating to Reclassification and Reassignment of Officers, Reclassification of Regular Army Brigadier generals and major generals, Entry NM 1022, Relief History of Brigadier General R. A. Brown, 130-84-2-5, August 21, 1918, 20.

88. Ibid., 21–22.

89. NARA, RG 120, AEF General Headquarters, G-3 Reports, Entry 270, 42nd Division, Folder 10.

90. *Americans All*, 493.

91. Watts, *Memoir*, 16.

92. *Americans All*, 346.

93. NARA, RG 200, Index and Case Files relating to Reclassification and Reassignment of Officers, Reclassification of Regular Army Brigadier generals and major generals, Entry NM 1022, Relief History of Brigadier General R. A. Brown, 130-84-2-5, August 21, 1918, 28.

94. Duffy, *Father Duffy's Story*, 157.

95. SHD 17 N 125, Rapport sur les opérations du 25 au 29 Juillet 1918, 30 Juillet 1918.

96. NARA, RG 200, Index and Case Files relating to Reclassification and Reassignment of Officers, Reclassification of Regular Army Brigadier generals and major generals, Entry NM 1022, Relief History of Brigadier General R. A. Brown, 130-84-2-5, August 21, 1918, 5.

97. Ibid., 28.

98. Ferrell, *The Question of MacArthur's Reputation*, 84–85.

99. Leach, *War Diary*, 107. Italics original.

100. Ibid.

101. John D. Brenner, "*Le* [sic] *Guerre*," 43.

102. *Alabama's Own*, 162.

103. Ibid., 164.

104. *Americans All*, 343.

105. *Alabama's Own*, 164.

106. Wolf, *Brief Story*, 34.

107. AMHI, World War I Veterans Survey, 42 Division, 167th Infantry Regiment, J. Douglas Brown, Private, 1st Battalion Medical Detachment.

108. *Americans All*, 493.

109. Paul F. Braim, *The Test of Battle* (1987; reprint, Shippensburg, PA: White Mane Books, 1998), 31.

110. Coffman, *War to End All Wars*, 255.

111. Tompkins, *Story of the Rainbow Division*, 31–32.

112. Ibid.

113. Janis, *The Big Show*, 183–84.

114. *Alabama's Own*, 165.

115. Sherwood, *A Soldier in World War I*, 58.

116. Wolf, *Brief Story*, 36.

117. *Alabama's Own*, 165–66.

118. General Order No. 73. Mahon, *History of the Militia and the National Guard*, 161.

119. The author's maternal grandmother kept the flag used when her son served in World War I. Neil Hanson also describes this tradition: "Since the first American troops had sailed for Europe, every American family had been entitled to display a blue star service flag, for each husband, father or son serving with the U.S. forces. Thousands of women sewed a blue star on to a piece of white fabric and hung it in their windows. On 28 May 1918, concerned at the negative impact that sight of thousands of American women in traditional mourning dress might have on public morale, President Woodrow Wilson had approved a proposal from the Women's Council on National Defense that the mothers or wives of dead American servicemen could display a gold star service flag and wear a black armband with a gold star to symbolize the honour and glory accorded for the supreme sacrifice for the nation" (Hanson, *Unknown Soldiers*, 250).

120. *Alabama's Own*, 167.

121. Hayes, *Heroes among the Brave*, 32.

122. The author received this message from a relative of John Hayes: "I had a great uncle, John B. Hayes originally from Notasulga who was in the Rainbow Division. . . . He was so disturbed by his experiences that when World War II came and his sons had to go, he spent the entire war in Bryce's in a catatonic state. After the war, he got better and could tell you everything that happened in the time he was incapacitated."

123. Hew Strachan, *The First World War* (2001; reprint, New York: Penguin Books, 2005), 316.

124. *Alabama's Own*, 167.

125. Peter Englund, *The Beauty and the Sorrow* (New York: Knopf, 2011), 474.

126. Farwell, *Over There*, 175.

127. *Americans All*, 522–23.

128. Despite such testimony, the historian David Homsher believes that the Rainbow Division displayed some "extremely aggressive battlefield behavior during World War I. It is also my distinctive impression that the investigation conducted by the AEF HQ was a total whitewash." Homsher, "Was the 'Rainbow' Tarnished by Its Behavior on the Battlefield?," 160.

129. Edward G. Lengel, *To Conquer Hell: The Meuse-Argonne, 1918*. (New York: Henry Holt, 2008), 68.

130. Mangin, *Les Américains en France*, 109.

131. Howard Vincent O'Brien and Karl Edwin Harriman, *Wine, Women, and War: A Diary of Disillusionment* (New York: J. H. Sears, 1926), 122. Italics original.

132. Pershing served thirty-three years in the army without a wife. He was secretly married to Micheline Resco by Father Jules A. Baisnee at Walter Reed General Hospital in Washington on September 2, 1946, and died on July 15, 1948. Smythe, *Pershing*, 307.

133. *Alabama's Own*, 168.

134. Ibid.

135. Brenner, *Le* [*sic*] *Guerre*, 52.

136. Fromkin, *In the Time of the Americans*, 174.

137. James H. Hallas, *Squandered Victory* (Westport, CT: Praeger, 1995), 86.

138. *Alabama's Own*, 169.

139. Ibid.

140. MacArthur, *War Bugs*, 128.

## Chapter 8

1. Hallas, *Doughboy War*, 197.

2. *Alabama's Own*, 171.

3. Ibid.

4. Ibid.

5. AMHI, World War I Veterans Survey, 42nd Division, 167th Infantry Regiment, J. Douglas Brown, Private, 1st Battalion Medical Detachment.

6. *Alabama's Own*, 172.

7. Ibid.

8. MacArthur, *War Bugs*, 137.

9. *Alabama's Own*, 173.

10. Ibid.

11. Thompson, *Trench Knives and Mustard Gas*, 164–65.

12. *Americans All*, 541.

13. Eisenhower, *Yanks*, 183–84, 194.

14. *Americans All*, 538.

15. Pershing, *My Experiences in the World War*, 2: 254–55.

16. Farwell, *Over There*, 222.

17. Hallas, *Squandered Victory*, 16.

18. Pershing, *My Experiences in the World War*, 2: 226.

19. *Alabama's Own*, 170–71.

20. *Americans All*, 542.

21. *Alabama's Own*, 174.

22. Ibid.

23. William W. Wright, *Meuse-Argonne Diary*, ed. Robert H. Ferrell (Columbia: University of Missouri Press, 2004), 17.

24. *Enzyklopädie Erster Weltkrieg*, s.v. "St Mihiel Bogen," 809. Quotation translated from the original German.

25. Webb, "Painting the Rainbow," 38.

26. *Alabama's Own*, 176.

27. William L. Langer, *Gas and Flame in World War One* (1919; reprint, New York: Knopf, 1965), 40.

28. Collins, *151st Field Artillery*, 122.

29. Wright, *Meuse-Argonne Diary*, 17.

30. Major Carroll's name does not show up in the records of the regiment after his being wounded on July 28.

31. Greene was the only officer of the Alabama regiment killed that day. At the Ourcq, he had a conversation with Screws (recorded in the Inspector General investigation into the possible relief of the brigade commander) at a time when the regiment was mentally and physically exhausted and stated that he had never quit nor been in the hospital. A Pell City lawyer and 1901 graduate of the George Washington University School of Law, Greene had organized the Pell City Guards in 1915. His body remains in the Saint-Mihiel American Cemetery at Thiaucourt, near where he fell. More information at http://www.archives .state.al.us/goldstar/images/Greene_JGardner/booklet.pdf, accessed July 29, 2013.

32. *Alabama's Own*, 177.

33. Wright, *Meuse-Argonne Diary*, 18.

34. *Alabama's Own*, 181.

35. Wright, *Meuse-Argonne Diary*, 18.

36. *Alabama's Own*, 177.

37. Ibid.

38. US Adjutant General's Office, *Congressional Medal of Honor*, 42.

39. *Alabama's Own*, 178.

40. Langer, *Gas and Flame in World War One*, 35.

41. Martin Blumenson, *Patton: The Man behind the Legend, 1885–1945* (New York: William Morrow, 1985), 113–14.

42. David Bonk, *St Mihiel 1918: The American Expeditionary Forces' Trial by Fire* (Oxford: Osprey, 2011), 29.

43. *Americans All*, 539.

44. *Alabama's Own*, 178.

45. Ibid., 181–82.

46. *Americans All*, 575.

47. Pershing, *My Experiences in the World War*, 2: 272–73.

48. MacArthur, *War Bugs*, 147–48.

49. Robert H. Zieger, *America's Great War: World War I and the American Experience* (Lanham, MD: Rowman and Littlefield, 2001), 99.

50. Pershing, *Final Report*, 43.

51. NARA RG 120.3.2, General Headquarters, American Expeditionary Forces, Second Section, General Staff, *Monograph*, March 24, 1919, 23.

52. Ferrell, *The Question of MacArthur's Reputation*, 53.

53. Eisenhower, *Yanks*, 210.

54. Bruce, *Fraternity of Arms*, 271.

55. Ibid.

56. Wright, *Meuse-Argonne Diary*, 45.

57. Pershing, *My Experiences in the World War*, 2: 300.

58. Ferrell, *America's Deadliest Battle,* 41.

59. NARA, RG 165, German Military Records 1917–1919, Entry 320, 52nd Jaeger Division. Quotation translated from the original German.

60. Bruce, *Fraternity of Arms*, 271.

61. George Marshall, *Memoirs of My Services in the World War, 1917–1918* (Boston: Houghton Mifflin, 1976), 165.

62. Eisenhower, *Yanks*, 254.

63. Marshall, *Memoirs*, 163.

64. Lengel, *To Conquer Hell*, 184. In *Over Here*, David Kennedy notes that Pershing, years later, discovered this and dismissed it then as "a purely political gesture" (Kennedy, *Over Here*, 198).

65. "Album de la Guerre," 2: 1002.

66. Wilhelm, *Memoirs of the Crown Prince of Germany*, 207.

67. Eisenhower, *Yanks*, 254.

68. Ibid., 235.

69. Ferrell, *America's Deadliest Battle*, 74.

70. Lengel, *To Conquer Hell*, 251.

71. Coffman, *War to End All Wars*, 323.

72. Eisenhower, *Yanks*, 237.

73. Alan D. Gaff, *Blood in the Argonne: The Lost Battalion of World War I* (Norman: University of Oklahoma Press, 2005), 4.

74. Smythe, *Pershing*, 207.

75. *Alabama's Own*, 191.

76. Cheseldine, *Ohio in the Rainbow*, 245.

77. *Alabama's Own*, 190.

78. Ibid.

79. Lengel, *To Conquer Hell*, 315.

80. Stewart, *Rainbow Bright*, 119.

81. Wren, *Letters*, October 8, 1918.

82. *Army and Navy Journal*, December 21, 1918; Leach, *War Diary*, 152–53.

83. *Americans All*, 658.

84. Ibid., 659.

85. Ferrell, *The Question of MacArthur's Reputation*, 11

86. *Alabama's Own*, 190.

87. Langille, *Men of the Rainbow,* 158.

88. *Alabama's Own*, 191.

89. Ibid.

90. NARA, RG 117, Records of the American Battle Monuments Commission, Entry A1 31, Correspondence with former Division Officers, 42nd Division, file 714.2-M/A, Letter to American Battle Monuments Commission dated November 23, 1926.

91. Eisenhower, *Yanks*, 226.

92. Ferrell, *American's Deadliest Battle*, 98.

# Chapter 9

1. Eisenhower, *Yanks*, 252.

2. Braim, *Test of Battle*, 125. "Kill 'em All Summerall," was used by Citadel cadets when Summerall was president. Tom McLemore, a cadet during Summerall's tenure, told the author about the nickname.

3. See Appendix B: Organization of the 42nd Division.

4. Smythe, *Pershing*, 206.

5. Accidentally burned in 2011.

6. Eisenhower, *Yanks*, 256.

7. NARA RG 120.3.2, General Headquarters, American Expeditionary Forces, Second Section, General Staff, *Monograph*, March 24, 1919, 30.

8. Ferrell, *The Question of MacArthur's Reputation*, 2.

9. *Americans All*, 516.

10. The splendid work of the telephone and telegraph servicemen in the Argonne is best described in Lavine, *Circuits of Victory*, 540–76. Lavine gives a detailed picture of the terrain and conditions.

11. D. Clayton James, *The Years of MacArthur: 1880–1941*, vol. 1 (Boston: Houghton Mifflin, 1970), 215.

12. *Americans All*, 648.

13. MacArthur, *War Bugs*, 173.

14. One can still see its tracks today.

15. *Americans All*, 677.

16. The late Floyd Gibbons, war correspondent from the *Chicago Tribune* during World War I, described him: "He wore his heavily brassed hat (when he wore a hat at all on the battlefield) with a rakish tilt, like a modern D'Artagnan, but it was just that jaunty tilt that permitted his grand personality to emerge, without violating any Army regulations." (Francis Trevelyan Miller, *General Douglas MacArthur: Fighter for Freedom* [Philadelphia: John C. Winston, 1942], 4). His Rainbow soldiers had a lifelong devotion for him (ibid., 101). The author's father, William Johnson Frazer, all of his life kept an unconditional admiration for MacArthur acquired on the French battlefields of 1918. During World War II, when the war in the Pacific was not going well and MacArthur was strongly criticized, Will Frazer kept defending him.

17. Hill 263 is presently known as the "Pain de Sucre."

18. George McIntosh Sparks, Walter Alexander Harris, Cooper Winn, and J. A. Moss, *Macon War's Work: A History of Macon in the Great World War*, ed. George Sparks (Macon, GA: J. W. Burke), 102.

19. The originals may be seen at AMHI, The Infantry, US 42nd Division.

20. *Americans All*, 713.

21. Hayes, *Heroes among the Brave*, 37.

22. Eisenhower, *Yanks*, 255.

23. "Robert H. Ferrell Papers," Royal Little Correspondance with ABMC, November 16, 1926, MAMA, RG 15, Box 75, Folder 5.

24. *Americans All*, 644.

25. "Douglas MacArthur, the American Experience: WWI: Côte de Châtillon," PBS: http://www.pbs.org/wgbh/amex/macarthur/maps/chatelion02.html, accessed December 29, 2009.

26. Ferrell, *The Question of MacArthur's Reputation*, 22.

27. *Alabama's Own*, 194.

28. Ferrell, *The Question of MacArthur's Reputation*, 27.

29. Ibid., 26.

30. Sherwood, *A Soldier in World War I*, 92.

31. Sparks et al., *Macon War's Work*, 102.

32. *Americans All*, 651.

33. Collins, *151st Field Artillery*, 146.

34. *Americans All*, 690–91. Donovan was wounded and evacuated two days later in action that caused his recommendation for the Medal of Honor. War Department, General Orders No. 56, December 30, 1922, http://www.militarytimes.com/citations-medals-awards/recipient.php?recipientid=3330, accessed July 30, 2013.

35. "Robert H. Ferrell Papers", Royal Little Correspondence with ABMC, November 26, 1926, MAMA, RG-15, Box 75, Folder 5.

36. Taber, *The Story of the 168th Infantry*, 2: 170.

37. AMHI, 42nd Division, Daily Intelligence Report, February 21, 1918–November 13, 1918, The Infantry, US 42nd Division, Box 17, US Army Military History Institute, Carlisle Barracks.

38. Taber, *The Story of the 168th Infantry*, 2: 177.

39. *Americans All*, 680.

40. NARA, RG 165, German Military Records 1917–1919: Entry 320, Folder 3, Copy 1, Copies of entries in the War Day Book of the Argonne Group, 44 and Entry 320, Kriegstagebuch mit Anlagen des Generalkommandos z.b.V. 58, 12. Quotations translated from the original German.

41. *Americans All*, 681.

42. Ferrell, *The Question of MacArthur's Reputation*, 47.

43. *Americans All*, 681.

44. Ibid., 682.

45. Ibid., 696.

46. *Alabama's Own*, 195.

47. *Americans All*, 678.

48. Ibid., 682.

49. Taber, *The Story of the 168th Infantry*, 2: 179–86.

50. Neibaur, "How Private Neibaur Won the Congressional Medal of Honor," 786.

51. *Americans All*, 678.

52. Ibid.

53. Ibid., 679–80.

54. Ibid., 682. Reilly misspells Bare's name as Baer throughout his text. The first use is marked here; subsequent misspellings from Reilly are not.

55. Ibid., 684. This chicane is not referenced on the ABMC military map Meuse-Argonne Offensive from 1927, and the author was unable to find this specific aerial photograph at NARA.

56. *Americans All*, 684.

57. Ibid., 682–85.

58. Mr. Brouillon wrote the following account after pouring over maps alone and with the author and after reading the primary sources about the attack the author provided to him:

> I keep thinking that the approximately 120 men could have gone from the South of the Musarde Farm along the big hedge, that I knew well and have cut and where there were left over remains of lines of barbed wire with "cornières" poles, therefore of French origin (on a crest line) at 400 meters in front of La Musarde.
>
> Therefore, through this hedge, using the trenches visible on your maps, they crossed in front of the Musarde in a west-east direction for 500 meters to reach the little wood "Petite Musarde" close to the Tuilerie and went back from there in a northern direction facing the wood to be attacked until they reached it. This wood, known as

the Musarde, was protected inside by barbed wire, there are numerous remains in earth and, also, there were poles of trenches "cornières," therefore of French origin. Through the exterior edge of the wood of big oak trees to the barbed wire, they could have passed to the exterior of the woods' edge until the buildings of the Musarde in a direction east–west, entered just behind the buildings (I think it is where the famous chicane was) where there are still big ditches going up toward the wood in direction of the summit of the Côte.

We are therefore on the west side, and these ditches could easily allow the 120 courageous men to wait for the morning and start the assault following the covering fire coming from Côte Blanche. If they had been forewarned, they could remain under these shots, without any risk, considering the depth of the ditches that may have been well-cut trenches at the time.

The assault would have been easily possible quickly as they were very close to the summit, less than 400 meters.

This is only a supposition, my reflections following your research and my knowledge of the terrain.

I hope that this proposition can advance the accuracy of your writings. Normally there should be documents of the French army on the maps of trenches and lines of barbed wire as this côte was protected by "cornières" poles. The poles "pig tail," the German ones, were laid on the east side between the woods of Bantheville toward the pasture of Beuil in direction of Romagne. They remind of the lines at the beginning of the fighting, at the time when the French held Landres et St. Georges, Sommerance, St. Juvin and beyond. (Quotation translated from the original French.)

59. Jean Pierre Brouillon inherited the Musarde Farm that his father had bought in 1950 and he himself bought the Tuilerie Farm in 1970.

60. Winter uniforms and underwear, overcoats and blankets only arrived on October 18. Ferrell, *The Question of MacArthur's Reputation*, 43.

61. *Americans All*, 679.

62. Taber, *The Story of the 168th Infantry*, 2: 187–200.

63. *Americans All*, 712.

64. Ibid., 684.

65. NARA, RG 117, Records of the American Battle Monuments Commission, Entry A1 31, Correspondence with Former Division Officers, 42nd Division, File 714.2-G/AM.

66. *Americans All*, 685.

67. Ferrell, *The Question of MacArthur's Reputation*, 59.

68. *Alabama's Own*, 334.

69. *Americans All*, 687, incorrectly reported the date as October 14, 1918. The correct date is October 16, 1918, as reported in US Adjutant General's Office, *Congressional Medal of Honor*, 37.

70. *Alabama's Own*, 335.

71. Royal Little Correspondence with ABMC, November 26, 1926, MAMA, RG 15, Box 75, Folder 5.

72. Ferrell, *The Question of MacArthur's Reputation*, 59.

73. *Alabama's Own*, 197.

74. Ferrell, *The Question of MacArthur's Reputation*, 60.

75. Neibaur, "How Private Neibaur Won the Congressional Medal of Honor," 787–89. Private Neibaur's exploits had been witnessed in full view of the entire attacking force. The Medal of Honor citation stated that he had killed four of the enemy with his pistol and captured eleven prisoners. He was the first private in the US Army and the first Mormon to receive the nation's highest decoration. The French conferred on him the Légion d'Honneur and the Croix de Guerre. Neibaur, after spending the next three months in various French hospitals, was decorated in Chaumont by General Pershing on February 9, 1919. He was twenty. Of the five Medals of Honor awarded in the Rainbow Division during the war, two went to Corporal Sidney Manning and Private Thomas S. Neibaur of the 167th Infantry, two went to Sergeants Richard W. O'Neill and Michael Donaldson of the 165th Infantry, and one went to an officer, Colonel William J. Donovan, also of the 165th.

76. *Americans All*, 686.

77. *Alabama's Own*, 335.

78. Ibid., 197.

79. Cheseldine, *Ohio in the Rainbow*, 255.

80. *Americans All*, 678.

81. Ferrell, *The Question of MacArthur's Reputation*, 62.

82. Ibid., 61–62.

83. It was not approved, as Bare was not directly engaged in the fighting. He was awarded the Distinguished Service Medal, an administrative award, by order of the secretary of war on August 26, 1921 (War Department, Office of the Adjutant General, *Decoration, United States Army: 1862–1927* [Washington, DC: GPO, 1927]) and promoted to brigadier general in the reserves in 1926 (Hartley A. Moon to Walter E. Bare, August 4, 1926, Box 2, Walter E. Bare Papers, ADAH).

84. *Alabama's Own*, 334.

85. As quoted in Pommois, *In Search of Rainbow Memorials*, 45.

86. Ferrell, *The Question of MacArthur's Reputation*, 2.

# Chapter 10

1. MacArthur, *Reminiscences*, 67.

2. Cheseldine, *Ohio in the Rainbow*, 257.

3. Ulrich and Zieman, *Frontalltag im Ersten Weltkrieg*, 131. Quotation translated from the original German.

4. Ibid.

5. *Alabama's Own*, 198.

6. Ibid., 201.

7. Ibid., 199.

8. Ibid., 203.

9. Gertrude C. Bray, "My Most Interesting Experience of the War," *Army and Navy Record* (April 1920): 14.

10. Mangin, *Les Américains en France*, 101.

11. *Alabama's Own*, 202.

12. Conversation with the author.

13. *Alabama's Own*, 202.

14. Eisenhower, *Yanks*, 264.

15. Kennedy, *Over Here*, 201.

16. Adam Hochschild, *To End All Wars: A Story of Loyalty and Rebellion, 1914–1918* (New York: Houghton Mifflin Harcourt, 2011), 331.

17. *Alabama's Own*, 203.

18. Ibid.

19. Ibid.

20. Ibid., 204.

21. MacArthur, *Reminiscences*, 69.

22. *Alabama's Own*, 205.

23. Eisenhower, *Yanks*, 283.

24. MacArthur, *Reminiscences*, 68.

25. Persico, *Eleventh Month*, 39.

26. Mead, *Doughboys*, 335.

27. MacArthur, *Reminiscences*, 68.

28. Ibid.

29. Eisenhower, *Yanks*, 270.

30. Ibid., 241.

31. Ibid., 277.

32. Kennedy, *Over Here*, 231.

33. Eisenhower, *Yanks*, 280.

34. Gilbert, *First World War*, 495–97.

35. Mead, *Doughboys*, 333.

36. *Americans All*, 778.

37. *Alabama's Own*, 206.

38. Collins, *151st Field Artillery*, 159.

39. *Alabama's Own*, 210.

40. Ibid., 410–14.

41. Ibid., 210.

42. Ibid., 210–11

43. Ibid., 211.

44. Ibid., 210.

45. Ibid., 211.

46. Ibid., 413.

47. Ibid., 212.

48. MacArthur, *War Bugs*, 220–21.

49. *Alabama's Own*, 212.

50. Ibid.,213.

51. http://www.archives.alabama.gov/goldstar/images/card/Killough_JosephC.pdf, accessed July 30, 2013.

52. *Alabama's Own*, 212.

53. He is buried in the Saint-Mihiel Cemetery. *Alabama's Own*, 214.

54. Eisenhower, *Yanks*, 283.

55. Ibid., 280–81.

56. Nicholas Best, *The Greatest Day in History: How on the Eleventh Hour of the Eleventh Day of the Eleventh Month, the First World War Finally Came to an End* (London: Weidenfeld and Nicholson, 2008), 80.

57. Persico, *Eleventh Month*, 307–8.

58. Wilhelm, *Memoirs of the Crown Prince of Germany*, 260.

59. NARA, RG 120, Box 2140, Index to Correspondence of the Adjutant General, AEF Headquarters, 1917–20, Backfile Drawer Telegrams, Records of the AEF, World War I, Telegram Number T-4181.

60. Persico, *Eleventh Month*, 330–31.

61. Ibid., 332.

62. *Alabama's Own*, 219.

63. James J. Cooke, "The American Soldier in France, 1917–1919," in *Facing Armageddon: The First World War Experienced*, ed. Hugh Cecil and Peter H. Liddle (London: Leo Cooper, 1996), 252.

64. Bruce, *Fraternity of Arms*, 282–283.

65. G. J. Meyer, *A World Undone: A Story of the Great War, 1914 to 1918* (New York: Delacorte Press, 2007), 704.

66. Wilhelm, *Memoirs of the Crown Prince of Germany*, 280. That last order issued by Kaiser Wilhelm's son to the German Army contained the seeds of World War II. Pershing, Mangin, and others had been right: the German Army had not been defeated on its own soil. The German people felt that the war had been lost by politicians, not by the army, which kept its glorious pride intact. Willingly, feeling undefeated, Germany would be ready to follow Hitler on his destructive path.

67. *Alabama's Own*, 220.

68. Ibid.

69. Ibid.

70. Cheseldine, *Ohio in the Rainbow*, 299.

71. *Alabama's Own*, 221.

72. Ibid.

73. Ibid., 223.

74. Ibid., 221.

75. Ibid., 221.

76. Straub, *A Sergeant's Diary*, 229.

77. Wren, *Letters*, November 29, 1918.

78. *Alabama's Own*, 222.

79. Ibid., 232.

80. "This is the Kaiser." Hallas, *Doughboy War*, 313.

81. Straub, *A Sergeant's Diary*, 237.

82. *Alabama's Own*, 224.

83. Brenneman, *Letters*, December 18, 1918.

84. *Alabama's Own*, 227–28.

85. *Stars and Stripes*, January 25, 1919.

86. *Alabama's Own*, 225.

87. *Americans All*, 862.

88. Conversation with the author in 1953.

89. Brenneman, *Letters*, December 31, 1918.

90. Straub, *A Sergeant's Diary*, 258. Another witness, Amos Brenneman, wrote about one killed and twelve wounded. Brenneman, *Letters*, January 17, 1919. Brenneman (1898–1956), Company C, 167th Infantry, had been injured at Croix Rouge Farm. He remained in the military after the war, eventually achieving the rank of master sergeant.

91. *Alabama's Own*, 235.

92. Vernon E. Kniptash, *On the Western Front with the Rainbow: A World War I Diary*, ed. E. Bruce Geelhoed (Norman: University of Oklahoma Press, 2009), 175. "Readying his shirt" is a process in which a soldier removed his shirt and searched for the lice in it.

93. *Alabama's Own*, 235.

94. Ibid., 232; Cooke, *The Rainbow Division*, 234–35.

95. Anne Cipriano Venzon, *The United States in the First World War: An Encyclopedia* (New York: Garland, 1995), 136.

96. *Alabama's Own*, 243.

97. Wren, *Letters*, March 31, 1919. Amerine in *Alabama's Own* lists citations and awards awarded to the members of the regiment (325–39) and a list of officers entitled to wound chevrons (408–9).

98. Langille, *Men of the Rainbow*, 184.

99. "Robert H. Ferrell Papers," Summary of Intelligence, March 31, 1919, By Command of Brigadier General Gatley, William N. Hughes Jr., Colonel, General Staff, Chief of Staff, Folder 1, MAMA, RG 15, Box 75, Folder 5.

100. Hayes, *Heroes among the Brave*, 43.

## Chapter 11

1. *Alabama's Own*, 251. Will Frazer recounted the welcome from Lewis's family.

2. As told to the author by his father.

3. W. T. Sheehan, "Lt. Gov Miller Voices a Welcome to Heroes of the Valiant 'Fourth Alabama,'" *Montgomery Advertiser*, April 27, 1919.

4. *Alabama's Own*, 253.

5. Ibid., 252.

6. Pommois, *In Search of Rainbow Memorials*, 45.

7. Besides the Donovan Archives at AMHI's archives at Carlisle Barracks, including his correspondence with his wife during World War I, more on Donovan's role in World War I can be found in Richard Dunlop, *America's Master Spy* (Chicago: Rand McNally, 1982) and Douglas Waller, *Wild Bill Donovan: The Spymaster Who Created the OSS and Modern American Espionage* (New York: Simon and Schuster, 2011).

8. Wright, *Meuse-Argonne Diary*, 1.

9. Ettinger and Ettinger, *A Doughboy with the Fighting 69th*, 241.

10. The chaplains of the regiments were proud of their men: "The question of whether the chaplain of the New York or the Alabama regiment was more militant is not for an outsider to decide" (Sullivan, *The History of New York State, XI*, 1304), yet in time of need they would serve all the men of the division as after the battle at Croix Rouge Farm when the Alabama, Iowa, and Ohio chaplains were at the aid station together (see chapter 6, "Aisne-Marne, Croix Rouge Farm," 121).

11. Sheehan, "Lt. Gov Miller Voices a Welcome to Heroes."

12. *Alabama's Own*, 253.

13. "One Section of 167th Regiment Passes Thru Huntsville This P.M.," *Huntsville Daily Times*, May 9, 1919.

14. *Alabama's Own*, 253.

15. "Alabama Rainbow Boys Parade Here," *Gadsden Times-News*, May 9, 1919.

16. *Alabama's Own*, 254.

17. Ibid.

18. Ibid.

19. W. H. Hendrix, "Warriors Arrive Amid Great Roar of Joyous Voices," *Birmingham News*, May 10, 1919.

20. Ibid.

21. Sig G. Bauer, "Streets Jammed as Troops Pass in Grand Review," *Birmingham News*, May 10, 1919.

22. Sig G. Bauer, "Pretty Maidens Make Prisoners of 167th's Men," *Birmingham News*, May 11, 1919.

23. *Alabama's Own*, 254.

24. Ibid.

25. Ibid.

26. Editorial, *Birmingham News*, May 10, 1919.

27. Bauer, "Pretty Maidens Make Prisoners of 167th's Men."

28. "Troops Depart; City Is Praised," *Birmingham News*, May 12, 1919.

29. *Alabama's Own*, 259.

30. Ibid.

31. "Welcome Home," *Montgomery Advertiser*, May 12, 1919.

32. *Alabama's Own*, 260.

33. Ibid.

34. Pommois, *In Search of Rainbow Memorials*, 45.

35. Hopper, *Medals of Honor*, 211.

36. *Rainbow Reveille*, October 1928, 2.

37. *Alabama's Own*, 262.

38. Ibid., 261.

39. Ibid.

40. Ibid.

41. Lillian Frazer Key, the author's cousin, told him in the mid-1970s that she had watched the parade from the capitol grounds as a grade school student and everyone, black and white, wore their best clothes.

42. "Battle-Scarred Veterans Paid Ringing Tribute," *Montgomery Advertiser*, May 13, 1919.

43. *Alabama's Own*, 262. Misses Thorington and McGough are pictured in photo 12.

44. Ibid., 263.

45. Ibid., 262.

46. Ibid., 263–67.

47. Ibid., 263.

48. "Huge Multitude Render Homage to 'Old Fourth,'" *Montgomery Advertiser*, May 12, 1919. The paper reported 75,000 people on the capitol grounds on May 12, 1919, when the regiment returned home. It reported 25,000 people when Dr. Martin Luther King Jr. held his triumphant march. J. Mills Thornton III, *Dividing Lines: Municipal Politics and the Struggle for Civil Rights in Montgomery, Birmingham, and Selma* (Tuscaloosa: University of Alabama Press, 2002), 489.

49. "Battle-Scarred Veterans Paid Ringing Tribute," *Montgomery Advertiser*, May 13, 1919.

50. *Alabama's Own*, 263.

51. Ibid., 263–65.

52. Ibid., 265.

53. For a complete list of the location of each reception, see *Alabama's Own*, 265–66.

54. "Toots and Shoots and Blare of Bands Greet 167th Heroes," *Mobile News-Item*, May 13, 1919.

55. "Mobile Falls to Alabamians Who Smashed Kaiser's Line; Conquerors March in Triumph," *Mobile News-Item*, May 13, 1919.

56. "Mobile's One Joyous Welcome to Heroes of Fourth Alabama Half Dozen Mardi Gras in One," *Mobile News-Item*, May 13, 1919.

57. "Here in Brief Is Tuesday's Program of Alabama Heroes," *Mobile News-Item*, May 12, 1919.

58. "Medals Pinned on Heroes' Brast [*sic*] by Mobile Girls," *Mobile News-Item*, May 13, 1919.

59. *Mobile News-Item*, May 13, 1919.

# Appendix D

1. Lisa M. Budreau, *Bodies of War: World War I and the Politics of Commemoration in America, 1919–1933* (New York: New York University Press, 2010), 51.

2. It also established one in England and one in Belgium.

3. This list of cemeteries and soldiers buried was kindly provided by Michael G. Conley, American Battle Monuments Commission and can be seen at the Croix Rouge Farm Memorial Foundation website under 167th (Alabama) Infantry Regiment.

4. List of Mothers and Widows of American Soldiers, Sailors, and Marines Entitled to Make a Pilgrimage to War Cemeteries in Europe. Washington, DC: GPO, 1930.

5. Budreau, *Bodies of War*, 7–9, 192–241.

6. One soldier, Private Patton, died at sea during the Atlantic passage and is buried at Brookwood Cemetery in England.

7. http://croixrougefarm.org/wp-content/uploads/2011/03/Members_167th_Alabama _Infantry_Regiment_buried_in_ABMC_Cemeteries.pdf, accessed July 30, 2013.

8. "Alabamians at War—Soldiers," in *Public information subject files*, Letters-Letters to/ from Dr. Owen, SG017101f02, ADAH.

9. http://www.archives.alabama.gov/goldstar/info.html, accessed July 30, 2013.

10. The bridge was rededicated on Veteran's Day, 1992 (Pommois, *In Search of Rainbow Memorials*, 48), and again on Memorial Day, 2012 ("Alabama Governor Robert Bentley Helps Dedicate Memorial for Alabama National Guard Battalion," *Birmingham News*, May 28, 2012). Today, only a battalion of the Alabama National Guard carries the glorious name of the 167th Alabama Infantry Regiment in World War I. This explains the confusion of the author of the article in calling the World War I unit a battalion when it was a regiment.

# Bibliography

## Abbreviations

| | |
|---|---|
| ADAH | Alabama Department of Archives and History, Montgomery |
| AEF | American Expeditionary Forces |
| AFB | Air Force Base |
| AMHI | Army Military History Institute, Carlisle Barracks, Carlisle, PA |
| GPO | Government Printing Office |
| MAMA | MacArthur Memorial Archives, Norfolk, VA |
| NARA | National Archives and Records Administration (US) |
| SHD/DAT | Service Historique de la Défense, Vincennes, France |
| UNLA | University of Nebraska–Lincoln, Archives and Special Collections |

## Archival Materials

### Alabama Department of Archives and History, Montgomery (ADAH)

The Adjutant General Quadrennial Report. 1919. SG021635.

Burr, Borden. Diary. LPR262. Box 1.

———. Scrapbook. LPR262 Box 3.

Hackett, Edmund F., First Lieutenant. *The Fight at Croix Rouge Farm*. Public Information Subject Files—Alabamians at War. "Battles and Histories: Reminiscences of 167th Infantry Member." SG017102.

Hayes, John B. *The Destiny of a Soldier: An Autobiography*. SPR91.

167th Infantry Regiment. SG17102; SG17103.

Roberts, Gary, Private. *Letters*. "Soldiers' Letters." PISF. SG017101.

Screws, William P. *Family Scrapbooks*. LPR260, Box 1.

Steiner, Robert E. *Military Record*. 1933. PISF. SG017093.

Watts, John Wade. *Memoir of Work with the Rainbow Division*. Circa 1920. SPR571.

## Army Military History Institute, Carlisle Barracks, Carlisle, PA (AMHI)

*The Battle of the 15th of July 1918*, explained by General Hug, Former Chief of the Bureau of Operations of the 4th Army, upon the Occasion of the Twentieth Anniversary of the Battle of Champagne. Box 17.

The Infantry, US 42nd Division, Boxes 1, 2, 15, and 17: Daily Intelligence Reports, Summary of Intelligence Reports, ABMC, and various collections of personal papers.

Patterson, Einar. Papers. The Infantry. US 42nd Division. Box 15.

World War I Veterans Survey. 42nd Division. 151st Machine Gun Battalion. Walker, Isaac G., Lieutenant, Company A.

World War I Veterans Survey. 42nd Division. 167th Infantry Regiment. Brown, J. Douglas, Private, 1st Battalion Medical Detachment. Campbell, Duncan, Lieutenant (Cold Spring, NY). Donaldson, John M., Lieutenant, Company B (Rhode Island, diary covering Plattsburgh and Camp Mills). Pickel, Robert D., Private First Class, Company D (Birmingham, AL). Summers, Norman L., First Sergeant, Company M (diary).

## Auburn University Special Collections and Archives, Auburn, AL.

Clark, Franklin Ashton. *Diary* and *Letters.*

Wren, Edward R. Collection. *Letters.*

## Birmingham Public Library, Alabama

Jordan, Mortimer. *Letters.* June 11, 1916–July 23, 1918.

## Crawfordsville District Public Library, Indiana

Brenneman, Amos D. C Company, 167th (Alabama) Infantry. *Letters.* RL 929.2 and RL 940.3 http://www.cdpl.lib.in.us/lh-ww1letters.php (accessed September 2, 2013).

## Indiana Historical Society

Tyndall, Robert H. Collections. Manuscripts and Archives Department, #M0280, Boxes 1 and 2.

## James Vann Collection, Macon, Georgia

Kennedy, Phipps. *Letters.* Courtesy of James Vann.

Vann, Daniel. *Letters.* Courtesy of James Vann.

## MacArthur Memorial Archives, Norfolk, VA (MAMA)

Allender, Ben Company G. 168th (Iowa) Infantry. *Diary of World War I.* RG 123.

Coulter, John. Scrap Book. Forty Second Division (Rainbow Division) Camp Mills, 1917. Vols. 1 and 2.

Journal des Marches et Opérations: 42ᵉ D.I.U.S. Mission Française: 15 Novembre 1917 au 19 Janvier 1919. RG-15. (Original at SHD/DAT.)

MacArthur, Douglas. Personal Correspondence. RG 10. Box 21. Folder 10.

———. *Reminiscences* manuscript. Personal correspondence. RG 15. Box 193a.

"Papers of the 42nd Infantry Division/National Archives". RG 15, Box 78, Folder 1.

"Robert H. Ferrell Papers." Photocopies from the National Archives, RG 15, Box 75, Folder 5.

## National Archives and Records Administration (US). National Archives Building, College Park, MD. (NARA)

### CARTOGRAPHIC REFERENCE BRANCH

*AEF maps*

*42nd Division operations*

### LIBRARY COLLECTION

*RG 117, Correspondence with the American Battle Monuments Commission.*

Entry A1 31. Summary of Operations, 42nd Division (plus 47th Infantry), Aisne-Marne, July 25–August 2, 1918. Box 230.

Entry A1 31. Summary of Operations in the Champagne, July 5–17, 1918. Box 231.

Entry A1 31. Correspondence with Former Division Officers. Box 233.

*RG 120, World War I Organization Records, Entry 1241.*

42nd Division Historical Record. (Location: 290/1/4/6, Boxes 13–15).

84th Infantry Brigade. (Location: 290/1/4/7, Boxes 25, 26).

167th Infantry Regiment. (Location: 290/1/51/1, Boxes 31, 32).

Backfile Drawer Telegrams. (Box 2140).

"Negro Personnel in the War," Statistical Section Report #138, Army War College Library. Brigadier General Paul B. Malone, "Report on Education." Folder #268; Reports of the Commander in Chief, 1917–20; Textual Records of the AEF 1917–23: National Archives, College Park, Maryland.

*RG 165, German Military Records 1917–19. Entry 320. (Location: 370/76/01/01, Boxes 90, 91, 135.)*

*RG 200, Index and Case Files Relating to Reclassification and Reassignments of Officers, Index and Case Files Relating to Reclassification and Reassignment of Officers, Reclassification of Regular Army Brigadier Generals and Major Generals, Entry NM 1022, Relief History of Brigadier General R. A. Brown, 130-84-2-5. (Location: 130/84/2/5–6, Box 8.)*

### SPECIAL MEDIA ARCHIVES SERVICES DIVISION

Mexican Punitive Expedition Signal Corps Pictures 111-SC.

World War I Signal Corps Pictures 111-SC.

World War I Signal Corps Motion Pictures 111-H and 111-M.

Service Historique de la Défense, Département de l'Armée
de Terre, Vincennes, France (SHD/DAT)

7 N 2323: Historique Divisions US.
17 N 124: 42$^e$ D.I.U.S.
17 N 125: 42$^e$ D.I.U.S.
17 N 126: 42$^e$ D.I.U.S.

JOURNAUX DES UNITÉS 1914–1918 (MÉMOIRE DES HOMMES ACCESSED
AT HTTP://WWW.MEMOIREDESHOMMES.SGA.DEFENSE.GOUV.FR.)

IVe Armée.
21e Corps.
13e Division d'Infanterie.
167e Division d'Infanterie.
170e Division d'Infanterie.
17e Régiment d'Infanterie.
109e Régiment d'Infanterie.
167e Régiment d'Infanterie.
10e Chasseurs à Pieds.
20e Chasseurs à Pieds.

University of Nebraska–Lincoln, Archives and Special Collections (UNLA)

Brenner, John D. *Le Guerre*. Rainbow Division Association Papers, Box 1, Folder 7, 1.
*Rainbow Division Veterans Association Papers, 1917–2000*. Spec MS # 104 RDVA Records World War I. Boxes 1, 73, 74, 80, 88.

## Books and Articles

"Album de la Guerre." *L'Illustration*. Vols. 1 and 2. Paris, 1929.
Allen, Hervey. *Toward the Flame: A Memoir of World War*. 1926; reprint, Lincoln: University of Nebraska Press, 2003.
American Battle Monuments Commission (ABMC). *American Armies and Battlefields in Europe*. Washington, DC: GPO, 1938.
———. *42nd Division, Summary of Operations in the World War*. Washington, DC: GPO, 1944.
Amerine, William H. *Alabama's Own in France*. New York: Eaton and Gettinger, 1919.
Armstrong, Vince O., ed. *World War One Soldiers: Training, Trenches, and Weapons*. WebWord, LLC, 2009.
Autric, Raphaëlle. "La rivalité franco-américaine: L'instruction des soldats américains en France (1917–1918)." *Revue Historique des Armées* 246 (2007): 22–32.

Babin, Gustave. "Sur le Champ de Bataille de Champagne: La Victorieuse Défense de Chalons." *L'Illustration* 76, no. 3934 (July 27, 1918): 92–95.

Barbusse, Henri. *Le Feu*. 1916. Reprint. Paris: Editions Gallimard, 2007.

Best, Nicholas. *The Greatest Day in History: How on the Eleventh Hour of the Eleventh Day of the Eleventh Month, the First World War Finally Came to an End*. London: Weidenfeld and Nicholson, 2008.

Blumenson, Martin. *Patton: The Man behind the Legend, 1885–1945*. New York: William Morrow, 1985.

Boghardt, Thomas. *The Zimmerman Telegram: Intelligence, Diplomacy, and America's Entry into World War I*. Annapolis, MD: Naval Institute Press, 2012.

Bonk, David. *St Mihiel 1918: The American Expeditionary Forces' Trial by Fire*. Oxford: Osprey, 2011.

Braim, Paul F. *The Test of Battle: The American Expeditionary Forces in the Meuse Argonne Campaign*. 1987; reprint, Shippensburg, PA: White Mane Books, 1998.

Brandt, Allan M. *No Magic Bullets: A Social History of Venereal Diseases in the United States since 1880*. New York: Oxford University Press, 1987.

Bray, Gertrude C. "My Most Interesting Experience of the War." *Army and Navy Record* (April 1920): 14, 50, 52.

Bristow, Nancy K. *Making Men Moral: Social Engineering during the Great War*. New York: New York University Press, 1996.

Brown, J. Douglas. "In Action with the Rainbow Division, 1918–19." *Military Review* (January 1978): 35–46.

Browne, George. *An American Soldier in World War I*. Edited by David L. Snead. Lincoln: University of Nebraska Press, 2006.

Bruce, Robert E. *A Fraternity of Arms: America and France in the Great War*. Lawrence: University Press of Kansas, 2003.

Budreau, Lisa M. *Bodies of War: World War I and the Politics of Commemoration in America, 1919–1933*. New York: New York University Press, 2010.

Bullard, Robert Lee. *Personalities and Reminiscences of the War*. Garden City, NY: Doubleday, 1925.

Burr, Borden. "Impressions." *Army and Navy Record*. April 1920, 16, 60.

Capozzola, Christopher. *Uncle Sam Wants You: World War I and the Making of the Modern American Citizen*. 2008; reprint, New York: Oxford University Press, 2010.

Carter, H. L. "Story of B. C. Dunlop: 'The Apostle of Sunshine.'" *Army and Navy Record* (April 1920): 28.

Chambrun, Colonel de, and Captain de Marenches. *The American Army in the European Conflict*. New York: Macmillan, 1919; reprint, La Vergne, TN: Kessinger Publishing, 2009.

Cheseldine, R. M. *Ohio in the Rainbow, Official Story of the 166th Infantry 42nd Division in the World War*. Columbus, OH: F. J. Heer Printing, 1924.

Churchill, Winston S. *Never Give In! The Best of Winston Churchill's Speeches*. New York: Hyperion Books, 2003.

Coffman, Edward M. *The War to End All Wars: The American Military Experience in World War I*. Lexington: University Press of Kentucky, 1998.

Collins, Louis L. *History of the 151st Field Artillery, Rainbow Division*. Vol. 1. Edited by Wayne E. Stevens. St. Paul: Minnesota War Records Commission, 1924.

Cooke, James. J. *Pershing and His Generals*. Westport, CT: Praeger, 1977.

———. *The Rainbow Division in the Great War, 1917–1919*. Westport, CT: Praeger, 1994.

———. "The American Soldier in France, 1917-1919" in *Facing Armageddon, The First World War Experienced*. Edited by Hugh Cecil and Peter H. Liddle. London: Leo Cooper, 1996.

Coulter, Ernest K. "Chasing History under Fire." *Quartermaster Review* 1, no. 5 (March–April 1922): 3–6.

Cox, Clarence W. "Private Clarence W. Cox, Hquarters Company, Relates His Most Exciting Experiences." *Army and Navy Record* (1920): 32.

Davis, Wade. *Into the Silence: The Great War, Mallory, and the Conquest of Everest*. New York: Alfred A. Knopf, 2011.

Duffy, Francis P. "Colonel Bill." *Rainbow Reveille* (October 1928): 2.

———. *Father Duffy's Story*. Garden City, NY: George H. Doran, Country Life Press, 1919.

Dunlop, Richard. *America's Master Spy*. Chicago: Rand McNally, 1982.

Eisenhower, John S. D. *Intervention! The United States and the Mexican Revolution, 1913–1917*. New York: W. W. Norton, 1993.

———. *Yanks: The Epic Story of the American Army in World War I*. New York: Free Press, 2001.

Englund, Peter. *The Beauty and the Sorrow*. New York: Knopf, 2011.

Esnault, Gaston. *Le Poilu tel qu'il se parle*. Paris: Editions Bossard, 1919.

Ettinger, Albert M., and A. Churchill Ettinger. *A Doughboy with the Fighting 69th*. New York: Pocket Books, 1993.

Farwell, Byron. *Over There: The United States in the Great War*. New York: W. W. Norton, 1999.

Ferrell, Robert H. *America's Deadliest Battle: Meuse-Argonne, 1918*. Lawrence: University Press of Kansas, 2007.

———. *The Question of MacArthur's Reputation: Côte de Châtillon, October 14–16, 1918*. Columbia: University of Missouri Press, 2008.

Fleek, Sherman L. *Place the Headstones Where They Belong: Thomas Neibaur, WWI Soldier*. Logan: Utah State University Press, 2008.

Fleming, Thomas. *The Illusion of Victory: America in World War I*. New York: Basic Books, 2004.

Ford, Nancy Gentile. *Americans All! Foreign-Born Soldiers in World War I*. College Station: Texas A&M University Press. 2001.

———. *The Great War and America: Civil-Military Relations during World War I*. Westport, CT: Praeger Security International. 2008.

Fromkin, David. *In the Time of the Americans: FDR, Truman, Eisenhower, Marshall, MacArthur—The Generation That Changed America's Role in the World*. London: Macmillan, 1995.

Gabriel, Kurt. *Die 4 Garde Infanterie Division: Der Ruhmesweg einer bewährten Kampftruppe durch den Weltkrieg.* Berlin: Verlag Klafing, 1921.

Gaff, Alan D. *Blood in the Argonne: The Lost Battalion of World War I.* Norman: University of Oklahoma Press, 2005.

George, Herbert. *The Challenge of War.* New York, Vantage Press, 1966.

Gilbert, Martin. *The First World War.* 1994; reprint, New York: Holt Paperbacks, 2004.

———. *A History of the Twentieth Century: 1900–1933.* Vol. 1. New York: Avon Books, 1998.

Glenn, George A. "Stops Counter Attack: Montgomery Man Spreads Death among Germans Charging with Stokes." *Army and Navy Record* (April 1920): 108.

Gouraud, Henri J. E. "My Memories of the Rainbow Division." *American Legion* (November 1933): 26–27, 56, 58–59.

Groc, Léon. *La Division des Loups.* Collection Patrie, 17. Paris: F. Rouff éditeur, 1919.

Grotelueschen, Mark Ethan. *The AEF Way of War: The American Army and Combat in World War I.* New York: Cambridge University Press, 2007.

Hallas, James H. *Doughboy War: The American Expeditionary Force in World War I.* 2000; reprint, Mechanicsburg, PA: Stackpole Books, 2009.

———. *Squandered Victory.* Westport, CT: Praeger, 1995.

Hanson, Neil. *Unknown Soldiers: The Story of the Missing of the First World War.* New York: First Vintage Books, 2006.

Harbord, James G. *Leaves from a War Diary.* New York: Dodd, Mead, 1925.

Hayes, John B. *Heroes among the Brave: A Story of East Alabama's Own Co. 1 and the Famous Rainbow Division of World War I.* Loachapoka, AL: Lee County Historical Society, 1973.

Hirschfeld, Gerhard, Gerd Krumeich, and Irina Renz, eds. *Enzyklopädie Erster Weltkrieg.* Paderborn: Verlag Ferdinand Schöning, 2009.

Historical Branch, War Plans Division, General Staff. *Brief Histories of Divisions, U.S. Army, 1917–1918.* Washington, DC: GPO, June 1921.

Hochschild, Adam. *To End All Wars: A Story of Loyalty and Rebellion, 1914–1918.* Boston: Houghton Mifflin Harcourt, 2011.

Hoffman, W. R. *The Famous 42nd "Rainbow" Division Who Helped Close the Lid of Hell.* Plattsmouth, NE: Hoffman and Steinhauer, 1919.

Holmes, Richard. *Acts of War: The Behavior of Men in Battle.* New York: Free Press, 1985.

Homsher, David. "Was the 'Rainbow' Tarnished by Its Behavior on the Battlefield?" *Military Collector and Historian* 58 (Fall 2006): 158–62.

Hopper, James. *Medals of Honor.* New York: John Day, 1929.

Hunt, Frazier. *The Untold Story of Douglas MacArthur.* New York: Devin-Adair, 1954.

*Illustrated Review Fourth Alabama Infantry, United States Army.* Montgomery, AL: Service Engraving and Paragon Press, 1917. N.p.

*Infantry Drill Regulations (Provisional).* Part 1. Paris: Imprimerie E. Desfossés, 1918.

*Infantry in Battle.* Washington, DC: Infantry Journal, 1939.

James, D. Clayton. *The Years of MacArthur: 1880–1941.* Vol. 1. Boston: Houghton Mifflin, 1970.

Janis, Elsie. *The Big Show: My Six Months with the American Expeditionary Forces*. New York: Cosmopolitan Book, 1919.

Joyce, Dan. "42nd Division Shoulder Sleeve Insignia, A.E.F." *Military Collector and Historian* 59 (Summer 2007): 149–51.

Kaspi, André. *Le temps des Américains, 1917–1918*. Paris: Publications de la Sorbonne, 1976.

Keegan, John. *The First World War*. New York: Vintage Books, 2000.

Keene, Jennifer D. *Doughboys: The Great War, and the Remaking of America*. Baltimore: Johns Hopkins University Press, 2001.

Kelly, Richard B. "Bravery of Sidney E. Manning." *Army and Navy Record* (April 1920): 68.

Kennedy, David M. *Over Here: The First World War and American Society*. Oxford: Oxford University Press, 2004.

Kniptash, Vernon E. *On the Western Front with the Rainbow: A World War I Diary*. Edited by E. Bruce Geelhoed. Norman: University of Oklahoma Press, 2009.

Langer, William L. *Gas and Flame in World War One*. 1919; reprint, New York: Knopf, 1965.

Langille, Leslie. *Men of the Rainbow*. Chicago: O'Sullivan Publishing House, 1933.

Lavine, A. Lincoln. *Circuits of Victory*. Garden City, NY: Country Life Press, 1921.

Leach, George E. *War Diary*. Minneapolis, MN: Pioneer Printers, 1923.

Lee, Clark, and Richard Henschel. *Douglas MacArthur*. New York: Henry Holt, 1952.

Lengel, Edward G. *To Conquer Hell: The Meuse-Argonne, 1918*. New York: Henry Holt, 2008.

Liggett, Hunter. *AEF, Ten Years Ago in France*. New York: Dodd, Mead, 1928.

*List of Mothers and Widows of American Soldiers, Sailors, and Marines Entitled to Make a Pilgrimage to War Cemeteries in Europe*. Washington, DC: GPO, 1930.

MacArthur, Charles. *War Bugs*. New York: Grosset and Dunlap, 1929.

MacArthur, Douglas. *Reminiscences*. 1964; reprint, Annapolis, MD: Bluejacket Books, Naval Institute Press, 2001.

Mahon, John. *New York's Fighting Sixty-Ninth: A Regimental History of Service in the Civil War's Irish Brigade and the Great War's Rainbow Division*. Jefferson, NC: McFarland, 2004.

Mahon, John K. *History of the Militia and the National Guard*. New York: Macmillan, 1983.

Manchester, William. *American Caesar: Douglas MacArthur, 1880–1964*. 1978; reprint, New York: Back Bay Books, 2008.

Mangin, Joël. *Les Américains en France, 1917–1919: La Fayette, Nous voici!* Saint-Cyr-sur-Loire: Alan Sutton, 2006.

Mason, Herbert Molloy, Jr. *The Great Pursuit*. New York: Random House, 1970.

Marshall, George. *Memoirs of my My Services in the World War, 1917–1918*. Boston, MA: Houghton Mifflin Company, 1976.

Mead, Gary. *The Doughboys: America and the First World War*. Woodstock, NY: Overlook Press, 2002.

Meyer, G. J. *A World Undone: A Story of the Great War, 1914 to 1918*. New York: Delacorte Press, 2007.

Miller, Francis Trevelyan. *General Douglas MacArthur: Fighter for Freedom*. Philadelphia: John C. Winston, 1942.

Miller, Roger G. *Preliminary to War: The First Aero Squadron and the Mexican Punitive Expedition of 1916*. Bolling AFB, DC: Air Force Historical Studies Office, 2003.

Millett, Allan R. *The General, Robert L. Bullard, and Officership in the United States Army, 1881–1925*. Westport, CT: Greenwood Press, 1975.

Neibaur, Thomas. "How Private Neibaur Won the Congressional Medal of Honor: A Thrilling and Wonderful War Story, Told in his His Own Words." *Improvement Era*, Vol. 22, July 19, No. 9: 782–790.

Neiberg, Michael S. *The Second Battle of the Marne*. Bloomington: Indiana University Press, 2008.

Newton, Wesley Phillips. "Tenting Tonight on the Old Camp Grounds." In *The Great War in the Heart of Dixie*, edited by Martin T. Olliff, 41–65. Tuscaloosa: University of Alabama Press, 2008.

O'Brien, Howard Vincent, and Karl Edwin Harriman. *Wine, Women, and War: A Diary of Disillusionment*. New York: J. H. Sears, 1926.

Olliff, Martin T., ed. *The Great War in the Heart of Dixie: Alabama during World War I*. Tuscaloosa: University of Alabama Press, 2008.

*Order of Battle of the United States Land Forces in the World War. American Expeditionary Forces: Divisions, 42nd Division (NG)*. Vol. 2. Washington, DC: Center of Military History, United States Army, 1988.

Owen, Thomas McAdory. *History of Alabama and Dictionary of Alabama Biography*. Vol. 1. Chicago: S. J. Clarke, 1921.

Pershing, John J. *Final Report*. Washington, DC: GPO, 1920.

———. *My Experiences in the World War*. Vols. 1 and 2. New York: Frederick A. Stokes, 1931.

Persico, Joseph E. *Eleventh Month, Eleventh Day, Eleventh Hour, Armistice Day 1918: World War I and Its Violent Climax*. New York: Random House, 2004.

Pommois, Lise M., with Charles Fowler. *In Search of Rainbow Memorials*. Bedford, PA: Aberjona Press, 2003.

Ready, Alma. *Open Range and Hidden Silver: Arizona Santa Crux County*. Nogales, AZ: Pimeria Alta Historical Society, 1973.

———, ed. *Nogales, Arizona, 1880–1990, Centennial Anniversary*. Nogales, AZ, 1990.

Reilly, Henry J. *Americans All: The Rainbow at War; Official History of the 42nd Rainbow Division in the World War*. Columbus, OH: The F. J. Heer Printing Co., Publishers, 1936.

Robb, Winfred E. *The Price of Our Heritage: In Memory of the Heroic Dead of the 168th Infantry*. Des Moines, IA: Kessinger, 1919.

Sadler, E. J., ed. *California Rainbow Memories: A Pictorial Review of the Activities of the 2nd Battalion, 117th Engineers during the World War*. N.p., 1925.

Sanders, Robert, Jr. "World War I: Catalyst for Social Change in Alabama." In *The Great War in the Heart of Dixie*, edited by Martin T. Olliff, 185–200. Tuscaloosa: University of Alabama Press.

Schaffer, Ronald. *America in the Great War: The Rise of the War Welfare State*. New York: Oxford University Press, 1991.

Sherwood, Elmer E. *A Soldier in World War I: Diary of a Rainbow Veteran, Written at the Front*. 1929; reprint. Edited by Robert E. Ferrell. Indianapolis, IN: Indiana Historical Society Press 2004.

Smythe, Donald. *Guerrilla Warrior: The Early Life of John J. Pershing*. New York: Scribners, 1973.
———. *Pershing: General of the Armies*. Bloomington: Indiana University Press, 2007.

Sondhaus, Lawrence. *World War I: The Global Revolution*. New York: Cambridge University Press, 2011.

Sparks, George McIntosh, Walter Alexander Harris, Cooper Winn, and J. A. Moss. *Macon War's Work: A History of Macon in the Great World War*. Edited by George Sparks. Macon, GA: The J. W. Burke Company, n.d.

Stewart, Lawrence O. *Rainbow Bright*. Philadelphia, PA: Dorrance Publishers, 1923.

Strachan, Hew. *The First World War*. 2003; reprint, New York: Penguin Books, 2005.

Straub, Elmer Frank. *A Sergeant's Diary in the World War: The Diary of an Enlisted Member of the 150th Field Artillery. October 27, 1917 to August 7, 1919*. Indiana Historical Commission, 1923.

Sullivan, James, ed. *The History of New York State, XI: New York in Seven Wars*. New York: Lewis Historical Publishing. 1927.

Taber, John H. *The Story of the 168th Infantry*. Vol. 1 and 2. Iowa City, IA: The State Historical Society of Iowa, 1925.

Teilhard de Chardin, Pierre. *Genèse d'une pensée: Lettres 1914–1919*, Paris: Bernard Grasset, 1961.

Thirion, André. *Revolutionaries without Revolution*. New York: Macmillan, 1972.

Tompkins, Raymond S. *The Story of the Rainbow Division*. New York: Boni & Liveright, 1919. The Digital Bookshelf, 1998.

Thompson, Hugh S. *Trench Knives and Mustard Gas: With the 42nd Rainbow Division in France*. Edited by Robert H. Ferrell. College Station: Texas A&M University Press, 2004.

Thornton, J. Mills, III. *Dividing Lines: Municipal Politics and the Struggle for Civil Rights in Montgomery, Birmingham, and Selma*. Tuscaloosa: University of Alabama Press, 2002.

Truss, Ruth Smith. "The Alabama National Guard." PhD diss., University of Alabama, Tuscaloosa, 1992.
———. "The Alabama National Guard's 167th Infantry Regiment in World War I." *Alabama Review*. Published in cooperation with the Alabama Historical Association by the University of Alabama Press (January 2003): 3–34.
———. "Military Participation at Home and Abroad." In *The Great War in the Heart of Dixie*, edited by Martin T. Olliff, 24–40. Tuscaloosa: University of Alabama Press, 2008.

Tuchman, Barbara. *The Zimmerman Telegram*. 1958; reprint, New York: Ballantine Books, 1994.

Ulrich, Bernd, and Benjamin Ziemann. *Frontalltag im Ersten Weltkrieg*. Essen: Klartex Verlag, 2008.

*United States Army in the World War, 1917–1919: Military Expeditions of the American Expeditionary Forces*, vol. 5. Washington, DC: Center of Military History, United States Army, 1989.

US Adjutant General's Office. *Congressional Medal of Honor, the Distinguished Service Cross, and the Distinguished Service Medal Issued by the War Department since April 6, 1917, up to and Including General Orders, No. 126, War Department, November 11, 1919*. Washington, DC: GPO, 1920.

Venzon, Anne Cipriano. *The United States in the First World War: An Encyclopedia*. New York: Garland, 1995.

Viereck, George Sylvester. *As They Saw Us: Foch, Ludendorff, and Other Leaders Write Our War History*. Garden City, NY: Doubleday, Doran, 1929.

Wallach, Mike. *"Farmer: Have You a Daughter Fair?"* New York: The Vanguard Press, 1929.

Waller, Douglas. *Wild Bill Donovan: The Spymaster Who Created the OSS and Modern American Espionage*. New York: Simon and Schuster, 2011.

Webb, Jas. A. "Painting the Rainbow." *Army and Navy Record* (April 1920): 10–84.

White, Miller G., and Arthur H. Peavy. *The 151st Machine Gun Battalion, 42d (Rainbow) Division: A Battalion History and Citations of the Rainbow, August 13, 1917, to April 26, 1919*. Macon, GA: J. W. Burke.

Wilhelm, Crown Prince. *Memoirs of the Crown Prince of Germany*. 1919; reprint, Uckfield, East Sussex: The Naval and Military Press Ltd, 2005.

Wolf, Walter B. *A Brief Story of the Rainbow Division*. New York: Rand McNally, 1919.

Wright, William W. *Meuse-Argonne Diary*. Edited by Robert H. Ferrell. Columbia: University of Missouri Press, 2004.

Zieger, Robert H. *America's Great War: World War I and the American Experience*. Lanham, MD: Rowman and Littlefield, 2001.

## Newspapers

*Birmingham News*

*Gadsden* (AL) *Evening Journal*

*Gadsden* (AL) *Times-News*

*Greenville* (AL) *Advocate*

*Mobile News-Item*

*Montgomery Advertiser*

*Montgomery Journal*

*New York Times*

*Nogales* (AZ) *Daily Herald*

*Rainbow Reveille*

# Index of Military Units

28th US "Pennsylvania" Division, 110–111

31st US "Dixie" Division, 195

32th US Division, 176, 179

34th US Division, 194

42nd "Rainbow" Division, XIII, 36–37, 40–44,
    54, 56, 58, 63, 65, 69, 74, 78–80, 86–87, 92,
    94–95, 102–104, 108–109, 111–112, 127,
    132, 137–139, 142, 150, 155, 160, 176, 182,
    188, 192–194, 198–199, 201, 205, 219, 225,
    280n41

78th US Division, 190

82nd US Division, 158

89th US Division, 150, 201

BRIGADES US 2ND DIVISION

Marine, 86

BRIGADES 26TH US DIVISION

51st F.A., 109

BRIGADES US 42ND DIVISION

83rd (165th and 166th Infantry Regiments), 109,
    127, 137–138, 179, 182, 190, 225

84th (167th and 168th Infantry Regiments,) xiii,
    xiv, 43, 72, 108–109, 124, 127–128, 134,
    136–138, 155, 160, 176, 183, 190–191, 194,
    198, 225, 281n77

REGIMENTS

*French*
17th French, 97

21th French, 95

32nd French, 61

43rd French, 98

60th French, 68

109th French, 95, 102

132nd French, 98

167th French, 68, 71, 77, 127

*German*
5th German Grenadier, 102

15th Bavarian, 103

20th Bavarian, 103

77th Bavarian, 72

*US*
1st Alabama Cavalry, 8

1st Alabama Infantry, 8, 22, 27, 35

1st Gas Regiment, 154

1st Iowa Volunteers, xiii

2nd Alabama Infantry, 8, 24, 27, 35, 60

2nd Idaho, 22

4th Alabama, xi, 8, 10–12, 14, 17, 21–24, 27,
    32–35

5th California, 20

10th US Cavalry, 24, 25

15th New York, 41

18th US Infantry, 160, 177

39th US Infantry, 139

47th Infantry, 134–136

59th US Infantry, 139

69th New York, 37

111th Infantry (Pennsylvania), 110–111

149th US Artillery, 84, 160

151st US Artillery, 61, 65,

165th (New York) Infantry xiii, 37, 40, 43–44,
    54–55, 71, 73, 85, 96, 127, 128, 133–134,
    138, 179, 181–182, 187–188, 201, 225,
    281n77

166th (Ohio) Infantry xi, xii, xiii, 35, 37, 51, 68,
    74, 81, 96, 121, 127, 128, 156, 179, 201, 225,
    281n77

167th (Alabama) Infantry xi, xii, xiv, 35–47, 52–
    56, 58–63, 66, 68–73, 75–77, 79–83, 86, 88–
    89, 93–98, 101–105, 108–117, 120–128,
    130–141, 144, 146, 150, 152, 154–156, 158–
    161, 177–188, 190, 192, 195–196, 198–199,
    200–208, 281n77

168th (Iowa) Infantry xiii, x1v, 37, 43, 57, 60, 63,
    72–73, 76, 82–83, 96, 98, 108–112, 114–
    117, 120–121, 125, 128, 130, 132, 134, 136–
    139, 154, 159, 179, 181–187, 190, 201, 225,
    281n77

328th US Infantry, 158

BATTALIONS

*US 167th Infantry*
1st Battalion 167th Infantry Regiment, 45, 49, 53,
    56, 68–69, 86, 88–89, 96–96, 110–114, 116–
    121, 126–127, 132, 134–136, 141–147, 153–
    155, 178, 180–181, 186, 192–193, 198, 205

2nd Battalion 167th Infantry Regiment, 45, 46,
    49, 53, 56, 88, 89, 94, 95, 103, 111, 127, 128,
    132, 134, 139, 141, 144, 153–155, 160, 178,
    180, 185–186, 192–193, 197, 205

# General Index

.